BEHIND THE TIMES

BEHIND THE TIMES

VIRGINIA WOOLF IN
LATE-VICTORIAN CONTEXTS

MARY JEAN CORBETT

CORNELL UNIVERSITY PRESS
Ithaca and London

First published 2020 by Cornell University Press

Library of Congress Cataloging-in-Publication Data

Names: Corbett, Mary Jean, 1962– author.
Title: Behind the times : Virginia Woolf in late-Victorian contexts / Mary Jean Corbett.
Description: Ithaca [New York] : Cornell University Press, 2020. | Includes bibliographical references and index.
Identifiers: LCCN 2020007235 (print) | LCCN 2020007236 (ebook) | ISBN 9781501752469 (hardcover) | ISBN 9781501752483 (pdf) | ISBN 9781501752476 (epub)
Subjects: LCSH: Woolf, Virginia, 1882–1941—Criticism and interpretation. | Woolf, Virginia, 1882–1941. | Women authors—Political and social views— 19th century. | Women authors, English—19th century. | Feminism and literature—History—19th century.
Classification: LCC PR6045.O72 Z578827 2020 (print) | LCC PR6045.O72 (ebook) | DDC 823/.912—dc23
LC record available at https://lccn.loc.gov/2020007235
LC ebook record available at https://lccn.loc.gov /2020007236

CONTENTS

PREFACE

        In the course of researching and writing this book, I have consulted a diverse array of sources and aimed to synthesize my findings to the best of my abilities. Providing an historicist account of Woolf's relation to the literature and politics of the immediate late-Victorian past, with particular emphasis on her engagement with older women writers and turn-of-the-century activist and advocacy movements, has required a deep dive into a number of different areas. I believed, for example, that reading the books that she was writing about, including early literary histories of the late-Victorian period, would enhance my analyses of Woolf's reviews and essays. Similarly, I have sampled the varied literary production of later Victorian women writers, including a large number who make only cameo appearances in this book, such as Alice Meynell, Vernon Lee, Clementina Black, and Elizabeth Robins; some who feature more substantially, including Sarah Grand, Mary Augusta Ward, and Lucy Clifford; and many more who barely feature at all, like Emma Brooke, George Egerton, and Ménie Muriel Dowie. Along my other main line of inquiry, I have consulted writings by and about late-Victorian philanthropy and philanthropists, social-purity activists, and suffragists, including memoirs of and biographies about key figures in the varied movements of the time. This wide range of reading would not have been possible without the digitization of nineteenth- and early twentieth-century materials, and so this would have been a far different book without the affordances of instant accessibility: in short, I have been able to identify and read far more material now online than I could ever hope to reference here.

    As access to digitized materials enabled me to locate a range of texts that would otherwise have remained entirely unknown to me, my travels on the Internet also somewhat unexpectedly led me to do more archival research than I have done for other projects. I have thus consulted the resources of seven different libraries or archives: the Bath Public Library, which contains a considerable amount of material by and related to Sarah Grand, most of it now published; the Berg Collection at the New York Public Library, where I read archival materials by Leslie Stephen and Stella Duckworth; the British Library, which provided access to unpublished letters between Leslie and Thoby Stephen, as well as some by the Stephen family friend Lucy Clifford, in addition to her application to the Royal Literary Fund; the Frances Willard House Library and Archives, housed at Northwestern University, which also includes unpublished letters by Lady Henry Somerset; the Surrey History Centre, home to the Lushington Family Archive; and the Women's Library, now located at the London School of Economics, where I read unpublished letters by Josephine Butler and other materials. I was also able to access reproductions of some unpublished letters included among the Elizabeth Robins Papers in the Fales Collection at New York University. I am grateful to the archivists and librarians at all these institutions. The fruits of these labors, while relatively modest, have persuaded me that there is still more to know and say about the past than even many specialists begin to realize.

That belief has also led me to adopt a particular approach to both the content and the organization of this book. First and foremost, it does not consist of a series of close readings of Woolf's fiction or make a comprehensive study of her enormous body of work. It attends primarily though not exclusively to her first two novels and to the last one published in her lifetime, but I would make no claims to providing definitive readings of even those works. Perhaps surprisingly, it does not consider *Orlando* (1928), *Flush* (1933), or *Freshwater* (perf. 1935) in any sustained way. Instead, it draws extensively on the large body of non-fictional writing that Woolf generated over the course of her life, including her letters, diaries, literary journalism, critical essays, prose polemics, and memoirs. This choice of primary sources should also indicate the decidedly biographical nature of my approach not only to Woolf's oeuvre, but to some of the key female figures I study, particularly when they are lesser-known or underappreciated. With the exception of my attention to Sarah Grand's *The Heavenly Twins*, my effort in representing literary figures such as Lucy Clifford or Mary Augusta Ward focuses less on analyzing their writing than on indicating—for Victorianists as much as modernists—their positions within literary discourse around the turn of the century. I have also sought to illuminate the complexities of feminist activism at the turn of the century by tracing the intra-, inter-, and multigenerational networks of women who participated in public life, including those who pursued both political goals and aesthetic interests, such as Lady Henry Somerset and Ray Strachey. The book thus combines narrative and analysis so as to tell a story about Woolf's relation to the immediate past, to provide some interpretation of it, and to contextualize that story as thickly as I can. A series of interludes branching off from the main lines of the argument provide some additional contextual material.

Above all, this project has taken time, and I have been lucky to have the support of institutions and individuals over the long course of completing it. I am grateful to the College of Arts and Sciences and the Committee on Faculty Research at Miami University for release time from other duties over the last decade. A fellowship from the American Council of Learned Societies in the spring of 2015 enabled me to make substantial progress, which I would not have been able to achieve without the collegiality of Regenia Gagnier and Ellen Rosenman, as well as LuMing Mao and Jerry Rosenberg. Our current chair, Madelyn Detloff, has been not only a tireless advocate for my work—and for the value of Virginia Woolf—but also a highly valued colleague and stalwart friend in hard times. I thank her in particular for her integrity and her commitment to our shared work.

I have also been incredibly blessed in having a wide-ranging network of people who have sustained my belief in this project and my capacity to complete it. Because I try to think about old friends the most, I am grateful first, last, and always to Kelly Hager, Barbara Leckie, Teresa Mangum, Kelly Mays, Lori Merish, Deborah Denenholz Morse, Lucy Norvell, John Plotz, Kate Ronald, Mary Rutkowski, Lynn Voskuil, and Ann Wierwille. The members of my writing group have cheered me on (and up) for the last several years: my thanks to Susan Griffin, Deborah Lutz, Maura O'Connor, Jill Rappoport, Ellen Rosenman, Marion Rust, and Susan Ryan. I am thankful as well to the two anonymous readers of the manuscript secured by Mahinder Kingra, and to him and his staff for their stewardship. Though they may not quite realize it, the support of other colleagues has been equally consequential: a special thank you to Andrew Miller and Yopie Prins for their kindness and camaraderie, and to Kathy Alexis Psomiades, whose incisive commentary on a rather large gap in my previous book led me to write this one. I am also indebted to those who invited or hosted me during presentations at different venues: at William and Mary, Suzanne Raitt; at the University of Exeter, Regenia Gagnier; at the Birkbeck Forum for Nineteenth-Century Studies, Hilary Fraser; and at two Eighteenth- and Nineteenth-Century British Women Writers Conferences, the first sponsored by Kirstyn Leuner at the University of Colorado at Boulder and the second by Livia Woods and Meechal Hoffman of the City University of New York, where Talia Shaffer also provided the warmest of welcomes. The debt I cannot now repay is to Drew Cayton, the memory of whose warmth, intellectual generosity, good humor, and exemplary collegiality continues to sustain me. I will never stop wishing that he were still here.

The book integrates a range of writing I have published over the last several years. Small portions of the introduction derive from three sources: "On *Crawford v. Crawford and Dilke, 1886,*" *BRANCH: Britain, Representation and Nineteenth-Century History,* edited by Dino Franco Felluga, branchcollective .org; and reviews of *Victorian Bloomsbury,* by Rosemary Ashton, *Victorians Institute Journal,* vol. 41, 2013, pp. 249–53, and *Roomscape: Women Writers in the British Museum from George Eliot to Virginia Woolf,* by Susan David Bernstein, *Nineteenth-Century Gender Studies,* vol. 9, no. 3, 2013, ncgsjournal.com/issue93 /corbett.htm. Chapters 1 and 2 draw primarily on revised material from two essays, "Virginia Woolf and 'the Third Generation,'" *Twentieth-Century Literature,* vol. 60, no. 1, 2014, pp. 27–58; and "Generational Critique and Feminist Politics in *The Heavenly Twins* and *The Voyage Out,*" *Generational Exchange and Transition in Women's Writing,* special issue of *Women's Writing,* edited by Doreen Thierauf and Lauren Pinkerton, vol. 26, no. 2, 2019, pp. 214–28. Chapter 1 also contains material from "Cousin Marriage, Then and Now," *Extending Families,* special issue of *Victorian Review,* edited by Kelly Hager and Talia Schaffer, vol. 39, no. 2, 2013, pp. 74–78; "Considering Contemporaneity: Woolf and 'the Maternal Generation,'" *Virginia Woolf and Her Female Contemporaries: Selected Papers from the 25th Annual Conference on Virginia Woolf,* edited by Julie Vandivere and Megan Hicks, Clemson UP, 2016, pp. 2–7; "The Great War and Patriotism: Vernon Lee, Virginia Woolf, and 'Intolerable Unanimity,'" *Virginia Woolf Miscellany,* no. 91, Spring 2017, pp. 20–22; "Virginia Woolf," *The Palgrave Encyclopedia of Victorian Women's Writing,* edited by Lesa Scholl, Palgrave Macmillan, 2019, doi.org/10.1007/978-3-030-02721-6_85-1; and "'Ashamed of the Inkpot': Virginia Woolf, Lucy Clifford, and the Literary Marketplace," *Nineteenth-Century Gender Studies,* vol. 11, no. 3, 2015, ncgsjournal.com/issue113 /corbett.htm, which forms the nucleus of chapter 3. A small portion of chapter 2 appeared in "New Woman Fiction," *Encyclopedia of Victorian Literature,* vol. 3, edited by Dino Franco Felluga, Pamela K. Gilbert, and Linda K. Hughes, Wiley-Blackwell, 2015, pp. 1111–19; while another small part of chapter 5 draws from Denise Eileen McCoskey and Mary Jean Corbett, "Virginia Woolf, Richard Jebb, and Sophocles' *Antigone,*" *A Companion to Sophocles,* edited by Kirk Ormand, Wiley-Blackwell, 2012, pp. 462–76. I am grateful for permission to reprint this material in revised form here.

BEHIND THE TIMES

Introduction

In "A Sketch of the Past" (1939–40), Virginia Woolf (b. 1882) marked a perceived temporal divide between her and her sister, on one side, and the male elders of the family, on the other, that poised an emergent future against a not-very-distant past. Describing herself and Vanessa Bell (b. 1879) as "explorers and revolutionists," she cast their father and their two half brothers as representative patriarchs "of a society that was about fifty years too old for us": "The society in which we lived was still the Victorian society. Father himself was a typical Victorian. George and Gerald were consenting and approving Victorians. . . . We were living in say 1910; they were living in 1860."[1] In the tableau that follows of "a single day as we lived it about 1900" (147), what marks the central differences between the two temporalities are the constraints of upper-middle-class English domesticity, represented as a set of gendered distinctions prescribing different roles for men and women. Though in the mornings Vanessa escaped to Sir Arthur Cope's in South Kensington or, later, to the Royal Academy, while Virginia retreated to her room to prepare for her Greek lessons—first with Clara Pater (b. 1841), then with Janet Case (b. 1863)—"Victorian society began to exert its pressure at about half past four," with tea, then dressing for dinner, then perhaps an evening party, all requiring "a certain manner" (148, 149): "the Victorian manner," enforced by the demands of male relatives and obedient to "the rules of the game of Victorian society" (150). "With eyes that were looking into the future" in the morning, the sisters had to live the second half of their day within the boundaries of an eternally "Victorian" present—not 1900, that is, but 1860—because they "were completely under the power of the past" (147).

In what had become one of her standard rhetorical moves, Woolf deems these male elders, identified as "typical Victorian[s]," entirely behind the times—out-of-date and old-fashioned—while locating herself and her sister as well ahead of them. Importantly, this temporal figure also has a latent spatial component: "behind" suggests that Leslie Stephen (b. 1832) and his stepsons, George (b. 1868) and Gerald Duckworth (b. 1870), were not truly of their own moment, but of one further back, such that "1860" attains an almost physical or material existence, located in the shared family home. Woolf would come to measure the distance she and Vanessa took from 22 Hyde Park Gate in South Kensington in years rather than kilometers, identifying their first Bloomsbury home at 46 Gordon Square (just a scant three miles away) with the future yet-to-be. And like any memoirist, Woolf constructs this division "from my present distance," in which she sees in the "now" of the time of writing "what we could not then see—the gulf between us that was cut by our difference in age" (147).

Yet, rather than follow her lead in staging this as a "struggle" between "the Victorian age," eternalized as 1860, and "the Edwardian age" of 1910, that landmark year in so many studies of Woolf—which occupies a place of importance in this work, too—I configure the conflict as generational (147). Following Wilhelm Dilthey and Karl Mannheim, David Scott describes the phenomenon Woolf invokes as an instance of "the *noncontemporaneity* of cotemporal generations" (163; emphasis in the original). Because "generations are successive and continuous as well as overlapping and cotemporal," Scott argues, people who live at the same time—some older, some younger—do not have the same experience of that time, and may not perceive those who are younger or older as even being of the same time (165). Virginia Stephen cited the view of Gerald Duckworth that this was indeed the case in their family when she wrote to her friend Violet Dickinson (b. 1865) some months before her father's death early in 1904: "He said he felt that he and Georgie were a generation older, and that we must make our own lives independently," even suggesting they take "a small house, Bloomsbury possibly," where the Stephen children could "be four together" (V. Woolf, *Letters* 1: 96).

Along these lines, we might say that while multiple generations coexisted and overlapped in the Stephen-Duckworth household, their experiences, shaped by age—and, as the adult Woolf articulated, by gender—sharply differentiated them. The blended family formed at 22 Hyde Park Gate on the marriage of Julia Duckworth and Leslie Stephen in 1878 contained four children from their first marriages, to which were added another four in the second marriage, with all eight children born over a period of just about fifteen years. Divisions among the siblings based on age were apparent and salient: as an instance of what Leonore Davidoff calls the long family, "age ranges between eldest and youngest children created an *intermediate generation*" between the parents and their latest-born offspring (82; emphasis in the original). From Woolf's perspective, clearly the three Duckworth siblings (with the mysteriously disabled Laura Stephen [b. 1870] making an uncertain fourth) played that part. But in positing a significant temporal distance not only from Leslie Stephen—"We were not his children," she writes, "we were his grandchildren"— but also from her half brothers, Woolf widened the gap between the Duckworth and the Stephen offspring ("Sketch" 147). The revealing metaphor she uses in George's case extends that distance in representing the shaping force exerted on his character by the times through which he had lived: "Like a fossil he had taken every crease and wrinkle of the conventions of upper middle class society between 1870 and 1900. . . . No more perfect fossil of the Victorian age could exist" (151). The implication is that in being behind the times— even a tad prehistoric—her half brothers in particular instantiated and upheld the dated gender norms of an earlier moment.

On the whole, then, the memoir pushes the Duckworth brothers, and George in particular, back into a mid-Victorian past and freezes them there. The Stephen sisters are forced to negotiate not only the outdated patriarchal norms for masculinity that their male elders embodied and performed but also the version of femininity that they inherited from the memory of both their mother (b. 1846), who died in 1895, and their half sister Stella (b. 1869), who died in 1897. As the story goes, it was only by leaving behind the essentially mid-Victorian site of South Kensington that they could enter into the modernity they associated with Bloomsbury. But generational thinking enables us to revise this narrative. Rather than cast Hyde Park Gate as identical in 1900 to what it would have been in 1860—thus collapsing some very significant differences between earlier and later Victorians—we might say instead that people of different ages and generations differently experienced and enacted gendered norms, while the norms themselves necessarily shifted over time. Thus, one significant strand of this introduction aims to reconstruct aspects of the specifically late-Victorian context that Woolf's own representations tend to elide—especially in terms of the opposition within Woolf criticism between South Kensington and Bloomsbury—so as to suggest both the differences and continuities of the world of her childhood and adolescence with the times before and after.

Locating Woolf's abiding preoccupations squarely in late-Victorian contexts, my larger argument in this book will take two main directions. In the first three chapters, I contend that Woolf's critique of selected elder female contemporaries—Anne Thackeray Ritchie (b. 1837), Sarah Grand (b. 1854; pseud. Frances McFall), Lucy Lane Clifford (b. 1846), and Mary Augusta (Mrs. Humphry) Ward (b. 1851; née Arnold)—constitutes part of a lifelong effort to create new norms for the work of the woman writer. She framed her own persona as responsive to readers, but above the marketplace; invested in literary tradition, but no slave to its conventions; engaged with politics, but not a propagandist; a "woman of letters," but not "a lady novelist" (Peterson). Having learned a view of literary production that privileged "great" male writers, Woolf disparaged or ignored writing by women of her parents' generation, distancing herself from what she perceived as powerfully negative and old-fashioned models. Yet such models were not easily relegated to the past, as most of the women writers I consider were still active during the first two decades of the new century, just as Woolf embarked on her own career and published her first two novels, *The Voyage Out* (1915) and *Night and Day* (1919). Connected either with her parents or with male writers whose work she knew and admired, these women helped to create the available paradigms for doing the work Woolf wanted to do, yet she dissented from the examples they offered and the positions they took. In the final two chapters, I turn away from Woolf's engagement with the literary scene to consider her changing relations to two other sites of middle-class Victorian women's emergence into public life, philanthropy and suffrage, as mediated by her ongoing antagonism toward their imperialist tenor and coercive absolutism. These related enterprises had very specific biographical referents for Woolf among the women of her family: a whole range of female relatives were actively involved in efforts to remediate the lives of the sick and the poor—efforts that Woolf associated, most famously in *Mrs. Dalloway* (1925), with the coercive tactics of proportion and conversion. Here my arguments thus emphasize the generational divisions between Woolf and what Molly Hite has called "the maternal generation" ("Public Woman" 524), even as I also look at her relationships with some closer contemporaries, such as Janet Case, Margaret Llewelyn Davies (b.1861), and Ray Strachey (b. 1887; née Costelloe), with whom she forged bonds in her adult life.

My ultimate goal is to challenge the force Woolf's constructions still exert by replacing her explicitly period-bound thinking with a more flexible generational framework, one which tacitly underlies much of her work. I seek to tell what I take to be a more historically grounded story about her relationship to some aspects of mid- and late-Victorian culture, conceived as something other than monolithic. For even now, Woolf's representation of the gendered conventions of *late*-Victorian life as anachronistically *mid*-Victorian, as Ana Parejo Vadillo has shown with reference to the representation of

Mrs. Ramsay in *To the Lighthouse* (1927), continues to exert a powerful pull on how feminist scholars think about the Stephen-Duckworth family; about Virginia Woolf's career; and, more generally, about the gender politics of the late nineteenth and early twentieth centuries ("Generational"). In minimizing substantive differences between 1860 and 1900, Woolf constructed a temporal disjuncture not only within her childhood home but also between it and the world outside its doors, which obscures the ways in which her half siblings, their parents, and their extended circle of kin, friends, and neighbors indeed participated in the shifting scenes of late-Victorian culture. Rather than situate her family at a remove from the late-nineteenth-century world to which, as I hope to show, it firmly belongs, I aim to illustrate in this introductory chapter and elsewhere in the book that the circles to which her older family members belonged were instead very much of their times.

Deconstructing the "Victorian"

Woolf's necessarily retrospective constructions coincide with some of the dominant motifs of her career, especially in their disavowal of a specifically late-Victorian context as a shaping force in the development of modern(ist) consciousness. They imply a thorough rejection of patriarchal and imperial values, which was, in actuality, only imperfectly achieved over time. They minimize or ignore the connections between her elders, whether the parental generation or the half siblings, and some of the progressive movements of the day. They posit the persistence of fixed gender distinctions that, by the time of Woolf's birth in 1882, were already in question in both the literary and political spheres. They assume a heterosexual and gender orthodoxy that had been challenged from within and beyond the family circle. As I argue below, they locate the South Kensington world in which the Stephen children were reared at a great remove from the free and modern urban environment to which the "four together" relocated after their father's death, thereby marking a severance from the past in both temporal and spatial terms. In Woolf's erasures of the new neighborhood's own past(s), moreover, Bloomsbury functioned for the sisters as that unmarked place in and of the future where members of their generation could live on their own terms. Woolf thus repeatedly emphasizes the break with that "Victorian" past—constructed in a highly stereotypical way—even as she also registers its persistence into the present.

Woolf's modes of characterizing the Victorians have had a profound effect on studies of her work and on the academic and popular concept of Woolf as an "icon," using Brenda Silver's term. Most importantly for my purposes, the

influential strand of feminist criticism that emerged in the 1970s and 1980s represented her as a forward-looking literary modernist for whom "Victorianism" signified a set of conventions ripe for critique and a system of subordination
she had to escape. But "the further we are from the first constructions of modernism," in the words of the eminent Woolf scholar Melba Cuddy-Keane,
"the more we realize that the early myths about its identity elided and obscured
many of its crucial elements" (*Virginia Woolf* 146). This book thus responds to
what Jane Goldman has characterized as the "recent critical impetus in modernist and Woolf studies to reconsider the ways our periodising definitions of
modernist aesthetics tend to rely on constructed notions of the Victorian
'other' of modernism . . . in part supplied by Woolf herself" ("Virginia Woolf"
38). For "Woolf did not simply reject the Victorians and their concerns, or re-
nounce them"; as Gillian Beer further argues, "she persistently rewrote
them" ("Victorians" 94). Since "the Victorian 'other'" that her writings construct is sometimes, though by no means always, the stuff of cliché, and the
received wisdom regarding the literary and cultural production and political
tenor of those years has depended, until quite recently, largely on those constructions, a rather limited set of ideas about "the Victorian" continues to circulate. Even though Steve Ellis, for example, aptly comments on "how willing
Woolf always was to use the term 'Victorian' as a designation with no misgiv-
ings that such labels might be reductive in encompassing broad and very varied historical periods," his own book on the subject, published in 2007, does
little to remedy that situation, given that he tends not to inquire very closely
into why it is that Woolf overlooks or diminishes the later Victorians or, sometimes, assimilates them to the Edwardians (6). In the meantime, critical understanding of the late-Victorian period in particular—the last two decades of
the century, which coincided with Woolf's early childhood and adolescence—
has been utterly transformed over the last thirty years, through its recon-
struction as an extended moment of "sexual anarchy" when the perceived
pieties of earlier Victorian generations were coming under attack, a development in Victorian scholarship of which Ellis also appears to have been unaware
(Gissing 113). Another aim of this book, then, is to create a more heterogeneous picture, especially of the late Victorian, than the one sometimes embraced either by Woolf or the scholars who have followed in her wake.

Although Woolf returned again and again over the course of her career to
the immediate past, as Jane Marcus, Jane De Gay, Emily Blair, Marion Dell,
and others have argued from different positions and to different ends, those
returns do not themselves acknowledge the full range of figures that populated it. Famously eschewing the Edwardians, who failed to provide "living heroes" for the writers of her generation "to worship and destroy," she cast her

own chief literary precursors among the later Victorians as Thomas Hardy, Henry James, and George Meredith, novelists who were both friendly with her parents and admired by her male Bloomsbury peers ("On Re-reading Novels," *Essays* 3: 336). With the exception of "the four great novelists"—Jane Austen (b. 1776), Charlotte Brontë (b. 1816), Emily Brontë (b. 1818), and George Eliot (b. 1819)—nineteenth-century women writers generally receive scant attention or credit in Woolf's criticism (*Room* 79). Dell in particular has highlighted Woolf's extended and complex engagements with the work of her father's first wife's sister, Anne Thackeray Ritchie, while Blair's work takes up Woolf's strategic dismissals of both Elizabeth Gaskell (b. 1810) and Margaret Oliphant (b. 1828). But Woolf also distanced herself from those popular and/or politically active late-Victorian women writers of her childhood and adolescent years who succeeded in the shifting conditions of the literary marketplace, some of whom were closely allied to her family. Helping to erase the work of writers that, for the most part, she did not care to read and whose potential influence on her own practice she sought to limit, the first "great" feminist writer of the twentieth century, I will contend, was complicit in the exclusion of others from the women's tradition she did so much to establish.[2]

The reasons for that exclusion are necessarily various, but I aim to highlight one central factor in analyzing the gender and sexual politics of late-Victorian culture that informed Woolf's stance. Briefly, she rejected not only the mixing of literature and politics by some women writers, and the marketplace tactics of others, but also the ideological underpinnings of the feminist activism of the 1880s and 1890s. Focusing on the discourses of New Womanhood, suffrage, and social purity, scholars who study the later Victorians have recovered an array of aesthetic, cultural, and political debates among fin-de-siècle intellectuals and activists with diverse ideological and aesthetic standpoints. Each of those discourses was inflected by both the emergence of eugenics within the frameworks of biopower and the rhetoric that framed women's "mission" in decidedly imperialist terms. Woolf's principled resistance to these formations provides one of the through lines for her career, even as it can be difficult at times to isolate her support for particular political positions from her broader rejection of yoking art to politics. I contend that her birth into an extended family with close ties to patriarchal institutions, on the one hand, and women's advocacy and activism, on the other, shapes her ambivalence about both literary professionalism and feminist politics. Yet, this book also emphasizes how, in the later part of her career, Woolf's attitudes to late-Victorian women's movements, especially philanthropy and suffrage, changed *with* the times, as she aged out of a younger generation and into an older one.

Approaching Woolf from a critical vantage point within Victorian rather than modernist studies, this book thus situates her creative work, critical pronouncements, constructions of literary history, and political positions in relation to the writing and political activism of women whom, with a few important exceptions, she did *not* think back through. In doing so, the analysis brings into view aspects of Woolf's profile different from those most feminist modernists have emphasized. I examine the literature and politics of the last two decades of the nineteenth century so as to contextualize her outlook on key issues of gender and sexuality within late-Victorian culture that emerged in her writing in the first two decades of the twentieth century. As noted in the introduction to an edited volume titled *Late Victorian into Modern*, "The writers we most often constitute as 'modernist' were . . . formed in and by the values of the late nineteenth century, and while they frequently sought, and fought, to break with the immediate past, their identities were, at least in part, shaped by it" (L. Marcus et al. 3). If at some moments they are romanticized, at others fiercely criticized, the mid- and late-Victorian antecedents of this modernist daughter and granddaughter have been both aggrandized and diminished. For we have seen them, for the most part, as Woolf saw them, even as she on occasion saw them differently: when the protagonist breaks through her mother's mediation to a more intimate view of her eminent grandfather in *Night and Day*; in Woolf's claim in her diary, some months after the publication of *To the Lighthouse*, that her father "comes back now more as a contemporary"; and at the moment when, queried by her nephew's wife about "the Victorians," the elderly Lucy Swithin responds, "I don't believe . . . that there ever were such people. Only you and me and William [Dodge] dressed differently" (*Diary 3*: 208; *Between the Acts* 125). Denying in these instances the temporal distinctions she elsewhere insists on, Woolf's shifting view of generational differences constitutes another focal point of my attention throughout this study. To contextualize this further, I turn now to the politics of place that underwrites her generational thinking.

South Kensington

Just as she represented the Duckworth brothers as stuck in a superseded past, Woolf configured her childhood milieu as remote from the currents of modernity that shaped her adult neighborhood of choice. She opposed her childhood home in "Victorian" South Kensington, understood as the site of an anachronistically structured domestic sphere and its attendant oppressive norms, to her adult home in "modernist" Bloomsbury, typically represented as the space of liberation. The temporal split, in other words, entails a spatial one: South Kensington is *behind* the times, off the map of modernity, while Bloomsbury is well *ahead* of them and lies at the very center of all new things.

Among the range of oppositions she constructs, one district connotes the familiar feminine plot of heterosexual marriage, while the other enables the pursuit of vocation for self-consciously modern women. Thus her early, unfinished story about two sisters named Phyllis and Rosamond, dated June 1906 in the typescript, renders its plot according to a divided urban geography. "The irreproachable rows of Belgravia and South Kensington" constitute "the type" of the protagonists' "lot" as "the daughters at home" who are living "a life trained to grow in an ugly pattern to match the staid ugliness of its fellows" (["Phyllis"] 24, 18, 24). But an evening party at the home of the Tristram sisters (one a writer, the other an artist) in "the distant and unfashionable quarter" of Bloomsbury opens a new perspective. There, Phyllis Hibbert imagines, "one might grow up as one liked" amid "the live realities of the world" (24). After only a year or so of life in Bloomsbury, comparable to that of the Tristram sisters, Virginia Stephen here makes strange the values she would associate with "the dreary streets of South Kensington" (*Night* 332; ch. 24). Even earlier, describing a walk with her cousin Marny Vaughn (b. 1862) in Kensington Gardens on 18 March 1905, she writes of that most familiar childhood haunt that it "seems to recall a very different age," identifying the place she had left with an "age" she had lived past (*Passionate* 253). And fifteen years later, she continued to identify South Kensington with the mercenary aspects of the marriage market: after reconnecting with Katie Cromer (b. 1865; née Thynne), wife of the fierce antisuffragist and former viceroy of India, and inviting this old friend to tea late in 1921, Woolf "told her how Kitty [Maxse]" (b. 1867; née Lushington) "was worldly, & wished me to marry into South Kensington"—an option that both Stephen sisters firmly rejected as antithetical to their goals (*Diary* 2: 144).

Understanding the Hibberts and the Tristrams as "two mentally and geographically separate sets of characters," Christine Froula observes that "this scenario doubles, mirrors, and contrasts the Stephen sisters' successive lives in two London neighborhoods as each pair of sisters regards the other across an almost unbridgeable social divide" (Homans 416; Froula, "French" 572). Ten years after abandoning that early story, Woolf cast the Stephens' removal from Hyde Park Gate in similar terms, as a passage across "the gulf between respectable mum[m]ified humbug" in South Kensington and the "life crude & impertinent perhaps, but living," that they found in Bloomsbury (*Diary* 1: 206). Suggesting a slightly more dialogical relation between the two, in the 1920s Woolf wrote, "46 Gordon Square could never have meant what it did had not

22 Hyde Park Gate preceded it" ("Old Bloomsbury" 182). But on the whole, she frames the divide quite starkly: the change of location—from one neighborhood to another—signified, in both occupational and ontological terms, a rejection of (mercenary) marriage in favor of (paid) work, and a resurrection from the "mummified" to the "living." Thus it has become a truism in Woolf studies that "had she not moved to Bloomsbury, . . . she would not have gained the experience, the confidence or the autonomy to write as she did" (Snaith, *Virginia Woolf* 25). That move putatively enabled Virginia Stephen both to distance herself from the values she identified with her adolescent context and to develop newer, more progressive ones. It represents, in Woolf's biography and Woolf criticism, the means of gaining access to a new plot that need not end in marriage but instead offered an encounter with "live realities," sealing her commitment to a modernist aesthetic practice. And this, we might say, is a key aspect of the foundational myth—from one time *and* place to another— of Woolf's career.

But constructing the gulf as "unbridgeable," or framing one set of sisters as altogether "mentally and geographically separate" from the other, reproduces rather than interrogates the terms of the opposition. "The exaggeration of distance," as Matthew Ingleby has argued, "was one of the chief rhetorical strategies throughout the nineteenth century by which Bloomsbury was constructed as peripheral to London's West End, its centre for social capital accumulation" (23).[3] How might the picture change if we challenged the rhetorical emphasis on sharp distinctions or looked for continuities between the neighborhoods of origin and of choice? The critique of the model of marriage, for example, that Woolf associates with South Kensington does not rest on the removal to Bloomsbury: it arises from within South Kensington itself. As Leila Brosnan observes of the Stephen family newspaper, "Issue after issue of the *Hyde Park Gate News* . . . deals with marriage, money, and social and moral matters, in which commentary is repeatedly filtered through Virginia Stephen's loosely fictionalised depictions of her own family's characteristics," with the knowing and cynical remarks of its reporters and columnists focused "firmly on the interrelatedness of marriage and money" (27; cf. Zwerdling, "Mastering" 171–73). The 14 March 1892 issue of this family newspaper characterizes cousin Millicent Vaughan (b. 1866), recently returned from Canada, as "searching the wide world in quest of matrimony"; a few months later, we find a "Letter from a Mother who wants to get a husband with plenty of money for her daughter"; while in January 1895, a "Miss Smith" who has preached "women's rights" as "a temperance lecturer" nonetheless settles down into marriage (Woolf et al. 42, 66, 165–66).[4] In this "licensed outlet for the subversion of Victorian family values," the marriage plot of much nineteenth-century fiction and of the lives of the Stephen-Duckworth women—no doubt gleaned from hearing and overhearing adult conversation as much as from the books Virginia read, whether on her own or aloud to Vanessa—is both an object of parody and a preoccupation (Alexander 32). Its repeated appearances suggest that, from an early age, Virginia Stephen understood the primary options open to her: she could enter the "matrimony market"; or she could earn her own living as a writer, as Leslie Stephen predicted to his wife that she might, "unless she marries somebody at 17" (Woolf et al. 65; Letter [27 July 1893]; qtd. in Hill 352). One path she associated with late-Victorian South Kensington, the other with modern(ist) Bloomsbury: the trick would be, as Rachel Blau DuPlessis observes, "to solve the contradiction between love and quest," with the latter understood as the pursuit of vocation (323).

In connecting heterosexual marriage less to romance, love, or sex than to money and material privilege, and in recognizing that it provided the presumed end or goal of a woman's life as well as a dominant form for fiction, Virginia Stephen both internalized and began to challenge the structure of opportunities for women of her class in her generation, whether or not they happened to live in South Kensington. Taking marriage as an object of critical investigation implies how closely her career is bound up from the outset in examining that structure, one that New Woman writers of the generation before had also been scrutinizing during her childhood and adolescence. Ever-larger numbers of "the daughters of educated men"—including any number of women she came to know quite well in later life—came to reject that older norm in favor of the values Virginia Stephen identified with Bloomsbury in the Phyllis and Rosamond story (Three 6; ch. 1): the pursuit of aesthetic goals and individual autonomy, the pleasures of "freedom and frankness" in mixed-sex conversation (["Phyllis"] 25). Understandably, the views of her home, family, and immediate milieu that Woolf developed then continued to shape her adult understanding of them. For example, in the posthumously published "Middlebrow," written in 1932, she facetiously noted that aesthetically speaking, Bloomsbury was "on high ground" and Chelsea "on low ground," but South Kensington was "betwixt and between" (Essays 6: 472). Middlebrow and conventional as she perceived it to be, the home neighborhood but rarely commanded her attention as an adult. Attitudes she developed in her youth toward values she identified with South Kensington—her hostility toward philanthropy, her disdain for commercialism in the arts, her resistance to heteronormative conformity—hardened over time. Nonetheless, as I show in chapter 3, Woolf still relied on friends and acquaintances from those early days when it came to launching her career. And as had also been the case for Anne Ritchie, who returned imaginatively to one of her best-loved childhood homes in the novel *Old Kensington* (1873), the associations of the past, which Woolf usually identified with bourgeois respectability, continued to dominate her vision of that neighborhood long after she left it.

Positing a thoroughgoing rejection of a respectable "middlebrow" South Kensington in favor of a bohemian "highbrow" Bloomsbury thus belies the continuing use Woolf made of both the opposition itself and those whom she knew from her early years who had constituted that world. The Booth family provides a salient example. A cousin of Beatrice Webb (b. 1858) and a niece of Thomas Babington Macaulay, Mary Booth (b. 1847) assisted her husband Charles in both his business and his extensive sociological work as lead architect of the seventeen-volume *Life and Labour of the People in London* (1889–1903), an extended project on which George Duckworth worked as an investigator.[5] During a 1907 visit to the Booths, Virginia Stephen described this formidable matriarch in slightly acerbic tones: "she sits upright and talks admirable sense . . . takes broad views of the church in France, quotes [Jacques-Bénigne] Bossuet, discusses politics, and meanwhile sympathises and advises with each daughter and son and baby, and keeps them all depended from her middle finger" (*Letters* 1: 277). Although she would disparage the Booths more roundly later on, the Stephen siblings had stayed with them in Marylebone, just across from Hyde Park on the edge of Belgravia, on their way out of South Kensington to their new quarters in Bloomsbury (*Passionate* 44n72). She reviewed daughter Meg's collection of stories, *The Brown House, and Cordelia* (1905) for the *Guardian*, just before Meg married Anne Ritchie's son Billy in 1906 (*Essays* 1: 74). And she continued intermittently to interact with them: attending a Booth dance in 1905 with Elena Rathbone (b. 1878), a friend of her youth who would marry Woolf's *Times Literary Supplement* (*TLS*) editor Bruce Richmond in 1913, she described the guests in what would become typical terms as "the usual representatives of a certain set, who are for the most part amiable but dull" (*Passionate* 225). She told Dickinson two years later, while staying at the Booths' country home, that "the whole place [is] flowing with cheerful domestic life, and kindness and sweetness." Her ambivalence about this form of family life comes through clearly: "none of them extraordinary and yet set in motion like this the whole effect is harmonious"; "how odd and simple all this is—and I suppose it is as good a way of spending ones [sic] life as another"; "it is a large family, and they marry, and produce children, and come and settle near, and you feel that the prolific power of the race is boundless" (*Letters* 1: 276, 277). Four years later, to Vanessa, she was a good deal more direct: "I was glad to find that they are as vapid and commonplace as we used to find them, so that we [were] right to hate them" (*Letters* 1: 468). Still, a sympathy note to

Mary Booth on her husband's death in 1916 recalls the comfort the Booths provided on the occasion of an earlier death in her own family: when Thoby Stephen died in 1907, Woolf wrote, with perhaps just a bit of an edge, "It was like finding our own home again to come into yours" (*Letters* 2: 127). Despite characterizing the Booths as dull companions, the affective pull toward them is sometimes apparent.

Return visits to South Kensington also generated imaginative capital for Woolf's fiction: she used the past of her adolescence as a resource, opportunistically rather than nostalgically, in *Night and Day* and *Mrs. Dalloway*, as in *To the Lighthouse* and *The Years* (1937). Just a week or so before finishing *Night and Day* late in 1918, she went to tea and then to a concert with Nelly (Lady Eleanor) Cecil (b. 1868), whom she had met through Kitty Maxse: "How much the annual income of the audience amounted to, I should not like to guess" (*Diary* 1: 220).[6] She regaled Vanessa Bell by letter with a vision of "our entire past, alive, incredibly the same as ever"—former neighbors, relations by marriage, "any number of people who weren't exactly George [Duckworth] but might have been." All "so nice, kind, respectable—so insufferable": "I enjoyed it immensely; but I couldn't help seeing us in white satin Mrs Young's [dresses] being taken down to supper" (*Letters* 2: 290–91). In a later letter, Woolf told her sister that "chiefly for your sake," she went to another concert, where she met up with the artist Ethel Sands (b. 1873), a friend who lived in Chelsea; reconnected with Katie Cromer; and was "overcome by [the] feminine charm" of Elena Richmond. Commenting sarcastically on "the atmosphere of opulent respectability and refinement of mind in that room," she remarked, "I'm very curious to discover exactly when and how they become [*sic*] so different from" those of their own set, "Carrington or [Mark] Gertler, or Roger [Fry]" (*Letters* 2: 301, 302). But when not seeking to amuse her sister, Woolf turns the lens back on herself: "I felt strange enough; but oddly familiar with their ways after the first" (*Diary* 1: 226). Having attended another of those Kensington concerts, this one at the Campden Hill home of the Booths' son George in March 1920, she criticized in her diary both the "mercantile smugness" of the decor and the comparable smugness of "the family system" the Booth clan represented. Yet she also portrayed her motives for going as somewhat self-interested: "to see [his] house—to take notes for my story—to rub shoulders with respectability" (*Diary* 2: 24, 25).

Published in *Monday or Tuesday* (1921), that story, "The String Quartet," consists mainly of dialogue among the respectable, as imagined or overheard by its narrator. The members of the concert audience are brought together from all over town by "Tubes and trams and omnibuses, private carriages not a few" that "weav[e] threads from one end of London to the other." The story's style clearly mimics the note-taking Woolf's diary references, reporting "facts"—the signing of the Treaty of Versailles; the weather; the difficulty of finding a flat at any price; the aftereffects of the flu; the narrator's leaving her "glove in the train"—yet it also registers a deeper unease among the crowd (138). "There are signs," says the narrator, "that we're all recalling something, furtively seeking something," something associated, perhaps, with the prewar past (139).

Significantly, the narratorial "I" occupies a position similar to the one Woolf held on her returns to South Kensington. Reaching forward "to accept cordially the hand which is perhaps offered hesitatingly"—it has been "seven years since we met," for "the war made a break" in more ways than one—the narrator yet feels compelled to do so by "the ties of blood." "Little arrows" of conversation stir "regrets, pleasures, vanities, and desires" that circulate amid "the hats, the fur boas, the gentlemen's swallow-tail coats, and pearl tie-pins" (138). The narrator expresses contempt not only for the other members of the audience—"it's all a matter of flats and hats and sea gulls, or so it seems to be for a hundred people sitting here well dressed, walled in, furred, replete"—but also for herself, "since I too sit passive on a gilt chair, only turning the earth above a buried memory" (139). The start of the Mozart quartet then breaks the tension and takes the story in another direction, yet as in the diary entries I have quoted, the implication of the narratorial "I" in what she might otherwise disavow—an identification with respectable concertgoers of the Booth kind—is striking. For all the distance achieved by the move to Bloomsbury, this return shows, at least in part, the persistence of South Kensington relations: not as something Woolf or her narrator can firmly locate in the past, but active in the narrative present; not the peculiar province of the Booths, but still operative in the narrator herself. To put it differently, we can say that, in more ways than one, the social and economic relations of South Kensington necessarily underwrote the new plot she identified with Bloomsbury.

South Kensington Connections

The use of South Kensington as a metonym for gender and (hetero)sexual conformity to an entirely conservative or mid-Victorian ethos also masks the more complex set of values, practices, and ideologies with regard to gender and sexuality that permeated late-Victorian culture, even in the respectable West End: here we must go a bit deeper than Woolf herself did to reconstruct some of the broader contexts in which members of her family and its circles were situated. Uncovering this material is important, I think, to challenging some of the entrenched notions of South Kensington as a backwater mired in traditionally or conventionally Victorian values and can open up a different vantage point on the late-Victorian world that as a young adult, Woolf did not know at first hand.

Available evidence shows, for example, that not all the neighbors and acquaintances of Leslie and Julia Stephen and the three Duckworth siblings were quite so straitlaced as Woolf perceived the Booths and their ilk to be; some of them were firmly identified with the progressive movements of the time. Take Emily Massingberd (b. 1847), who like more than a few of their family and friends indeed preached "women's rights" as "a temperance lecturer," albeit after rather than before her marriage, which ended with her husband's death in 1875 (Clement). Hers must have been a familiar name at 22 Hyde Park Gate, as the mother of four young adults ("the three Miss Montgomeries," as Woolf misremembered them in "22 Hyde Park Gate" [165], and their only brother) who were close friends of the Duckworth siblings.[7] A little like the heroine's mother in *Dear Faustina* (1897) by Rhoda Broughton (b. 1840), the highly unconventional Massingberd adopted menswear, as reported in the press, and lived apart from her son and daughters after her husband's death ("London's Woman Club"; A. Curtis 5–6). Perhaps providing a model for the Stephen siblings to follow, the four young Massingberds made a home of their own near the Lushington family, also close friends of the Stephens and Duckworths, in Kensington Square. Interviewed in 1889 by the *Women's Penny Paper*, which asserted that "her name is a household word for Temperance," their mother worked alongside Julia Stephen's first cousin, Lady Henry Somerset (b. 1851), in the British Women's Temperance Association (BWTA) and was the honorary treasurer for the farm colony at Duxbury that Somerset started as a rehabilitation center for women alcoholics ("Interview with Mrs. Massingberd" 1; Clement).

As for so many other activists of the time, Massingberd's commitment to temperance went hand in hand with her support of votes for women: she "made her first speech in favour of women's suffrage" in 1882; ran for a seat on the Lincolnshire County Council in the late 1880s, losing by only twenty votes; and served on the executive of the Women's Liberal Association in 1893 (Clement; Hollis 319). But her chief accomplishment was founding the Pioneer Club in 1892, "the only temperance club in London," which charged a subscription fee of three guineas; it hosted lectures and debates and provided a site for both women's leisure and networking (Clement). Notably, the New Woman novelist Sarah Grand took up the founder's suggestion that she "try the effect" of her breakthrough novel, *The Heavenly Twins* (1893), "upon people who were unprepared for it" by "inviting a number to the Pioneer Club, and read[ing] portions aloud," which "produced quite an extraordinary sensation," as Grand told William Blackwood in June 1892 (*Sex* 2: 26). Although presumably not among the audience at that event, Margaret Lushington (b. 1869) noted in her diary at least two occasions when she went as part of a large group to the Pioneer—even if the debate she attended on fox hunting wasn't much to her liking (15 June 1893). Just after Julia Stephen's death, Margaret married Stephen Massingberd, with Gerald Duckworth as his best man; not much later, with Emily Massingberd's death in January 1897, the Pioneer Club was thrown into chaos. Unlike some other figures I will consider in this book, who carried on the progressive political work of their immediate elders, none of Massingberd's daughters publicly advocated her political interests in any perceptible way—although Mildred (b. 1868), an aunt by marriage to Woolf's friend Gwen Raverat (b. 1885; née Darwin), became "a fanatical teetotaller" who subscribed to the *Journal of Inebriety* and was, "in her own way, . . . an ardent feminist" (Raverat 199, 200).

In founding the Pioneer Club, Massingberd clearly forwarded the creation of some of London's multiple, intersecting feminist networks of the 1890s. Her affiliations with temperance and suffrage also imply her connection to the efforts to moralize the public sphere, especially in relation to sex, that began to take hold in the 1880s under the heading of "social purity"; and one of the nearer neighbors on Hyde Park Gate attracted significant attention from Massingberd's allies on this front. Harry Cust was a Cambridge Apostle, a member of "the Souls," briefly editor of the *Pall Mall Gazette*, and a notorious rake (Atkinson).[8] Spearheaded by Millicent Garrett Fawcett (b. 1847), the unsuccessful campaign to block his candidacy for Parliament in 1894 rested on the allegation that, having already fathered the child of a married woman, he had impregnated Nina Welby (b. 1867), daughter of the well-known and well-connected philosopher of language Victoria, Lady Welby (b. 1837).[9] Drawn into the social purity movement in the wake of the 1885 "Maiden Tribute" incident engineered by W. T. Stead, which was supported by Josephine Butler (b. 1828), Fawcett believed in an equal standard of sexual morality for men and women; but whereas Butler was not inclined to insist that private deviations from the norms should disqualify men from public office, her younger colleague brought that standard strongly to bear on their sexual conduct.[10] Although she made her home in Bloomsbury, Fawcett, too, was something more than a passing acquaintance of the Stephens: after her husband Henry's death in 1884, Woolf's father wrote the life of his former Cambridge colleague at the widow's request. Leslie Stephen's position as editor of the *Dictionary of National Biography* (*DNB*) and the two men having been contemporaries at Trinity Hall mattered more, it seems, than whatever ideological differences had opened up between them over time. But that before Henry Fawcett's death, in Leslie Stephen's words, "our intercourse had ceased to be so frequent as before" may imply an even broader gulf between their wives, who were on opposite sides of the women's suffrage question (*Life* v).

That said, we can perhaps assume that Julia Stephen would have shared Fawcett's objection to Cust's behavior, if not to his candidacy—and perhaps even knew something about the circumstances of his hasty marriage to Nina Welby, since Virginia Stephen certainly did.[11] Unlike her husband's friend's wife or her own cousin Lady Henry (hereafter, Isabel), Julia Stephen did not take a public position on the sexual politics we now associate with the social purity movement. She nonetheless recognized, as I will show in chapter 4, the problems that men's sexual behavior could and did create for women, especially but not exclusively for women of the servant class. Like Fawcett, she "believed in female 'purity' and the family"; one of her unpublished essays argues that it was part of the privileged woman's domestic mission to exert her influence—or what she calls "a long and patient continuance in well doing . . . joined to intense love and sympathy"—so as to lead "a father or son to pause in their career of indulgence or vice" (Rubinstein 84; J. Stephen, ["Servant Question"] 245). This conventional stance places at least part of the responsibility for restraining men from pursuing "vice" on the women who love them. But in the changing circumstances of the late nineteenth century, these norms for feminine conduct were also breaking down, as other high-profile sex scandals of the time made clear.

The Cust affair did not achieve quite the level of notoriety that characterized those involving Charles Stewart Parnell or Oscar Wilde, but it was not the only one in which a near neighbor played a part. Another contretemps that emerged in 1885 with some bearing on Hyde Park Gate was revived first in 1889 and then again in 1892, when a large number of women including Fawcett and Somerset as well as some men, including Stead, protested Sir Charles Dilke's effort to return to public office (Niessen 103).[12] Living just next door to the Stephens, Maye Ashton Dilke (b. 1856) was both Charles Dilke's widowed sister-in-law and the eldest sister of Virginia Crawford (b. 1863), whose husband (also an MP) had filed for divorce in 1885, naming Dilke as co-respondent.[13] The ensuing controversy effectively ended Dilke's chances at becoming prime minister, thus leveling a blow to the women's movement. A longtime advocate for "the Cause," he had "supported Jacob Bright when he introduced the first women's suffrage measure to be put before the House of Commons in 1870" (S. Holton 73). Ironically, according to her early biographer Ray Strachey, the young Fawcett had made her first public speech in favor of suffrage while sharing a platform with Dilke in 1868 (*Millicent* 46).

While most analyses of such scandals consider the political effects of men's sexual improprieties, the scandals also had serious implications for women's politics. The elite women involved could be pitied as victims of male lust or castigated for their errant ways, yet the public nature of their trials—indeed, the very breach of the boundary between publicity and privacy—challenged the norms for female purity that were upheld by figures as opposed in other respects as Millicent Garrett Fawcett and Julia Stephen. Greater sexual freedom for women, in or out of heterosexual marriage, was by no means part of the social purity agenda, even if it was associated with some iterations of the New Woman. The discursive circulation of the trials of these and other "women who did," to adapt Grant Allen's phrase, forwarded the establishment of their equivalence with "public women," a term associated with prostitution, publication, and political activism, as I explore in subsequent chapters.[14] Thus, in describing a neighbor who lived at 17 Hyde Park Gate (L. Goldman), "Mrs Biddulph Martin, the rich American"—better known to posterity as the spiritualist and feminist Victoria Woodhull (b. 1838), notorious in the United States for her advocacy of free love—as "tarnished," like Maye Ashton Dilke, "by some connection with women's rights," Woolf alluded to the liminal status of the public woman, as viewed from the South Kensington standpoint she did not altogether leave behind ("Sketch" 120).

If from a child's perspective Maye Dilke was mainly noteworthy for her wealth and her wardrobe, some of her feminist contemporaries indeed considered her also "tarnished" by her association with extramarital sex.[15] "Active in Liberal feminist and suffrage political circles," she was a well-known orator, commended in the press for her "truly womanly eloquence," who continued her political activities (though not her public speaking) after her second marriage in 1891 to William Russell Cooke (Israel 201; Dolman 676).[16] She was one of two prominent feminists—the other being Fawcett—called on to rebut the "Appeal against Female Suffrage" published in *The Nineteenth Century* in the summer of 1889, the handiwork of Stephen family friends Mary Augusta Ward and Louise Creighton (b. 1850), to which Mrs. Leslie Stephen was, infamously, a signatory. Their political differences notwithstanding, Woolf's mother still made "kind enquiries" of their neighbor's governess when Maye Dilke was hit by a stone at one of her public speaking engagements ("Sketch" 120). Others inside the women's movement were not so supportive. Dilke's recruitment as a British delegate to the first meeting of the International Council of Women, held in Washington, D.C., in 1888, "so outraged Helen Taylor" (b. 1831), stepdaughter of John Stuart Mill, "that she made it the grounds for her own withdrawal from participation in the international conference," ostensibly owing to the "speculation and gossip" that surrounded Dilke's private life before her second marriage (S. Holton 74). Such rumors were perhaps circumstantially substantiated by the "tarnished" reputation of not only her sister but also her mother.[17] Because Dilke was simultaneously censured by other feminists and rendered suspect in the eyes of her neighbor for her advocacy of women's rights, her status as a public woman—politically and perhaps sexually active, someone who spoke out in public and was spoken publicly about—differed from that of Massingberd or Fawcett. Yet each of them transgressed the mid-Victorian norms for femininity to which members of the Stephen-Duckworth circle ostensibly adhered.

The presence of all three (alongside Isabel Somerset, who similarly achieved notoriety as a result of an earlier sex scandal) within the broader Stephen-Duckworth network constitutes a powerful counterexample to the dominant image of South Kensington as located somewhere beyond the currents of modernity; the social and sexual ferment that critics and historians now identify as a leading feature of late-Victorian culture surely extended even to Hyde Park Gate. Yet the conservative ethos of much late-Victorian feminist activism must be acknowledged, indeed as a part of modernity itself. Associated mainly with social purity and the demand that men and women adhere to a single sexual standard—as in the suffragette battle cry of Christabel Pankhurst (b. 1880), "Chastity for Men"—it could condemn the perceived excesses of free love, or "free unions." Not all those we might now call feminists, in other words, sought an end to marriage as it had been constituted, as conveyed by Nora Helmer's slamming the door on her dollhouse or by the emergence of New Women, real and fictive, in the public sphere. Locating Woolf's family of origin within this cultural context requires an effort to look beyond her (and thus our) relatively narrow point of view on her background, as forged in her adolescence, and to interrogate the geographical division her adult writings installed. Doing so gives us a more complex view not only of the women of her mother's generation but also of the use she made of the South Kensington/Bloomsbury divide.

Reverse Migration: From South Kensington to Bloomsbury

While both the Phyllis and Rosamond story and "The String Quartet" represent South Kensington as a site where culture is consumed but not produced in the homes of the elite, the Stephen-Duckworth set had actually been located amid a literary and artistic scene that did not fade away with the onset of the twentieth century. During the decades when the Stephen sisters were growing up, not only did Henry James, Walter Pater, and the much older Robert Browning all live in the neighborhood, but so, too, did many important late-Victorian women writers, including Alice Meynell (b. 1847), Olive Schreiner (b. 1855), Katharine Tynan (b. 1861), and the best-selling Marie Corelli (b. 1855; pseud. Mary Mackay). Although often represented as the place from which the Stephen sisters necessarily had to escape in order to become artists, for a London newcomer like the American Ezra Pound in the 1910s, "the 'village' of Edwardian Kensington" constituted the "small world" of avant-gardism to which he initially migrated from the United States (Brooker 47). Like Chelsea, home to Woolf's friends Desmond and Molly MacCarthy (b. 1882; née Warre-Cornish)—"where," as Vanessa Bell later wrote, "at least as many of the 'high-brows' lived and always have lived"—Kensington, too, was a key spot for a modernist fraction in the new century ("Notes" 103).[18] At South Lodge on Campden Hill, not far from George Booth's home and about a mile's walk from 22 Hyde Park Gate, Violet Hunt (b. 1862) gave writerly garden parties throughout the first years of the new century. Her guests included Pound, her erstwhile lover Ford Madox Ford, Walter de la Mare, Amy Lowell (b. 1874), May Sinclair (b. 1863), H. D. (b. 1886), Richard Aldington, D. H. Lawrence, and Rebecca West (b. 1892), indicating "the broad sociality, across different arts, different moral and political opinions and different generations, of this Kensington-based circle" (Brooker 57). Beyond Kensington, Woolf's friend Hugh Walpole gestured toward the diverse sites around London where writers gathered early in the new century: "the Sidney Colvins at the [British] Museum, [Marie] Belloc Lowndes' exciting teas at Rumplemayer's [sic], . . . Somerset Maugham in Charles Street[, Mayfair], H. G. Wells out at Hampstead" (40).[19] None of these figures was among Woolf's close associates: in August 1922, for instance, she characterized an invitation from the painter Dorothy Brett (b. 1883) to a party in Hampstead as a missive from "the heart of the enemies [sic] camp" (Diary 2: 192). Nor do they feature for the most part in the annals of high modernism any more than Walpole himself does. But identifying multiple locations where writers lived, worked, and came together—as in Catherine Clay's mapping of middlebrow women writers in the interwar period, which includes Chelsea and Hampstead figures (15–26)—enables us to reframe the familiar South Kensington–Bloomsbury opposition on a larger canvas and to establish a broader range of writerly sites of sociability.

The networks that Woolf's predecessors and contemporaries constructed and in which they participated can be understood and represented in a variety of ways. Like the very "concept of modernity," networks are "spatial as well as temporal" (Pykett, Engendering 7). Where one lives, who one lives with or near, what public or semipublic institutions (like mass transport and lending libraries) support or constrain interactions and intersections—all these play a part in shaping the possibilities for making or breaking connections and facilitating or hindering professional advancement. In the ongoing scholarly project of "remapping the turn of the twentieth century," the shifting geographical networks of literary London, as traced in Parejo Vadillo's work on late-Victorian women poets or Peter Brooker's study of modernist bohemians, can be concretely specified (Ardis, *Modernism* 1). Woolf's own place(s) on the map between 1882 and 1919 may be calibrated in relation to those inhabited by other writers then living and working in the city, its suburbs, and/or the countryside. In tracing what Regenia Gagnier calls "interpenetrating and mutable domestic, artistic, and political circles," we should recognize, too, that these geographies also shift, in that neighborhoods change over time (19).

Recent literary historians have thus incorporated urban geography as a tool for mapping writerly locations at the turn of the last century without neglecting the salience of the temporal axis, which tells us that the South Kensington, Bloomsbury, and Chelsea of 1882 are not quite the same places they would become by 1904, or that they had been in 1860. That insight enables us further to revisit some of the generational divisions or splits that Woolf famously installed among Victorians, Edwardians, and Georgians. Locating cotemporal writers spatially or geographically as living and working in close proximity to one another can prevent us from seeing them as fully cut off from one another by generational (or period) difference. For example, that the New Woman writer most frequently seen as a stylistic precursor of Woolf, George Egerton (b. 1859; pseud. Mary Chavelita Dunne), was also a Bloomsbury neighbor, living as of 1922 first at 59, then at 44 Ridgmount Gardens, just off Gower Street and less than half a mile from 52 Tavistock Square, suggests another way of placing the two on the same map (White 99). That said, as it was no doubt Woolf's "hereditary position in English letters" that made South Kensington her starting point rather than her final destination, her trajectory is something of an anomaly within a larger framework (T. S. Eliot 121). As Parejo Vadillo establishes, "Bloomsbury . . . was the favored place for aspiring artists" at the fin de siècle, which was perhaps a factor in Gerald Duckworth suggesting and Vanessa Stephen ultimately choosing to relocate to that neighborhood; but "once they became financially successful, they tended to move to Kensington, the preferred place for the economically successful artist" (*Women* 119). Leslie Stephen's first father-in-law, William Makepeace Thackeray, had done just that, two generations before the Stephen siblings left Hyde Park Gate for Gordon Square, by resettling his daughters in Kensington in 1846 after they had lived around Russell Square from 1838 to 1843.

In hindsight, the Stephen sisters clearly believed that reversing course had liberated them from their own recent past. "We knew no one living in Bloomsbury then and that I think was one of its attractions," Vanessa Bell wrote in 1951; "people did live there whom we might easily have known," women like Fawcett (also a younger sister of Stella Duckworth's doctor, Elizabeth Garrett Anderson [b. 1836], who lived and worked in Marylebone), "but they were of the older generation" ("Notes" 98). Interestingly, among all the London locales Virginia Stephen records visiting in her 1897 journal, which gives the fullest extant account of any year of her life before 1916, Bloomsbury is conspicuously absent, although Marylebone and Regent's Park to the west, Covent Garden to the south, and the City to the southeast all appear as regular destinations. Inconceivable though it is that she had never been to the British Museum prior to the Stephens moving to Gordon Square late in 1904, either with her father on one of his research trips or with her siblings to see its collections, no Bloomsbury sites figure in her 1897 journal. Perhaps this explains in part the sense of wonder and happiness she experienced at making a home in what was virtually a new neighborhood for her, seemingly free of all associations with the seven unhappy years between the death of Stella Duckworth Hills and that of Leslie Stephen. But once we place the movement from South Kensington to Bloomsbury within the broader spatial and temporal contexts of the turn of the century, the Stephen siblings' relocation to this part of town may itself look a bit behind the times. As Ruth Livesey puts it, "Woolf's early twentieth-century Bloomsbury . . . overlay an earlier Bloomsbury of the mid-1880s like a palimpsest"; and that earlier Bloomsbury—itself diverse and heterogeneous—was every bit as progressive, if not more so, as the one she later encountered (*Socialism* 205).[20] Most strikingly, it was a Bloomsbury she did not much care to know.

Late-Victorian Bloomsbury

Although new to the Stephen siblings, Bloomsbury had been a key site of progressive action and experiments in living for much of the nineteenth century, and particularly hospitable to those "daughters of educated men" with aspirations beyond the domestic sphere. Much feminist fiction of the late century registered these facts, but one example will have to serve here. Published in 1895 but set about a decade earlier, *On the Threshold* by Isabella O. Ford (b. 1855) dramatizes, and to some extent ironizes, the position of two young middle-class women who come to Bloomsbury from the provinces to study art and music.[21] Swept up in "the idealism and millenarian optimism" of socialist activism in the 1880s, the first-person narrator Lucretia and her roommate Kitty experience Bloomsbury as "a magic blind-spot beyond the panoptic gaze of parents, which enables [them] to discover their political identities and express themselves as independent young women" (Livesey, *Socialism* 47; Ingleby 189). As Carolyn Steedman has argued, building on Franco Moretti's analysis in *Atlas of the European Novel* (1998), *On the Threshold* belongs to a late-century subgenre of urban investigation novels, comparable in part to James's *The Princess Casamassima* (1886), that "mapped the great city of the world . . . by their [characters'] walking of it: by the same hurried passage through its streets to the same kind of meeting . . . somewhere in the fictional and real square mile of Bloomsbury" (26). The women rent "three small, dark rooms" located "not far from . . . Gordon Square" (Ford 10, 78). Together they attend meetings and pursue their studies at an historical moment "in which the socialist aesthetic ideals of fellowship and comradely labour . . . could be lived in the city in pursuit of the cause" (Livesey, *Socialism* 47). This is not, then, the same district represented by Woolf's mid-Victorian male predecessors, whether in Johnny Eames's triumphant escape from Burton Crescent in *The Small House at Allington* (1864), as he marches "down through the squares—Woburn Square, and Russell Square, and Bedford Square—towards the heart of London" (567; ch. 51); or, still earlier, in Amelia Sedley's return from boarding school to the comfortable Russell Square mansion her family occupies thanks to the fortune her merchant father made, then loses, in *Vanity Fair* (1847–48).[22] From her reading rather than her experience, Woolf knew those earlier and specifically literary versions of her future neighborhood much better than she did the Bloomsbury of the 1880s or 1890s. Thus it is probably no accident that the mid-Victorian Miss Willatt, of "Memoirs of a Novelist" (1909), winds up "living in a poor neighbourhood," "[keeping] house for her brothers in a Bloomsbury Square" after her father's death in 1855 (75, 74).

Long before the Stephen siblings arrived at 46 Gordon Square, Bloomsbury had been home territory not only for such novelists as Thackeray, Trollope, and a host of others but also for cultural and social institutions founded by the liberal vanguard of the age that laid the foundation for the neighborhood's association with progressive politics, which was facilitated by material changes in the area itself. By the end of the century, as detailed in Rosemary Ashton's *Victorian Bloomsbury* (2012), the upwardly mobile had moved to the suburbs or more fashionable locales like Belgravia and Regent's Park; former single-family residences were converted to office space or to boardinghouses and other multiple-occupancy accommodations for students, travelers, and unmarried women. "Following on more than two decades of feminist popular fiction" comparable to Ford's "that registered the phenomenon of middle-class radicalism and the texture of women's daily lives in Bloomsbury" (S. Blair 820), Woolf obliquely referenced this aspect of its immediate past when she sends Katharine Hilbery on a visit to Mary Datchet's suffrage society office in Russell Square, which had been, many years earlier, Mrs. Hilbery's childhood home. And twenty years after *Night and Day*, Woolf also chose to set a suffrage scene in *The Years* at a location on the edge of Bloomsbury, in an "old square off Holborn," probably the historic Red Lion Square (*Years* 156; "1910"). (It is, of course, also a Bloomsbury boardinghouse "off the Tottenham Court Road" from which Septimus Warren Smith makes his fatal leap in *Mrs. Dalloway* [79].) Yet such references in Woolf's fiction to the neighborhood are few and far between.

Although the Stephen sisters, like the Hibberts, surely thought of Bloomsbury "as 'distant' from the world of fashion, . . . both spatially and in terms of social class," Ashton shows that the point about reverse migration notwithstanding, they were "following a well-documented mental map trodden by plenty of their predecessors," including a generation of women artists and activists like Ford's Kitty and Lucretia, in moving to Gordon Square (7). Bloomsbury was "neither very fashionable, nor very much the reverse," the *Times* commented in 1894, "not so far removed from the centre of things as to become provincial, not so much immersed in the bustle of life as to kill tranquillity"; by 1906 E. V. Lucas could term it "a stronghold of middle class respectability and learning," making it a most desirable place for emancipated women to live (qtd. in Ashton 12, 13). Drawing on the poverty maps Charles Booth and his team—including George Duckworth—generated for *Life and Labour of the People in London*, Sara Blair similarly characterizes the district "at the fin de siècle . . . [as] the site of snug middle-class life"; albeit also traversed by transnational currents, it was populated by "the class of bankers, merchants, and legal professionals made via the business of empire and acceding to the former freehold property of the landed aristocracy" (818). As Angelica Garnett points out, when her mother selected the neighborhood, she "chose a district marked in yellow" on the 1897 version of Booth's poverty map, "the same colour as Hyde Park Gate and one that designated the highest income bracket" (22). Yet, just a few minutes' walk from their new home—as had also been the case in South Kensington, as the Booth maps show—lived some of the city's poorest residents.

If the Bloomsbury of 1905 was mildly bohemian, class-diverse, and more racially and ethnically mixed than some other London districts, twenty years earlier it had been the site of modes of living and working that anticipate yet diverge from those the Stephen siblings practiced, as scholars have demonstrated with reference to feminist and socialist-feminist networks of the

1880s. For example, in *Roomscape: Women Writers in the British Museum from George Eliot to Virginia Woolf* (2013), Susan David Bernstein refutes Woolf's iconic view of the Reading Room as a patriarchal space where the narrator of *A Room of One's Own* (1929) encounters evidence only of "the mental, moral, and physical inferiority" of her sex, highlighting instead the community of women writers, translators, and activists who populated the library in the last decades of the nineteenth century (*Room* 31).[23] Many of the women of this Bloomsbury generation, like the fictional Lucretia and Kitty, pursued both aesthetic and political interests. In the Reading Room, Eleanor Marx (b. 1855) completed the first English translation of Gustave Flaubert's *Madame Bovary* (1857), published by Henry Vizetelly in 1886; translated *Reuben Sachs* (1889), by the Newnham-educated Amy Levy (b. 1861), into German; and taught herself Norwegian to translate several Ibsen plays. All the while, she was developing a network of colleagues and connections centered in the neighborhood where she lived alongside Levy and the Brighton transplants, Constance and Clementina Black (b. 1861 and 1854). After marrying Edward Garnett, Constance translated the great Russian novelists into English and thus became the conduit for their immensely important influence on late-Victorian and modernist writers, including Katherine Mansfield (b. 1888) and Woolf herself (Bernstein 63). But before her marriage, and after a stint teaching Charles and Mary Booth's daughter Antonia, "spending the summer with them in Leicestershire and coaching the eldest boy [Thomas] in Latin," she engaged in other kinds of translation (Jefferson 11). She contributed to *Labour and the Life of the People in London* (as Booth's work was titled when the first volume was published in 1889) and held the position of librarian at the People's Palace in the East End, a form of "cross-class translation work" that enabled her to transgress a gendered line at a moment when librarians were almost always men (Bernstein 59).

Living without servants on Fitzroy Street in the 1880s, Constance shared quarters with her sisters, including Clementina, a novelist, journalist, and secretary of the Women's Protective and Provident League (later called the Women's Trade Union League) from 1887 to 1889 (Livesey, *Socialism* 54). The League had its first offices at Clark's Buildings, south of Great Russell Street in the Rookeries, one of the pockets of poverty found in and about the district on the Booth maps; later it moved to Mecklenburgh Square, where it was housed alongside the People's Suffrage Federation, for which Virginia Stephen volunteered in 1910 (Glage 26). Clementina Black's adopted home neighborhood constituted a site of intersection among contemporary activist practices: in the words of a character from one of her novels, *An Agitator* (1894), who attends a meeting of the Russell Square Socialist Society, "Socialism in the West

End . . . is enthusiasm; in the East End it's revolt; in Bloomsbury it is business" (48). And Black herself continued her varied political work alongside her literary and journalistic output from her Bloomsbury base for many years, intersecting at points with both Julia Stephen and Isabel Somerset.

Along with many other women, then, Marx and the Black sisters experienced their Bloomsbury as a place for connecting with other cultural workers. By late century, as Emma Francis notes, Bloomsbury constituted "one of the most significant interfaces between socialism and feminism in British history" (50). Yet, though we have come to think of Woolf as both a socialist and a feminist, with the exception of the references in *Night and Day* and *The Years* noted above, this aspect of Bloomsbury history appears to have remained invisible to her; the question is, why? In Bernstein's analysis, which resonates with the one I will offer in chapter 1, Woolf disavowed and disregarded the progressive collectives of the generation that intervened between her and George Eliot, who died just over a year before Virginia Stephen was born. In the early part of her career, she chose instead, like her "great" predecessor, to privilege individual privacy over shared publicity, the solitude and security of one's own room and the privileges of a lending institution like the London Library—founded by Thomas Carlyle and of which her father was for a time president—over the heterosocial spaces of contact with others (Bernstein 150–56). For Livesey, "the surviving traces of the political aesthetics of 1880s," which emphasized the development of an ethically aware sympathy that Clementina Black had no trouble endorsing, "threatened [Woolf's] tentative steps towards forming an individualist and autonomous radical aesthetic" in opposition to "a nineteenth-century world of purposive literary realism" ("Socialism in Bloomsbury" 135, 141); indeed, Livesey's broader analysis in *Socialism, Sex, and the Culture of Aestheticism in Britain, 1880–1914* (2007) goes a long way toward explicating Woolf's erasure of this aspect of Bloomsbury history from the record. Woolf's objections to the whole idea of "purpose" also forms a major node in her resistance to yet another set of writer-activists of the time, the New Woman novelists of the 1880s and 1890s, as I explore in chapters 1 and 2.

Woolf probably never read *On the Threshold*, or *An Agitator*, or any of those novels by late-Victorian women with Bloomsbury connections, only recently recovered and significantly underread even now. And although one of her most astute and historically minded readers, Anna Snaith, has provided a brief overview of some Bloomsbury fictions produced early in the new century, by Olive Birrell (b. 1848), Radclyffe Hall (b. 1880), and Violet Hunt, among others, it does not seem likely Woolf would have read these books, either (*Virginia Woolf* 28–29). It is far more plausible that her literary knowledge of the district in the two decades before she moved there would have derived from her reading of two other writers at work in the 1880s and 1890s, only one of whom she admired. On the one hand, Woolf saw the late-Victorian Bloomsbury depicted by George Gissing, a sometime-resident of the neighborhood, in such novels as *Workers in the Dawn* (1880), *The Nether World* (1889), and *New Grub Street* (1891), as "a world of fog and four-wheelers, of slatternly landladies, of struggling men of letters, of gnawing domestic misery, of gloomy back streets, and ignoble yellow chapels" ("George Gissing," *Essays* 5: 534). Though in general Woolf scorned the fiction of purpose, with which she classes some of his work, "because Gissing was always thinking, he was always changing. In that lies much of his interest" (537). On the other hand, the depiction of the district in *Marcella* (1894) by another Bloomsbury dweller of the 1880s, Mary Augusta Ward—a family friend and precursor Woolf disliked and disavowed—drew on some of the same tropes Gissing deployed, but from a very different angle. Renouncing first art, then politics, Ward's protagonist trains as a district nurse. When the narrative picks up after a year's interval, Marcella Boyd is caring for a Jewish woman in a house that is "one of a type familiar all over the poorer parts of West Central London—the eighteenth-century house inhabited by law or fashion in the days of Dr. Johnson, now parcelled out into insanitary tenements, miserably provided with air, water, and all the necessaries of life, but still showing . . . signs of the graceful domestic art which had ruled at the building and fitting of it" (341; bk. 3, ch. 3). Such "signs" showed, too, in both the affordable house Ward and her family leased in Russell Square starting in 1881 and the one the Stephen siblings occupied in Gordon Square late in 1904, each being among "the well-to-do squares which made the centre of this poor and crowded district" (345).

When Virginia Stephen herself began to walk the streets of Bloomsbury, then, early in 1905, she was following in the proverbial footsteps of the members of multiple nineteenth-century generations with whom she had some real and perceived affinities: the "great" mid-Victorian male novelists, including Charles Dickens, who lived on Doughty Street from 1837 to 1839; the intellectuals and activists of the liberal vanguard who built Bloomsbury's institutions; the progressive feminists of the 1880s and 1890s who engaged in both collective action and aesthetic pursuits, as she for the most part did not; and those late-Victorian novelists who were her immediate precursors. In her fiction, essays, and other writing, these predecessors are unevenly acknowledged at best, yet their presence in that past can be felt and at times heard in her work. By taking "a small house, Bloomsbury possibly," at Gerald's suggestion and on Vanessa's initiative, the Stephen siblings were, as the cliché goes, seeking to leave their past behind them; but so, too, did that place have its own multiple pasts.

Yet here again we might say that the distance between South Kensington and Bloomsbury was not quite so pronounced as Woolf retrospectively deemed it. In *Marcella*, the protagonist's future husband walks south from one of those stately eighteenth-century Bloomsbury houses and crosses High Holborn to Little Queen Street, which was literally built over during the next decade in the making of Kingsway, the setting for one of Katharine Hilbery's most memorable walks in *Night and Day*. With a policeman for a guide, Aldous Raeburn visits "a street behind Drury Lane" that just a few years later George Duckworth would also visit in his work for Booth's project, "a black street," according to the color code of the poverty map, with "filthy gutters and broken pavements" and "a variety of other horrors, social and sanitary" (*Marcella* 416; bk. 3, ch. 10). Both Ward and George Duckworth, that is, had been there in Bloomsbury—before either Katharine Hilbery and Mary Datchet of *Night and Day*, or Vanessa and Virginia Stephen. Less than half a mile from this slum, in a district George would also visit for Booth's purposes—as he indeed visited all the streets and squares of West Central from 1897 to 1898, including the ones where his half siblings came to live for the better part of their lives—Gerald Duckworth would set up his publishing firm at 3 Henrietta Street in Covent Garden in 1898, from which he would publish his half sister's first two novels. Gerald, too, then, had preceded them in traveling ground that Virginia would later mark out as her home territory. Despite all efforts to banish it to the past, such traces of late-Victorian South Kensington persisted nonetheless in modernist Bloomsbury.

CHAPTER 1

Gender, Greatness, and the "Third Generation"

> As the current answers don't do, one has to grope for a new one; & the process of discarding the old, when one is by no means certain what to put in their place, is a sad one. Still, if you think of it, what answers do Arnold Bennett or Thackeray, for instance, suggest?
>
> —Virginia Woolf, *Diary*, 27 March 1919

> The old are as mysterious as idols in a temple; we take off our shoes before we approach them. The whole of our tradition is against unpremeditated intercourse with them; before we speak we sort out what it is proper to say to them as if they were newly made acquaintances, although in fact they may be related to us by the closest ties.
>
> —Virginia Woolf, "Old and Young," 1916

> At any given period of transition there are always three generations actively in being: the great old men on the heights in the background, still wielding authority from their achievement, and in some cases still achieving, the men in their fifties, sixties, seventies, and even eighties, in the full vigour of their maturity, occupying the middle distance, and the young men in the foreground dreaming and plotting the creation of the future.
>
> —Richard LeGallienne, *The Romantic 90's*, 1925

When T. S. Eliot remarked after her death on "the particular advantage" Virginia Woolf had possessed in holding "a kind of hereditary position in English letters" and garnering "the incidental benefits that position bestowed," he identified one of the contexts that consistently shaped her fictional and critical output in the first two decades of her career (121). To an ambitious American like Eliot, who may have perceived that position as an entirely good thing, those "incidental benefits" would have included actual and symbolic access to personal and professional networks of "great" writers and artists as well as their descendants, intersecting networks created by relationships on both sides of her family and by her father's first marriage. But for her part, Woolf recognized not only the positive benefits but also the incipient drawbacks of her situation. Thus in noting the unearned privilege of Katharine Hilbery's birth with a quick nod to Francis Galton's *Hereditary Genius* (1869), the narrator of *Night and Day* makes it clear that prestigious ancestors constitute a very valuable but potentially unnerving endowment.[1] They confer on later generations what the historian of anthropology Adam Kuper calls the "powerful competitive advantage" of "sustained alliances," which results from the fictional Alardyces having "married and intermarried" among themselves ("Changing" 721; *Night* 31, ch. 3). Their descendants form part of an elite stratum that Noel Annan memorably if problematically termed "the intellectual aristocracy."[2]

Dissecting the key features of that structure, Woolf's narrator asserts, "No very great merit is required, once you bear a well-known name, to put you into a position where it is easier on the whole to be eminent than obscure" (30–31). One's individual "merit" aside, knowing the right people makes all the difference for the sons and grandsons of the "eminent," who can always count on cousins in high places: "One finds them at the tops of professions, with letters after their names; they sit in luxurious public offices, with private secretaries attached to them; they write solid books in dark covers, issued by the presses of the two great universities, and when one of them dies the chances are that another of them writes his biography"—as did Leslie Stephen on his brother James Fitzjames's death. "And if this is true of the sons," the narrator intones, "even the daughters, even in the nineteenth century, are apt to become people of importance—philanthropists and educationalists if they are spinsters, and the wives of distinguished men if they marry"— unless they become "lamentable exceptions" to the rule, as Woolf herself feared she might (31).[3]

Despite her embrace of obscurity in the 1930s and her skepticism about eminence—apparent in the allusion to *Hereditary Genius*, in which we find six entries for male Stephens but none for their mothers, sisters, wives, or daughters—Woolf labored in her first decades as a professional writer to turn her family legacy to her own uses, rather than suffer under its weight (Galton 185).[4] More broadly, she returned repeatedly in the early years of her career to preoccupations and problems that had exercised two prior Victorian generations of writers, both acknowledging and denying the significant impact of their concerns on her own writerly practice. During the first two decades of the twentieth century—marked by her continuing work as a book reviewer; the long-protracted making of *The Voyage Out*; and the publication of such short fictions as "The Mark on the Wall" (1917) and "Kew Gardens" (1919), which constituted her breakthrough into experimental form—Woolf's relations to prior yet still palpable generations had real urgency.

Even as she aimed to set aside the putative advantages of her "hereditary position," we can feel some ancestral pressure at work. Parodying the halting manner in which Henry James spoke, as she would again in the first chapter of *Night and Day*, she reported to Violet Dickinson in 1907 that when this eminent family friend addressed her as "your fathers daughter nay your grandfathers grandchild—the descendant I may say of a century—of a century—of quill pens and ink—ink—ink pots," "I felt like a condemned person, who sees the knife drop and stick and drop again": "Never did any woman hate 'writing' as much as I do" (V. Woolf, *Letters* 1: 306).[5] Whatever the "incidental benefits," and doubtless there were many, to be the daughter, niece, and granddaughter of writers, and to choose the writer's path—rather than the more conventionally feminine role of philanthropist, educationalist, or wife—meant laboring under high expectations and high standards and thus encountering some significant obstacles as well.

I argue in this chapter that *Night and Day* marks an effort on the part of this third-generation daughter to represent and work through the literary and personal legacy of her antecedents. Discriminating between "great" mid-Victorians and their lesser descendants, Woolf excised significant parts of a late-Victorian legacy from the literary-historical narrative that this novel, along with her critical writing, shaped for its readers, a tactic with lasting effects. And in creating a tie between grandfather and grandchild that cuts out the intermediate, specifically "maternal generation," we can read Woolf's deliberate framing of her own relation to a dominant strand of the English novelistic tradition.

The view of late-Victorian literary production that Woolf thus helped to construct is far more homogeneous than the one that such scholars as Ann Ardis, Sally Ledger, Lyn Pykett, Talia Schaffer, Margaret D. Stetz, and many others have created over the last several decades, in which the end of "Victorianism" is seen to be already well under way at least two decades before Victoria's actual demise. These and many other recent critics working on the contested terrain of fin-de-siècle literary and cultural history would agree that Woolf's essays, reviews, and first two novels not only created a gulf between the Georgians and their immediate predecessors, the Edwardian materialists, but also diminished both the male and, more problematically, the female writers whose careers took shape at the end of the nineteenth century. Still, the motivating factors in Woolf's erasure of the late Victorians have yet to be fully explored. Rethinking Woolf's relationship to the immediate past leads to new conclusions about where and how she does or does not borrow from, resist, or reject its legacy, conclusions that ought to enable us to understand her own legacy more precisely.

Reviewing the 1890s

According to Steve Ellis, Woolf did not start using the word "Victorian" as a term of contrast with present time until around 1916, in "A Man with a View," a review of a book about Samuel Butler, who frequently figures in her writing as anticipating the iconoclastic spirit of the new century (Ellis 7; *Essays* 2: 34–39). But when she does use the term, her construction of distinctions among Victorians, Edwardians, and Georgians sometimes subordinates continuities to differences in a reductive or parodic way. Casting her mother's friend Elizabeth Robins (b. 1862) as "a pre-war writer" in reviewing the short stories collected in *The Mills of the Gods* (1920), for example, Woolf puts the periodizing principle firmly in place as a means of denying this older contemporary any purchase on the shared "modern" present. "At the end of each [story]," she writes, "one can pencil a date—any date between 1895 and 1910 will do; the date that is quite out of the question is the date 1920," here creating what Bonnie Kime Scott calls "a complicated scenario of generational and stylistic difference" (*Essays* 3: 228; Scott 62).[6] At other moments, however, as in a letter to Janet Case from 1925, Woolf rejected her own somewhat glib use of period shorthand: "I don't think you settle the matter by labelling the elderly Victorians and the young Georgians" (*Letters* 3: 211).

More often than not, Woolf is highly self-conscious, even strategic, about such "labelling." Much later in her career, the unfinished essay "Anon" (1940) casts the Georgian writers' turn away from the Edwardians as not so much a "predicament," as she calls it in "On Re-reading Novels," (1922), as a conventional writerly tactic for coping with the immediate past (*Essays* 3: 336). "The modern writer attacks the actual work of some one of the generation that has just gone"—or not quite "gone," in the case of Arnold Bennett, H. G. Wells, or John Galsworthy, writers who were among her older contemporaries; indeed, more or less exact contemporaries of her half brothers ("Anon," *Essays* 6: 590). On the basis of this late, unfinished essay, we might posit that Woolf became increasingly skeptical of the period labels she had once deployed as a means of attack or containment. But rather than presume in advance a one-directional movement over time away from them, a properly historicist understanding of Woolf's own historicizing practices ought to take note of the contradictory impulses that punctuate her narratives about the recent literary past, and to see those impulses as responding to shifting circumstances and particular contexts.[7]

When Woolf juxtaposes Edwardians to Victorians in "On Re-reading Novels," for instance, an essay to which I return at the end of this chapter, the latter clearly come out on top. But when she shifts her attention to consider multiple Victorian generations and to make distinctions among them, the "greatness" factor comes into play, as for Woolf not all Victorian generations are equal. One critic claims that modernist "hostility was directed, almost exclusively, at the early and mid-Victorians" and that "to be a late Victorian was to escape the contempt directed at the earlier generations," while another notes that "the *fin de siècle*, because of its doubts, skepticism, and rejections of identity and one Truth, was more often annexed to modernity than Victorianism" (Keating 93; Gagnier 143). To be sure, Woolf and her circle, like Victorianists today, routinely differentiated between the mid-Victorian Dickens and Thackeray and the later, longer-lived, yet still "Victorian" novelists Meredith and Hardy. The latter were among the living writers whom the Cambridge men at the core of Bloomsbury most admired for "breaking away," in the words of Leonard Woolf, "from the cosmic and social assumptions" of Dickens and Thackeray by "challenging their standards of morality" (*Sowing* 181). But while the "great" later Victorian writers who survived into the twentieth century—Meredith, Hardy, James, and the slightly younger Gissing and Joseph Conrad—were mostly free from the contempt of the "third generation," their lesser male contemporaries were not.

The collective portrait of 1890s artists that Woolf considers in her review of *Nights* (1916) by Elizabeth Robins Pennell (b. 1855), for example, includes such divergent figures as William Ernest Henley, leader of the manly Young Men, and the decadent Aubrey Beardsley, each of whom the author, herself a participant in multiple aestheticist networks of the time, recalls in some detail.[8] Countering Pennell's vision, which conjoins these highly disparate men with their Pre-Raphaelite precursors as activist rebels against "Victorian sham prudery and respectability," Woolf describes the literary output of the 1890s as a diminished thing (Pennell 190; qtd. in "The Fighting Nineties," *Essays* 2: 45). And its makers were similarly ephemeral (Beardsley died before the end of the decade and Henley did not last much longer) and effeminate (a label that would have sent the latter rolling over in his grave): "The little shelf of books bequeathed to us by the writers of that age has always seemed the fruit of an evening time after the hot blaze of day, when swift, moth-like spirits were abroad; a time of graceful talent and little thin volumes whose authors had done with life long before they were old" (45). Here Woolf clearly participates in the modernist construction of a late-Victorian twilight, even as her remarks recall Holbrook Jackson's contemporary representation of the Decadence as "a movement of elderly youths who wrote themselves out in a slender volume or so of hot verse or ornate prose, and slipped away to die in taverns or gutters" (84).

Ten years later, Woolf's review of *The Romantic '90s* by Richard Le Gallienne, who was aligned with John Lane's circle rather than Henley's, changes the metaphor but not the meaning. Works by Ernest Dowson and Oscar Wilde—and by Arthur Symons and John Davidson, both of whom Woolf had positively reviewed in the mid-1910s—fail to justify the assertion that the decade witnessed a burst of "creative revolutionary energy" (Le Gallienne 137; qtd. in "Romance and the 'Nineties," *Essays* 4: 359). "We have got into the way of thinking of that 'amazing decade,'" she continues, "as the sophisticated, elongated, tapering tail to the body of the robust lion" (360). Crediting Le Gallienne for his "reasoned and defended point of view," Woolf nonetheless quotes only so as to contest his claim that "all our present-day developments amount to little more than pale and exaggerated copying of the 'nineties" (Le Gallienne 137; qtd. 359). Terming it "a curious overstatement," she yet concedes that writers she refers to elsewhere as Edwardians—Wells and Bennett, or Rudyard Kipling and W. B. Yeats—"can all be made to fall within the decade if we choose," a concession that might but does not lead to further reevaluation of the period concept (360). Although Woolf partially accepts the arbitrariness of these designations, she avoids comment on Le Gallienne's own fullest periodizing claim, one echoed by both Peter Keating and Regenia Gagnier: "It is plain that here was not so much the ending of a century as the beginning of a new one. Those last ten years of the nineteenth century properly belong to the twentieth century" (Le Gallienne 136). "'The '90s' are usually spoken of as if they had only one colour," he complains, which constitutes a "tempting" but "misleading" effort "to compress a period into a formula" (162).[9]

Woolf does sometimes reject that "formula" for compression. Her review of *Streaks of Life* (1921), the second volume of memoirs by Ethel Smyth (b. 1858), specifically references men who were at once Smyth's immediate contemporaries and friends of her own father, characterizing the 1890s as "the age of . . . Henley and Stevenson." Albeit at first "inclined to risk a theory that the prominent artistic figures of that time were racy, slangy, outspoken men and women; very patriotic, very combative, and very warm-hearted: differing in all these respects, not necessarily for the worse, from those who now occupy the stage," she recants it rather than "impute to an age what is, as a matter of fact, true only of one individual," the memoirist herself, whom Woolf would not get to know personally for another ten years ("Ethel Smyth,"

Essays 3: 298). Proffering but rejecting this equally partial version of the decade—albeit a far more "robust" and "combative" image than the lion's sinuous tail or those "moth-like spirits"—Woolf indicates her awareness that she could construct multiple versions of a contested past.

Writing just around the same time, another, older commentator also denied there was much difference between the 1890s and the 1920s. In the words of Smyth's good friend, Maurice Baring, who had close ties to the birth family of Molly MacCarthy as well as to Vernon Lee (b. 1856), "The 'nineties were, from the point of view of art and literature, much like any other period. If you want to know what literary conversation was like in the 'nineties you can hear it any day at the Reform Club. If you compare the articles on literature or art that appeared in the *Speaker* of 1892–3 with the articles in the *New Statesman* of 1921, you will find little difference between the two" (147). By contrast, the younger Woolf clearly had a stake in maintaining a sense of difference. Thus she concludes the Le Gallienne review of 1926, for example, with brief summaries of some of his more trifling anecdotes regarding Pater and Swinburne. On the whole she tends to reproduce "the language of effeteness and effeminacy" so as to distance late-Victorian writers from the "modern" present without commenting on how this discursive construction of the decade implicitly derides both the feminine and the feminized (Freedman xvi). She even adopts this idiom herself in some of her critical works: if "modern literature . . . had grown a little sultry and scented with Oscar Wilde and Walter Pater," she writes in the explicitly gendered tones of "Poetry, Fiction, and the Future" (1927), she "revived instantly from her nineteenth-century languor when Samuel Butler and Bernard Shaw began to burn their feathers and apply their salts to her nose" (*Essays* 4: 434).

Differentiating herself and her generation from this array of male precursors, Woolf diminishes the writers of the fin de siècle primarily as a means of clearing out a space for more direct communication and communion, I will contend, with the "great." Commenting on "the effacing of the 90s generation" from her generational map of "recent literary history," which ranges "the great Victorians" against the disappointing Edwardians, Ellis asserts that Woolf's "ancestral position in the 'respectable' literary establishment is a totally other world to the late Victorian decadence," thus implying that her exclusion of later Victorians from the map had its sole origins in her family background (59, 58). To be sure, Virginia Stephen's position as the daughter of an eminent but elderly literary critic born five years before Victoria came to the throne forms one basis for understanding what she did and did not constitute as part of the "great" literary tradition, as I will explore in the next chapter. That position creates a platform from which she made her earliest judgments on those male predecessors who were active in the later nineteenth century. Such judgments can be glimpsed in both her novels and her reviews and also shapes her less-than-sympathetic perspective on New Women writers who took up issues of sexual morality in their work. But the active disavowal of what I will call second-generation writers, while certainly shaped in part by familial context, is just one facet of a broader and deeper drive in the first decades of her career to establish connections with an earlier, "greater" Victorian group while bypassing this intermediate and imperfect one. If Dickens and Thackeray are rejected—albeit only partially, in the case of the latter—for their sentimentality and "their cosmic and social assumptions," their greatness is seldom called into question. Indeed, as I will demonstrate below, Woolf's attitude on artistic greatness was itself very much of a piece with second-generation Victorian attitudes on the subject, including her own father's.

To some extent, Woolf's exclusion of virtually all late-Victorian women writers from such discussions may have been contingent on the literary history of the fin de siècle as it was being written in the first decades of the twentieth century. Looking more closely at the books by Pennell and Le Gallienne, for example, we can see that each represents the 1890s primarily though not exclusively as a male affair, supporting the claim that "the neglect of women's writing began with the first histories of aestheticism" (Schaffer and Psomiades 13). Women writers make only token appearances in each text. Pennell just mentions in passing A. Mary F. Robinson (b. 1857), Rosamond Marriott Watson (b. 1860), and Violet Hunt while spending many pages on Henley (whose *Essays* Woolf reviewed in 1921) and his "Young Men" (129, 157, 158). Le Gallienne recalls meeting Michael Field (pseud. Katharine Bradley [b. 1846] and Edith Cooper [b. 1862]) at Meredith's home; seeing Marriott Watson and E. Nesbit (b. 1858) at John Lane's teas—debarred by sex, one supposes, from the publisher's "masculine evenings"; and even going so far as to read Alice Meynell, whom he credits, along with her husband Wilfrid, with establishing "one of the many influential groups . . . of that energetic seminal period . . . independently contributing to the creation of a new age" (45, 165, 136). But not one of these well-known, successful women writers gets the sustained attention that both Pennell and Le Gallienne give to their male peers, a fact that Woolf's reviews do not acknowledge, as we might expect them to, even given the constraints of periodical publication as she experienced them. A picture of the 1890s as effete and effeminate yet simultaneously undisturbed by actual writing women perhaps better serves Woolf's own purposes at this point in her career than either wrestling with unruly precursors or making public value judgments on women's writing.

Older Female Contemporaries and the Contest between Generations

It may also be the case, however, that some of her elder female contemporaries occupied the privileged position that Woolf sought to achieve for herself, a phenomenon that Pierre Bourdieu analyzes in "The Field of Cultural Production," in which a contest between generations helps to structure the literary field.[10] In the early stages of her career, as a reader, reviewer, and would-be novelist, Woolf can be located among "the newcomers" who, in Bourdieu's words, "must assert their difference, get it known and recognized, get themselves known and recognized ('make a name for themselves'), by endeavouring to impose new modes of thought and expression, out of key with the prevailing modes of thought" (58). Bourdieu considers this contest or struggle, which consists of what he calls "position-takings," not as voluntarily chosen but as structurally inevitable: "Because position-takings arise quasi-mechanically—that is, almost independently of the agents' consciousness and wills—from the relationship between positions, they take relatively invariant forms"; "the history of the field arises from the struggle between the established figures and the young challengers" (59, 60). If we apply this to her critique of Robins, for example, Woolf shows herself to be one of "those who cannot make their own mark without pushing into the past those who have an interest in stopping the clock, eternalizing the present stage of things" (60). Whether early or late in her career, however, the "struggle" or "contest" in which she engages publicly, through her essays and reviews, almost always involves only men. Why is that? She offers one answer in a cancelled passage from *Women and Fiction*: she will name no women writers, for that would be "discourteous"; "one should keep one's preferences among the living to oneself" (110). But Bourdieu suggests another: "Adversaries whom one would prefer to destroy by ignoring . . . cannot be combated without consecrating them" ("Field" 42).

Within that framework, Woolf enhances the status of Wells, Bennett, and Galsworthy even as she takes them down. Ignoring those older female contemporaries signifies an effort to "destroy" them by other means. "By refusing to mention . . . female writers in her great canon-forming polemics," Molly Hite argues, "Woolf helped make them forgotten by much of twentieth-century literary history, or at best, regarded as minor" ("Public Woman" 523; cf. E. Blair 16–19). In other words, she fails to "consecrate" them, the term Bourdieu uses to sum up the impact of prizes, awards, or other markers of success on the reputations of those you admire or emulate. Building on Terry Lovell's account of Bourdieu's potential uses for feminist theory, we could count Woolf among those who embrace "forms of social and intellectual life which are not exclusively agonistic, as Bourdieu's seem to be; not structured around hierarchy, male domination, cut-throat competition, [and] symbolic violence" (27). There is, of course, substantial evidence to think this is the case, as Woolf persistently criticized these foundational aspects of patriarchy. That Woolf is, however, one of the few women writers Bourdieu himself ever mentions—in his reading of *To the Lighthouse* in *Masculine Domination*—supports the very point he makes (69–80). She managed to achieve "exceptional status" in part by understanding and even enforcing the rules of a game (or struggle, or battle) that might well otherwise have excluded her.

By considering Woolf's public and private comments from earlier and later in her career on her older contemporaries among women writers, as I do here and elsewhere in this book, we can register both her tactics of disavowal, in their "relatively invariant forms," and her subsequent revaluation of at least some of the work of "the maternal generation" as she moved over time from one position to another, from young challenger to established figure. For example, early in her career she characterized Alice Meynell—a serious candidate for the laureateship vacated at Tennyson's death in 1892—as very much behind the times, which was not at all the way Meynell's male contemporaries saw her. Considering her essays rather than her poetry in 1898, Bennett wrote, "Among modern writers, Mrs. Alice Meynell has a style unsurpassed in simplicity, fineness, and strength" (*Journalism* 39). Meredith called her "a great Englishwoman of Letters"; Wilde dubbed her "the new sibyl of style" (qtd. in Peterson 174, 201). Although Woolf might have found female antecedents for "Bloomsbury's self-conscious aestheticism" in the "intense explorations of interdependence" conducted by Meynell—who undertakes, in Gagnier's words, "a critique of linearity and progress as profound as the modernism of Woolf and Joyce"—she did not (75, 77). In this context, Woolf's tactic as a "newcomer" was to posit "a wider chronological and cognitive space between herself and her predecessor"—or older contemporary—"than actually existed" (Schaffer 193). Yet, as she aged, Woolf engaged in a more sustained manner with this figure of the writing woman, and with at least some of Meynell's writing.

At the age of twenty-seven, Virginia Stephen met Meynell during a luncheon with Bernard and Mary Berenson (b. 1864; née Smith) at the Villa I Tatti outside Florence. Her journal describes this still-eminent writer as "a lean, attenuated woman, who had a face like that of a transfixed hare" and seemed primed for "chaste expression" (*Passionate* 398).[11] Apparently familiar with and appreciative of Meynell's poetry, she expresses disappointment at finding the source of "even such words as Mrs. Meynells [*sic*]" to be "a lank slightly absurd & altogether insignificant little body" (399). Whereas "once, no doubt, she was a poetess, & trod the fields of Parnassus," the meager flesh now declares a falling off (398–99). For her part, Meynell recorded this meeting in very different terms: as one of Coventry Patmore's closest confidantes in the last years of his life, she took note of the Stephen sisters only as the granddaughters of Mia Jackson, one of Patmore's other longtime female intimates (Badeni 198).[12]

But once she ages out of the newcomer group and becomes an established figure herself, Woolf's position in relation to Meynell's shifts. Recalling that visit to Italy in her diary for 21 August 1929, Woolf takes a different tack twenty years later, by reflecting back on the person who made those remarks. Referring to her younger self as "rustic, provincial & badly dressed," she admits, "I was unhappy that summer; & bitter in all my judgments" (*Diary* 3: 243). Just a few days later, while skimming Viola Meynell's recently published memoir of her mother, which Leonard was reviewing for the *Nation and Athenaeum*, she records that she has had to "read a page or two of Samuel Butler's notebooks to take the taste of Alice Meynell's life out of my mouth" (*Essays* 5: 483n1; *Diary* 3: 250). Yet even here, in reading about Meynell, she owns herself "interested; a little teased by the tight airless Meynell style; & then I think what they had that we had not—some suavity & grace" (250). Reading the memoir recalls the 1909 meeting with Meynell and even leads her to reread her account of that meeting, which then results in further revision of a prior judgment: "I recorded my regret that one ever saw poetesses in the flesh. For she was a poetess too—it strikes me that one or two little poems will survive all that my father ever wrote" (251).[13] While this might sound like damning with faint praise, it does suggest that as Woolf aged out of one group and into another, she came to rate Meynell's achievement more highly. And this indicates that, for all her explicit and implied criticism of it, Woolf saw her predecessor and her work differently with the passage of time—Alice Meynell had reached R, we might say, while Leslie Stephen had remained stuck at Q—and, perhaps, in the mellowing light of her own consecration.[14]

Another older contemporary—"the caustic, the fastidious, the learned, the well-loved and the very 'difficult'" Vernon Lee—met with similar treatment from Woolf, despite, or perhaps because of, the fact that the two had much in common (Swanwick 257).[15] Admired by Roger Fry and Desmond MacCarthy, Lee is among the very few living women writers Woolf mentions in *A Room of One's Own* (Smyth, *What* 27; Cecil and Cecil 209–10; *Room* 78). In a letter of 1922, she remembered her visiting Talland House in St. Ives thirty years earlier as "a dashing authoress" who "gave my father her books" (*Letters* 2: 550). He had published Lee's work in the *Cornhill*, and she had been to the Stephens' South Kensington home on at least two occasions, in 1882 and 1883, the latter of which she described as "very dull" (V. Lee 94, 127). Woolf met Lee again both in 1904 and during the Stephen sisters' 1909 trip to Florence, "when [Lee] fell in love with Nessa," at least in Virginia's estimation (*Letters* 2: 550).[16] Politically speaking, they were in many respects fellow travelers. An early member of the Union of Democratic Control alongside such Bloomsbury associates as Goldsworthy Lowes Dickinson, Bertrand Russell, Phillip and Ottoline Morrell (b. 1873), Adrian and Karin Stephen (b. 1889; née Costelloe), and Leonard Woolf, Lee attended meetings, appeared on platforms, and wrote letters to editors, protesting the demonization of all things German. "Lee's vehement advocacy of pacificism brought her into conflict with many of her feminist friends and associates," as Gillian Beer has established, during the militant phase of the suffrage campaign ("Dissidence" 111). If it is the case that "Woolf considered the Great War a completely masculine occupation," and thus found it difficult at the time of the war to reconcile "her belief that war is antithetical to female nature" with the positions and actions of so many Englishwomen, Lee did not: the critical pacifist position she occupied then clearly anticipates the one at which Woolf would arrive in later life (Wussow, *Nightmare* 37, 38).

Woolf nonetheless almost always approached Lee's work with ambivalence. Reviewing *The Sentimental Traveller* in 1908, she deems its method "purely impressionist," filled with "egotistical diversions" (*Essays* 1: 157). "With much of the curiosity, the candour, and the sensitiveness to trifles of the true essayist," this writer "lacks the exquisite taste and penetrating clearness of sight" that characterizes Charles Lamb (often a touchstone) or James (158). Privately, in a contemporary letter to Violet Dickinson, she confessed, "I am sobbing with misery over Vernon Lee, who really turns all good writing to vapour. . . . I put her on my black list, with Mrs. Humphry Ward. But though this is true as truth . . . still it can't be said in print" (*Letters* 1: 320). In her review of another collection of essays the following year, Woolf again criticizes Lee's egocentrism: "Her statements have none of the Divine impersonality which stamps the myths and visions of Plato, but they are expressions of individual opinion. The very qualities of her style get in the way of any clear sight of the matter which she discusses; images and symbols, unless they spring from a profound understanding, illustrate not the object but the writer" ("Art and Life," *Essays* 1: 279). A long diary entry from April 1919 that reflects on diary writing itself posits Lee's "slack & untidy" writing as an example to avoid: "Her ligaments are too loose for my taste" (*Diary* 1: 266). It's not until "The Modern Essay," revised for *The Common Reader* (1925), that she has an unambiguously good word to say about Lee, placing her in the company of Lamb, Bacon, Beerbohm, Pater, and her own father as essayists who "reach[] the farther shore" by their "fierce attachment to an idea" (*Essays* 4: 224).

As Christa Zorn has argued, "The discord between Lee and Woolf is best understood as a conflict between two generations of women writers," while other scholars have also begun to think about the relationship between the two as a function of the temporal dynamics of periodization (75). Angela Leighton is surely correct that to writers of Woolf's generation, "Vernon Lee presented the puzzle of an eminent Victorian who, not only had not quietly passed away, but was sometimes, in her sheer formal inventiveness, as avant-garde as they" (100). And as Kristin Mahoney puts it, "Lee is at once of the past and the future, a remnant of Victorian aestheticism who is devoted, almost stubbornly, to innovative thinking" (314). Although matters of periodization are certainly important, making Lee a modernist—or Woolf a Victorian, for that matter, as Jane Goldman has criticized Ellis for doing—isn't quite what I'm aiming at here (Goldman, "Virginia" 37–38). Instead, I follow Bourdieu in positing that "the agents engaged in the struggle" that constitutes the literary field "are both contemporaries—precisely by virtue of the struggle which synchronizes them—and separated by time and in respect of time": "Consecrated writers," he concludes, "recognize their contemporaries only in the past" ("Field" 60). It's on this ground and in these terms that an aging Woolf comes to see Lee and perhaps Meynell, too, "more as a contemporary," the phrase with which she described her new sense of relationship to Leslie Stephen on what would have been his ninety-sixth birthday, a year and a half after the publication of *To the Lighthouse* and about twenty-five years after his death. Having authored her own consecration by her close attention to the established rules of the game made Woolf, in the second half of her career, less inclined to wage the "struggle" to exclude others, because she had already won it. By investigating her location as a member of the "third generation"—an early title for *Night and Day*—we can begin to comprehend the contours of that shift over time, in exploring the complex mix of distance and proximity that structures her early-career relations to male and especially female writers of a very immediate past.

"Ancestor-Worship"

Woolf problematizes her own position in an extended family of writers in *Night and Day* especially through her representation of Katharine Hilbery. In a key instance of thinking back through (or with) the Victorian grandfather, occurring about two-thirds of the way through the novel, Woolf's heroine achieves momentary communion with her long-dead maternal ancestor,

Richard Alardyce—a fictive version of William Thackeray, described by the narrator as "a poet eminent among the poets of England"—in a way that is paradigmatic for understanding the structuring antagonisms of Woolf's early career (30; ch. 3). "Feeling unable to decide" whether a newly received "proof-sheet" should be framed and hung "on the staircase" or displace another "relic" in the overcrowded room dedicated to "ancestor-worship," Katharine "glance[s] at the portrait of her grandfather, as if to ask his opinion." Looking at it, she wonders if his dreams had ever resembled her own, while the narrator remarks that his "expression repeated itself curiously upon Katharine's face as she gazed up into his," suggesting a reciprocal influence:

> The young man who was her grandfather looked vaguely over her head. The sensual lips were slightly parted, and gave the face an expression of beholding something lovely or miraculous vanishing or just rising upon the rim of the distance. . . . She wondered what he was looking for; were there waves beating upon a shore for him, too, she wondered, and heroes riding through the leaf-hung forests? For perhaps the first time in her life she thought of him as a man, young, unhappy, tempestuous, full of desires and faults; for the first time she realized him for herself, and not from her mother's memory. He might have been her brother, she thought. It seemed to her that they were akin, with the mysterious kinship of blood which makes it seem possible to interpret the sights which the eyes of the dead behold so intently, or even to believe that they look with us upon our present joys and sorrows. (337–38; ch. 24)[17]

As Aaron Jaffe argues in his work on modernism and celebrity, following the lead of the art historian Paul Barlow, the nineteenth-century "portraiture ideal . . . draw[s] on a myth of unmediated contact between sitter and portraitist" that enables the spectator to glimpse "lived identity as once experienced first-hand" (172). In this textual form, representing the portrait of Alardyce as "vaguely" looking out at the world, as his descendant does so often in the novel, with a gaze fixed on "something . . . rising upon the rim of the distance," the novel imaginatively revivifies the famous dead man, making him share in the "perplexities" of the present. Crucially, Katharine imagines that they look not so much at one another, but outward and together. Envisioning Alardyce as a younger man of about her own age, she construes him almost as "her brother," indicating his potential as a partner or peer, rather than an indifferent witness or a remote influence, in the effort to resolve the open questions in Katharine's life and in Woolf's novel. Unlike her mother, Katharine does not do "homage" to the dead eminence. Instead, she offers him her "doubts, questionings, and despondencies" regarding the course her life should take.

Chief among her "perplexities" at this point in the novel is not just whom to marry but whether to marry at all, or, if not, what else to with "the life which [the dead] had given her, the life which they had lived": her grandfather's portrait seems to ask in return only "some share in what she suffered and achieved" (*Night* 338).

The passage thus weighs the grandfather's potential role in resolving both the heroine and her author's dilemma even as *Night and Day* "allegorically recovers" Woolf's relationship to those she classed among her literary ancestors (Zemgulys 186). While "great" writers, from Shakespeare to Fielding to Dostoevsky, all have a "share" in the novel, so, too, do those literary figures associated with the familial past.[18] Adopting "the courtship narrative," which inserts this novel into the tradition of domestic fiction in which Austen had set the standard, not only indicates the novel's "vexed commitments to both tradition and novelty" but also provides for its author "a way of immersing herself in, and examining in writing, the social order into which she had been born" (Outka 130; De Gay, *Virginia* 45). More specifically, it sizes up the multigenerational literary family to which Woolf belonged, casting parts for Leslie Stephen's first father- and sister-in-law in this fiction. Confronting the literary import of her extended family legacy and analyzing it in self-conscious fashion, Woolf also appropriated it for her own ends, a tactic she commends in her review of a memoir by Augustine Birrell of his mid-Victorian father-in-law, the poet Frederick Locker-Lampson, published just a year after *Night and Day*. Commenting on Birrell's capacity for bringing back the dead, she asserted that he "reduces these nineteenth-century phantoms"—"Tennyson and Thackeray, Browning and Ruskin, George Eliot and Matthew Arnold"—"to human scale": "Thackeray, in particular," she writes, "inspires the fancy that one could have talked to him as to a human being" ("A Character Sketch," *Essays* 3: 256, 257). Revivifying the "phantoms" of a "great" Victorian tradition, Birrell makes them available, as Woolf also tried to, for everyday use.

At the same time, *Night and Day* conceives the intersubjective relations between grandfather and granddaughter as a matter of both what is handed down—as we usually figure matters of (literary) tradition—and what is given back, suggesting an interest in contributing to and constructing that tradition. Previewed in *The Voyage Out*, Woolf's strategy in *Night and Day* for making use of a "great" tradition involves excising an intermediate generation, which is largely but not entirely feminized. While Alardyce's portrait is itself a representation and so instantiates the inevitability of mediation, the passage emphasizes that "for the first time in her life," Katharine "realized him for herself" and not through "her mother's memory," another detail that we may read in allegorical terms. We might take "the sight of [the] concord" between granddaughter and grandfather, that is, as a sign of a breach between this daughter and her mother ("On Re-reading Novels," *Essays* 3: 336). Mrs. Hilbery, who "lament[s] the passing of the great days of the nineteenth century," shapes her daughter's experience of both the family and the literary tradition and indeed combines the two in her own person (*Night* 32; ch. 3). Even as the scene stages the desire for a direct encounter with an "eminent" Victorian man of letters, then, the intervening mother seems to stand in her daughter's way. Katharine's effort to see with Alardyce thus encodes several layers of critique, directed not so much at the mid-Victorian grandfather as at the long-lived late-Victorian mother. In its "constructive and purposeful retrieval of the past," *Night and Day* yet aims, then, to bypass the feminized mediations of the second generation by way of Katharine's cross-generational and cross-gender appeal (Ellis 4).

As Mrs. Hilbery dates the end of her parents' marriage to some "sixty years" before the action of the novel, itself set a few years before the Great War, we can see that Woolf deliberately chose to place the grandfather in the early- or mid-Victorian past, thus making him safely remote rather than uncomfortably close (102; ch. 7). Bringing him back as a peer rather than a patriarch, she also cuts him down to a manageable size: Katharine perceives him as a friend rather than an antagonistic elder, and the fact of his own marital unhappiness makes him something of an ally. While children, parents, and grandparents may indeed be "dressed differently," members of each generation all struggle with questions of marriage, sexuality, and conventional morality, a primary focus of the novel for more than a century. And in the two or three decades prior to the appearance of Woolf's first novels, those questions had been given even greater prominence in fiction not only by Hardy and Gissing but also by such New Woman writers as Sarah Grand and Mona Caird (b. 1854). Indeed, one of the key continuities of *Night and Day* with both "the tradition" *and* "the counter-tradition," to adapt Joseph Allen Boone's formulation, lies in its debt to and argument with the conventions of the marriage plot. Considered in this light, that Katharine's appeal to the ancestor is both cross-generational and cross-gendered suggests a perceived need to think back beyond the women and the women writers of the second generation. And since Mrs. Hilbery's real-life prototype was one of Leslie and Julia Stephen's closest friends, Thackeray's daughter, Anne—whom the highly discriminating James called "a woman of genius"—it is arguably the first-generation writer that both novel and novelist look back to and befriend ("Art" 11).[19] Working on multiple levels, this scene thus stages a desire for an unmediated encounter with an "eminent" Victorian man of letters from the perspective of a member of the "third generation." *Night and Day* here represents and assesses a multigenerational literary legacy, articulated in familial terms, as Katharine moves from relying on her mother's mediation of Alardyce to claiming him as an ally.

Woolf's tactics in the novel also include adopting an aesthetic of impersonality and neutrality with partial but significant roots in the critical writing of both Leslie Stephen and some male writers of the second generation. Favoring values and techniques evinced by "great men" rather than their female counterparts, she recasts the conflict between fictional practice and sexual politics in modernist terms that obscure continuities between her work and that of two antecedent generations. Andrea Zemgulys rightly characterizes Woolf's position that "only by writing *impersonally* . . . can women writers produce as many literary masterpieces as have been produced by men" (156; emphasis in the original); indeed, as Hite has argued, Woolf "made impersonality a defining characteristic of great works of literature" (*Woolf's Ambiguities* 101). This recasting has significant implications, in generational and gendered terms, for Woolf's account of literary history. Turning now to her fictive portrait of Anne Thackeray Ritchie in the mother-daughter relation depicted in *Night and Day* and the novel's nuanced and thoughtful deliberations on the work of literary/familial biography these two female characters undertake, I will explore the difficulty of achieving an impersonal distance on a past that seems at once very much mediated and all too immediate.

Thackeray's Daughter

Although Woolf was ambivalent about her "hereditary position in English letters," Ritchie repeatedly emphasized that being "Thackeray's daughter" was a good thing. "The sons and daughters of men and women eminent in their generation are from circumstances fortunate in their opportunities," she wrote in a memoir of Robert Browning: "From childhood they know their parents' friends and contemporaries, the remarkable men and women who are the makers of the age, quite naturally and without excitement," including in her case almost all the celebrated writers, artists, and thinkers of the day (*Records* 129).[20] Professional as well as personal benefits accrued to Ritchie's position. Her father had facilitated her entrée into literary production, publishing her first essay, "Little Scholars" (1860), during his tenure at the *Cornhill Magazine*.[21] When she gave up writing fiction and turned to memoir, which draws on her "childhood memories, and the privileges associated with being her father's daughter," Ritchie continued to mine the resources provided by her place in a far-reaching literary network. Born in the year of Victoria's accession to the throne and outliving her Stephen brother-in-law by about fifteen years, she capitalized on these connections throughout her career as the legal and literary heir to her father's estate; her long "life enable[d] her to mediate between past and present, to affirm continuities and to explore change" (Debenham 89). Her centrality to Victorian literary culture is nicely epitomized in her place at Tennyson's Westminster Abbey funeral service in 1892, between an inconsolable Ellen Terry (b. 1847) on one side and her close friend Margaret Oliphant on the other (Gérin 228).[22]

Via the friendships she forged and her writing about them, as Woolf commented in her obituary, Ritchie became an "unacknowledged source of much that remains in men's minds about the Victorian age," "the transparent medium through which we behold the dead": "Again and again it has happened to us to trace down our conception of one of the great figures of the past not to the stout official biography consecrated to him, but to some little hint or fact or fancy dropped lightly by Lady Ritchie in passing" ("Lady Ritchie," *Essays* 3: 18). While that way of framing Ritchie's position downplays her considerable cultural capital, it accurately registers the circumstances that shaped her life and career; moreover, it recalls the relation that Katharine is momentarily able to achieve when she envisions her eminent dead grandfather as an "ordinary" man, suggesting an ongoing debt to Ritchie's capacity for providing imaginative access to the "great." In her diary, however, Woolf also addressed the gap between the woman she always called "Aunt Anny" and the younger generation, commenting that the elder "had the wits to feel how sharply we differed on current questions": "I admired her sincerely; but still the generations certainly look very different ways" (*Diary* 1: 247).

Woolf's tribute to Ritchie, however, differs significantly from the role assigned to Mrs. Hilbery in *Night and Day*, whose memories mediate her daughter's access to Alardyce's past in a fashion by no means "transparent," as first emerges in the novel's commentary on the difficulties of writing the eminent poet's biography.[23] Although Alardyce is long dead, the past he represents isn't really over for either Katharine or her mother in that they work together daily on composing his life. They thus undertake the kind of memorializing project at which Woolf would try her hand many times over the course of her career, from the pages she wrote in 1905 for F. W. Maitland's biography of Leslie Stephen (474–77); and the mock biographies with nineteenth-century content like "Memoirs of a Novelist," *Orlando*, and *Flush*; to her full-length biography, *Roger Fry* (1940). And so "a great part of [Katharine's] time was spent in imagination with the dead," sorting through materials for the book, among which "the most private lives of the most interesting people lay furled in yellow bundles of close-written manuscript" (34; ch. 3). Katharine had first experienced her family ties to "the glorious past, in which men and women grew to unexampled size," as "matter for satisfaction," but subsequently they become a stultifying force: "As the years wore on, the privileges of her lot were taken for granted, and certain drawbacks made themselves very manifest," such as "the risk of comparison" between figures of "the great age" and those of the diminished present (33). Described by the narrator as "half crushed," "sometimes [Katharine] felt that it was necessary for her very existence that she should free herself from the past; at others, that the past had completely displaced the present, which, when one resumed life after a morning among the dead, proved to be of an utterly thin and inferior composition" (38). And the mother's situation further intensifies the weight of the past for the daughter. Mrs. Hilbery not only has difficulty in writing "for more than ten minutes at a time" (34) but also is at a loss as to whether or not to include the facts of her parents' "most private lives." Refusing "to face the radical questions of what to leave in and what to leave out" in telling her father's story, she "could not decide how far the public was to be told the truth about the poet's separation from his wife" (35).[24]

Although such problems of biographical tact were commonplace in Victorian literary culture, Trev Lynn Broughton reminds us that the question of what biographers should or should not tell about "the most private lives" of their subjects received renewed attention late in the nineteenth century. To take a notable example, James Anthony Froude's candid revelations about Jane and Thomas Carlyle's marriage, based on the written materials each left behind, created a scandal that continued to garner attention well into the first decade of the new century in the wake of further speculation about whether his impotence was one source of their joint misery (T. Broughton 140–72; cf. Booth, *Homes* 209–11). That biographical contretemps would have resonated with Woolf because of Carlyle's long association with her grandfather, her father, and her uncle (a coexecutor of Carlyle's estate).[25] But Mrs. Hilbery's quandary also draws on another highly charged strand of extended Stephen family lore. It reconfigures the circumstances of Thackeray's marriage in the early 1840s, when his wife Isabella's postpartum suicide attempt and subsequent mental illness led him ultimately to put her away under close supervision, as Leslie and Julia Stephen would later do when Thackeray's granddaughter, named for the heroine of *Pendennis* (1848–50), was deemed incompetent for family life. Thackeray's anomalous position as a married man with close female friends—like Jane Brookfield, married to a Cambridge classmate, with whom he fell in love—but no available wife famously fueled the furor surrounding Charlotte Brontë's dedication of the second edition of *Jane Eyre* (1847) to him.[26] For this father was then in need of something like a governess for his two daughters: Minny (b. 1840), who married Leslie Stephen in

1867; and Anne, who remained close to Leslie after Minny's death in 1875, living in his house and helping to care for Laura.

Because Ritchie obeyed her father's command *not* to write his biography, although she twice produced biographical introductions to lavish and lucrative editions of his collected works, she was spared some of Mrs. Hilbery's difficulties but struggled nonetheless with the whole question of biographical tact. She quoted her father as saying, "Mind when I drop there is to be no life written of me," an injunction Leslie Stephen supported (Ritchie, *Anne* 130). But as Virginia R. Hyman points out, "the series of scandalous biographies" that appeared during the 1880s so impugned her father's reputation that Ritchie "could do little to restore the damage that had already been done" ("Concealment" 123). As she wrote in 1892 to Hallam Tennyson, another surviving child entrusted with shaping and protecting a literary father's legacy, "in [my father's] case there were so many complications—not the least my Mothers [*sic*] illness & possible recovery"—that "to write a true life was alas impossible & a make up one omitting all that was most real was no good" (qtd. in Aplin 59).[27] These sentiments differ hardly at all from those Froude would express, in a posthumous publication that defended the candor with which he had depicted the Carlyle marriage: "The biographies of the great men of the past . . . are generally useless. They are idle and incredible panegyrics, with features drawn without shadows, false, conventional, and worthless. The only 'Life' of a man which is not worse than useless is a 'Life' which tells all the truth so far as the biographer knows it" (40). Virginia Stephen made the same point herself in 1909: since "the most interesting event" of the biographical subject's life in "Memoirs of a Novelist," "owing to the nervous prudery and the dreary literary conventions of her friend, is thus a blank," the resulting volume resembles "a wax work as it were of Miss Willatt preserved under glass" (73, 74). And thirty years later, Virginia Woolf said much the same thing about "Victorian biographies": they are "like the wax figures now preserved in Westminster Abbey that were carried in funeral processions through the street—effigies that have only a smooth superficial likeness to the body in the coffin" ("The Art of Biography," *Essays* 6: 182).

While Ritchie could not "write a true life" without potentially incurring scandal or dishonoring her father's wish, she nonetheless refused to write a "make up one" that would falsify "what was most real" about her parents' lives, including her mother's mental illness. Viewed in this light, we might construe Mrs. Hilbery less as an incompetent writer, as Leslie Stephen cast Anne Ritchie in his *Mausoleum Book* (e.g., 13–15), or an entirely dutiful daughter than as, like Froude or Woolf herself, resistant to the "stout official biography" in two or three dull volumes and the related conventions that would substitute euphemisms for plain speaking or gloss over the facts. Without taking this history into account, most critics argue that *Night and Day* caricatures Ritchie's incapacity for sustained narrative. The novel relies on Leslie Stephen's authority in presenting her as a nincompoop; as Marion Dell notes, "much of Woolf's material and attitudes about Ritchie are inherited" from her father (57). But if the novel parodies Mrs. Hilbery's situation as a writer, it does sympathize with what she experienced as a daughter, for whom telling "the truth" about the past is not so easy a proposition as it may sound.

Katharine's account of her visit to Mary Datchet's suffrage society office in Russell Square—the Bloomsbury locale where Katharine's grandmother had lived after the Alardyce marriage broke up, and where Thackeray had kept a house—probably inspires her mother's further reflections on her childhood.[28] The narrator remarks that as "Mrs. Hilbery grew old she thought more and more of the past, and this ancient disaster seemed at times almost to prey upon her mind, as if she could not pass out of life herself without laying the ghost of her [father's] sorrow to rest" (102; ch. 7). As Mia Carter has also noted, Mrs. Hilbery's "difficulty in completing her father's history is, in part, related to her inability to come to terms with the imperfect and human aspects of his life—especially the part of his story that relates to his marital difficulties and separation from his wife" (79). With a mother whose infidelity (rather than madness) is hinted at, in her having lived "a rather reckless existence" (*Night* 101), and a father who gave up drink but "whose inspiration had deserted him," as Thackeray's had arguably deserted him after *Henry Esmond* (1852), Mrs. Hilbery makes a "tragic story" from her unresolved grief, a "legend" of which "Katharine would have been glad to hear the details . . . and to have been able to discuss them frankly." But in a telling metaphor, Mrs. Hilbery relates the story as a housekeeper might tidy a room, "as though by a touch here and there she could set things straight which had been crooked these sixty years" (102). Unlike the materials she sorts, the details that Katharine wishes to know and "discuss . . . frankly" cannot be rearranged or made right. The story of this unhappy marriage may not be delivered to the reading public insofar as it departs from what *Night and Day* implicitly represents as a monolithic Victorian domestic ideal.

Yet it would seem, too, that without being told, its "ghost"—the story itself—cannot be laid "to rest." The novel thus suggests that the "real" Alardyce/Thackeray cannot be accessed, in part owing to the silence that surrounds sexual irregularity, especially but not exclusively when it involves women, and in part because of second-generation mediation. While Mrs. Hilbery cannot fix through narrative the somewhat traumatic childhood events she experienced, the third-generation granddaughter yet aims to place herself on a level with the first-generation ancestor, as I argued above, positioning herself as wanting to connect with Alardyce, seeking advice rather than information. Although the conventions for what could and could not be told had changed somewhat, or had at least been challenged over time, Woolf implies in representing Mrs. Hilbery's dilemma that communicating candidly with the living about the dead is much more difficult, if not impossible, to achieve than the cross-generational communion with the dead that Katharine effects by identification or projection. In this context, then, the turn to the eminent literary ancestor brings together several different strands of Woolf's relation to an earlier Victorian past, both as it was mediated for her by the late-Victorian perspective of a woman writer/relative and as she aimed to shape it for her own purposes.

To be sure, Woolf went on record early and often about her disaffection from first-generation precursors. As she wrote in a 1916 essay commemorating the centenary of Charlotte Brontë's birth, "The mid-Victorian world . . . is the last that we of the present moment wish to see resuscitated" ("Charlotte Brontë," Essays 2: 27). In the very year Night and Day was published, she ventured the view that "there is no single characteristic that so alienates the present generation from Dickens and Thackeray as their insistence upon . . . 'domestic purism,'" an ideal neither man maintained in his personal life despite promulgating it in his fiction ("Dickens by a Disciple," Essays 3: 27). As Woolf would learn in writing Roger Fry, however, modern biographers faced comparable challenges in representing the sexual lives of their own contemporaries, as in E. M. Forster's book on Goldsworthy Lowes Dickinson,[29] or in the effort made by Katharine Furse (b. 1875) "to write a true life" of her father, John Addington Symonds.[30] In her own time, that is, life writers more often than not also found themselves "omitting all that was most real"—with "the real" seemingly always signifying sexuality, as Eve Kosofsky Sedgwick suggests in Epistemology of the Closet (1990)—regarding "the most private lives" of their subjects, whether or not they were sexual dissidents like Dickinson and Symonds.[31] I want to suggest nonetheless that in this regard, the novel critiques the second-generation daughter for her disfigurement of an earlier Victorian past, her inability to tell "the truth" about it, and her complicity in the silence about sexuality. Yet, at the same time, despite the third-generation daughter's impatience with her mother's inability to be "transparent" about her grandparents' private lives, in both her fiction and her reviews Woolf internalized and enacted a range of objections to the critique of sexual morality that had already been mounted by late-Victorian writers. She advanced instead an ideological and aesthetic position that eschewed all argument, even those arguments with which she might have agreed, and in so doing, took up a position that aligns her with the "great" men, not women, of the prior generation.

Impressions, Not Arguments

Positing "the moral timidity of the usual English novelist" in "The Art of Fiction" (1884), James pointed to the "traditional difference between that which people know and that which they agree to admit that they know, that which they see and that which they speak of, that which they feel to be a part of life and that which they allow to enter into literature" as a shaping force in the fiction of his time; thematizing this difference, he created some of his finest late novels.[32] Challenging the claim of Walter Besant, James "directly reverse[s] his] remark" to "say not that the English novel has a purpose," or explicit aim, "but that it has a diffidence," or tacit silence (21). That distinction differentiates the reformist valence of much of the fiction of the time from the impersonal position taken up by James and some of his contemporaries.[33] For Arnold Bennett, whose *Books and Persons* Woolf reviewed in 1917 (*Essays* 2: 128–32), the gap between knowledge and expression figured somewhat differently: it signified not only "moral timidity" but also pervasive censorship. "Between Fielding and Meredith," Bennett wrote on the death in 1909 of the latter, who published his final novel but one in 1895, "no entirely honest novel was written by anybody in England"; he cited "fear of the public, the lust of popularity, feminine prudery, sentimentalism, Victorian niceness" as the "things [that] prevented honesty" ("Meredith" 135). From his earlier vantage point and in the idiom of his day, Thackeray had said much the same thing in the preface to *Pendennis*, in a statement to which Woolf would allude in the first footnote to *Three Guineas* (1938): "Since the author of Tom Jones was buried, no writer of fiction among us has been permitted to depict to his utmost power A MAN. We must drape him, and give him a certain conventional simper" (Thackeray, *Pendennis* 34; *Three* 6n1, ch. 1). While James never wavered on the aesthetic value of significant silences, Bennett implied both that impediments to candor in fiction were ethically detrimental to the novel and that they had been eliminated in the modern present.

However much Woolf differed from Bennett in some respects, his list of causes for the novel's failure to be "entirely honest" itemizes many of her own concerns at the onset of her career. Becoming modern in the first decades of the twentieth century surely entailed a farewell to "Victorian niceness" of the kind that Ritchie and most other women of her family had practiced, however difficult that was made by what Woolf called her "tea-table training" ("Sketch" 150). Frank discussion of the sort that Katharine Hilbery fails to achieve with her mother had become a Bloomsbury ideal for intragenerational relations—though it would be difficult to say for sure how often it was accomplished. That Terence Hewet of *The Voyage Out* plans to write a novel about "the things people don't say," while Rachel Vinrace believes "only a few things can be said even by people who know each other well," suggests Woolf's ongoing concern with the possibilities of, and the prohibitions on, both interpersonal and novelistic expression (224, ch. 16; 147, ch. 11).[34] The fear that she and/or her work would be perceived as "sentimental," moreover, recurs repeatedly in her diary and letters. To take a relatively late and personal example, a 1931 letter to Ethel Smyth admits that "everyone I most honour is silent . . . and so I have trained myself to silence; induced to it also by the terror I have of my own unlimited capacity for feeling" (*Letters* 4: 422). The tension between what is and is not said subtends Woolf's life—and, to a great extent, her writing—almost from start to finish. Thus an ethic or aesthetic of entire honesty and what that might entail—the representation of "views," arguments over politics and morality, the substitution of frankness for euphemism—is not actually part of the program in Woolf's early fiction and reviews. Quite the opposite: Woolf identifies such tactics as the purview of some late Victorians.

Her objections to the work of Olive Schreiner, for example, do not concern its politics, but how the inclusion of politics of any stripe skews the novelist's point of view. Reviewing a volume of letters posthumously published in 1925 by "this rather distant and unfamiliar figure," Woolf asserts that the one "famous book"—which Meredith had persuaded Chapman and Hall to publish (Showalter, *Literature* 198–99; Waller 851)—recalls "in its brilliance and power . . . the Brontë novels" ("Olive Schreiner," *Essays* 4: 4, 5).[35] But *The Story of an African Farm* (1883) "has the limitations of those egotistical masterpieces without a full measure of their strength": "The writer's interests are local, her passions personal, and we cannot help suspecting that she has neither the width nor the strength to enter with sympathy into the experiences of minds differing from her own, or to debate questions calmly and reasonably" (5). In representing "local," "personal" interests and passions, the novel dates and damns itself. "Unfortunately for her fame as a writer," Schreiner's ideological project damages the aesthetic bearings of her work: "It was into debate and politics, and not into thought and literature, that she was impelled, chiefly by her passionate interest in sex questions," making her "a diamond marred by a flaw" (5, 6). A few years later, both echoing James's definition of the novel as "a personal, a direct impression of life" and citing Hardy's claim in the 1892 preface to *Tess of the D'Urbervilles* (1891) that "a novel is an impression, not an argument," Woolf uses the words of the latter—the writer who "stood for more to this generation than it is possible for any single voice to say"—to make a more general point (James, "Art" 8; Hardy 5; "Thomas Hardy's Novels," *Essays* 4: 507). But she goes on to turn those words against Hardy's own final fiction, *Jude the Obscure* (1895): "At his greatest, [Hardy] gives us impressions; at his weakest, arguments" (*Essays* 4: 514). And in the case of both *Tess* and *Jude*, Hardy's "passionate interest" in relations between the sexes fueled those "arguments."[36]

As novelists who represent and, to differing extents, advocate the gender and sexual politics associated with New Womanhood, both Schreiner and Hardy criticize heterosexual marriage in particular, as do Woolf's own first novels in a less polemical way. Indeed, those books share with those of Schreiner and Hardy the "preoccupation with the institution of marriage" that characterizes so much New Woman fiction (Ledger, *New Woman* 20; cf. Hite, *Woolf's Ambiguities* 85). But despite exhibiting the same "flaw," Hardy is praised and remembered while Schreiner was, until fairly recently, almost entirely forgotten. Whereas his stature and output ensured frequent reissues of Hardy's fiction well into the twentieth century, and his friendship with her father underwrote Woolf's ongoing attention to it, a "desperate freethinker"—as Leslie Stephen called Schreiner in 1887 on meeting her in Switzerland in Lucy Clifford's company—could easily remain a "distant and unfamiliar figure" to Woolf because of the cultural forces at work in the reception of writing by women with "advanced" views on "sex questions" (*Selected Letters* 2: 344).

In a groundbreaking essay from the late 1970s that treated Woolf's attitudes to women writers in a comprehensive way, Michèle Barrett argues that the "bias" Schreiner's novel evinced was "to Virginia Woolf an aesthetically undesirable element in a work of literature"; her "conception of artistic integrity precluded the possibility of an acceptable *explicit* treatment of political questions, including the question of the position of women" (Introduction 11, 21; emphasis in the original). Whereas Barrett writes that Woolf's work "reveals a deep-seated ambivalence to the rival claims of art and politics" (24), Toril Moi subsequently identified "the politics of Woolf's writing *precisely in her textual practice*" and emphasized "the political nature of Woolf's aesthetics" (16, 17; emphasis in the original). Acknowledging the spirit of both positions, Hite very persuasively demonstrates how Woolf deploys narrative techniques that enable her narrators to take and keep their distance from characters and events without directing her readers to a particular position; she also identifies the alternative means by which Woolf represented "sex questions" in developing "passionate and sensuous female characters"—Clarissa

Dalloway, Mrs. Ramsay—"without embroiling them in the societal consequences of female eroticism that had shaped the romance plot" (*Woolf's Ambiguities* 1–28; "Two Bodies," para. 3). From this point of view, Woolf did not
so much set aside "sex questions" as challenge the conventional means for representing and addressing them. Over time, she achieved a massive transformation of the form—but only over time, for it is certainly fair to say, with
Barrett, that the aesthetic norms Woolf internalized and disseminated in the
early part of her career had more than a grain of patriarchal second-generation
thinking at their core, particularly in their emphasis on impersonality as the
key conduit to greatness.

In one of the very first books she reviewed, Virginia Stephen encountered
an instance of the power of the critical establishment to invalidate political
fiction by women writers. *The Feminine Note in Fiction* (1904) by W. L. Courtney, editor of the *Fortnightly Review* from 1894 until his death in 1928, considers a range of second-generation women authors including Robins, Ward, John
Oliver Hobbes (b. 1867; pseud. Pearl Craigie), and Lucas Malet (b. 1852; pseud.
Mary St. Leger Kingsley).[37] According to Lois Cucullu, the Cambridge Apostles had discussed this book at one of their meetings, but probably not until
well after Virginia Stephen had reviewed it (95n7). And as Jane Goldman establishes, it also formed the jumping-off point for a talk titled "The Feminine
Note in Literature" that E. M. Forster gave in two different versions, one to
an all-male gathering of Apostles and the other to the mixed-sex Friday Club,
founded by Vanessa Bell, both in 1910.[38] While some critics see *The Feminine
Note* as "moderately sympathetic" to female aesthetes, Pykett argues that
"Courtney's equivocations on the subject of the New Woman writing, and indeed women's writing more generally, are based on a masculinist, proto-
modernist aesthetic designed to protect English fiction from the destructive
incursions of the feminine" (Schaffer and Psomiades 13; Pykett, *Engendering*
65). Its remarks on late-nineteenth- and early-twentieth-century fiction contain some nuggets of received gender wisdom that may have given pause to
the aspiring woman novelist.

Aside from George Eliot—"essentially a masculine genius"—Courtney
opines that "it would be difficult . . . to think of any feminine rival to George
Meredith, in the scope and range of his creative work; still less is it possible to
find any feminine successor to Scott, Thackeray, and Dickens. It is the neutrality of the artistic mind which the female novelist finds it difficult to realize," mired as she is in the data of personal experience and lacking the
impersonality that Shakespeare or Dickens maintains "towards all his puppets"
(xii). Such a standard aims at "discrediting the subjective and historically contingent," with which, as I suggested above, late-Victorian writers are frequently

associated by masculinist moderns to distance themselves from male and female precursors alike (Ardis, *New* 57). "Even a cursory glance at the misogynist rhetoric that attended the male modernists' anti-Romantic program,"
Cassandra Laity remarks, "suggests familiar dismissals of effeminate men's and
women's writing" (2).

In her review, the critic (rather than his subjects) takes the lion's share of
Virginia Stephen's censure, in that despite Courtney's professed "certain[ty]
that there is such a thing as the feminine note in fiction," he "has done nothing" to illuminate or isolate it ("The Feminine Note in Fiction," *Essays* 1: 15).
Of his general points, she notes that he singles out most women writers' "passion for detail," with the exception of the mature works of Charlotte Brontë
and Eliot, as disqualifying any claim to their being "artists" because that passion "conflicts with the proper artistic proportion of their work" (Courtney
xi; qtd. 16). She counters with the "great" examples of Sappho and Jane Austen and goes on to surmise that it is "possible that the widening of the [woman
novelist's] intelligence by means of education and study of the Greek and Latin
classics may give her that sterner view of literature which will make an artist
of her"; she here foregrounds her own preferred course of reading, a mode
of self-education that numerous female aesthetes and New Women had undertaken as part or in lieu of university study (16).[39]

Yet, if she persistently confronts and contests it over the course of her career,
sometimes in worried tones, Woolf herself goes on to adopt Courtney's standard in the manner Bourdieu would suggest.[40] "If a novelist take [*sic*] sides,"
Courtney writes, "he or she is lost. Then we get a pamphlet, a didactic exercise, a problem novel—never a work of art" (xii). As for New Woman writers
in particular, he focuses on the sensational political content of the writing as
the reason for dismissing it: "At the time when problem plays and problem novels were rife, . . . novelists like Sarah Grand, Mona Caird, George Egerton,
and others were . . . giving the worst possible pictures of the lengths to which
rebellious womanhood would go" (xxvi). Anticipating Terence's critique of Rachel's reading in *The Voyage Out* as "trash" even as he assigns the impetus for
its production to Hardy's influence, Courtney constructs that sort of thing as
outmoded or, to use Terence's word, "exploded" (304; ch. 22): "Problem plays
and problem novels were the fashion of an hour which has already passed. . . .
They had unlovely characteristics which we are only too glad to forget" (xxvi–
xxvii).[41] In passing over such remarks without comment in her brief review
of Courtney's book, Woolf may have been bound by considerations of space,
or by the gendered pressure to be "nice" that she describes in "Professions for
Women" (1931). But it is nonetheless striking that these very recent female
precursors—Grand, Caird, and Egerton, all presumed to be writing "with a

purpose"—are consigned to the dustheap both by Courtney and, ten years later, by characters in *The Voyage Out*, as I will explore in chapter 2.

Such attitudes not only reflect the side Woolf would aim to take in the struggle for preeminence in the literary field but also have deep roots in late-Victorian debates about the aesthetics of the novel. As James put it with a clear bias toward a position not unlike Courtney's, "Questions of art are questions (in the widest sense) of execution; questions of morality," presumably those that touch on sexual politics, "are quite another affair" ("Art" 20). James's friend Leslie Stephen, who rejected "the categorical disjunction between literature and morality" that characterized the writings of Pater and James and instead "simply assumed their interdependence," yet affirmed that it was less the content than the stance of the writer toward that content that would determine the moral bearings of the artwork (Avery 303). Anticipating and perhaps influencing Courtney, Stephen wrote in his essay on Henry Fielding's fiction in the third series of *Hours in a Library* (1879), "The highest morality of a great work of art depends upon the power with which the essential beauty and ugliness of virtue and vice are exhibited by *an impartial observer*" ("Fielding's Novels" 85; emphasis mine). And as Stephen argued more generally of both the critic and the novelist, in an essay on Charlotte Brontë in the same volume, "When we are seeking to justify our emotions, we must endeavour to get for the time into the position of *an independent spectator*, applying with rigid impartiality such methods as are best calculated to free us from the influence of personal bias" ("Charlotte Brontë" 326; emphasis mine).

Such formulations, indebted to the precepts of Adam Smith, recur in the writings of many other fin-de-siècle critics. For example, the publisher Arthur Waugh—father of the novelists Alec and Evelyn—asserts in "Reticence in Literature," which appeared in the first volume of *The Yellow Book* in 1894, "It is only when we regard life with the untrammelled view of the impartial spectator, when we pierce below the substance for its animating idea, that we approximate to the artistic temperament," having first claimed that a woman can only achieve that "temperament" once "she throws off the habit of her sex, and learns to rely upon her judgment, and not upon her senses" (210). As John Kucich notes, Waugh here promotes "the moral superiority of male artists" who articulate "the moral and aesthetic importance of reticence" (*Power* 247). Despite its gendered bias, the idea that the artist should be (or at least appear to be) "an impartial observer" or "an independent spectator" surfaces repeatedly in Woolf's early fictional and nonfictional writing, in the reviews of Schreiner and Hardy cited above, and in the narrator's critique of the way-too-angry Charlotte Brontë in *A Room of One's Own*. Like her father, she, too, found "novels with a purpose . . . proverbially detestable" (Stephen, "Art" 101). As he wrote in the very last paragraph of "Art and Morality" (1875), which Perry Meisel calls a "bitter denunciation of aestheticism," while "even a novel should have a ruling thought, . . . it should not degenerate into a tract," further arguing that such a "thought should be one which will help to purify and sustain the mind by which it is assimilated, and therefore tend to make society so far healthier and happier" (101; Meisel 1).[42] Although Woolf would not have construed her own aesthetic practice as an instrument of either social hygiene or moral contamination—though as subsequent chapters will show, she did lay that charge against other books and writers—*Night and Day* yet engages the question of literature's relation to sexual conduct, though without taking sides. Eschewing what it implicitly constructs as the partisan tactics of fiction with a purpose, its multiple scenes of reading suggest the complex legacy of second-generation debates around the representation of sexuality for the third-generation reader and writer.

Impartial Observers

Following its exposition of the "ancient disaster" of the Alardyce marriage, chapter 7 of *Night and Day* concludes with Katharine Hilbery's failed effort to "to interest her parents in the works of living and highly respectable authors" (103). While we could take this failure merely as a sign of a generational split between the Hilberys' preferred reading and the contemporary works delivered to their house twice a week by library subscription—a split that perhaps also operated within the Stephen home, where the collected works of Sir Walter Scott constituted a good part of "healthy" family reading—the elders' reactions obliquely touch on a broader cultural discussion regarding the "respectable."[43] Mrs. Hilbery is "perturbed by the very look of the light, gold-wreathed volumes, and . . . make[s] little faces as if she tasted something bitter as the reading went on"; Mr. Hilbery "treat[s] the moderns with a curious elaborate banter such as one might apply to the antics of a promising child" (103–4). "Highly respectable" as these moderns are, it may be precisely their respectability, putatively assured by lending libraries like Mudie's, that the Hilberys (and / or their author) find so cloying.[44] Katharine answers her mother's complaint that "it was all too clever and cheap and nasty for words" and the request that Katharine "read us something *real*" by taking down from the bookshelf "a portly volume in sleek yellow calf" to calm her. Until the evening mail arrives, the daughter entertains her parents with "the periods of Henry Fielding" (104; emphasis in the original), whose grave in Lisbon Clarissa Dalloway photographs in *The Voyage Out* (36; ch. 3) and who was, not incidentally, both Bennett's exemplar of the "entirely honest" and Thackeray's favorite novelist.[45]

Perhaps Katharine's choice is "that mystic book" (*Jacob's Room* 122; ch. 10), *Tom Jones* (1749). One of Woolf's essays, titled "Hours in a Library" (1916) after her father's multivolume critical collection, imagines a serious young man "read[ing it] . . . at the age of twenty" alongside Meredith, Hardy, and the Elizabethans (*Essays* 2: 56), while the protagonist of *Jacob's Room* (1922) blithely recommends it to the prostitute Fanny Elmer. Albeit "not so elevated in tone as might be desired," Fielding had earned Leslie Stephen's respect for his capacity to touch pitch without being defiled: his "mind had gathered coarseness, but it had not been poisoned. He sees how many ugly things are covered by the superficial gloss of fashion, but he does not condescend to travesty the facts in order to gratify a morbid taste for the horrible" ("Fielding's Novels" 89, 67–68). Criticizing the writers of his time in "The Decay of Literature" (1882) and regretting the lack of "successors" to Dickens and Thackeray, he praised Fielding for possessing the power, "in an eminent degree, of laying bare the real working forces of society. . . . We do not want tracts or blue-books in the shape of fiction; but we do want to get a downright masculine insight into living realities" (610). With all the hetero manliness lacking in, say, Pater, along with the "healthy" taste Stephen despaired of finding in Balzac, Fielding would thus appear ideally appropriate for adult consumption, or at least adult male consumption ("Balzac's Novels" 347).[46] His "greatness," that is, did not prevent recurring inquiries into his suitability for younger and/or female readers: "The bicentenary of Fielding's birth in 1907 generated a profusion of articles debating whether he was an offensive writer," while in 1913, a provincial public library went so far as to ban *Tom Jones* (Waller 253; Wilson 54–55). Both incidents indicate the persistence of the discourse on literary propriety and respectability into the new century.

That controversy, moreover, recalls an earlier chapter in the debate on the morality of Fielding's fiction from a point of view associated with the social-purity wing of the late-Victorian women's movement. Early in *The Heavenly Twins*, which I will consider at length in the next chapter, one of its heroines criticizes Tobias Smollett's *Roderick Random* (1748) and "dismissed [*Tom Jones*] with greater contempt, if possible," for their representations of "the self-interest, the injustice of men"; she describes Fielding's male protagonists as "steeped in vice," with the vicious hero of each novel nonetheless going on to marry "a spotless heroine" (20; bk. 1, ch. 3). These remarks spawned an exchange between the novel's reviewer in the *Pall Mall Gazette*, who suggested that the author "would be better to 'study life from Tom Jones's point of view'" than the perspective she takes in *The Heavenly Twins*," and the redoubtable

W. T. Stead, who countered in his *Review of Reviews* "that to suggest that Grand adopt the view of Tom Jones was to suggest that a woman become a promiscuous scoundrel in order to understand life" (qtd. in Youngkin 60). But within the context of Woolf's novel, the invocation of Fielding functions less as a referendum on the sexual conduct of his male characters and rather more as an index to the disinterested distance *Night and Day* aims to take on the characters and events it describes. For what the post that interrupts the reading from Fielding brings are "two letters which each told the same story differently," a story the eighteenth-century male novelist would have told very differently than his nineteenth- or twentieth-century counterparts (*Night* 105; ch. 8).

Confirming that he has fathered two children outside of wedlock with a third on the way, Katharine's cousin Cyril Alardyce writes a letter "full of quotations" not from Fielding but from those late-Victorian analysts of sexual morality, "Ibsen and Butler" (110). The other letter, from Aunt Celia Milvain, argues that Cyril "must be made to marry the woman at once," although, as an advocate of the right *not* to marry that Cyril appears to be, he "would not own that he had any cause to be ashamed of himself" (105–6). Katharine is "left to do the disagreeable work" of relating the facts to her mother, a duty "which belonged, by rights," to her father—who, like Austen's Mr. Bennet, maintains a literal distance on the matter by retreating to his study (112). Katharine herself "shrank, nervously . . . from all that would have to be said on the occasion," which both jars with her earlier-expressed wish for frank discussion of her grandparents' failed marriage and foreshadows the silence that she will maintain with her parents on the topic of her own romantic entanglements. But Katharine's reserve in this instance also indicates her dissent from the position she attributes to her elders. Anticipating her mother's reaction while reflecting on "Cyril's misbehaviour . . . she saw something which her father and mother did not see, and the effect of that something was to suspend Cyril's behaviour in her mind. . . . They would think whether it was good or bad; to her it was merely a thing that had happened" (113; ch. 9). Refusing to pronounce on the morality of the affair—with Woolf simultaneously signaling through her citation of Fielding that questions of sexual morality are susceptible of different treatment at different historical moments, in literature as in life—Katharine herself aims, albeit not as successfully as her father or the narrator, to take up the stance of impartial observer.

In Katharine's characterization of her female elders' conversation as moralizing we can identify another trace of Woolf's discontent with some second-generation writers whose example *Night and Day* seeks to challenge. Once Aunt Celia arrives to spill the beans, the narrative fleetingly expresses Katharine's dissent, contained in her spoken wish "to realize Cyril's point of view"

before judging his conduct, and her disappointment that "Cyril had not confided in her" (123, ch. 9; 110, ch. 8). Mrs. Hilbery purports to be "more hurt
by the concealment of the sin than by the sin itself," and Katharine "felt an
immense relief and pride" at this initial response; only the arrival of another
cousin interrupts her effort at "speaking directly to her mother, as if to a contemporary" (123; ch. 9). Although Aunt Celia and Cousin Caroline soon disagree on what the latter calls "the rights and wrongs of the affair," they coincide
on the main point, which the latter presses home to Mrs. Hilbery: the child
about to be born "will bear your name . . . your father's name, remember"
(124; cf. 106). Katharine is then "much disappointed in her mother," who goes
on to equate being "born out of wedlock" with having "Jewish blood" as a
spur to future achievement, an obstacle for Cyril's children to overcome (124,
125): "How they talked and moralized and made up stories to suit their own
version of the becoming" (125). As Wussow notes of the discussion among
the female elders, "The women weave verbal fictions to escape the unpleas-
antness of reality" ("Conflict" 69). The views of this older generation of
women on "the rights and wrongs of the affair," however, are implicitly mea-
sured against both the fuller and freer fictional representation of sexuality available to Fielding in an age represented as less moralizing, or more "real," and
the iconoclasm of "Ibsen and Butler" in the decades just before the publication of the novel.

In contrast with the women of the second generation, Katharine responds
to "Cyril's misbehaviour" by discarding the moral polarity of "good" or "bad."
Her attitude to it is consistent with her pleasure in reading Dostoevsky: she
enjoys the freedom of sampling a "book which neither her father or [sic]
mother had read, and keeping it to herself, and gnawing its contents in privacy, and pondering the meaning without sharing her thoughts with any one,
or having to decide whether the book was a good one or a bad one" (138; ch.
11).[47] While male and female writers alike conducted a critique of conventional
sexual morality as enforced by literary and social convention in the latter part
of the nineteenth century, Woolf tends to identify the challenge to the right-
or-wrong, good-or-bad way of thinking with such writers as Ibsen and Butler,
who do *not* insist on the morality or immorality of a given act or of its representation in an artwork. The more dogmatic "Wells and Shaw" of *Jacob's
Room*—who vigorously indicted (hetero)sexual morality, thus offending literary respectability, and whose books line the shelves of the Cambridge don
George Plumer—belong instead among the moralizers (35; ch. 3).[48]

Significantly, Woolf does not name any women writers at all in this context, such that the views of the female relatives in *Night and Day* stand in, to
some extent, for those expressed in books they would probably never read.

For when Cousin Caroline "blame[s]" Cyril, while Aunt Celia claims that *"she entangled him,"* they rehearse the argument on sexual morality perceived to dominate New Woman fiction, differing only on whose shoulders, male or female, the responsibility lies (124, ch. 9; emphasis in the original). Though these female relations are hardly New Women, they perpetuate the moralizing point of view for which not only "Wells and Shaw" but also those late-century New Woman writers who were associated with the social purity movement were criticized, in seeking to lay blame for sexual transgression, whether on men or women. In the meantime, like both her father and her author, and as "an avatar of both modernity and modernism, Katharine seeks detachment and impersonality" (Hite, "Two Bodies," para. 13). As does her father, she "took up her position at some distance, . . . as though by so doing she could get a better view of the matter"—though it should be noted that Mr. Hilbery is not quite so diffident when his own position as father of a newly wayward daughter is involved, and that Katharine herself loses her composure more than once under the pressure of her own difficulties (120; ch. 9). But in representing her protagonist's effort to be "an impartial observer," "dispassionate" and removed, rather than an advocate or opponent of a progressive or conservative stance, Woolf again signals her generational rejection of the use of fiction as a platform for inculcating or challenging sexual morality. She modifies her father's position with the aestheticist principles he deplored while also dismissing out of hand a large and important body of late-nineteenth-century fiction. By locating *Night and Day* in relation to this debate among writers and critics of the second generation, we can apprehend more clearly why Woolf's third-generation heroine, in an extended moment of author/character identification, looks back to—and even thinks back through—the first.

Constructing recent literary history as a family affair became a habit for Woolf, who over the course of her career intermittently deployed a "familial metaphor for literary succession" in her critical writing and reviews (Fogel 105). For example, in attributing to her contemporaries a preference for "fat Victorian volumes" over the slimmer Georgian alternatives, the opening paragraphs of "On Re-reading Novels" use a generational thematic to claim that such a preference "speaks very well" of modern readers, yet redounds "still more to the credit of the Victorians" (*Essays* 3: 337, 336). "The grandchildren, it seems, get along very nicely with the grandparents; and the sight of their concord points inevitably to the later breach between the generations," since the Georgians "are in the odd predicament of turning for solace and guidance not to their parents who are alive, but to their grandparents who are dead." By the logic of this metaphor, however, "the failure of the Edwardians, comparative yet disastrous," must also be at least in part a failure of the Victorians. For would "the year 1860" have been "a year of empty cradles"—and "the reign of Edward the Seventh" thus "barren of poet, novelist, or critic"—if the mid-Victorians had done their generative job properly (336)? What were the wives of all those great men doing if not birthing the geniuses of the next generation? Did the childless women writers somehow fail to do their part? And wouldn't the living Edwardian fathers—or "uncles," as Bonnie Kime Scott terms Woolf's older male contemporaries (19–34)—be less disappointing and conventional, more energetic and inventive, if the Victorians had managed things better, had not squandered their own inheritance from "Defoe and Fanny Burney . . . the parents of the modern novel," or left something for their descendants to do or create (337)? Positing ongoing conflict between Edwardian (or late-Victorian) uncles and their Georgian heirs, Woolf here positions the dead first generation as benevolent benefactors who shower largesse on their grandchildren, even as she implicitly wonders why they failed to (re)produce an intermediate generation of "great" creative artists. Locating Woolf's position in the context of an adjacent set of debates, Ruth Livesey rightly claims that "it is [the] reduction of aesthetics to a functional social good by Shaw's Edwardian Fabian generation that Woolf dramatizes as the cause of her orphaned amorality" (*Socialism* 195).

As is the case in "Mr. Bennett and Mrs. Brown" (1923) and "Character in Fiction" (1924), "the Edwardians" look to be the odd men out in this family circle. Emphasizing Woolf's variable views of "the Victorians," Ellis notes that "the stress on linking the generations—of a generational consciousness—with regard to both the family and the literary tradition, is a permanent feature of Woolf's writing" in that "she seeks to establish relations between contemporary writers and the great Victorians across the 'barren' interval of the Edwardian years" (38, 32). Yet, as I have already suggested, that impulse to associate with "the great Victorians" also relegates a host of lesser, later Victorians to obscurity. When Woolf wrote in "How It Strikes a Contemporary" (1923), which borrows its very title from the eminent Robert Browning, that "no age can have been more rich than ours in writers determined to give expression to the differences which separate them from the past and not to the resemblances which connect them with it," it was perhaps any potential "resemblances" to, or identification with, the not-so-great of the prior generation she was most eager to minimize (*Essays* 3: 357).

Although Woolf resented Katherine Mansfield's characterization of her work ("A decorous elderly dullard she describes me; Jane Austen up to date" [*Diary* 1: 314]), *Night and Day* not only participates in but implicitly constructs a nineteenth-century tradition, which clearly includes "Jane Austen and the

Brontës and George Meredith" but excludes many, many more for some of
the reasons I have established here ("On Re-reading," *Essays* 3: 336). Woolf thus
not only acknowledges "great" novelists such as Thackeray but also enlists
them as her allies in the critique of "fiction with a purpose," which I will explore more fully in the next chapter. The "great" writer who famously claimed
that "we think back through our mothers if we are women"—an assertion
"contradicted by her own writing"—signally failed to identify potential models among those of the generation just preceding her own (*Room* 75; Vanita
39).[49] Most poignantly, she chose "actively to diminish and to obscure Ritchie's
achievements," treating her as if she were one of Katharine's interfering aunts
rather than a potentially enabling force in Woolf's own success (Dell 67). *Night
and Day* also turns away in particular, as I have argued, from those late-century
women writers who had also grappled with the representation and the regulation of sexuality. In the first two decades of her career, that is, Woolf turned
again and again to the second-generation Victorians Hardy, Meredith, and
James rather than their female contemporaries, partly because older works of
the "great" men were reissued and newer ones still reviewed, partly because
she privileged their aesthetic over the varied experiments of New Woman writing. And in so doing, she helped to secure a version of literary history as
generational family history that long denied a place to her late-Victorian aunts.

INTERLUDE I

Grand Reads Woolf

While I have not found any evidence that Woolf read the works of New Women writers aside from Schreiner and Robins, we do know that at least one of those disowned foremothers read her. As a subscriber to the feminist periodical *Time and Tide*, Sarah Grand might have seen both its admiring review of *A Room of One's Own* by Theodora Bosanquet (b. 1881) and the excerpts from the essay it published over the course of November 1929 before she got her hands on the book itself, which she certainly did within just a few months of its publication on 24 October 1929.[1] In a thank-you note for a gift from her "devoted friend" Gladys Singers-Bigger, Grand promised her "a copy. . . . There was none to be had in Bath so I had to order it," perhaps by writing to the proprietors of the Hogarth Press (*Sex* 2: 129). Singers-Bigger's journal for 14 January 1930, which noted the book's arrival, reports that Grand "had written in the book, copying a eulogistic critique" (perhaps Bosanquet's) "with characteristic generosity to a fellow author, ignoring the fact that she herself had said it all long before" (qtd. in Kersley 213). As if to underline that last point, Singers-Bigger concluded her journal entry with a quotation from Grand's *Babs the Impossible* (1901): "More women have distinguished themselves than men in a state of subjection. Aesop is the only slave I can think of who distinguished himself in literature. A subjugated race produces no great work of art: why do you expect a subjugated sex to produce more than a subjugated race under similar circumstances?" (*Babs* 345, ch. 36;

qtd. in Kersley 213). But she omitted the sentences immediately following, which might be still more pertinent to Grand's favorable view of Woolf's book: "So far, woman has been the thrall of law and custom, and she has only been able to indicate the possession of power. But you will see that as soon as women begin to let themselves go in art, so soon as they cease to respect hampering laws and try for the expression of fine ideas, they will succeed" (345).

The gaps in Singers-Bigger's reporting of her objections to *A Room*, which she "criticized adversely" in conversation with Grand, make it difficult to gloss subsequent references (qtd. in Kersley 219). But we can infer from the context that it was not only that Grand "had said it all long before" that bothered her adoring and much younger friend. About two weeks thereafter, in another letter, Grand asked her, "Why should you apologize for differing from me just because I gave you the book? . . . Differences of opinion are interesting, not irritating to discuss; they keep up the conversation and give point to it"—a sentiment that Woolf, I think, would have endorsed. That "there are wide differences of opinion on the subject of this book, some of them curiously unexpected," as Grand goes on to say, becomes a keynote of the discussion with the more conservative Singers-Bigger, born in the United States in 1889 and thus much closer in age to Woolf than to Grand. Yet it is her younger friend who, in Grand's view, is behind the times: "Your first impression was unexpected enough to be a shock," she wrote, because "it had never struck me that you were an ultra Victorian," "too content ever to be aware of how some were being cramped and suffering by being forcibly kept in places in which they had no room to expand" (*Sex* 2: 130). Here and elsewhere in their discussion of *A Room*, Grand situates herself by contrast as having always been well ahead of her own moment.

This is not to say that, as time passed, Grand necessarily felt herself or her work to be in fashion: "When 1933 mocks the 1890s for phrase-makers," she told Singers-Bigger that year, "it may be that 1933 is saying 'sour grapes'" (*Sex* 2: 196). But she maintained her sense that even though the 1890s went in and out of style, she had always been in the vanguard. In July 1937, just a few months after Woolf published *The Years*, the best seller that took the vestiges of the late-Victorian world as a major focus, Grand remarked that "the Victorians are coming into the new again now"; and, further, "I was among them though not of them. I was before my time, a reformer and prophet who made such a big noise and was so tenacious there was no ignoring me or casting me out" (242).[2] Even in Woolf's own day, then, at least one of the mothers whom she might have thought with, rather than "back through," who occupied the same space and time, however differently experienced, was not quite gone—and thus still had the capacity to respond.

Yet there is at least one way in which Grand and Woolf do converge over time. For her part, in the foreword to the 1923 reissue of *The Heavenly Twins* (not reissued again until its centenary year), Grand raised questions about what the late-Victorian feminist movement had really accomplished, questions that would also come to preoccupy Woolf in her final years. "Is [the novel's] reappearance," Grand wondered, "a sign that people are fundamentally the same, in change unchangeable, and pretty much where they were; with their old needs upon them again, their old problems still unsolved, and their old advisers and props and stays still in demand as the most reliable, in spite of all that is being said to the contrary?" (397). Maybe, or maybe not; but by the time of writing *Three Guineas*, Woolf might well have agreed with Grand on how little had changed. Comparing "the battle of Harley Street in the year 1869," when women fought for the right to become doctors, to "the battle of Cambridge University at the present moment," with the women's colleges still being denied membership in the university, Woolf found men's resistance to women's emancipation "so familiar" as to make it seem "as if there were no progress in the human race, but only repetition": "On both occasions there is the same waste of strength, waste of temper, waste of time, and waste of money. Almost the same daughters ask almost the same brothers for almost the same privileges. Almost the same gentlemen intone almost the same refusals for almost the same reasons" (*Three* 80; ch. 2).

Forty years earlier, in the aftermath of another failed push to grant degrees to women at Cambridge, Grand had more optimistically forecast a feminist future in an essay of 1898: those who opposed the move, she wrote in "The Modern Young Man," "will be held to have been extraordinarily primitive by their own great-grandchildren."

> In fifty years' time even undergraduates will make merry over the record of the significant exhibition of abject terror displayed by their predecessors in 1897 when the prospect of being brought into competition with women's wit was imminent. By the end of our own day, in fact, if the present rate of progress continues unchecked, there will remain but a few bald-headed representatives of that sort of young man—antiquated bores—such as survive from every period, with eyes turned inwards, so that they are unaware of other ideas than their own. (59)

But "the present rate of progress" did not "continue unchecked." The "extraordinarily primitive" young men of 1897 and the "antiquated bores . . . such as survive from every period" remained in the ascendant, so much so that Woolf would feel compelled to call them out in 1938, as Grand had in 1897. If "human character changed" in 1910, from the perspective Woolf expresses in "Character in Fiction," then I would submit that from the perspective of the 1930s—the decade in which Woolf turned back once more to the later Victorians in both *The Years* and *Three Guineas* (and in *Roger Fry*, "A Sketch of the Past," and *Between the Acts*)—"human character" may have looked very different in looking, as Grand might say, very much the same (*Essays* 3: 421).

CHAPTER 2

New Women and Old

Sarah Grand, Social Purity, and *The Voyage Out*

> I have read the Maria Tellier, and the Rouge et le Noir
> [*sic*], but as for the rest, you know I plod consistently
> behind the times, in the worn rut of convention.
>
> —Virginia Stephen to Clive Bell, 18 August 1907

> Having a room of my own always has been a great
> advantage.
>
> —Sarah Grand, *The Heavenly Twins*, 1893

In chapter 22 of *The Voyage Out*, Terence Hewet lectures his fiancée, Rachel Vinrace, for reading "trash": "And you're behind the times, too, my dear. No one dreams of reading this kind of thing now—antiquated problem plays, harrowing descriptions of life in the east end—oh, no, we've exploded all that. Read poetry, Rachel, poetry, poetry, poetry!" (341).[1] Throughout the novel, what the heroine reads receives a lot of attention: indeed, as Ann Ardis points out in her persuasive reading of this key passage in the novel, "Rachel is encouraged by everyone she knows to read *something else*" (*Modernism* 1; emphasis in the original).[2] Aboard the *Euphrosyne*, Richard Dalloway promises to send her a volume of Burke (*Voyage* 79; ch. 5). Her new friend St. John Hirst recommends Gibbon's *Decline and Fall*, which Adrian Stephen had gifted to his bookish sister (172, ch. 12; King and Miletic-Vejzovic 85). The classics scholar Ridley Ambrose first suggests Plato and Sophocles, and Swift, "Wordsworth and Coleridge. Pope, Johnson, Addison, . . . Shelley, Keats" complete the list (192; ch. 13). Aside from Miss Allan, the schoolteacher at the hotel in Santa Marina, and Rachel herself, who brings along a copy of *Wuthering Heights* (1847), only Clarissa Dalloway appears to read fiction written by women, albeit long-dead ones—Jane Austen, the Brontës—and she reads aloud from *Persuasion* (1818) only in order to put her husband to sleep (59, 64; ch. 4).[3]

But in chapter 10, at the villa, where she inhabits "a room cut off from the rest of the house, large, private . . . a fortress as well as a sanctuary," Rachel makes her own choices from among the books Terence will call "trash" (136). Described more neutrally by the narrator as "modern books, books in shiny yellow covers, books with a great deal of gilding on the back," they include the *Works of Henrik Ibsen* and Meredith's *Diana of the Crossways* (1885), loosely based on the scandalous life of Caroline Norton (b. 1808), both a novelist and an advocate for women's rights to child custody and divorce. Rachel performs Ibsen plays "for days at a time . . . then it would be Meredith's turn and she became Diana" (137). She acts out, that is, male-authored versions of the New Woman she so decidedly is not. Among the unnamed books are some, the narrator tells us, that her elderly paternal aunts back home in Richmond would deplore, "tokens in [their] eyes of harsh wrangling and disputes about facts which had no such importance as the moderns claimed for them" (137–38). More progressive than her Richmond counterparts, even Helen Ambrose would rather Rachel choose "Defoe, Maupassant, or some spacious chronicle of family life" than the novel she is actually reading in this chapter, "whose purpose was to distribute the guilt of a woman's downfall upon the right shoulders" (137, 138).[4] The next clauses of this sentence and the one that follows migrate from Helen's point of view toward the narrator's to indicate Rachel's response to this particular book: Its "purpose . . . was achieved, if the reader's discomfort were any proof of it. She threw the book down, looked out of the window, turned away from the window, and relapsed into an armchair" (138).

The unnamed book makes its second and final appearance much later in the novel, in the chapter in which Rachel and Terence announce their engagement, after he recommends poetry in place of "trash" and imagines their married life to come in London. Her response to a scenario that gives her "the horrors"—perhaps because her fiancé has just identified their class privilege, the prospective "thousand a year and perfect freedom," as unavailable to all but a very few—is mediated by its continuing presence: "She looked grudgingly at the novel which had once caused her perhaps an hour's discomfort, so that she had never opened it again, but kept it on her table, and looked at it occasionally, as some medieval monk kept a skull, or a crucifix to remind him of the frailty of the body. 'Is it true, Terence,' she demanded, 'that women die with bugs crawling across their faces?'" (351; ch. 22). What distinguishes *this* book, which makes Rachel feel uncomfortable and vulnerable, from the ones she acted out? And why does *this* book, which Rachel never finishes, function as a memento mori?

Considering Helen's dismissive attitude toward this novel and the "discomfort" that reading it causes Rachel, I would suggest that this particular book might well be an article of New Woman fiction by a woman writer. Its "purpose" would be to critique both male heterosexual behavior and gendered inequality; and it would have been written by one of those "critically-acclaimed and widely-read group of female and often feminist writers," in Molly Hite's words, "who produced novels that were aggressively 'modern' in their attitudes and subject matter" ("Public Woman" 523; cf. *Woolf's Ambiguities* 62–63). While Hite nominates Elizabeth Robins's *My Little Sister* (1913; original English title *Where are You Going . . . ?*) as a candidate for the unnamed book, the best-known and best-selling New Woman novel of a generation before, Sarah Grand's *The Heavenly Twins*, would perhaps be even more directly pertinent to Rachel's circumstances in the novel.[5] For had she read it on the boat to Santa Marina, Rachel certainly would have known, without Helen's having to tell her, that the women she has seen in Piccadilly are prostitutes, and that their presence there is why she "can't walk alone" anywhere, at any time (*Voyage* 87; ch. 6). And had she finished the book, she might have picked up a hint or two as to how her own story would end.

My identification of *The Heavenly Twins* as Rachel's unread book is avowedly conjectural, as Woolf's diaries, letters, and essays contain no references whatsoever to New Woman writers, aside from the reviews I have already cited.[6] By the time Woolf was choosing her own reading and reviewing books for publication, New Woman fiction itself was largely out of print and out of fashion: on Franco Moretti's bar graph "British Novelistic Genres, 1740–1900," it constitutes one of the latest entries with one of the shortest durations (*Graphs* 81).[7] Its tenets were inevitably absorbed and reframed by a range of Edwardian feminists, as Jane Eldridge Miller and others have established, though *The Heavenly Twins* was itself reissued six times after its initial publication, including in 1912 (Bonnell, "Legacy" 470). But by 1915, fiction with a feminist purpose could readily be represented as unquestionably behind the times. Unduly polemical to Helen, who aims to guide Rachel away from reading about sex to discussing it, and firmly out of date to the aspiring novelist Terence, the Cambridge man who directs Rachel away from late-Victorian fiction or drama, both characters (frequently understood as fictive versions of Vanessa and Clive Bell) reject literature with an explicit "purpose" as a thing of the recent but outmoded past. And in so doing, they not only consign a large body of writing, especially by women of the prior generation, to a superseded time, but also position the reading heroine herself as never quite in synch with the present moment, always somewhat "behind" it. Terence's use of the phrase "behind the times," then, implies that both what Rachel is reading and Rachel herself—like Virginia Stephen in this chapter's epigraph, however sarcastic her claim to Clive Bell—lag behind the contemporary moment, putting her and her books at some distance from the present.[8]

In the context of this novel, to call a literary work "behind the times" is to deploy a temporal-spatial figure that extends the distance between the recent past and a fast-moving, iconoclastic present, thus discarding the social-realist aesthetic of the 1890s in particular. Yet, as Terence implies, Rachel, too, is belated and backward: the narrator says that "her mind was in the state of an intelligent man's in the beginning of the reign of Queen Elizabeth," suggesting her absence of experience or knowledge, a blankness that both resonates with some elements of Grand's sprawling novel and, perhaps, exaggerates the conditions of young ladyhood as Virginia Stephen and her sisters knew them (*Voyage* 31; ch. 2). Both unformed and uninformed, Rachel Vinrace thus ironically figures the imaginary young lady reader at the center of so much late-nineteenth-century literary discourse, whose ignorance or innocence could be shattered or preserved depending on what she did or did not read. The almost comical yet simultaneously deadly state of not knowing that Rachel's character inhabits forms an ironically melodramatic backdrop, as I will demonstrate, for the three heroines of Grand's most successful and widely read novel.

In its effort to convey knowledge about sexuality to its female readers, *The Heavenly Twins* provides an important counterpoint to the elaboration of the "impartial" or "objective" narrative stance that Woolf inherited from the late-nineteenth-century discussion I sampled in chapter 1. Both her critique of Schreiner and Hardy and Katherine Hilbery's stance on her cousin Cyril's "misbehavior," for example, imply Woolf's lifelong opposition to novelistic "preaching" toward some definite end—including what she saw as a good or desirable end, such as the sexual education of young women.[9] But in parallel fashion, Grand's novel itself registers some dissatisfaction with the work of the women writers and political activists of the generation prior to her own. The commodification of sex was a major and persistent concern in mid- and late-Victorian feminist discourse and activism, not just for the second-generation Grand and her contemporaries but also for the first-generation Elizabeth Gaskell and the social reformer Gaskell's fiction influenced, Grand's older contemporary Josephine Butler. A key figure in *Three Guineas*, Butler had a decided impact on both Grand and Woolf, and it is this first- rather than second-generation figure that came to occupy a central, visible place in Woolf's thinking. In considering the ways in which Grand, like Woolf, resisted and rearticulated the stance of her elder contemporaries, I will show a generational dynamic at work quite comparable to the one I identified in chapter 1.

In what follows, then, I bring some of the central motifs of *The Voyage Out* into extended conversation with *The Heavenly Twins*. Considering Woolf's formation as a reader during her early years, before her father's death, I locate that reading in the context of debates about what young women should and shouldn't know, turning back in time to comparable material in *The Heavenly Twins* to show how Grand, too, addresses these debates. By the date of *The Voyage Out*—after three decades of increasingly explicit cultural discussion of sexuality in fiction—we ought to see Rachel's sexual ignorance as the exception, not the rule, as does her aunt Helen, who "could hardly restrain herself from saying out loud what she thought of a man who brought up his daughter so that at the age of twenty-four she scarcely knew that men desired women and was terrified by a kiss" (86; ch. 6).[10] That Rachel's relative ignorance of male heterosexual desire is presented as exceptional rather than normative owes something to the unacknowledged efforts of the writers and reformers of Grand's generation. For even as it downplays some of its family resemblance to this work by her older contemporary and for all the formal differences between them, in its resistance to and revision of late-Victorian matter *The Voyage Out* yet betrays a deep investment in many of the issues that preoccupied eminent and not-so-eminent female (and male) novelists at the fin de siècle.

Hours in a Library

Whether or not Leslie Stephen gave his youngest daughter "a solid grounding in English literature and history" and "trained her" in both emerging disciplines, and even taking into account the discovery of her attendance at courses run by the Ladies' Department of King's College at 13 Kensington Square, there can be little doubt that in her early years, Virginia Stephen's reading was mainly limited to the contents of her father's library (Hill 351; Kenyon Jones and Snaith).[11] Although Ellis contends that the metaphorical trajectory of Woolf's career took her from her mother's garden to "the paternal study as the key Victorian locale . . . in her quest for fact and documentation rather than romance," I would suggest instead that we ought to regard "the paternal study" of her actual readerly experience during her adolescence as having a significant influence on both her lack of access to the varied literatures of her parents' time and the course her career would take (145). If her father did informally school her through his library holdings, as many scholars have suggested, then it is nonetheless apparent that the selected nineteenth-century texts he offered his daughter were not those of the immediate present.

With an eye to his daughter's future, Leslie Stephen constructed authorship as "a thing for ladies," as he told Julia Stephen, seeing it as a growth profession for women (qtd. in Hill 351). Well before the vituperative attacks on the feminization of literature that punctuated the late-century literary scene, he had predicted that "the art of novel-writing will pass altogether into feminine hands. It may be long before the advocates of women's rights will conquer other provinces of labour," he accurately claimed in 1874; "but they have already monopolized to a great extent the immense novel manufacturing industry of Great Britain" ("Richardson's Novels" 64–65). Even before their marriage, he told his future wife in July 1877 that he believed "women ought to be as well educated as men": his daughter "Laura, for example, ought to learn something thoroughly when she grows up, thoroughly enough to be able to make her living at it, if it is of the paying kind, as to be an authority on it, if it is not" (*Selected Letters* 1: 214). He took a different tack years later, however, when he told Thoby Stephen that despite receiving "piles of . . . indignant letters ordering me to go" to the vote on "women's degrees at Cambridge," "I shall not go, because I don't very much care" (Letter [15 May 1897]).

Leslie Stephen's scattered comments on educating his daughters signal the value he attributed to their acquiring a professional ethos. And developing disciplined habits of mind as a reader and writer did enable Woolf to operate in an increasingly competitive and diversified literary marketplace that was relatively open to women. In representing a career as a writer as the alternative rather than the complement to an unpaid career as a mother and wife, her father was also of course very much of his time. Married women of the Stephens' class, for some decades to come, did not typically work for money while also running a home and/or raising children, unless they had to. But certainly, many of the women writers with whom Leslie Stephen was friendly, such as those two whose careers I will explore in chapter 3, were in precisely that position, since writing was one of the few occupations that "daughters of educated men" might combine with heterosexual marriage and family life.

We can speculate, then, that insofar as Leslie Stephen directed his daughter's reading, he did so with an eye to her taking up authorship, as had any number of women he knew quite well. Supportive as he may have been to some, however, he did not have any particular interest in contemporary women's writing: "It is startling to see how few women appear" in the catalogue of his library, although we must consider what remains of it with a skeptical eye rather than draw firm conclusions from it (Daugherty, "Learning" 14; cf. De Gay, "Exploring"). This caveat aside, it is clear that most of the close working relationships he established in his years as editor of the *Cornhill* were with men: Hardy, James, Meredith, Henley, Symonds, and Robert Louis Stevenson. His published criticism of nineteenth-century writers also tends, unsurprisingly, to focus on the "great," as in the volume on George Eliot for John Morley's ironically titled "Men of Letters" series in 1902. He steered clear of contemporary fiction when he left the editorship of the *Cornhill* in 1882 to take the helm at the *Dictionary of National Biography*. He was close to fifty when his youngest daughter was born and not in the best of health; "father's deafness," Woolf wrote, "cut off his intercourse with the younger generation of writers." At least in the 1890s, "young writers, young painters never came to Hyde Park Gate," though many older ones did ("Sketch" 157).[12] The long list of nineteenth-century books that Virginia Stephen mentions reading in her 1897 journal also skews heavily toward works by "classic" figures—Scott, Carlyle, Tennyson, Charlotte Brontë, Kingsley, Gaskell, Macaulay, as well as Trollope, Dickens, Thackeray, and Eliot—all safely dead and most suitably "great." Her grounding in that tradition, its gender politics notwithstanding, was a clear asset in her career, in which first book reviews and later review-essays constituted both much of her published work and a substantial part of her earned income.

What if any late-Victorian works did Leslie Stephen's library contain? Janis M. Paul concisely makes the salient point: "While James Joyce was discovering Ibsen," his exact female contemporary "was reading Sir Walter Scott" (20).[13] That primer for mid-Victorian femininity, *The Daisy Chain* (1856) by Charlotte Mary Yonge (b. 1823), to which Virginia Stephen alluded in a number of the *Hyde Park Gate News*, was another favorite, at least among the daughters of the house (160).[14] The later Victorian books from Leslie Stephen's library that were still in Leonard Woolf's possession at his death in 1969—no doubt many fewer than when Stephen died in 1904—include only a presentation copy of Pater's *Imaginary Portraits* (1887), signed by the author; a first edition of Swinburne's *Poems and Ballads* (1866), which may have belonged to Herbert Duckworth; and the short-story collection *Celibates* (1895) by George Moore, which could have belonged to either Leslie Stephen or the Woolfs. The most controversial nineteenth-century title is Émile Zola's *Nana* (1880);[15] the very advanced Evadne Frayling reads it in *The Heavenly Twins* (221; bk. 2, ch. 11), and surely Stephen did, too, even if he did so, like Grand's heroine, without much relish for a writer he classed among "the modern would-be satirists who make society—especially French society—a mere sink of nastiness" ("Fielding's Novels" 88).[16]

Both the limits of her father's library and the likely limits on what volumes she might have read from it lead me to infer that, unlike her contemporaries Strachey, Woolf, or Joyce, the teenaged Virginia Stephen had little to no immediate access to late-Victorian literature in a naturalist, aestheticist, and/or protofeminist vein.[17] Even assuming that Stephen was inescapably aware of the changing dynamics of contemporary print culture, it is difficult to imagine him reading Grand or Egerton; purchasing *The Yellow Book* or *The Savoy*;

allowing his teenage daughter to peruse *Nana*; or sampling Moore's *Celibates* or the Zolaesque *Esther Waters* (1894), which Woolf appreciatively reviewed on its reissue in 1920 ("A Born Writer," *Essays* 3: 250–52). As there is no reference in her early journals to reading Hardy until 1903, his fiction may, too, have been off-limits, despite Leslie Stephen's admiration for it (*Passionate* 205). For as editor of the *Cornhill*, Stephen had "deleted on his own initiative passages" from *Far from the Madding Crowd* (1874) and refused *The Return of the Native* (1878) altogether, in deference to the sensibilities of Mrs. Grundy and "the Young Person" (Keating 258).[18] "Suppose the ladies and children always present": so Thackeray had mandated as first editor of the *Cornhill*, and his son-in-law continued to heed that imperative (qtd. in Debenham 20).[19] As Stephen wrote in 1872, invoking the watchwords of Podsnappery, his job as editor was "to provide healthy reading for the British public & to be sure that our Mag. may lie on the table of the most refined female without calling a blush to her cheek" (*Selected Letters* 1: 109).

With editors and contributors alike increasingly chafing against such restrictions, prohibitions on content constituted an important node in literary discourse of the time, aligning the female reader with the forces of censorship—as in Moore's "Literature at Nurse" (1885), the forum on "Candor in Fiction" that appeared in *The New Review* in January 1890 with Hardy, Besant, and Eliza Lynn Linton (b. 1822) as contributors, and numerous other contemporary polemics regarding the proper boundaries of literary representation.[20] The New Woman writers that father and daughter did not apparently read also played an important role in this debate. Even as the lively periodical conversation on "the Woman Question" shifted the ideological terrain of gender norms for later Victorians, New Woman fiction problematized both the form and content of realist writing. As this diverse body of work became a key site for critiquing the social and narrative structures that had confined both actual women and their fictional counterparts to particular kinds of plots, contemporary critics simultaneously argued that novels had failed to represent the potential and actual problems of heterosexual marriage, especially for women, with the frankness and clarity they warranted. By late in the century, challenges from all sides to the aesthetics of domestic fiction in particular, perceived as patently unrealistic, especially targeted the circulating libraries as the purveyors of a prudery that purported to keep literature safe for English girls and women; and such challenges certainly remained in play during the first decades of the new century.

From the point of view of many writers, limits on expression and representation constrained artistic freedom and achievement while also suppressing or omitting any view of "things as they are"; ironically, daily newspapers were perceived as having a degree of license that literature lacked (Linton 10). As the fledgling novelist Mary Erle realizes in *The Story of a Modern Woman* (1894) by Ella Hepworth Dixon (b. 1857), who was the daughter of a well-known Victorian journalist, no reader of the daily press could secure "protection" from the "dangers" of sexual knowledge.[21] Yet, even as her editor takes a telephone call from his paper's photographer and urges him to get good shots of all the players in the latest celebrity divorce case, he tells Mary that only "thoroughly healthy reading" will do for the fiction-reading public (146). In many respects, *The Voyage Out* continues and extends this late-Victorian debate about tacit and explicit censorship as it affects both the young lady reader and the would-be woman writer at the turn of the century. As noted above, Woolf represents the impressionable Rachel as subject to a wide variety of advice about what she should and shouldn't read, and the narrator of *The Voyage Out* further comments on, while some second-generation characters enforce, the particular gendered constraints that shape her reading. I suggest here that such constraints shaped Virginia Stephen's reading as well.

Describing the heroine as having "been educated as the majority of well-to-do girls in the last part of the nineteenth century were educated"—that is to say, quite imperfectly—the narrator further states that Rachel had "never troubled her head about the censorship which was exercised first by her aunts, later by her father" (*Voyage* 31, 32; ch. 2). "Brought up with excessive care," she thus remains "completely ignorant," particularly of sex and its conventions (32). In words the narrator of *Mrs. Dalloway* uses to describe Clarissa Parry, about a generation older than the protagonist of this novel, at Bourton in the 1890s, Rachel, too, "knew nothing about sex—nothing about social problems" (30). At the same time, *The Voyage Out* carefully distinguishes the regime of Rachel's home life in Richmond—described most closely in chapter 16, which was radically trimmed for the 1920 U.S. edition of the novel—from the laissez-faire attitude of her uncle Ridley, whose traveling library includes the improper Balzac (DeSalvo 344–49). Although he remarks that "if you read Greek, you need never read anything else," Ridley encourages Rachel's desultory reading of works typically prohibited to young ladies: "She chose for herself a volume at random, submitted it to her uncle, who, seeing that it was *La Cousine Bette*, bade her throw it away if she found it too horrible" (*Voyage* 192, 193; ch. 13). Ridley's giving his niece more or less free rein to choose any book from his shelves (although she still "submitted" it for his inspection) anticipates Woolf's much later claim in a centenary tribute to Leslie Stephen, often quoted by critics, that she had had "the free run of a large and quite unexpurgated library" ("Leslie Stephen, the Philosopher at Home: A Daughter's Memories," *Essays* 5: 588).

While *The Voyage Out* paints Ambrose as a less censorious figure than his brother-in-law Willoughby, the historical Leslie Stephen was perhaps closer to Willoughby's position than Woolf's retrospective characterization of her father asserts. In an 1893 letter written to his wife while staying with Symonds and his family in Switzerland, Stephen describes *La Cousine Bette* (1846) as being about "the lady who has 5 men to dinner & tells each of them that he is about to become a father ie. [*sic*] by her having a baby" (*Selected Letters* 2: 415). He further reports that Symonds authorized his daughter Madge (b. 1869) to request in his name the Balzac novels she wanted. Leslie Stephen responded to Symonds's perceived paternal permissiveness with censure: "If Stella had said the same to me, I should instantly have told her *not* to write for them. . . . I don't think it pretty reading for young ladies" (415; emphasis in the original). (By contrast, Beatrice Webb writes that when she and her sisters "complained to my father that a book we wanted to read was banned by the libraries[,] 'Buy it, my dear,' was his automatic answer" [55]). Both Stella Duckworth and Madge Symonds were twenty-four at the time of this letter, precisely the same age as the fictional Rachel, and only a trifle younger than Virginia Stephen herself was as she began drafting the novel. Rachel's reading thus extends beyond the range that Leslie Stephen would ostensibly have permitted. Ridley's "opposition to censorship notwithstanding," his "deft insinuation of Victorian moral codes" that might make Balzac "too horrible" for a young lady reflects the persistent turn-of-the-century concern with middle- and upper-class women's knowledge of sexuality (Schlack 9).

If exposure to sexual matters was perceived as a risk to the young lady reader, then Stephen may have construed the severance of art from morality identified with such male aesthetes as Pater and Wilde as an even more serious threat to the would-be woman writer, as I suggested in chapter 1. Though Woolf recalls reading *Marius the Epicurean* (1885)—"for which I then had a passion"—in her bedroom at 22 Hyde Park Gate before her father's death in 1904, Perry Meisel has argued that "until Virginia's late adolescence, Leslie monitored her reading very closely" and that "it was clearly authors precisely like Pater whom [he] sought to guard his daughter against"; he further speculates that Stephen's perceived distaste for sexual dissidence undergirded his hostility to Pater ("Old Bloomsbury" 182; Meisel 5). But Stephen's preference that young ladies read and, perhaps, that grown women write only "pretty" books was not unique to him, of course. According to one advice writer of the 1890s, a respectable governess "should not understand what 'decadent' and *fin-de-siècle* mean: the implication being that if such information is not imported into one area of the house, its contamination cannot spread" (J. E. Panton; qtd. in Flint 105).

To be sure, during "a decade when *David Copperfield* [1850] and *Adam Bede* [1859] could still be considered risqué reading" from a middle-class standpoint because of their representation of sex outside heterosexual marriage, Virginia Stephen records reading both in the summer of 1897 (Flint 300; *Passionate* 120, 122). Yet, when she reports that "I may read Vanity Fair & Jane Eyre," the latter of which Leslie Stephen had charged with "some coarseness" and which Kitty Malone's mother in *The Pargiters* deems "immoral," the "may" could mean "I might" or, more likely, "I am now allowed to" (*Passionate* 121; L. Stephen, *Selected Letters* 1: 123; Woolf, *Pargiters* 99). Provocatively, Woolf's "Hours in a Library" describes "the books we read in childhood" as having been "purloined . . . from some shelf supposed to be inaccessible." Though there is no way of knowing for sure, Woolf may be drawing on her own experience here, invoking both the prohibition and its surreptitious circumvention. Owing to the paucity of records between the end of the 1897 journal and the onset of her professional career in 1905, it is difficult to say at exactly what point she began to read not according to her father's lights, but by her own. Yet, "the later reading," according to "Hours in a Library," "is quite a different matter. For the first time, perhaps, all restrictions have been removed, we can read what we like" (*Essays* 2: 56).

Woolf's tastes as a reader of the later Victorians, when she did come to read some of them, coincided in good part with those of her male contemporaries, albeit with certain differences. While we have to reconstruct her knowledge (and ignorance) of fin-de-siècle literature from the incomplete historical records of her reading that we possess, and can only trace how it did or did not change over time from her reviews, essays, letters, and diary entries, Leonard Woolf left behind five volumes of autobiography, the first of which identifies the writers favored at the turn of the century by the Cambridge men who formed the nucleus of old Bloomsbury. If we should not assume that his wife's tastes were identical to his own, then his representation of the shared preferences of his classmates still suggests a good deal of overlap with what we do know about her judgments. He notes in *Sowing* (1960) the "tremendous effect of Henry James's later novels," for example, though he qualifies that group consensus by adding that he admired James "always with a reservation"—as did Virginia (123, 119).

But Leonard Woolf did not emphasize the value of particular writers on the aesthetic grounds that his wife consistently adopted. He praised them instead for their role in the struggle with "bourgeois Victorianism," the "revolt against a social system and code of conduct and morality" whose "protagonists" were all later Victorians, many of whom survived into the new century: "Swinburne, Bernard Shaw, Samuel Butler in *The Way of All Flesh*, and to some extent Hardy and Wells" (*Sowing* 166). Characterizing these writers as the first to rebel against the earlier Victorians, he situated himself and his Cambridge friends as part of "the second generation in this exciting movement of men and ideas," "out to construct something new" rather than being "part of a negative movement of destruction, against the past" (175). He thus asserts that the rebellion against the received "system and code" was prosecuted by artists, not activists; by men, not women; and in literature first, one might say, and only then carried out in life. Classing him among his own "contemporaries," Leonard reports that "the first to mean something to us was George Meredith," friend of the Stephen family, whose fiction experienced an enormous vogue starting in the 1880s after decades of laboring in obscurity. But their "leaders" were Hardy (whose *Tess* and *Jude* had outraged "the most degraded and hypocritical elements in Victorianism"), Shaw, and Ibsen (181–82).[22] To a great extent, then, the writers Leonard prizes for their wholesale challenge to "bourgeois Victorianism" were among the writers whom Virginia repeatedly identified as her chief immediate (male) precursors, yet she treats these figures with definite differences, differences that gender makes.

For Virginia as for her ally Vanessa, the revolt against "bourgeois Victorianism" and its associated "code of conduct and morality" decidedly involved making "something new"—first and foremost, themselves. Books alone would not do much to ease the passage from being a late-Victorian young lady to a modern woman, for which the typical (and, I have argued, misleading) shorthand is the move from South Kensington to Bloomsbury. Certainly James, Hardy, Meredith, Shaw, and Ibsen were of some help in jamming the works of "that great patriarchal machine," which ground out proper ladies and gentlemen ("Sketch" 153); indeed, all the writers Leonard Woolf cites as key figures for himself and his Cambridge contemporaries were critical to some degree of the sex/gender system of their day. Yet, in her public and private writings about these male authors, Virginia Woolf rarely assessed them in the terms that her husband would adopt: she read them as writers, not as "leaders" of a movement; she evaluated them not from an explicitly political point of view, but in terms of their style and technique. She studied them so as to make "something new" of herself not as a woman, but as a writer; not an activist, but an artist.

Dangerous Reading

Given this context, we can juxtapose the reading of both Rachel Vinrace and Virginia Stephen with that of Evadne Frayling, the most knowledgeable of *The*

Heavenly Twins' three heroines, as a way of both conjoining and differentiating Woolf and Grand's respective projects. Evadne's reading both does and does not educate her about life, which the works she reads represent in a particular light.[23] As mentioned in chapter 1, the eighteen-year-old Evadne criticizes *Roderick Random* and *Tom Jones* for their representation of male sexual conduct after hearing her misogynist father—"a bigoted Conservative, narrow and strongly prejudiced rather than highly principled," yet sounding a bit like Leslie Stephen all the same—praise them as "true to life in every particular, . . . and not only to the life of those times, but of all time" (Grand, *Heavenly* 6; bk. 1, ch. 1; 19; bk. 1, ch. 3). Evadne records her perceptions of these two novels in the commonplace book that she keeps "between the ages of twelve and nineteen": "It may be good to know these things," she concludes, "but it is not agreeable" (13, 20). Having read Smollett and Fielding does her no good at all, however, when she meets the man who becomes her first husband: only after her marriage does she learn that his "mode of life has very much resembled that of one of those old-fashioned heroes, Roderick Random or Tom Jones, specimens of humanity whom I hold in peculiar and especial detestation" (84; bk. 1, ch. 15).[24] Impelled by sexual desire, unprepared by her parents, and unable to connect what she finds in literature to her experience—and thus in some ways a definite forerunner of Rachel Vinrace—Evadne enters into a marriage with a man she desires that she will nonetheless never consummate, unarmed by understanding of her own sexuality, even if relatively well-versed (better-versed than Rachel, that is) by her reading about the sexual conduct of men.

Although John Kucich has argued that "the novel explicitly sees [Evadne's] quest for unmediated knowledge to represent her overidentification with male cultural authority," even as a teenager, Evadne reads from what critics including Teresa Mangum and Ann Heilmann would call a feminist point of view ("Curious" 200). Brought to her home by the progressive mother of the title characters, Lady Adeline Hamilton-Wells, *The Subjection of Women* (1869) takes pride of place in Evadne's commonplace book, establishing the important influence of John Stuart Mill on both author and heroine (Grand, *Heavenly* 14; bk. 1, ch. 3). But so, too, is *The Vicar of Wakefield* (1766) an early favorite: on rereading it when she is slightly older, Evadne observes that the "one thing in the book that strikes me first and foremost and above all others, . . . is that the men were educated and the women were ignorant" (16). She subsequently concludes, "Withholding education from women was the original sin of man" (24; bk. 1, ch. 5). Evadne goes on to read mathematics, like Katharine Hilbery, and then somewhat serendipitously turns to anatomy, physiology, and pathology. We later learn that she has attained extensive knowledge on subjects in which even elite young women were not typically schooled, but the narrator takes pains to describe her as no second Eve: she is "enlightened by knowledge, not corrupted" (23). Finally, on "the verge of womanhood," Evadne's "liberty of action was sensibly curtailed, but," significantly, "all supervision in the matter of her mental pursuits was withdrawn. She had received the accustomed education of a girl in her position, which her parents held, without knowing it themselves, perhaps, to consist for the most part in being taught to know better than to read anything which they would have considered objectionable." And though "from this time forward," as the narrator concludes the chapter, "there is less literature and more life in the 'Commonplace Book,'" Evadne has already read material that her parents "would have considered objectionable" even if she hasn't drawn many conclusions from it, owing to what the narrative portrays as her pure-mindedness and lack of sexual feeling (24–25). Writing to Lady Adeline, Evadne's mother states that her daughter "is perfectly innocent. . . . At eighteen she knows nothing of the world and its wickedness, and is therefore eminently qualified to make somebody an excellent wife" (39; bk. 1, ch. 8). But Lady Adeline reframes Evadne's pure innocence as *dangerous ignorance*: "In the matter of marriage especially an ignorant girl may be fatally deceived," and "she may, in these plain-spoken times, obtain a wholly erroneous theory of life and morality from a newspaper report" (40; emphasis in the original). Lady Adeline's line of thought coincides precisely with one of Hite's key points regarding *The Voyage Out*: "Feminine innocence is sustained by a calculated withholding of exactly the information that might allow women to protect themselves" (*Woolf's Ambiguities* 115).

And so it unfolds, at least in part. When the pious Evadne meets the army man Colquhoun, having previously rejected the suit of the local clergyman, the narrator makes clear that while she is not sexually drawn by the latter, her attraction to the former is something for which her reading could not have prepared her; indeed, Helen Ambrose's prescription for Rachel of "talk that was free, unguarded, and . . . candid" would have done Evadne far more good than books in this respect (*Voyage* 137; ch. 10).[25] As Grand's younger contemporary Ménie Muriel Dowie (b. 1867) made this eugenically inflected point in *Gallia* (1895), "The first man is never a woman's free choice": "He is an accident; neither science, skill, nor selection has a hand in landing him" (62). "Overcome by a feeling stronger than reason" and having "formulated the desire for a sign, for some certainty by which she might know the man whom the dear Lord intended to be her husband," Evadne's "heart bounded—her face flushed" at Colquhoun's first glance: "She had full faith in the sign"; "she clasped her hands to her breast, and reveled in sensations" (Grand, *Heavenly* 52, 53; bk. 1, ch. 11). Here as elsewhere in the text, Grand's own signs—or ways of signifying women's erotic feelings—are relatively muted and subtle, in accord with the context of the times. But they would have been unmistakable, I think, to an attentive or knowing reader; as Sally Ledger agrees, "It is made clear that [Evadne] desires her husband sexually even though she is determined to reject" his advances after marriage ("New" 158). Reading those bodily signs, as Grand represents them, thus leads to the conclusion that Evadne's mistake lies in taking sexual desire as the primary basis for marriage; here Grand "instructs her women readers," in Iveta Jusová's words, not only "to inspect their future husbands for signs of moral corruption" but also to interrogate their own bodily responses (20).

The letter Evadne receives just after the wedding ceremony shatters her "dangerous ignorance" for good. Abandoning Colquhoun at the train station, she telegraphs to her parents that she has "received information about Major C.'s character and past life which does not satisfy me at all, and am going now to make further inquiries" (Grand, *Heavenly* 68; bk. 1, ch. 12). Unlike, say, George Eliot's Gwendolen Harleth, who receives disturbing news about her husband-to-be's sexual past before the wedding day yet ultimately marries him anyway, Evadne seeks primarily to know and act on the truth. Her actions lead her parents to conclude that she knows too much, rather than too little. Although Grand does not explicitly state what Evadne learns from her mysterious correspondent, her "further inquiries" confirm that her new husband is "a disreputable man," "a moral leper" (78, 79; bk. 1, ch. 14). (When Evadne had "timidly" but explicitly asked about Colquhoun's past before the wedding, her father told her there was nothing objectionable in it, while her mother tells Lady Adeline, but not Evadne, only that Colquhoun had been "rather wild" [56, 55; bk. 1, ch. 11].) Writing to her parents in hopes of securing a legal separation after she (presumably) learns the details of her husband's sexual career, Evadne implicitly rebukes their low standard: "I find that I consented to marry him under a grave misapprehension of his true character—that he is not at all a proper person for a young girl to associate with" (84; bk. 1, ch. 15). When her father indignantly refuses his help and her parents jointly bully her into staying married, Evadne agrees only on the condition that while she will live with Colquhoun to save face, she will not have sex with him, an act of protest that also betrays the eugenic strand of Grand's feminism.[26] And she registers a more explicit protest against the sexual double standard in a letter to her mother: "Having been kept in ignorance, I consider that I was inveigled into consenting, that the vow I made was taken under a grave misapprehension, that therefore there is nothing either holy or binding in it, and that every law of morality absolves me from fulfilling my share of the contract" (89).

His daughter's disobedience indirectly sends Mr. Frayling to the bookcase in her former sitting room, where the sun shines in "on the backs of a row of well-worn books" with "scars of use and abuse." What he finds is not primarily fiction, but is certainly compared to fiction of a particular kind in its scandalizing effect *on him*:

> Without deliberate intention, Mr. Frayling followed the ray, and read the bald titles by its uncompromising clearness—histology, pathology, anatomy, physiology, prophylactics, therapeutics, botany, natural history, ancient and outspoken history, not to mention the modern writers and the various philosophies. Mr. Frayling took out a work on sociology, opened it, read a few passages which Evadne had marked, and solemnly ejaculated, "Good Heavens!" several times. He could not have been more horrified had the books been "Mademoiselle de Maupin," "Nana," "La Terre," "Madame Bovary," and "Sapho"; yet, had women been taught to read the former and reflect upon them, our sacred humanity might have been saved sooner from the depth of degradation depicted in the latter. (104; bk. 1, ch. 16)

Following her earlier discovery of a box of books in the lumber room, Evadne had, unbeknownst to her parents, read science and medicine (including works on the prevention and treatment of disease), history, philosophy, and unnamed "modern writers," a pursuit that the narrator unequivocally endorses. Comparable in kind if not in degree to Stephen's sense of Balzac as inappropriate reading for a twenty-four-year-old woman, Mr. Frayling's horror not only betrays his desire that his daughter not know such things but also highlights his creator's "unfeminine" knowledge of them, and of French literature, too.

The narrator's comparison of how Mr. Frayling responds to what Evadne actually reads with how he would respond to her reading Gautier (whose preface to *Mademoiselle de Maupin* [1834] first articulated the doctrine of *l'art pour l'art*), Zola, Flaubert, and Daudet—decadents all in Grand's eyes, regardless of the differences among them—at first levels the distinction between facts and theories, on the one hand, and the (sexual) knowledge fiction conveys, on the other. But the narrator's subsequent reflection corrects the misperception under which Mr. Frayling labors. By denying women access to useful knowledge, including the knowledge of how female and male bodies work and how they may come to suffer, men persist in multiplying the horrors of prostitution, adultery, and sexually transmitted disease that French fiction accurately, dispassionately reports. Making little to no distinction here between literature and life, Grand's narrator represents *Nana*, *Sapho*, and the rest as true representations of "the depth of degradation" which men's vice may plumb and which women's "dangerous ignorance" prevents them from perceiving.

Evadne does eventually read those French books when she makes her own voyage out, to her husband's station in Malta. Having agreed to the terms of cohabitation Evadne has negotiated, Colquhoun is not without "a hope [that] her determination to live up to [her views] was merely an infantile disease of which society would soon cure her," with the tone of "society" among the officers of the Maltese regiment being represented as decidedly low (173; bk. 2, ch. 1). He arranges two rooms of their house "with all the beloved possessions, books, pictures, and ornaments" from her childhood home, with particular emphasis on the volumes that he has added to her library: "I captured all the old ones, and I've got a lot more for you; see, here's Zola and Daudet complete, and George Sand. You'll like them better, I fancy, when you get into them than Herbert Spencer and Francis Galton"—the latter perhaps among the unnamed "modern writers," associated with the origins of eugenics, whose works her father had seen on her bookshelves (175–76). Although Evadne is naïvely touched by his consideration, the narrator knowingly parses Colquhoun's motives: "He had arranged the books himself, placing Zola and Daudet in prominent positions, and anticipating much entertainment from the observation of their effect upon her. He expected that she would end by making love to him" (176). But when he asks her later if she has read them, her response is not what he had hoped: "What has struck her most in" *Nana* and *Sapho*, she replies before bursting into "passionate sobs," is *"the awful, needless suffering."*[27] With Colquhoun's stratagem for seduction falling decidedly flat, "the whole of those dangerous works of fiction had disappeared" from her bookshelves within a few days (221; bk. 2, ch. 11; emphasis in the original).

Though her husband anticipated that French fiction would turn her on, Evadne's tearful response instead recalls the narrator's earlier remark that women's reading and reflecting on works of science, history, and theory would save "our sacred humanity" from "the depth of degradation" that French fiction realistically documents and that decadent men like Colquhoun avidly pursue. That rather than being titillated or tantalized, Evadne responds to "dangerous" reading with "passionate sobs" of sympathy thus challenges the assumptions that underpinned the idea of "the Young Person." Grand's point is that the pure- and healthy-minded Evadne remains so regardless of what she reads; it is life rather than literature that leads to her subsequent illness and breakdown. And here we might think, too, of the far less knowing Rachel Vinrace, whose nightmare following her first sexual experience—being kissed by the married Richard Dalloway—generates a claustrophobic, subterranean image of "barbarian men" that leaves her "still and cold as death" (*Voy-*

age 82, 81; ch. 5). Insofar as reading leads to greater understanding of the worlds in which Evadne and Rachel live, nothing ought to be off-limits. Yet, as Marilyn Bonnell observes of *The Heavenly Twins*, while "innocence never brings happiness . . . neither does knowledge" ("Legacy" 468). Books themselves are limited in what they can convey or correct, in their tacit censorship and failure to address matters of bodily experience.

Evadne's subsequent fall into hysteria, as diagnosed by her second husband Dr. Galbraith, has numerous causes.[28] It is effected partly by the repression of her sexuality that her celibate marriage entails, and partly by her first husband's interdiction on her pursuing any political or public activity during his lifetime. And it also registers the impact of the fate of her friend Edith Beale Monteith, who learns too late that her new husband had seduced a servant-class Frenchwoman, abandoned that woman after fathering her child, and transmitted syphilis to both women and each of their sons. One consequence of Edith's death for Evadne is that "she gave up reading. . . . She burnt any books she had with repulsive incidents in them. She would not have them about even, lest they should remind her" (349; bk. 3, ch. 15). Yet, ultimately, Grand also locates a share of the responsibility for the "dangerous ignorance" of two of her three heroines not only in patriarchal prohibitions on reading and male sexual "vice" but also with the novel's maternal generation, who fail to equip daughters with the knowledge of sexuality that would enable them better to navigate their lives. And on this very point, the generational dynamic the novel traces also extends beyond it, to include Grand's relations with her own female predecessors.

Conspiracies of Silence

In the foreword to the 1923 edition of *The Heavenly Twins*, Grand retrospectively suggested that her critique in the novel was directed less at men than at a certain kind of woman. Reporting a conversation about the book with a member of her own generation, "a delightful grandmother of the conservative Victorian type" who lamented "the state of ignorance in which we were kept," Grand remarks, "It was the best sort of woman that yielded to the Conspiracy of Silence," a phrase I return to below, "the purest minded, the highest principled, the most devoted" (398, 399). In the novel itself, one pertinent passage describes Edith's mother Mrs. Beale "and all the gentle mannered, pure-minded women among whom [Edith] had grown up" as "neglect[ing] the good they might have done here in order to enjoy their bright and tranquil dreams of the hereafter. . . . The kind of Christian charity from which they suffered was a vice in itself. To keep their own minds pure was the great object of their lives, which really meant to save themselves from the horror and pain of knowing" (Grand, *Heavenly* 155; bk. 1, ch. 21). Quoting Milton in the 1923 foreword, Grand glosses this attitude a bit less judgmentally in asserting that "the Victorian was robbed of the right to question a single dictum of her 'author' and 'disposer'; full faith was exacted of her on pain of sinning against God and man. If she ventured to doubt she was scourged by her family, by public opinion, by her own conscience" (*Paradise Lost* IV, ll. 635–38; qtd. 399).

Given Grand's recognition of the dangers of "doubt" for many middle-class and elite Victorian women and their consequent adherence to the "vice" of purity, it is all the more striking that one other book Evadne reads in the year before she marries—one of very few books by a woman that she reports reading at all—receives short shrift from both character and author. An important intertext for the representation of women's sexuality in *The Heavenly Twins*, Elizabeth Gaskell's *Ruth* (1853) was among the most controversial books of its day. It focuses on the fall and redemption of a dangerously ignorant seamstress who is seduced and abandoned by a rake. Poor, homeless, and pregnant, Ruth Hilton is saved from suicide first by the care of the stranger who takes her into his home, and then by her love for her child and her god. Burned by two men of Gaskell's acquaintance, despite what some contemporary readers recognized as its relatively orthodox religious tone, the novel by no means indicts the sexual double standard with the vigor of *The Heavenly Twins*. But in its mid-Victorian moment, it precipitated serious conversation and has since been repeatedly credited with spurring the public work undertaken by Josephine Butler. "Icon of the suffrage movement and a feminist exemplar" to both Grand and Woolf, Butler listened with silent disgust as her husband's Oxford colleagues discussed *Ruth*, "which seemed to me to have a very wholesome tendency, although dealing with a painful subject": "A moral lapse in a woman was spoken of as an immensely worse thing than in a man; there was no comparison to be formed between them" (Eberle 217; J. Butler, *Recollections* 95–96).[29] Gaskell's exposure of that double standard famously made so powerful an impression on Butler that she and her husband began to bring "fallen" women into their home to minister to them.

Yet despite her own hostility to the sexual double standard that Gaskell and Butler had identified, Evadne remarks somewhat sententiously that "Mrs. Gaskell must have been a very lovable woman," and copies just a single quotation from *Ruth* into her commonplace book (Grand, *Heavenly* 33; bk. 1, ch. 7). "The story seems to me long drawn out, and of small significance," she writes, just before recording her central criticism: "Full of food for the heart, but the head goes empty away, and both should be satisfied by a work of fiction, I think"

(34). One of the very few authorial footnotes to *The Heavenly Twins* suggests that Grand shared these opinions, legitimating them by reference to those of Gaskell's "great" contemporary Eliot, who predicted in February 1853 that *Ruth* "will not be an enduring or classical fiction" because Gaskell "agitates one for the moment, but she does not secure one's lasting sympathy; her scenes and characters do not become typical" (*Letters* 86). The footnote goes on to emphasize Eliot's acuity as a reader, whose response anticipates Evadne's own: "George Eliot thought so too, years before Evadne was born, and expressed the thought in a letter in which she also prophesied that 'Ruth' would not live through a generation. The impression the book made upon Evadne is another proof of prescience in the great writer" (Grand, *Heavenly* 33).[30] Indeed, Grand assigns to Evadne precisely the view of Gaskell as a personality that Eliot articulated: "Mrs. Gaskell has certainly a charming mind, and one cannot help loving her as one reads her books" (*Letters* 86).

Like Grand, Woolf would go on to give Gaskell a lower place than Eliot in the canon of nineteenth-century women's writing, for as Margaret Homans observes, "Eliot was the closest thing to a model of great female authorship Woolf was ever to find" (413). Alison Booth puts it even more precisely in the aptly titled *Greatness Engendered*: "Woolf needs to discover a precursor at once truly great, by masculine standards she is unwilling to abandon, and truly feminine" (55). She thus compared Gaskell not to Eliot or the Brontës, but to the Edwardian uncles. Reviewing a Gaskell biography in 1910, Virginia Stephen finds it "surprising that we should still be reading her books"; she contrasts Gaskell's depiction of a strike in *North and South* (1854–55) to one by Galsworthy in his play *Strife* (1909) as showing the difference between "a sympathetic amateur [and] a professional in earnest" ("Mrs. Gaskell," *Essays* 1: 341). And she further quotes Anne Ritchie's positive judgment from *The Blackstick Papers* (1908) on the character of Molly Gibson in *Wives and Daughters* (1864–66) only to disagree with it (343). Yet Woolf, too, retained a kind of affection for the "lovable" Gaskell, whose books she had read aloud to Vanessa during their teenage years. On rereading *Sylvia's Lovers* (1863) in 1915, she exclaimed to Nelly Cecil, "What a modest capable woman!"—though she went on to confess herself "rather bored" by it (V. Woolf, *Letters* 2: 64, 66). Eight years later, after consuming a "white dimity rice puddingy chapter of Mrs Gaskell" in the middle of a windy, sleepless night, she concluded that *Wives and Daughters* "must be better than [Bennett's] Old Wives Tale all the same" (*Diary* 2: 263).[31] But another fifteen years after that, Woolf praised *Ruth* for "its stillness, its unconsciousness, its lack of distraction, its concentration & the resulting 'beauty,'" "as if the mind must be allowed to settle undisturbed over the object in order to secrete the pearl" (*Diary* 5: 229). Though she still casts her mid-Victorian predecessor as somewhat artless, Woolf here breaks with not only her own earlier judgment but also the critical line on *Ruth* that Eliot initiated and Grand echoed.

Although their criticisms differ, both Woolf and Grand, thinking back to their literary foremothers, would clearly privilege Eliot over Gaskell, casting the latter as entirely "lovable" but not among the "great" women writers of the nineteenth century. But if Eliot, Grand, and Woolf, too, all condescend to Gaskell, Grand alone criticizes her for her complicity with the "Conspiracy of Silence" she mentions in the 1923 foreword. The one passage from early in *Ruth* that Evadne copies into her commonplace book speaks directly to the ideological project of Grand's novel: "The daily life into which people are born, and into which they are absorbed before they are aware, forms chains which only one in a hundred has moral strength enough to despise, and to break when the right time comes—when an inward necessity for independent action arises, which is superior to all outward conventionalities" (Gaskell 6; ch. 1; qtd. in Grand, *Heavenly* 33; bk. 1, ch. 7). "Independent action" is presumably what Evadne seeks but does not find in *Ruth*, while the novel's adherence to formal and social "conventionalities" may be what draws Grand's fire.

Along with Harriet Martineau (b. 1802), Butler first named the "Conspiracy of Silence" in 1869 as part of the countercampaign against the omissions of press coverage of the agitation to repeal the Contagious Diseases (C. D.) Acts and the double standard such silence supported. The "abolitionist" movement, as Butler called it so as to highlight perceived links between prostitution and chattel slavery, aimed to combat male sexual "vice" not only by publicly advocating for repeal of the statutes but also by disseminating information through the media that would expand women's knowledge of sexuality both in their own defense and as a means of defending others. Her further use of the phrase in a speech to the Ladies' National Association in 1880 commemorating the first decade of repeal agitation asserts that as "every great cause is propagandist in its spirit," "the conspiracy of silence of the press has done us this service . . . it has forced us to create a literature of our own" (qtd. in *Personal* 401, 402).[32] While Butler is referring specifically to her founding of *The Shield* as an official organ for fomenting opposition to the C. D. Acts, we might construe her claim more broadly as invoking, even inciting, the range of late-Victorian women's writing devoted to reform that feminist scholars have recovered over the last several decades. By taking the representation of the sexual double standard and the promulgation of information that would protect Englishwomen against venereal disease as its chief aims, much New Woman writing shattered that silence—but in ways that Butler and Woolf, for different reasons, would find somewhat uncomfortable.

Like her heroine in marking Gaskell as artistically inferior to Eliot, Grand also takes "the side of the overtly political rather than sentimental writer" in foregrounding Evadne's preference for Mill over Gaskell (Heilmann 108). She thus aligns herself with liberal culture's "club of reasonable men," in Elaine Hadley's terms, rather than with "the melodramatic mode and its often female cast" headed up by Butler, even though it is very much the case, as Mangum has established and I will explore below, that melodrama plays a key role in *The Heavenly Twins* (Hadley 184).[33] More directly, as Roxanne Eberle argues, Gaskell's casting of Ruth's fall and redemption in "embedded narratives that disguise the details of Ruth's sexual knowledge" both keeps silence on most aspects of her "seduction" and fails to target male vice as the "real" problem (137). Although as Deborah Epstein Nord points out, "The danger of contamination from the sexually tainted woman is proved to be an illusion" in *Ruth*, the "reality" of men's sexual predation is largely obscured according to the gendered conventions of the time: here we might imagine Grand indicting Gaskell's reticence for its complicity with those conventions (*Walking* 164).[34] Her reaction against Gaskell, comparable to Woolf's diminishment of New Woman writers though based on different criteria, thus suggests how the terms of engagement shift over the course of a generation, and so make the writing of one's foremothers appear behind the times.[35] Yet it also portends another generational division, between the tactics and rhetoric of the first generation and those adopted by their second-generation descendants.

Many scholars would locate the origins of Grand's own activist stance in her marriage to an army surgeon who ran one of the lock hospitals where prostitutes were quarantined under the C. D. Acts and through whom she putatively learned the facts that Evadne Frayling picks up from her reading. But in a speech she made as mayoress of Bath in honor of the Butler centenary in 1928, Grand herself identified the emergence of her political consciousness somewhat earlier, in the movement to repeal the C. D. Acts.[36] Describing her school experiences from 1868 to 1871, which coincided with the beginning of Butler's campaign, Grand claims that she had "set to work to form a society to rescue Josephine Butler"—"who had done something," according to her critics, "which no truly womanly woman would have done"—from her "unfair[]" treatment at the hands of her medical adversaries ("Heavenly" 318). Aiming "to rescue" a woman who had rescued others, Grand reports that she learned of Butler's campaign by eavesdropping on adult conversations at the home of a cousin of her mother's, "an eminent surgeon in London" (317). Maybe Grand also had a peek at this doctor's medical and scientific library, just as Evadne pores over the forgotten books in the lumber room only a few years before young Rose Pargiter, after her experience at the pillar box, "began to hunt about in the little book case [sic] in her father's study," choosing some volumes "because they had certain pictures" (V. Woolf, *Pargiters* 51).[37] Allegedly making classmates and teachers uncomfortable by her political fervor, Grand soon left that school, with a last half report deeming her performance "unsatisfactory"; but she did not stay long at her next school in Kensington, either, marrying in 1871 at the age of sixteen (qtd. in Kersley 28).[38] The adolescent Grand thus took Butler as a hero who bore public scorn in defense of the truth by advocating the spread of information about male sexuality and female suffering as a remedy for the "dangerous ignorance" of which Grand went on to write.

Yet, Butler snubbed Grand in person, as Grand had snubbed Gaskell in print. Regarding her speech for the Butler centenary, which doubles as a partial account of how she came to write *The Heavenly Twins*, a Bath newspaper reported Grand as saying that although she "never met Josephine Butler," "on one occasion, she saw her" at a restaurant in London's Berkeley Hotel:

> She would so have liked to have gone up to her and shaken hands with her; but being so much younger than [Butler] was, she thought it was not in her place to make the first advance. Josephine Butler looked very hard at her, but not sympathetically, and she told a friend of [Grand's] she did not approve of her book, and her words were, "There is no God in that." . . . She admitted that the book was not written in the way Josephine Butler would have written it, [but] Josephine Butler was mistaken. Had she read the book, she must have noticed that it was permeated from beginning to end with the belief that, through it all and through all the suffering, God was watching and it would work right in the end. ("Heavenly" 319–20)

Deferential to Butler's age and authority despite their apparent discord on ideological and religious grounds, Grand yet aims to defend her position as a writer with a purpose by correcting the misreading of even so eminent a reader as Butler. She obliquely registers the difference in their respective positions as based on age, implying not just deference to Butler but a difference of view between them, and presumably a difference of politics as well as aesthetics: for Butler, *The Heavenly Twins* was, sadly, no *Ruth*.[39]

Grand's reception by the very "womanly woman" of the first generation whom she had set out as a schoolgirl "to rescue" thus forms an interesting analogue to Woolf's seeming ignorance of, or indifference to, the New Woman writers of the second generation. Butler's apparent disapproval of *The Heavenly Twins* limns the deeper generational rift and broader disagreements among the late-Victorian feminist communities in which she, Grand, and so many others worked, as I will consider in chapter 4. But that generational rift also has a specifically literary dimension, to which I turn now in a comparative analysis of *The Heavenly Twins* and *The Voyage Out* that focuses on the role played by the prostitute in these texts.

Naturalism and Melodrama in *The Heavenly Twins*

By contrast with the view Evadne takes of Gaskell, the woman novelist depicted in *The Heavenly Twins* seeks to give an explicit, unmelodramatic account of contemporary evils. Also resident in Malta as a military wife, Mrs. Malcomson defines herself as "a naturalist": she "had seen some things which had made a painful impression on her," but "had not met any of those perfect beings" or "terrible demons" that populate prose fiction, characters presumably like Gaskell's redeemed magdalen Ruth or her unrepentant seducer Bellingham (Grand, *Heavenly* 333; bk. 3, ch. 14). Although she has "positive ideas of right and wrong," she never "denies, on the one hand, that wrong may be pleasant in the doing, or claims, on the other, with equal untruth, that because it is pleasant it must be, if not exactly right, at all events, excusable" (333–34). Instead, "she endeavoured to represent things as she saw them, things real, not imaginary" (333). And so Malcomson's aesthetic commitment—and, at least in part, Grand's own—to representing "things real" brings a degree of scandal on herself: "She was too independent to be conventional, and it was therefore inevitable that she should . . . be much misunderstood. . . . It was said, among other things, that she evidently could not be moral at heart, whatever her conduct might be, because she made mention of immorality in her book. Her manner of mentioning the subject was not taken into consideration, because such sheep cannot consider; they can only criticise" (334).[40] Deflecting the charge that the woman who writes of "immorality" must be "guilty" of it—a charge leveled at Gaskell and Grand alike[41]—Malcomson pursues her "naturalist" aesthetic and "independent" aims without concern for her more "conventional" readers, those "sheep" who fail to grasp that the "manner" of novelistic presentation obviates any unsavory matter.[42] In this sense, to adapt Ardis's observation regarding New Women novelists more generally, Mrs. Malcomson is "determined to complete the naturalists' project" (*New* 37).

The "positive ideas of right and wrong" Mrs. Malcomson possesses and seeks to convey in representing "things real, not imaginary"—ideas that Helen Ambrose, like Virginia Woolf, would find inimical to fiction—might well be summed up in the Tennysonian phrase "art for man's sake,"[43] which Grand used to vaunt the significant power of "popular writers" to effect social change:

The "novel with a purpose" and the "sex novel" are more powerful at the present time, especially for good, than any other social influence. Great teachers and preachers have a very limited audience compared to the audience of popular writers; and the most influential writers are those who set themselves to do some good in the world. For one reader that Robert Louis Stevenson has, Mrs Humphry Ward has a thousand; which shows that story books [sic] no longer satisfy us if they contain nothing more than the story. We appreciate art, but not art for art's sake; art for man's sake is what we demand. (*Sex* 1: 190)

Far from being either the sentimental advocate of Christian charity she sees in Gaskell or the detached aesthete here exemplified by Stevenson, Grand pursued a trajectory in which separating art from life was anathema—although her refusal of that aestheticist axiom certainly does not give her the position of "impartial observer" that Stephen and others mandated or that Woolf would go on to adopt as a preferred narrative strategy. The contemporary journalist Helen C. Black cast Grand's aim in *The Heavenly Twins* as congruent with that of the naturalist Malcomson: "She sat down, not to write what is ordinarily meant by 'a novel with a purpose,' but to depict a neighbourhood with its group of characters, types evolved by close observation, with the idea of developing them on natural lines, treating them without prejudice, or making them answer to foregone conclusions" (324).

Yet Grand's emphasis on the broad reach of "popular writers" like Ward, as opposed to the much smaller audience for "great teachers and preachers," suggests a highly intentional plan "to do some good in the world" via her fiction, much like the novelists of purpose that Amanda Claybaugh aligns with the mid-century coalescence of Anglo-American realism (31–51). Grand's frankly politicized aesthetic may have led her to deem Gaskell insufficiently committed to what we would today call an activist platform, and it would subsequently lead to her own temporary erasure from literary history, as she seemed to recognize: when she used that Tennysonian phrase again, in a letter of August 1929, Grand ruefully remarked that "Art for Man's sake is vetoed as being Victorian nowadays" (*Sex* 2: 120). In the 1890s, however, she sought to advance her ideological project by representing the scope and limits of individual action among members of her novel's maternal generation in their quest to end the traffic in women and girls. And she also aimed to combat what Kucich characterizes as the "belatedness" that faced all women writers at the fin de siècle, when "the necessity of formal choice was constructed for women as a trap, since both realist and antirealist writing by women could be stigmatized as forms of intellectual imitation and inadequacy" ("Curious"

202). Casting herself as very much ahead of her times, Grand might, on this reading, be understood as an avatar of Woolf herself two decades later, confronted with the challenge of how to bend to her own ends the novel form, deeply overdetermined by the intentions of others. Grand "deliberately exploits the conjunction of realist and antirealist writing," I would suggest, by intermittently differentiating her own "naturalist" strategies from the "melodramatic mode," which Hadley calls "a vehicle of expression for censored or repressed voices"; she both uses and, to a great extent, parodies it (Kucich, "Curious" 198; Hadley 194). But, more significantly for my purposes, she identifies it with Gaskell and thus by implication with Butler as well.

The critique of the female elders in *The Heavenly Twins* varies based on their degree of willingness to know, and then to act on that knowledge of "things real." When Evadne's aunt Mrs. Orton Beg learns that Edith has contracted syphilis from her husband, she renounces her prior disbelief "in the danger to which all women in their weakness are exposed" and pledges to "alter all this" by working alongside others (Grand, *Heavenly* 349; bk. 3, ch. 15). But the mothers of both Evadne and Edith instead turn away from male "vice" and female suffering, in order "to save themselves from the horror and pain of knowing" to which Grand referred in the 1923 foreword, with bad consequences for their daughters. Grand's narrator makes it clear that if Mrs. Beale had done something to assist the mother and infant that she and her daughter saw lying by the side of the road, then Edith might not have gone on to marry the man who seduced that woman, thus to contract syphilis and transmit it to her child. As the narrator reflects, quoting Tennyson on Merlin's sorry state after his seduction by Vivien in *Idylls of the King* (1859), "It had not occurred to either" Edith or her mother, "gentle, tender, and good as they were, to take the poor dusty disgraced tramp into their carriage, and restore her to 'life and use and name and fame' as they might have done"—and as both Thurstan Benson of *Ruth* and Josephine Butler did ("Merlin and Vivien," l: 968; qtd. in 160; bk. 1, ch. 22).[44] Although "Edwards, the old footman, could have told his mistress the girl's whole history," Mrs. Beale "would not have heard the story for the world": she had "scented something 'unpleasant' in the whole affair" and "very gladly dismissed the whole matter from her mind" (160, 170). Thus, even though the dying Edith indicts only professional men—her doctor, her father the bishop, and her soldier-husband—for "the arrangement of society which has made it possible for me and my child to be sacrificed in this way," the mother's unwillingness to know is actually a proximate cause of her daughter's death (300; bk. 3, ch. 8). As a result of the "dangerous ignorance" her parents did nothing to remedy, Edith "missed the opportunity to save her own life" (Mangum 98).

If some elite mothers prefer not to know, at least one aunt visibly takes action: Grand makes the novel's chief agent of rescue the unmarried Lady Fulda, who interacts with two very differently positioned streetwalkers, and situates her philanthropic work in the context of melodrama. Fulda is a daughter of the Duke of Morningquest, a dubiously reformed rake and Catholic convert who "in his youth . . . had filled Morningquest with riot and debauchery" (*Heavenly* 252; bk. 3, ch. 2). Like those she aims to save, Lady Fulda walks the streets at night, attending to "the spiritual welfare of that class of women which in former times [her father] had been accustomed to countenance in quite another way." Although as readers we never see or enter the "refuge" Fulda establishes, it gains support not only from her wealthy father but also from the progressive friends and relatives of her own generation, all "deeply interested in the success of the undertaking" (257). Described by the heavenly twins' tutor as a "beautiful abstraction," Fulda ministers chiefly to Marie Cruchot, the Frenchwoman who, as Angelica later learns through her friendship with Edith, had "sold her sister Louise to Mosley Menteith," Edith's husband (258, 378; bk. 4, ch. 4). The only extended scene between Fulda and Marie also precipitates the first nocturnal meeting of the Tenor, a stranger to Morningquest who joins the cathedral choir, and the Boy, the male persona based on her twin brother Diavolo that Angelica adopts as a newly married and deeply bored young woman.

While many analysts of the novel have focused on this "interlude," as Grand called it, for how it "strikingly breaks the novel's realist frame" and its other transgressive features—Angelica's transvestism, the Tenor's homoerotic feelings for the Boy, details that many readers now would consider in relation to Woolf's *Orlando*—the parallel between Fulda's rescue of Marie and her subsequent rescue of Angelica has gone largely unnoticed (Kucich, "Curious" 198). But when Marie solicits the cross-dressed Angelica, who "stepped back to avoid her, with an unmistakable gesture of disgust," and thus literally bumps into the Tenor for the first time, Grand sets up a relation between the two that cuts across their different positions, uniting them in their transgression of womanly norms (*Heavenly* 375; bk. 4, ch. 3). Importantly, "the very first effects of the cross-dressing are sexual as [the Boy] is approached by a prostitute"; at the same time, Grand also differentiates the potentially diseased Marie from Angelica, as part of the broader eugenicist strain in her thinking (Taylor 31; Jusová 30–31). This episode both initiates the reader's awareness of Angelica's nightly excursions in the guise of the Boy and marks the end of Marie's streetwalking.[45] Not named by Angelica or the narrator, Fulda suddenly appears "as though [she] were a heavenly visitant," speaks "earnestly" to Marie, and takes her to the local convent after gaining her priest's blessing on his "'wandering sheep,'" as the Boy surreptitiously follows them (Grand, *Heavenly* 377).

The melodrama of this moment evokes a matter-of-fact response from the cross-dressed Angelica: "'Humph!' said the Boy, who was lurking up an entry opposite: 'So that is what they do at night, is it?'" Having wondered earlier why Fulda appears at breakfast in the same clothes she wore the night before, the Boy exclaims, "Now I am beginning to know the world; and what an extraordinary old world it is, to be sure! One half seems to be always kept busy mending the mischief the other half has made" (378). Angelica's disguise thus enables her to see the world in a more knowing way.

But as it turns out, Fulda perceives and thus partially forestalls the consequences of Angelica's own protracted mischief-making in adopting the persona of the Boy and fraternizing with the Tenor. When he and the Boy fall in the river during a boat ride, the Tenor dies from his exposure to the freezing water, the chilling "truth" of the Boy's identity, and his own homoerotic desire. After she learns of the Tenor's death and visits his grave, Angelica in her despair wanders back to the riverbank and contemplates suicide:

> She remembered that after the first plunge [from the boat] there had been no great pain—and even if there had been, what was physical pain compared to this terrible heartache, this dreadful remorse, an incurable malady of the mind which would make life a burden to her forevermore, if she had the patience to live? . . . she turned to gather her summer drapery about her. . . . In the act, however, she became aware of someone hastening after her, and the next moment a soft white hand grasped her arm and drew her back.
>
> "Angelica! how can you stand so near the edge in this uncertain light? I really thought you would lose your balance and fall in." (519; bk. 4, ch. 5)

When Fulda prevents her niece's second "plunge" into the river, the context recalls other desperate young women on the verge of suicide in nineteenth-century fiction—Eliot's Hetty Sorrel or Mirah Lapidoth, to be sure, but especially Gaskell's Ruth Hilton. Here the rescuer is, significantly, female, and her rescue work encompasses both the Frenchwoman and her own errant English niece.[46] Subsequently comparing the Tenor's death to Christ's, Fulda's intervention sets Angelica on the path that will lead to her embracing her marriage to her much-older husband, whom she perversely calls "Daddy." Moreover, Angelica will ultimately mend her ways by taking up a very limited yet putatively meaningful role as a "public woman"—in the sense of that term as Woolf would go on to use it, in describing Margaret Llewelyn Davies or Ray Strachey, rather than in its other sense, as a euphemism for prostitute.

Grand's self-consciousness in these scenes—the staginess, so to speak, of Angelica's "fall" and "redemption"—suggests an authorial awareness of working within and even reworking well-established novelistic and theatrical conventions. While Kucich concludes that Grand evinces "an aesthetics more indebted to sensation fiction than to the English realist tradition," Pykett argues that "Angelica's recuperation" is "marked by a melodramatic excess which verges on the parodic and comic" (*Power* 262; "*Improper*" 160). And Grand assigns that self-consciousness about the plot in which Angelica finds herself to her errant heroine as well: if Angelica is described as disordered and "morbid" in the averted suicide scene, then her characterization of Fulda's sudden appearance as "absurd"—"like an incident in a melodrama, the arrival of the good influence"—is still quite apt (521, 520; bk. 5, ch. 5).

In calling attention to the antirealist elements of her own narrative, in its "absurd" coincidences, Grand in effect parodies the plot conventions that Gaskell had so earnestly established and that Woolf would later mainly reject. These were conventions on which Butler, too, had capitalized, both in her writing and in her public performances, as Judith Walkowitz illustrates (*City* 87–93). Butler "made ample use of the melodramatic mode's polemical tools of resistance," while "Grand both uses and refuses the dictates of good and evil, individual and social culpability, and upheaval and restoration of order in the melodramatic plot" (Hadley 183; Mangum 93–94). Perhaps, then, it is in the way that Angelica foregrounds her aunt's interventions as drawn from a fictional template, rather than exclusively from the "real things" that Mrs. Malcomson purportedly translates into fiction, that we can begin to see some of Grand's own resistance to the prior generation's aesthetic tactics, for despite the seemingly positive treatment of this character, her Roman Catholicism notwithstanding, Lady Fulda is the central object of these parodic moments in the text.

Subsequent metafictional interjections, in which Angelica again reflects on melodramatic conventions, underline this aspect of Grand's critique. In one, Angelica tells herself that "had I been the heroine of a story . . . it would have been left to the reader's imagination to suppose that I remained forever in the state of blissful exaltation up to which Aunt Fulda wound me by her eloquence yesterday": Fulda had then argued that the Tenor died "not for you alone . . . but for all the hundreds upon whom you, in your position, and with your attractions, will bring the new power of your goodness to bear" (540; bk. 5, ch. 8; 535; bk. 5, ch. 7). That Angelica's movement into this new life is not nearly so immediate, straightforward, or grandiosely successful suggests a rejection of the simple plot of sin, conversion, and redemption that Fulda preaches and that Grand might well be attributing to Gaskell, or even to Butler. In another metafictional moment that arises in that same discussion, after Angelica tells her aunt that she had hoped to ask the Tenor's forgiveness for her deception, only to learn instead of his death, Fulda replies that such "good resolutions would only have lasted until you had bound him to you—enslaved him." Here Angelica compares the femme-fatale figure her aunt invokes to "the evil-minded heroine of a railway novel" (536). Such a book would conventionally feature, in the words of the American newspaper poet Ernest LaTouche Hancock, "a beauteous maid, / A hero full of pluck," and "[a] villain, deeply, deeply vile" ("The Railway Novel," ll. 5–6, 9). Fulda surely implies that had she succeeded in securing the Tenor's pardon and regaining his attentions, the street-walking, cross-dressing Angelica would have become just such a villain, the seducer rather than the seduced, soliciting the Tenor as Marie Cruchot had once solicited the Boy—thus becoming, in other words, a variant on the other sort of "public woman."

Recognizing Fulda's role in her plot as shaped by the conventions of melo-drama, Angelica characterizes her aunt's rescue work in terms that not only denigrate the one-on-one ministry Fulda undertakes but also undercut the po-larized struggle between good and evil that Grand via Mrs. Malcomson iden-tifies with things "imaginary" rather than "real." When Angelica herself takes action in women's interests, it is not as a rescue worker, engaged in an indi-vidual pursuit of limited scope, or as one of the "great teachers and preach-ers," but as a woman who writes speeches for her husband to deliver in Parliament, even though she aspires to become an activist, whether "on the platform or otherwise engaged in *Unwomanly* pursuits" (603; bk. 6, ch. 10; em-phasis in the original). "Art for man's sake," in this case, means assaulting the literary and social conventions that maintain silence and subordinate women, with Grand preferring some combination of Mrs. Malcomson's naturalism and Angelica's potential for activism to the melodramatic mode as a more com-plex and up-to-date view of conveying "things real" in a public forum.

In their own day, the women of Grand's generation who broke the "con-spiracy of silence," in a way much different than Butler did, thought of them-selves as not behind but ahead of their times, as avatars of modernity, even as Woolf and her contemporaries arrogated that status for themselves. Thus in the next generation, Woolf would subject both the naturalist and the activist mode to irony rather than parody, as when Evelyn Murgatroyd of *The Voyage Out* announces that "we've talked enough about art, and we'd better talk about life for a change. Questions that really matter to people's lives, the White Slave Traffic, Women's Suffrage, the Insurance Bill, and so on" (289; ch. 19). In this context, pursuing art for man's—or even woman's—sake could only be con-strued as "Victorian." For by the time Woolf indicts "the established catego-ries for containing and conveying reality" through the experience and consciousness of her heroine in *The Voyage Out*, Grand's version of "things real" constitutes part of what Woolf is consigning to the past (Hite, "Public

Woman" 533). In "leaving the description of reality more and more out of their stories," as she wrote in "The Mark on the Wall," and "taking a knowledge of it for granted," future novelists would invent or discover "not one reflection but an almost infinite number" (86, 85). But if Woolf can mainly leave behind or leave out Grand's tactical feminist "description of reality," the representation of the prostitute in *The Voyage Out* still affords a site at which generational continuities and differences play out.

Figuring Prostitution in *The Voyage Out*

As Celia Marshik has demonstrated, Woolf's attitudes to prostitution are themselves continuous with rather than sharply separated from late-Victorian debates: she places Woolf's writing on this issue in the first half of her career (including *The Voyage Out*, *Jacob's Room*, and *Orlando*) in a line that stretches back to Dante Gabriel Rossetti and Shaw—the latter of whom Mangum describes as Grand's "greatest male advocate" (89)—as well as forward, to Joyce and Jean Rhys (b. 1890). And she also shows that the concerns about social purity and the sexual double standard that preoccupied Grand continued well into the twentieth century. Marshik nonetheless constitutes that movement as part of "the *resistance* to modernity contemporary with literary modernism," thus casting this strand of feminist activity as itself behind the times (9; emphasis mine).[47] Both Woolf's neglect of late-Victorian women writers and the critical view of the late-Victorian and early-twentieth-century social purity movement as old-fashioned have certainly made the continuities between her concerns and those of her female predecessors difficult to grasp.[48] She appears to descend, so to speak, from Rossetti and especially Shaw, which may well be how she would have wanted it.

Yet, while marking its differences from the immediate past, *The Voyage Out* clearly represents prostitution in ways that extend the late-Victorian critique, albeit with a much sharper focus than *The Heavenly Twins* evinces on the continuity between heterosexual marriage and prostitution. For the most part, Grand represents prostitution largely as a site of philanthropic and religious activity for the elite women of the maternal generation and as a threat to their daughters and nieces: Gaskell and Butler's "sympathetic" focus on the "fallen" of the working classes is not at all her concern. Moreover, the framing of prostitution as a form of economic exchange closely related to marriage is scarcely evident in Grand's text, a framing that pervades so much other late-Victorian writing—*The Story of an African Farm*, for example, or Mona Caird's essays on marriage—and that is extremely prominent in *The Voyage Out*.

In Woolf's novel, two female guests in the dining room of the Santa Marina hotel observe the presence of "a tall woman dressed conspicuously in white, with paint in the hollows of her cheeks, who was always late [for lunch], and always attended by a shabby female follower." Their brief discussion about her pivots on the ways that an elder and a younger woman speak of, or keep silent about, selling sex. "Well over seventy," Mrs. Paley implies her own knowledge of the woman in white's status even as she withholds that knowledge by a coy locution: "'I shouldn't like to say what *she* is!' she chuckled." Her niece and paid companion keeps her thoughts to herself, and they focus less on the tall woman than on the aunt: Susan Warrington "blushed, and wondered why she said such things," disavowing an awareness of prostitution even as her blush betrays it (*Voyage* 130; ch. 9; emphasis in the original). The elderly widow, financially comfortable enough to travel abroad attended by a follower of her own, can quite literally afford to chuckle at "what *she* is"; conscious of her dependency on the aunt who is also her employer, the niece cannot. For Susan has been musing earlier in the chapter over her chances of marriage to Arthur Venning: "She was thirty years of age, and owing to the number of her sisters and the seclusion of life in a country parsonage had as yet had no proposal of marriage" (114). Once Arthur does propose to Susan, thus initiating "the various changes that [Susan's] engagement would make"—including an "escape" from "the long solitude of an old maid's life"—the "tall woman" turns up again, in the days just before their engagement dance (155; ch. 11). Euphemistically characterized by the narrator as "the lady of doubtful character," she is classed among "the outsiders" not invited to the dance. Hewet feels that, like the "obscure lonely gentlemen" he approaches, "delighted to have this opportunity of talking to their kind," the lady "showed every symptom of confiding her case to him in the near future" (167; ch. 12). By placing Mrs. Paley and Susan in such close proximity to the prostitute and her "shabby female follower," both in the space of the dining room and in terms of the economic relations that obtain in each pair, yet excluding the latter from the legitimating rituals of heterosexual union, the novel establishes relations among paid work, prostitution, and marriage that will obtain not only throughout *The Voyage Out* but across Woolf's career.

In imagining himself as the lady's future confidant, Terence is mistaken. He does not see the woman again until she appears fleetingly—"a figure in a bright dressing-gown . . . crossing from one room to another"—at the end of his conversation with Evelyn M., who instead confides *her* case (218; ch. 14). Born out of wedlock to a pair of cross-class lovers who never married, the "self-dramatizing" Evelyn M. figures an alternative to Susan as a function of her own "doubtful character," owing to the illegitimacy of her birth and her indiscriminate romantic attachments (Froula, *Virginia Woolf* 49). She estimates that "perhaps ten [marriage proposals] was the right figure," but protests that "it really was not a high one" (215). Thus Evelyn confides in Hewet—"as if," in the narrator's words, "she were facing a real problem which had to be discussed between them"—that she's let one man kiss her and "gave him half a promise" of marriage, despite her ongoing relationship with another (213). When Hewet suggests that she "go on liking them" both and "wait and see" how it all turns out, she asks if he's "one of the people who doesn't believe in marriages and all that," invoking the possibility of what in the 1890s would have been called a "free union," an alternative to marriage that Katharine Hilbery also briefly considers (214; *Night* 509–12, ch. 33). Although Evelyn M.'s errant confidences inspire "a mixture of liking, pity, and distrust" in Terence, the narrative ironizes her unconventional pose by presenting both the possibility of marriage and her alternatives to it in rather conventional terms (*Voyage* 215). If she can't find someone to marry who is "great and big and splendid," "some one greater and nobler than I am," then perhaps she "really might *do* something" instead (216, 217, 216; emphasis in the original).

Evelyn presents her version of doing something during a conversation with Rachel. In an ironic allusion to the work of Isabel Somerset, to which I will return in chapter 4, she tells the largely indifferent Rachel about her friend Lillah Harrison, who "runs a home for inebriate women" and "goes among them at all hours of the day and night." Pointedly, Rachel distances herself from both activist work and heterosexual romance when she immediately "conceive[s] an equal dislike for Lillah Harrison and her work in the Deptford Road, and for Evelyn M. and her profusion of love affairs" (288; ch. 19). In another Bloomsbury in-joke, Evelyn M. also tells Rachel that she belongs to "the Saturday Club"—rather than the Friday Club, founded at 46 Gordon Square—and imagines that on her return to London, she will persuade her fellow members to make a difference on important issues like the sex trade:[49]

> "I'm certain that if people like ourselves were to take things in hand instead of leaving it to policemen and magistrates, we could put a stop to—prostitution"—she lowered her voice at the ugly word—"in six months. . . . We ought to go into Piccadilly and stop one of these poor wretches and say: 'Now, look here, I'm no better than you are, and I don't pretend to be any better, but you're doing what you know to be beastly, and I won't have you doing beastly things, because we're all the same under our skins, and if you do a beastly thing it does matter to me.'" (289)

That Evelyn goes on to cite clerical authority in support of her argument, however, when Rachel has lost her faith just that morning while listening to the

Reverend Bax's sermon, underlines the joint critique of religion and philanthropy that shapes Woolf's satirical stance. For his "remarks seemed to be directed to women," and "indeed Mr Bax's congregations were mainly composed of women and he was used to assigning them their duties"—which might well include ministering to inebriates in the Deptford Road (268; ch. 17).[50]

If Susan's character demonstrates how the middle-class woman is positioned by both the conventions of the marriage plot and her own economic dependency, with her fate thus figuratively bordering on prostitution, then Evelyn M.'s doubtful familial past and dubious romantic present imply a kind of meaningless mobility. She flits from one lover to another, and from one possibility of political action to another, as if the two were parallel options. Ironizing the character's romantic entanglements by treating them "as if she were facing a real problem" rather than actually facing one, Woolf's narrator also casts Evelyn M.'s attention to "questions that really matter" as something of a joke. Both her distinction between talking "about life" and talking "about art"—a distinction that, in another context, we might expect Woolf to endorse—and her ensuing plan for putting an end to prostitution in Piccadilly are patently subjected to ridicule. Yet for all that, the narrator also locates Evelyn M. alongside the women in Piccadilly, in the details of her background and behavior. Moreover, as Marshik notes, that she "lowered her voice" in saying "the ugly word" out loud, even in the privacy of her own room, implies how difficult Evelyn finds it to name the thing she seeks to eliminate (100).

Like Grand's Marie Cruchot, the prostitute herself "remains a device in the novel: readers do not hear her speak and know very little about her experiences" (Marshik 101). Her very expulsion from the text happens offstage, incidentally illustrating another generational difference, this one between men, and serving as an occasion for reflections on the hypocrisy of the English bourgeoisie. When Rachel and her party return from their trip up the river, St. John Hirst learns that in their absence, two of the older male guests have had "the Signora Lola Mendoza" removed from the hotel after one of them saw her "cross the passage in her nightgown." "No one seems to have enquired into the truth of the story, or to have asked Thornbury and Elliot what business it was of theirs," Hirst comments, further complaining parenthetically that "no one seems to have asked [Thornbury] what *he* was up to" in the middle of the night. Hirst alludes to the possibility that her accusers have themselves patronized Signora Lola, even as the older men publicly represent themselves as guardians of sexual morality by patrolling the hotel hallways; against their position first Hirst and then Helen define their own. The former wants to "insist upon a full enquiry," while the latter "burst[s] out" in Shavian tones against "[t]he hypocritical smugness of the English": "A man who's made a fortune in trade as Mr. Thornbury has is bound to be twice as bad as any prostitute." The rest of their conversation "as to the steps that were to be taken to enforce their peculiar view of what was right . . . led to some profoundly gloomy statements of a general nature. Who were they, after all—what authority had they—what power against the mass of superstition and ignorance?" (*Voyage* 358; ch. 23; emphasis in the original). Their final reflections occasion a critique of the nation, from which they notably exclude themselves—"It was the English, of course; there must be something wrong in the English blood" (358–59)—thus turning the tables on eugenicist fears that indiscriminate reproductive sex would taint the nation's moral stock. Like Sally Seton reproving Hugh Whitbread ("She told him that she considered him responsible for the state of 'those poor girls in Piccadilly'"), Helen and Terence take the older men's treatment of the prostitute as exemplifying "all that was most detestable in British middle-class life" (*Mrs. Dalloway* 66).[51] Yet Hirst's final comment on how "you couldn't trust these foreigners" also turns the critique he would otherwise evade back on himself and the members of his group (*Voyage* 359).

The varied representation of prostitution in *The Voyage Out*, then, figures the intersection of gender, sexuality, empire, and class in important ways. Connected to "respectable" marriage, prostitution demonstrates women's economic dependence on men; compared to other kinds of labor, like Susan's position as her aunt's paid companion, it reveals the exploitative basis of all capitalist relations. As a focus of Evelyn's projected political activity, it forms an object, albeit an ironic one, of social-purity intervention; as a target of Thornbury and Elliott's prurient interest, it constitutes a site at which those characters that form the novel's inner circle can disavow their own implication in the imperial structures of "British middle-class life." Rather than insert her heroine even more fully into those structures, Woolf kills her off.

In one last instance in which one of her heroines comes into close proximity to a prostitute, Grand further plays with the trope of streetwalking, this time without parody. Like Angelica but lacking the protection of a female "good influence," the unlucky and unhappy Evadne walks the streets of London, running the risk of being perceived as that other kind of "public woman," the kind that makes it impossible for Woolf's Rachel to walk alone. The single scene of Evadne's urban wandering is narrated in the novel's final section from the point of view of her future second husband. Dr. Galbraith sees Evadne, as Evadne comes to see herself, primarily as a case: the shift from Fulda's philanthropic care to Galbraith's pathologizing gaze bespeaks a gendered opposition in how the streetwalker is conventionally viewed. In an episode that is, again, "like an incident in a melodrama," Galbraith happens to observe Evadne getting off a bus at Piccadilly Circus, "between nine and ten at night, and calmly taking her way alone up Regent Street": "Such a proceeding was hardly decent, whatever her excuse, and it was certainly not safe" (*Heavenly* 616; bk. 6, ch. 11).[52] By chance, again, Galbraith runs into Evadne's current husband, who assumes that Galbraith is "following a lady" (in a Peter Walsh sort of way); but the doctor shakes off Colquhoun, intent on pursuing Evadne in her trance-like but "dignified" state, "so very unlike the women and girls who were loitering about the street, peering up anxiously into the face of every man they met" (617).

Although Evadne knows "what . . . those women in Piccadilly" are, the constraints she has suffered over the course of the novel produce her hysterical trance: she is rendered unknowing and unseeing, and thus vulnerable to the attentions of men by her presence alone at night on a city street.[53] That she is, however, simultaneously seen by Galbraith as "very unlike" the "loitering" women and girls she passes, who must observe "the face of every man" they encounter, and yet also like them, from a reader's point of view, suggests the equation Grand makes here between the hysterical wife who has been no wife, in the sexual sense, and the hypersexualized whore who trades her body for money. Both are driven to desperation within a patriarchal context, as was Edith Beale, whose syphilitic madness led her melodramatically to indict masculinist norms and institutions on her deathbed. In the contest between the reality Evadne has come to know and the conventions that have circumscribed her existence, her character's ultimate fate, which borders on insanity, clearly dramatizes, even melodramatizes, the cost of resisting those conventions. And so, too, does Rachel's comparable ending in *The Voyage Out*, with her death foreshadowed early in the novel by her revelation about the meaning of "the women in Piccadilly" to her own life to come. For once Helen Ambrose, trusting to talk, tells Rachel who those women are, "by this new light [Rachel] saw her life for the first time a creeping hedged-in thing, driven cautiously between high walls, here turned aside, there plunged in darkness, made dull and crippled for ever—her life that was the only chance she had" (87; ch. 6), the fleeting slice of time that the 1920 U.S. edition of the novel memorably calls "the short season between two silences."[54]

More than two decades later, Woolf would argue in *Three Guineas* that both the granting of the vote and the opening of the professions to women had revealed that the possession of "influence" over men—the chief string to the nineteenth-century domestic woman's bow—was no better, and perhaps worse, than prostitution. Citing the views of Sir Ernest Wild, she concludes that "if such is the real nature of our influence, . . . many of us would prefer to call ourselves prostitutes simply and to take our stand openly under the lamps of Piccadilly Circus rather than use it" (19; ch. 1). As Woolf repeats throughout the text, now that the daughters of educated men have won the right to earn their livings, their (effort at) exercising indirect influence over men is no longer necessary.

But the old and the new dispensations are not entirely different. Vara Neverow suggests that "Woolf's reference[s] to [Josephine] Butler's biography," coauthored by Millicent Garrett Fawcett, imply that "because of deliberate restrictions on women's earning power—and despite the vote—all women who are not economically independent are coerced into various forms of prostitution" (16).[55] Yet if the sale of the body in sex work is the metaphorical equivalent of the sale of the brain in the law, the clergy, or the academy, as Shaw had suggested in *Mrs. Warren's Profession* (1893; perf. 1902), then the oldest and newest professions for women disturbingly resemble one another, making the initial distinction between women's "influence" and their new economic "weapon" less hard and fast that it would otherwise appear.

What disappears from Woolf's analogy, however, is the question of sexuality itself, the sale of sex as opposed to the sale of the brain. As Naomi Black has pointed out regarding *Three Guineas*' use of tropes of prostitution and adultery, each one "redefined to mean contamination by market demands," these specifically sexual forms of "vice," a word that both Woolf and Grand used in different contexts, "have their fullest discussion as images of the co-opted literary life" (186). As I will explore in the next chapter in considering Woolf's attitudes to two women writers of her parents' circle, this metaphorical sleight of hand surely conditions her stance toward any writer whom she perceives to have "sold her brain, her very admirable brain, prostituted her culture and enslaved her intellectual liberty in order that she might earn her living and educate her children," as Woolf characterizes Anne Ritchie's close friend, Margaret Oliphant (*Three* 109–10; ch. 2).[56]

Butler appeared to Woolf to epitomize disinterestedness, as against the perceived economic interestedness of Oliphant or the political interestedness of Grand, because she ostensibly spoke out and acted up from the purest of motives; all the problematic elements of her philanthropic and political activity—including her evangelical Christianity and its imperialist tenor—went unacknowledged in Woolf's analysis. By contrast, second-generation New Woman writers who also contested "the conspiracy of silence," in print and in person, by intervening in the discourses of gender and sexuality do not merit even a footnote in *Three Guineas* or *A Room of One's Own*. That omission might be glossed by reference not solely to Woolf's ambivalence about those who were both progressive and popular during her youth and earliest years as a writer, but also to "the conspiracy of silence" as Grand rather than Butler represented it. For if by the time of Woolf's late-Victorian adolescence the New Journalism and the New Woman had put sex into discourse in the periodical, the newspaper, and the novel, then we might take "the purest minded, the highest principled, the most devoted" woman who chose not to know— and aimed to insure that her daughters would not, either—as the real site and source of Virginia Stephen's own unknowing.

Disinterestedness

When discussing how "vice" spreads in *Three Guineas*, Woolf turned to literature not for its cure, but as its cause. In her dismissive remarks on Margaret Oliphant—who functions as "a rhetorical figure for Woolf, standing in for the woman writer [she] disavows"—she singles out women's writing in particular as a source of "vice" rather than as an agent of its eradication (E. Blair 3). Expanding in *Three Guineas* on Shaw's critique of the professions, Woolf argues that "to sell a brain is worse than to sell a body, for when the body seller has sold her momentary pleasure she takes good care that the matter shall end there"—a questionable claim, to be sure, although the greater availability of prophylactics in 1938 than in, say, 1868 would at least have protected some actual sex workers from sexually transmitted diseases or pregnancy (111–12; ch. 3).[1] "But when a brain seller has sold her brain," she continues, "its anaemic, vicious and diseased progeny are set loose upon the world to infect and corrupt and sow the seeds of disease in others" (112). The writer who prostitutes herself gives birth to "diseased progeny": to put it baldly, the whorish author spreads "vice" through her books, and those books "infect" those who read them. Plying the argument that Grand and her allies—as well as Woolf's immediate contemporary, the suffragette leader Christabel Pankhurst—had used to indict the impact of heterosexual men's promiscuity on naïve women and their offspring, she takes "the political rhetoric against prostitution" in a wholly different direction (Chan 90).[2]

In light of Josephine Butler's opposition to the C. D. Acts, not to mention second-generation New Women's advocacy of what Pankhurst would call "chastity for men," this is quite an extraordinary repurposing of the prostitution metaphor, in that it makes at least some women's writing a source of, rather than a prophylactic against, "vice." Following Shaw, those who sell their brains, like those who sell their bodies, are fully implicated in the system Woolf criticizes. So, too, does the equation of (bodily) chastity with intellectual freedom as one of "the four great teachers of the daughters of educated men" repurpose the rhetoric of the social-purity campaigns of the 1880s, 1890s, and beyond, campaigns that Woolf, for the most part, ignored or tacitly rejected, even when she came to revisit the late-Victorian past in her research for *The Years* and *Three Guineas* (*Three* 96; ch. 2). It is not surprising, then, that Woolf's response to Butler focuses far less on the specifics of the causes she championed— she describes her as having led both "the campaign against the Contagious Diseases Act to victory" and, a bit less accurately, "the campaign against the sale and purchase of children 'for infamous purposes,'" an oblique reference to the "Maiden Tribute" scandal of the 1880s—and far more on what she approvingly represents as Butler's principles (92).

Citing Butler as an example of "the lives of professional women," while simultaneously noting that she "was not strictly speaking a professional woman," Woolf lauds the fact that she "refus[ed] to have a life of herself written" (91, 92).[3] Butler's memoir of the movement, *Personal Reminiscences of a Great Crusade* (1896), instead praises those nameless others who prosecuted the campaign against the C. D. Acts for "the utter absence in them of any desire for recognition . . . and the utter purity of their motives" (189; qtd. in *Three* 92). Woolf terms this "a negative quality": "not to be recognized; not to be egotistical; to do the work for the sake of doing the work" (93).[4] Unlike those women writers who prostituted their talents for money, "commit[ting] adultery of the brain," Butler and her allies, Woolf asserts, proceeded in a "disinterested" and selfless way, committed to ideals of "Justice and Equality and Liberty" rather than more narrowly personal goals like supporting themselves or their children (112, 108; ch. 3).[5] As I will show in chapter 5, Woolf's emphasis on the "purity of their motives" takes fictional form in the philanthropic Eleanor Pargiter of *The Years*, whose lack of egotism is implicitly contrasted with the self-regard and mixed motivations of her younger sisters, the more politically active Delia and Rose.

This representation of Butler and her nameless coworkers thus upholds elements of at least two closely related and quintessentially "Victorian" ideological formations with which we can identify some of Woolf's very own commitments. First, she both acknowledges and disavows her debt to the

Arnoldian representation of disinterestedness as a necessary precondition for the critical stance of the intellectual toward his—or her—culture, a position we might once more identify with that of the "impartial observer." As Eleanor McNees argues, Matthew Arnold is "the key critic with whom . . . Woolf would continually converse throughout her career" ("Stephen" 133). Though she differentiates her own ideas of "culture and intellectual liberty" from Arnold's—"for [his] definition would apply to paid-for culture" as opposed to the "unpaid-for culture" of the daughters of educated men, who can only "read and write their own tongue"—*Three Guineas* "also recall[s] Arnold's *Culture and Anarchy* in [its] indictment of blind patriotism, thoughtless conformity, and an inadequate educational system" (*Three* 108; ch. 3; McNees, "Stephen" 133). As ambivalent about Arnold's legacy as about her own father's ideas, Woolf nonetheless clearly framed her thinking about disinterestedness in relation to this "great" Victorian critic.

Second, and perhaps less immediately if also less ambivalently, the image of Butler as the selfless Victorian woman who "do[es] the work for the sake of doing the work" appears to translate some of the qualities typically associated with the figure of the Angel in the House into a public, political context. As Evelyn Tsz Yan Chan makes the point, following the Victorianists Mary Poovey and Amanda Anderson on the relation between the domestic woman and the professional man, "Woolf is drawing upon the ideology of the private house" especially in "fashioning" her ideas about female professionalism as normatively "based on the values of disinterest of nineteenth-century domestic ideals" (110, 111). Seemingly the very antithesis of the prostitute, although acknowledging her ethical and moral kinship with that real figure, Butler extends her unselfish sympathy to one perceived to be most in need of it. As I will show in chapter 4, as critical as Woolf was of those many women philanthropists who took up their moralizing mission beyond the home, in *Three Guineas* she casts as exemplary what she takes as Butler's dedication to abstract ideals (liberty, justice, equality), her preference for personal obscurity, and her commitment to "the work" as an end in itself. And in this move, the contrast between the virtuous Butler and the prostituted Oliphant could not be more complete.

CHAPTER 3

"Ashamed of the Inkpot"
Woolf and the Literary Marketplace

> Now Swinburne is dead, Meredith dumb, and Henry
> James inarticulate, things are in a bad way.
>
> —Virginia Stephen to Lady Robert Cecil, 12 April 1909

> I do hate to be classed with Mrs Clifford; at the same
> time, a little praise, being my father's daughter,
> pleases.
>
> —Virginia Woolf to Violet Dickinson, 30 March 1922

> Even the most superficial student of letters must be
> aware that in the nineteenth century literature had
> become, for one reason or another, a profession rather
> than a vocation, a married woman rather than a lady
> of easy virtue.
>
> —Virginia Woolf, "Edmund Gosse," 1931

In turning back near the end of her life to But-
ler and Oliphant, positioning the one as an unpaid, disinterested, and deeply
committed advocate of libertarian ideals and the other as degrading both herself and her work by her participation in the market, Woolf reproduces a
tension within her own career that had dogged it from the beginning.[1] As this
chapter will argue, she criticized those women who wrote for money especially in her representations of two elder female contemporaries, Lucy Clifford and Mary Augusta Ward, the former a close friend of her parents, the
latter a family friend as well as Matthew Arnold's niece. Those letters, diary
entries, and reviews that reference Clifford or Ward evince a complex mix of
emotions and beliefs about commercial success and mass-market popularity.[2]
Having already traced the imbrication of sexual and market exchange in *The
Voyage Out*, where the prostitute figures an array of socioeconomic relations for unmarried and married women, we should also note the persistence
of this metaphor not just in Woolf's thinking, but in the literary tradition.

Catherine Gallagher's classic 1986 essay on the prostitute and the Jewish question in George Eliot's *Daniel Deronda* (1876) analyzes the historical associations between the female author and the whore, which took on heightened implications in the late-nineteenth-century explosion of the print sphere; such associations, I contend, also shadowed much of Woolf's own personal writing about being a literary professional well into the twentieth century. For being a "professional" is almost the last thing that Woolf wanted to be. "The figure of the artist who practiced art for art's sake and who wrote without being tainted by the corrupting influence of money," as Evelyn Tsz Yan Chan asserts, "was the counter-image to professionalism," a figure that is disinterested and, significantly, desexualized (79).

What further complicates this situation is gender; or, as Jane Garrity puts it more precisely, "the ambivalent position of the woman writer for whom the lure of mass culture was arguably a more complex, if not strictly enabling, historical development" than it was for her male contemporaries ("Selling" 31). Following a path charted by Andreas Huyssen, Rita Felski has persuasively argued that the fin-de-siècle "division between elite and popular culture gradually acquired an explicit gender subtext"; "the ostensibly distanced and unemotional aesthetic stance embraced by both naturalists and modernists was explicitly valorized over the feminine sentimentality associated with popular fiction" (80). As we have already seen, Woolf "embraced" the former in part and feared association with the latter. At the same time, some writers rendered the substantial economic rewards of the best seller, sentimental or not, as inversely related to such a book's aesthetic value: "When it comes to minority culture," as Aaron Jaffe wryly puts it in the wake of Bourdieu's analysis, "nothing fails like success" (159). And when we factor in the increasing association of the publicity apparatus, especially for women writers, with the potential rewards and pitfalls of self-commodification, we can also grasp a central reason for Woolf's ongoing hostility toward the female elders who had deployed such mechanisms for financial gain—and largely without the visible ambivalence that marked Woolf's own relationship to the market.

As Jeanne Dubino astutely notes in her introduction to *Virginia Woolf and the Literary Marketplace* (2010), "Woolf was clearly a literary professional, but this was a title she eschewed"; "she felt uneasy about joining the ranks of professional working women who were increasingly involved" in mass-market literary production (3). The "characteristics of self-interest which Woolf attributed to professionalism," Chan argues, "led to her aversion towards the concept in art" (96). By contrast with T. S. Eliot, for whom "professionalism provided the conditions necessary for disinterestedness" (Kaufmann 141), Woolf formulated a critique of this institution over the course of her career, a critique from which she sometimes exempted herself, just as Helen Ambrose and St. John Hirst seek to distance themselves from "all that was most detestable in British middle-class life." In the years between the founding of the Hogarth Press and the publication of *Mrs. Dalloway*, which significantly shifted her relations to the market, Woolf largely displaced her concerns about literary professionalism onto other writers, and especially onto her older female contemporaries.

In this chapter, then, I identify the industrious Clifford and the well-connected Ward—the two professional women writers most closely associated with her childhood milieu, aside from Ritchie, herself "a successful, professional woman whose writing gave her an independent income, and a wide, admiring readership"—as Woolf's chief models for understanding the turn-of-the-century contours of women's authorship (Dell 40).[3] Each lived well into Woolf's twentieth-century present, continuing to publish while she was just beginning her career. Overlapping as they did in time and space, and connected to her by a variety of networks, including the ones they created and maintained in their own interests, these later Victorians had made their way in the new conditions of the mass marketplace in the 1880s and 1890s, while young Virginia Stephen was still reading *Tit-Bits*—itself a product of the late-Victorian diversification of literary markets and publication venues—and writing the *Hyde Park Gate News* (McDonald, *British* 144–52). Not identified with modes or styles she found conducive to her own practice, each yet exemplified an available paradigm for doing the work Woolf herself wanted to do and formed models for a literary career that she could have embraced. But in rejecting their example, she provides us with another case study of giving second-generation women writers no quarter.

Woolf's Apprenticeship

With her literary sensibility shaped in part by mid-Victorian ideals, by early 1905 Virginia Stephen was choosing her own volumes from Dr. Williams's Library in Gordon Square; purchasing a complete set of Pater's works; and penning her first book reviews for the *Guardian* (Snaith, *Virginia Woolf* 27; Meisel 17). She was, in other words, starting her career as a writer. Considering her approach to what her father had called "that line," she recorded in her diary for 13 March 1905 her trip "to Hatchards to buy Stevenson and Pater—I want to study them—not to copy, I hope, but to see how the trick's done. Stevenson is a trick—but Pater something different & beyond" (Letter to Julia Stephen [3 August 1893]; *Passionate* 251). Though she was already privately practicing the composition of higher-toned essays, the "trick" she had to learn was how to review books for publication and pay.[4] While continuing her reading in Greek and the classics of English literature and starting on their French and Russian equivalents, she was also diligently reviewing the works of contemporary writers, most of whose names are relatively unfamiliar to us now. For every James or Wharton or Howells novel she reviewed in her first decade of work as a literary journalist, there is one by a Hergesheimer or a W. E. Norris: as Melba Cuddy-Keane has calculated, "mainly forgotten" or "'ordinary' novels . . . accounted for eighteen of the thirty-five essays she published in 1905" (*Virginia Woolf* 173; cf. Dubino, "Virginia" 35). Entering into periodical publication, Virginia Stephen thus reviewed many books that she surely would not otherwise have read. Some of them, like the steamy romance novels Elinor Glyn (b. 1864) published with Duckworth and Company, no doubt would qualify as "vicious" in the sense of that word as Woolf used it in *Three Guineas*.

Such books differed quite dramatically, in their aims and audiences, from the steady diet of nineteenth-century volumes, among other "great" books, that constituted the basis of her own (self-)education as a reader and writer. If she was quickly disabused of the idea that reviewing for the *Guardian* or even the *TLS* would afford her the scope of Pater or Stevenson at this point in her career, then it is also clear that from the beginning Virginia Stephen aimed high, embracing models closely associated with late-Victorian aestheticism. She also, of course, discriminated between the two male essayists, affiliating her own efforts-to-come not with the trickery of Stevenson, but with the "different & beyond" of Pater—famous (or infamous) for his essays, yet himself once a book reviewer for the Anglo-Catholic *Guardian*, after leaving Oxford for London in the 1880s (Brake, "Pater").[5]

Two diary entries from March 1905, as she prepared for a trip to Spain with her brother Adrian, clarify still further Virginia Stephen's approach to professional literary work. Running into the editor of the *Guardian*'s women's section, to which she "contributed more than thirty articles" in the first three years of her career, she reports that Kathleen Lyttelton (b. 1865) "asked me to write her articles about my 'personal experiences' in Spain; which I suppose I must do" (Gualtieri, *Virginia* 23). The scare quotes suggest some diffidence about this commission, presumably à propos only to the women's section of the paper; and the slightly grudging tone of the "must do" also implies (à la Bartleby) that she would prefer not to. The next day, however, she had gone so far as to make "a paper book . . . for my Spanish Diary" and brought herself around to seeing it as an opportunity "by means of which I hope to pay some at least of my travelling expenses" (*Passionate* 256). The final sentence on the subject names a cause for the diffidence while also casting the work as having potential aesthetic value: "It is a Grub St. point of view—but all the same, rather a nice little bit of writing might be made out of the sea & land" (256–57). Writing for money summons up the specter of Grub Street with all the implications it had gathered over time, from Johnson to Gissing—and she is clearly not quite comfortable with that. Thus she revises the terms of Lyttelton's request: by substituting a travelogue of "sea & land" for the "personal experiences" for which the editor asked, she both casts the task as aesthetically valuable ("a nice little bit of writing") and shifts the focus from the observer to what she might observe, thus avoiding the invitation to be "personal."

Redirecting the task away from one kind of writing to another might readily be interpreted as part of the aesthetic of impersonality promoted in both *The Voyage Out* and *Night and Day*. It may augur the distaste for publicity that Woolf evinced after she became famous for both her fiction and her essays. And it can also be understood as an early indicator of her sense that obscurity was closely connected to creativity, a tenet she began to articulate more and more strongly in the last decade of her career. But we can also read this episode as not so much a stage in Woolf's developmental plot as a relatively conventional response in the context of turn-of-the-century literary production, in which the opposition between aesthetic value and economic value had been at the forefront of contemporary debate and discourse for a generation or more.

Seeming to accept that opposition, the aspiring writer clearly seeks to position herself on one side of it. A year after her encounter with Lyttelton, in reviewing *The Author's Progress* (1906) by Adam Lorimer (pseud. William Lorimer Watson), she sums up its exposition of "the ugliest form of 'shop'" as a set of publicity tactics, concluding that "the confusion between art and trade must always be ugly . . . since writing is sold as boots are sold" (*Essays* 1: 117).[6] Noting the commodification of the aesthetic even as she calls it "ugly," she similarly terms *The Author's Progress* "a most depressing and ugly book [that] treats Literature like a trade" in a roughly contemporary letter to Nelly Cecil. But if the aspirant to literary "greatness" would prefer to keep distinct lines between "art and trade," the literary journalist knows she cannot. Promising Cecil on her next visit to "talk shop as much as you like," she further describes the book as "the kind of thing we talk put into print," self-consciously implicating both herself and her correspondent in the "confusion" that the review deplores (V. Woolf, *Letters* 1: 176). As Rachel Bowlby writes in another context, "As much as it also surfaces frequently as an assumption to be taken for granted," here the "division between writing as a job and writing as art is . . . a question and a problem" (224).

Virginia Stephen thus undertook the paid, professionalizing activity of book reviewing, which included "reading up" on the topic at hand, alongside the unpaid labor of self-education in the practice of reviewing that she initiated, somewhat incongruously, by buying those volumes of Pater and Stevenson (each of whom had been dead for about a decade in 1905). Discussing Woolf's apprenticeship as a reviewer, Beth Rigel Daugherty shows that "she did this learning on the job and on her own" ("Reading" 30). "Until 1925," as Hermione Lee notes, "literary journalism was the main source of income and her main job" ("Crimes" 118). And it was a job at which she worked hard, even as she complained about the effort expended in reviewing a volume of Jane Carlyle's letters in 1905: "What a mercy it would be if one could write without reading—or read without writing, but a wretch of a journalist never can separate the two" (*Letters* 1: 195). As she was starting out, however, such were the conditions of Virginia Stephen's literary labor, as for virtually all those who aimed to earn money through literary journalism.[7] Less obviously, however, reading books for review also offered her an informal education in vectors of the contemporary literary field not fully visible from the vantage point of her father's study, or of Thoby Stephen and his Cambridge-educated friends.

The limits of her earlier reading also continued to inflect her understanding of the market. Almost two decades after she began her career, Woolf implied in "The Patron and the Crocus" (1925) that the diversity of the current literary scene was a phenomenon entirely of the new century, in that "the present supply of patrons is of unexampled and bewildering variety": "There is the daily Press, the weekly Press, the monthly Press; the English public and the American public; the best-seller public and the worst-seller public; the highbrow public and the red-blood public; all now organised self-conscious entities capable through their various mouthpieces of making their needs known and their approval or displeasure felt" (*Essays* 4: 212–13). "In the nineteenth century," she writes somewhat wistfully, "the great writers wrote for the half-crown magazines and the leisured classes" (212). But we can more precisely date the expansion of the reading public "from a small audience of cultivated people to a larger audience of people who were not quite so cultivated," and the emergence of mass media culture, with its concomitant divisions among high- middle-, and lowbrow readers, to the last quarter of the nineteenth century, with the passage of W. E. Forster's Education Act in 1870 playing a tremendous role in expanding the literacy of the English people ("The Modern Essay," *Essays* 4: 220).[8] Illustrating that the growth of a mass readership reshaped late-Victorian literary production, Peter Keating's survey of the years 1875 to 1914 adduces a crucially important fact that was also to affect Woolf's entry into the field: "The rapid expansion and diversification of the literary market" produced "the splits and factions, the cliques and exclusive groupings, that were already dividing up the new market" (31), including those emergent groups, as Bourdieu's analysis suggests, that would define their own positions as *beyond* the market. At the beginning of her career, then, Woolf first indirectly encountered readerships for fiction as a reviewer of recently published, now-forgotten books by "low moderns" (DiBattista and McDiarmid). She thus also encountered a more diverse and heterogeneous market than that of the "great" writers of two generations before, but not so different than the one into which her immediate predecessors had entered. As Peter D. McDonald puts it, "The modernists were not responding to a wholly new set of conditions. They were the inheritors of a late-Victorian legacy which included both a highly volatile cultural climate and a range of possible reactions to it" ("Modernist" 226).

Here again we might see Virginia Stephen as a bit behind the times, that is, for women writers had already populated—some, like her father, said overpopulated—the diversified late-nineteenth-century marketplace, even if their fuller entry into literary production had met with resistance on different fronts.[9] Alongside other, newer means of paid employment for "the daughters of educated men," expanded opportunities for publication at the turn of the century gave many women the chance to construe literary work, pitched at variable audiences and appearing in a wide range of venues, as a viable and potentially lucrative way of supporting themselves and their dependents, whether or not their work aspired to or achieved "greatness." Nonetheless, gender certainly formed one fault line among the "cliques and exclusive groupings" about which Woolf read in reviewing literary histories of the fin de siècle.

As McDonald's survey of the literary field in the 1890s makes clear, the increasing prominence of women writers in literary culture generated hostility from their male peers. Many at the time would have identified what James called "the extinction of all conception of privacy"—"that mania for publicity which is one of the most striking signs of our time" in "this age of advertisement and newspaperism, this age of interviewing"—with the personal element of the New Journalism and the increasing feminization of public life (*Complete Notebooks* 19, 40, 86). Contests between men and conflicts within the discourse of masculinity certainly matter here as well, so that the attacks of the highly influential Henley coterie on Pater, Wilde, and James himself underline "the importance of being virile"; Nathan K. Hensley has noted that Andrew Lang's version of the "*fin-de-siècle* media environment" in particular was "masculine in the extreme" (McDonald, *British* 35; Hensley, para. 10, 11). On the other side of this gendered divide, Linda K. Hughes has shown that when women took a page from the men's book in founding a women writers' dining club in 1889, it "raised a virulent response from male authors in the *Scots Observer* under the editorship of W. E. Henley and in *Punch*" ("Club" 233). As Margaret D. Stetz concludes, "The world of print . . . continued to resist the full integration of women" (125).

As such examples demonstrate, entering into literary production also meant accessing available networks—some gender-specific, some not—and here the young writer made some very particular choices with particular effects. "Virginia Stephen might have begun publishing through her father's connections," Jane Lilienfeld remarks, but "significantly, she did not" (39). She turned instead to women who had been intimate with her sister Stella: Madge Vaughan, Violet Dickinson, Kitty Maxse, and, later, Kitty's relation by marriage Nelly Cecil. Daughter of Symonds, Vaughan was herself a published author who supported her younger friend's aspirations (Dell 43). Dickinson introduced her to Lyttelton of the *Guardian*, who was also involved in the contemporary suffrage campaign (Kelly).[10] Daughter of Leslie and Julia Stephen's old friends Vernon and Jane Lushington and one of the Stephen-Duckworth family's favorite young women, Maxse gave Woolf a limited entrée to her husband Leo's conservative paper, *The National Review*. More importantly, this putative model for Clarissa Dalloway connected Woolf to Cecil, with whom she talked shop and alternated essays for a monthly column in the *Cornhill*, edited by Leslie Stephen until 1882 and from 1905 by Reginald Smith, son-in-law of its founder George Smith. Facilitated mainly by women—who "were *not* professional writers" (Daugherty, "Reading" 30; emphasis mine)—these connections constituted less a complete break with South Kensington or its values than a means of mobilizing its resources to promote the new ends of "freedom and friends" (["Phyllis"] 28). If Vanessa Bell had aimed to sever those ties completely by the move to Bloomsbury, her sister continued to maintain them, thereby providing herself with access to paid work for the next decade.

Significantly, as I suggested in the introduction, Woolf continued to draw on and revisit that past long after the move, in part to inspire her fiction; her visits with her *TLS* editor Bruce Richmond's wife Elena, for example, generated imaginative capital for fictions to come. Beginning to reimagine the figure of Clarissa from *The Voyage Out* in the months just before composing "Mrs. Dalloway in Bond Street," she concluded a February 1922 diary entry written after such a visit by saying that "when she comes again, I shall try to discuss the Lushingtons" (*Diary* 2: 162). And noting "the Lushingtons" as a point for further discussion follows on more or less directly from Woolf's sketch of Richmond's interests as a reader, which suggests another continuing use for South Kensington: "I find her sympathetic—so maternal, quiet, kindly; & liking literature as a lady does; & saying such unexpected things about it, as a lady does. She doesn't like representation in fiction; can't stand Wells & Bennett; attempts Dorothy Richardson; is puzzled; reverts to Scott; hasn't heard of Joyce; comfortably waves aside indecency; I should guess that she represents the top layer of the <Mudie> general public very accurately" (161).[11] Although Woolf crossed out the mention of "Mudie," we should note that in summing up her friend's position as a reader, she places her within a particular market segment. Elena Richmond's literary "tastes" are hardly those "of a school-boy," as Woolf described them to Vanessa Bell, but they do represent a particular fraction, "the top layer," of a book-reading, book-buying "general public"—a public that Woolf's writing would increasingly reach in the years ahead (*Letters* 2: 505). If making marriage a trade had been the dominant practice of South Kensington in the minds of the Stephen sisters, then we can also see that Woolf made trade of South Kensington in the art it helped to inspire.

Capitalizing on her long relationship with Richmond, Woolf sized her up as a reader from the point of view of the market even as both women objected to trade being made of them, as Woolf had reported in an earlier diary entry of January 1920. After describing a visit to Leonard's brother Edgar and his wife Sylvia in their Putney home ("sitting in the dining room with a large table, reading novels"), she recounted a conversation with the editor of the *London Mercury*, J. C. Squire, who tried to persuade her to plant her book reviews in his monthly's "very fertile soil." Publicly defending the "honesty" and "high standard" of the *Athenaeum*, edited by John Middleton Murry, against Squire's attribution to it of a "hard sceptical tone," she privately cast herself as "equally able to write for Murry, Squire or Desmond [MacCarthy]—a proof of catholicity or immorality, according to your taste," and subsequently noted an impending bill for "£200 perhaps on drains," a "low" household expense that reviewing would defray. Finally, relating some of the literary "shop" that she both enjoyed and detested, Woolf remarked that over "tea with Elena," "we broached, delicately, the subject of the Supplement": "She said that people were nice to her in order to influence reviews. She said they made Bruce's life a burden to him" (*Diary* 2: 15–16).

Making an equal return for Richmond's candor about her husband's subjection to importunate authors, Woolf described her own recent "interview with Mrs Clifford" in what we can infer were comparable tones: "It was all known to her, I could see; she knew Mrs Clifford's methods." Although Woolf characterized Richmond as "more clearminded & innocent than I am," asserting that her friend viewed such "methods" with "the simple brown eyes of the nicest, most modest, of collie dogs," she also wrote that she "liked Elena for sharing my feeling of repulsion" for these marketplace tactics (16).[12] Here South Kensington and Bloomsbury, despite the differences Woolf constructed between them, stand together in "repulsion" against "methods" Woolf associated with a literary underclass—a category to which she would at times assign both Squire and Murry, despite her defense of the latter here, as well as Katherine Mansfield, a category she associates with "Mrs Clifford." But what were those "methods"? Why do they inspire such "repulsion"? And who was Mrs. Clifford, anyway?

Lucy Clifford's Career

Lucy Clifford conducted her professional life under very different auspices than did Virginia Woolf. Novelist, children's author, and playwright, she counted on publishing to support herself and her two young daughters after the death from tuberculosis in 1879 of her husband, the Cambridge mathematician, free-thinker, and "celebrity iconoclast" W. K. Clifford, a friend and protégé of Leslie Stephen, who held a chair in mathematics at University College London on Gower Street in Bloomsbury (Dawson 168).[13] Writing to their mutual friend Oliver Wendell Holmes Jr. just before the Cliffords sailed for Madeira in a last-ditch effort to reverse the course of the illness, and less than a year after his second marriage, Leslie Stephen described the Cliffords' circumstances: "I have been sitting with him a good deal in some poor little lodgings where they have been for the last three months & seen him visibly failing. He has been admirably brave & cheerful, though poor fellow, he will leave a wife & 2 little babies with next to nothing" (*Selected Letters* 1: 236). According to Noel Annan, "It was Stephen who got up a subscription to send [the Cliffords] to Madeira in the vain hope that he might recover" (*Leslie* 100). On the dying man's last night in England, Lucy Clifford later reported, the Stephens came to say their goodbyes, "tall and grave and thin, as if they remembered a world of sorrow and understood ours, and were half-ashamed of their happiness" (qtd. in Annan, *Leslie* 81).[14] When the widow returned alone to England, Leslie Stephen later wrote, "Julia of course went to see her. They became close friends": "few people, I think, loved my darling better" (*Mausoleum* 80).

   After her husband's death, other friends rallied around Lucy Clifford, especially solicitous, perhaps, in view of her financial situation, which they—and she—aimed to remedy. Anne Ritchie passed on the news to Marian Evans Lewes, herself recently bereaved, who "promptly sent £10" to a memorial fund and, unusually for her, offered to go and see the widow if she were not able to come to the Priory (Haight 525). Charles Darwin gave £50 to the same fund, which ultimately amounted to £2,300, yielding about £90 income a year (Dawson 166; Chisholm, *Such* 69).[15] With Fred Pollock, a close Cambridge friend of W. K. Clifford, Leslie Stephen edited a posthumous two-volume collection of Clifford's *Lectures and Essays* (1879), the proceeds from which may be the £65 that Lucy Clifford mentions in her application to the Royal Literary Fund in February 1880, supported by letters from Thomas Henry Huxley and William Spottiswoode, then-president of the Royal Society ("Application"). She received a grant of £200 from that fund and, more substantially, a Civil List pension of £80 per year. When all was said and done, Lucy Clifford had an annual income of just over £200 after her husband's death on which to support herself and her daughters (Demoor, "Where" 34n5). As Gowan Dawson notes of a process that continued long after her husband's death, "It was necessary for [Clifford], who now owned the copyright of her late husband's works, to maximize the potential sales of his posthumous publications by not only keeping [him] in the public eye, but also by ensuring that it was a generally positive—and thus marketable—portrayal of him that was presented," a task made more delicate by Clifford's reputation for atheism (165).[16] But having published quite a bit of serialized fiction in *The Quiver*, founded in 1861 by the evangelical temperance reformer and businessman John Cassell, in the years before her marriage, Lucy Clifford got back into print.[17] As Marysa Demoor points out, she turned again to "writing as the only profession which she could combine with the raising of children" ("Self-Fashioning" 276).[18]

The difference between Lucy Clifford's situation in 1879 and that of Woolf's own mother about ten years earlier, as widows with young children, is striking. The death of Herbert Duckworth—whom Leslie Stephen described as "so far independent of his professional prospects that he scarcely devoted himself to his work in the spirit of a man who has his living to make by it"—was much more sudden and unexpected than W. K. Clifford's, but unlike her future friend, Julia Duckworth was left financially secure (*Mausoleum* 39). The probate record of her first husband's will states that he bequeathed to her "effects under £5000," in addition to whatever she may have had settled on her separately on marriage.[19] At the death of her father-in-law in September 1876, "she was given forty thousand pounds in trust," presumably for her three children though she could draw on the interest, "and an additional sum of five thousand pounds" (Rudikoff 151). Thus while Julia Stephen went on to do a good bit of writing during her second marriage—stories for children; an entry on her aunt Julia Margaret Cameron for the *DNB*; an unpublished essay on women and agnosticism as well as another that responded to Clementina Black's published essay on "the servant question," which I will consider in chapter 4; a pamphlet on nursing, published by Smith, Elder in 1883—she did not need to earn a living by it.[20] By contrast, Clifford appears to have been estranged from most members of her birth family—which was, significantly, a family of writers—noting in her application to the Royal Literary Fund, "I have no expectations & no relations able or willing to help."[21] Unlike Julia Duckworth, she lacked wealthy, supportive kin on whom she could rely, and thus she had almost immediately to turn her husband's connections and her own writing to account.

A further contrast with a member of the next generation is also instructive. While Clifford had that £200 a year after her husband's death in addition to whatever she could earn, the £2,500 inheritance from her aunt Caroline Stephen (b. 1834) that Virginia Stephen received in 1909 provided her with the further support of a secure if relatively modest annual income (*Letters* 1: 391). "By the time she married Leonard in 1912," Elena Gualtieri estimates, "her capital totaled more than £9,300 and yielded an income of around £400 a year," just a bit shy of the figure she names in *A Room of One's Own* as requisite for a woman to establish writerly autonomy and thus aesthetic "integrity" ("Woolf" 184; *Room* 72). Whatever else we might say about the differences between them, Lucy Clifford quite literally could not afford Virginia Stephen's ambivalence about writing for money. "Left with two infant girls and in straitened circumstances that could only be partially relieved by the efforts of Clifford's friends," Thoby Stephen's Cambridge classmate John Pollock considered their fathers' mutual friend, who did what she did out of necessity, as being nonetheless as "remarkable for character as for talent" (78).

In order to make her way, Clifford both accessed and enhanced her own and her husband's professional networks by continuing after his death to host "at homes"—as Julia Stephen and her daughters did—that brought together members of her intersecting circles, for her advantage as well as theirs.[22] "I have always thought," Ella Hepworth Dixon wrote in her memoir, that Clifford "had more of an idea of the *salon* than most Englishwomen" (*"As I Knew Them"* 93). Friend of Darwin, Huxley, and Spencer, Edward Clodd recalled his own visits, both before and after W. K Clifford's death: Fred Pollock, Leslie Stephen, and the Huxleys "were often" present and, "more rarely," Grant Allen, Hardy, and Lynn Linton; Clodd described Lucy Clifford as still keeping up "the old tradition" of "at homes" even at his time of writing in 1916 (37). In 1881, armed with a letter of introduction from Linton, whom she had met in Florence, the London newcomer Vernon Lee traveled from her Bloomsbury base in Gower Street, at the family home of A. Mary F. Robinson, "to see Mrs. Clifford," who "lives at the world's end" in Bayswater (Colby 50; V. Lee 66). There Lee met the *Athenaeum* editor Norman MacColl, one of Leslie Stephen's "Sunday Tramps," who left £2,000 to Lucy Clifford's daughters at his death in

1904, as well as the "hideously shy" Stephen himself, who had been publishing Lee's work in the *Cornhill* since 1879 (Chisholm, *Such* 71; V. Lee 66).

Subsequently invited again to Clifford's home, Lee dined with the freethinking Mathilde Blind (b. 1841), a former associate of W. K. Clifford and a member of radical circles, who, for a time, lived just across the road (Dawson 167; Diedrick 164). She met Helen Zimmern (b. 1846), "author of the first critical English biography of the philosopher" Arthur Schopenhauer and a close friend of Amy Levy, Fred Pollock, and Mark Pattison (Parejo Vadillo, *Women* 40; V. Lee 73). Lee continued the connection with Clifford on her successive summer returns to London at least until the end of the decade. If her "too obvious interest in promoting herself" irritated some of Lee's new London associates, especially after the appearance of her aestheticist roman à clef, *Miss Brown* (1883), then in the somewhat sensational aftermath of its publication Clifford was still willing, as many others were not, to maintain the relationship (Colby 114).[23] As Lee wrote to her mother in 1883, "If any set claims me . . . it is the Clifford one," describing it as composed of "people of some weight" (V. Lee 130). The Clifford-Lee connection might in the end have been broken only on Lee's publication of "Lady Tal," in the collection *Vanitas* (1892), a short story that features a parodic portrait of one of Clifford's closest literary friends of all, Henry James.[24]

Certainly Lucy Clifford knew, or knew of, virtually everyone in the turn-of-the-century literary world worth knowing. But like Andrew Lang, if for different reasons, she has come down to posterity mainly as a footnote. It is worth stating, however, just how broad and deep her connections were, in that they give a clear sense of how very definitely Virginia Stephen chose against making use of them. Although a personal falling-out severed them for many years, Clifford had a strong professional relationship with Rudyard Kipling: indeed, one history of the Macmillan publishing house claims "there is good reason to believe, though no documents confirm it, that what brought [Kipling] to the firm was the benign and invaluable influence of Mrs. W. K. Clifford" (Morgan 148).[25] The writer Marie Belloc Lowndes (b. 1868) described her as "the dear and honoured friend of men as different as Huxley, Browning, Tyndall, John Morley, Henry James, and . . . James Russell Lowell"; "a number of remarkable people were to be met every Sunday afternoon in her cottage-like, ground-floor sitting-room," including "the young, unknown Bernard Shaw" (63; cf. Demoor, "'Not'" 240). John Pollock includes among her guests in the new century Ford Madox Ford, Elizabeth Robins, Violet Hunt, and Somerset Maugham as well as "authors, literary agents, publishers"—like Gerald Duckworth—while Clifford's biographer notes that Theodora Bosanquet even met Ezra Pound there (Pollock 80; Chisholm, *Such* 80). According to Hugh

Walpole's memoir, *The Apple Trees* (1932), it was Clifford who took him to tea with Hardy in Kensington, initiating the friendship that Maugham would scandalously parody in *Cakes and Ale* (1930; Walpole 44–45). And like John Pollock, who wrote that both Walpole and Noel Coward "got a helping hand from Lucy Clifford in their upward climb" (81), Lowndes called her a "generous woman who did so much for others," singling her out for "the active help [she] was always eager to give unknown writers" (65, 63). "Nothing could have been kinder than she was to young authors," in Hepworth Dixon's estimation, "whom she would go out of her way to help" (*As I Knew Them* 94). She was generous as well to her peers: in an undated letter to Frederick Macmillan, probably from the early 1880s, Clifford recommends that he consider publishing a novel by Blind, with the comment that "Leslie Stephen has just returned it with a *very strong* letter saying it is not adapted for a magazine but speaking of it as . . . remarkable in offering to introduce it to Smith & Elder" (emphasis in the original).[26] While she obviously counted many men in her network, her professional and personal relationships with women writers were just as numerous: friends among her older contemporaries included Ritchie, Oliphant, Broughton, and Mary Elizabeth Braddon (b. 1835), while she also maintained ties with Mary Cholmondeley (b. 1859), Sinclair, Robins, Meynell, and Ward (Gates 59, 138; Chisholm, *Such* 123–24). She served as president of the Women Writers' Society in 1902 (Demoor, "Where" 35).

Making a career for herself and a living for her children meant that Clifford used all available means at her disposal to promote her friends' work and to publicize her own, marking her as a conscious and active participant in the marketplace. That involved a fair amount of what Woolf was to call the "slightly discreditable" practice of "literary gossip," not only in her conversation and private letters, but also in print (*Diary* 1: 254). Examining the column titled "Literary Gossip" that regularly appeared in the *Athenaeum* between 1885 and 1901, Demoor establishes that Clifford frequently contributed to this weekly roundup of literary news, which served as "a preferred instrument to let the world know what she had heard, what she was doing or . . . was not doing," pointing in particular to "the very good use she made of this outlet to promote her own writings" ("Where" 34).[27] Clifford further "embraced the possibilities of the contemporary mass media" by sitting for publicity photos such as the one that accompanied an interview with Mary Angela Dickens (b. 1862), eldest grandchild of the novelist, which appeared in the *Windsor Magazine* in 1899 (Demoor, "Self-Fashioning" 278).

Although Demoor characterizes her as having "no qualms about self-advertisement," Clifford does at times evince some hesitation about publicity ("Self-Fashioning" 278). Presumably on the basis of their conversation, Dickens reports that "the temptation to advertise herself and her wares, as is nowadays too much the fashion, passed Mrs. Clifford by": "So keen and so delicate was her feeling with reference to her husband's name that . . . she published all her earlier books anonymously rather than run the faintest chance of being thought to make capital out of Professor W. K. Clifford's reputation" (484). Such claims do not quite square with scholarly analysis: for example, the head-shot that illustrates the interview signals Clifford's availability for public consumption in the commodification and circulation of her image.[28] Whatever she might actually have thought or felt on this score—and the evidence here is mixed—the rhetoric Dickens uses to describe Clifford's stance provided her with a way of positioning herself for readers of the 1880s and 1890s as a respectable and ladylike writer who observes the old-school proprieties. At the same time, the interview also goes on to declare that she is proud of what she has accomplished on her own as a working woman: "Happily, Mrs. Clifford says, the feeling that work of any sort is a degradation, provided it is necessary or advisable to do it, has vanished or is vanishing, and that is one great step in the right direction." Being careful not to offend the sensibilities of gender traditionalists while yet staking a claim for the "great" woman writer, Clifford reportedly told Dickens, "There is no honour or credit in doing men's work less well than they themselves can do it"; but "if a woman has genius, or even real talent in any direction, that is another matter" (485).

Assisted by the networks she helped to create, Clifford "became famous overnight" on the publication of *Mrs. Keith's Crime* (1885), which earned praise from Browning, Hardy, and Besant (Demoor, "Self-Fashioning" 276; Demers 190). "Clearly inspired by the agonizing end of her own married life," the novel concerns "a strong, independent woman who, against all odds, establishes herself professionally as an artist" (Pollock 79; Demoor, "Self-Fashioning" 285). It closes with a shocking turn when the main character, after the death of her husband and son, chooses to euthanize her daughter in advance of her own fast-approaching death.[29] A later novel, *Aunt Anne* (1892), takes up the doubly sensational topic of an older woman who marries a much younger fortune hunter, who happens already to be married to someone else. Although such plots connect Clifford's writing to sensation fiction, *Aunt Anne* in particular earned a good deal of critical esteem. The poet William Watson wrote in the *Bookman* that the novel "clearly established her claim to be looked on as a writer of a high order of fiction" (qtd. in Stetz 126).[30] In her "Book Gossip" column in *Sylvia's Journal*, Rosamond Marriott Watson praised it for its "just and righteous scorn of our modern pharisaism," also calling Clifford "a woman who *thinks* . . . [and is] fearless and unshrinking . . . of the facts" (qtd. in Hughes, *Graham R.* 183; emphasis in the original). The U.S. trade magazine *Publishers*

Weekly went still further, ranking it above two other of its books of the year—Ward's *History of David Grieve* and Hardy's *Tess*—and significantly commending its success on two usually opposed counts: "We think it will be generally acknowledged that Mrs. W. K. Clifford's 'Aunt Anne' was the most brilliant and original English novel of 1892 and the one which achieved the greatest popular success" ("Books" 172). And years later, in his preface to *The Old Wives' Tale* (1908), Arnold Bennett described himself as "a convinced admirer of Mrs W. K. Clifford's most precious novel, *Aunt Anne*," and its "story of an old woman" (32).[31] Based on these two books alone, and the responses to them, one can see that Clifford clearly had a strong sense of the late-Victorian market for fiction that spoke to women's changing status and particular issues.

Like her terrifying stories for children, "The New Mother" (1882) and "Wooden Tony" (1891), both *Mrs. Keith's Crime* and *Aunt Anne* are compelling reads, if somewhat difficult to place within generic categories. Each seeks to engage readers with a taste for what theater historian Kate Newey calls "sensation melodrama," while exploring the interior life of a central female character (158). Though not quite high-end realism, Clifford's technique does reflect the increasing emphasis in the last quarter of the century on representing women's psychic states. And though her work was not quite "fiction with a purpose" either, Clifford did position it in relation to contemporary debates around gender and sexuality, and certainly takes up protofeminist themes and topics. Invoking the key terms by which Hugh Stutfield had infamously criticized Egerton, Caird, and Grand alongside such male contemporaries as Allen, Le Gallienne, and Wilde, Clifford's friend Clodd yet classed her "among those who maintain the high standard of English fiction, unsoiled by the erotic, neurotic and Tommyrotic" (37).

Yet even if she was not what her contemporaries would have called a New Woman, Clifford located another of her novels, *A Flash of Summer* (1896), in relation to the issues that preoccupied so many readers and writers in the 1890s. In its preface, Clifford claims the main character and plot "suggested themselves to me a few years ago, before marriage problems and questions had attained their present importance in fiction," and so the story "does not in any way belong to recent controversial discussion" (n.p.). Calling up the associations of the novel with a hot topic she simultaneously (and maybe disingenuously) disavows, Clifford treads lightly through something of a minefield, navigating a position that would court some readers without alienating others, including critics or fellow writers. Demoor implies as much in noting that "unlike [Marie] Corelli, [Clifford] did not reject the New Woman novel," but that she "refused to go as far as Ward since she did not take the side of the antisuffragists in their campaign" ("Self-Fashioning" 279). Indeed, in a later letter to Robins, Clifford described her relation to the suffrage movement in very similar terms: "I sit *on the fence* and don't want to be identified with the movement either way," adding *"if* I topple over it will be on yr. side" (Letter [27 November 1911]; emphasis in the original).[32] Clifford likewise frames her career as steering a middle way that might win her readers from otherwise opposed political and/or aesthetic camps.

Yet, in a tactic drawn from Ward's playbook, Clifford does represent herself, in an unpublished letter to William Gladstone, as taking a position on one strand of the "controversial discussion" about "marriage problems."[33] Presumably including the letter with an advance copy of *A Flash of Summer*, Clifford first thanks the former prime minister for the "kind things" he had reportedly said to James Knowles, founder and editor of *The Nineteenth Century*, about *Aunt Anne*. Then she seeks his opinion of the new novel, in which a young, inexperienced girl enters into a marriage, which she subsequently flees, to an older man who has pursued her solely for her money: "All the more do I venture to send it because of what you say concerning divorce," which Gladstone had vigorously opposed in 1857 and to which he had reiterated his opposition as recently as 1889 in the *North American Review*. Claiming to agree with his views "entirely," Clifford says she "would not for worlds in any book of mine plead for greater facility of divorce; but only for greater difficulty in marriage," for in the fortune hunting of the husband—as well as what Grand would term the ignorant innocence of the wife—"seems to me to lie the secrets of the 'problems' that novelists and others have so zealously set before us." Anticipating Gladstone's approval, she asks for a favorable blurb or review even as she castigates the practice: "*Please* do not think . . . that I would publish your words (unless it were your wish) for it seems to me so terrible that no private utterance is safe now-a-days, but must needs appear in the next day's papers" (Letter [14 November 1895]; emphasis in the original). In making a case for marriage reform, while both courting and scorning publicity, Clifford comes across as fully of her times.

So, too, in her turn to writing for the theater in the mid-1890s, which continued well into the next century, Clifford drew on protofeminist themes, sought new markets, and continued to expand her networks. With its title drawn from Swinburne's "A Ballad of Burdens" (1866), her best-known play, *The Likeness of the Night* (1899; perf. 1900), was produced by Madge and William Kendal and received a respectable sixty-three performances at London's St. James's Theatre in 1901. Derived from a story she first published in *Temple Bar*, "The End of Her Journey" (1887), this bigamy drama was also produced in 1921 for the cinema, the new medium to which Clifford was eager to contribute adaptations (Newey 159). She continued to deploy the generic mix of sensation melodrama in *The Searchlight* (1904), which traces the afterlife of a woman released from prison after serving her sentence for murdering her husband. The actor-manager and suffragette Lena Ashwell also staged Clifford's one-act, "The Latch," at the Kingsway in 1908, during the same season as Cicely Hamilton's *Diana of Dobson's*. Building her networks, in her later years, Clifford sought the advice and support of the wildly successful J. M. Barrie by sending him drafts of her plays-in-progress, like the theatrical adaptation of *Miss Fingal* (1919), which he thought would be "especially interesting to women." Clearly responding to a claim of her own, this letter from Barrie asserts that theater managers would not "really care twopence whether [a play] is by a man or a woman" (Letter [31 October 1920]). But Clifford seems to have persisted in believing in the sexism of the theatrical system, having argued this point ten years earlier in a letter to Frederick Macmillan: "As the fiends of managers won't have plays by women, I am going to publish a volume containing three, with Gerald Duckworth, the first week in October" (12 August 1909).

Clearly conscious of gender as a factor in determining her access to the theater, Clifford wrote stage comedies, too, such as the one-act "A Honeymoon Tragedy," which contains "sharp observations of the consequences of unequal power relations between the sexes" (Newey 161). Commenting on it in the *Saturday Review* of 21 March 1896 alongside "a couple of [Florence] Bell's drawing room pieces," which he described as "trivial," Shaw comparatively deemed Clifford's play "of much more serious merit" (Shaw 545). One can only wonder if Shaw's review preceded or postdated his acquaintance with Clifford—especially as another member of that matinee audience, Stella Duckworth, having attended with the "Vs," wrote in her pocket diary for that date that the plays were "not very good." Although we do not know what either of the "Vs" may have thought, this event constitutes, to the best of my knowledge, Woolf's only firsthand encounter with any of Clifford's work. Did she read "the cheap flaring books" that Clifford gave her years later, when she and Leonard visited her home for tea early in 1920 (*Diary* 2: 12)? If so, we have no evidence of that: indeed, despite announcing to her sister, with her customary sarcasm, "I suppose I shall have to review [*Miss Fingal*] after all—her courage and fertility move my heart to tears," Woolf did not comment either privately or publicly on any of her work, as Clifford doubtless hoped that she would (*Letters* 2: 427).[34]

Woolf was deeply ambivalent about the standard practices of Lucy Clifford and so many other writers at the turn of the century. She associated the commodifying and self-publicizing tenor of "literary gossip" with a mode of professional authorship that she sought to keep at arm's length, even as she perceived its advantages. Writing to Roger Fry in May 1923, as she returned to work on *Mrs. Dalloway* after a holiday abroad, she asked for advice on "how to acquire the social manner. . . . What irritates me is to see—anybody, Mrs. W. K. Clifford it may be—possessed of a sense which I have not," calling it "essential for a writer. I think Proust had it" (*Letters* 3: 39). If we can read Woolf's deeming "the social manner" as "essential"—as it presumably was for Clifford, who needed to make and affirm the kinds of relationships that would keep her working life in order—her (perceived) inability to "acquire" it seems (to her) like a detriment: if even someone like Lucy Clifford has it, then why doesn't she? At the same time, from the perspective of both South Kensington and Bloomsbury, Clifford was decidedly déclassée. Although Gerald Duckworth supported her efforts to publish her work, Vanessa Bell recalled her as a "vulgar, rollicking" woman "who gossiped endlessly about the literary underworld," while the socially ambitious George Duckworth considered her, as Woolf wrote, not sufficiently "nice" for his half sisters to know (V. Bell, "Life" 75; "22 Hyde" 169). Even Leslie Stephen, himself "closely involved in the marketplace," described his friend as "a little too much immersed in the journalistic element" (H. Lee, "Crimes" 117; *Mausoleum* 80).

Read from a particular angle, these (and other) class-based judgments about the relatively successful Clifford certainly support Demoor's more general claim that Woolf was, on the whole, "unable to feel any sympathy for professional women writers" ("'Not'" 246). Given the challenges that Clifford faced and met in restarting and then maintaining a viable career after her husband's death, Woolf's attitude toward her, which ranges from mild indifference to outright hostility, should trouble feminist sensibilities. Her pouring scorn on someone whom James once referred to as the "bravest of women and finest of friends" suggests that Woolf wholly failed to contextualize this sort of writerly career within either Clifford's personal circumstances, which were far worse than they were for Woolf's own mother, or the exigencies of the turn-of-the-century literary marketplace, in which Woolf herself had, as a beginner, a very tenuous foothold (James qtd. in Demoor and Chisholm 15n8). Here again, a woman writer of the second generation comes in for rather a drubbing. But in the late 1910s and early 1920s, it is Woolf's uncertainty about her own status, I submit, that partially generates these and other unflattering references.[35] She typically conjures up Clifford in her letters or diaries, that is, only when she confronts her own position in the marketplace, in comparing herself to—and competing with—other women writers.

Classifying the Hack

Written just a few months before Gerald Duckworth accepted *Night and Day* for publication and as Middleton Murry was assuming the editorship of the *Athenaeum*, a diary entry of March 1919 evokes one of Woolf's childhood memories of Lucy Clifford. She is primarily writing about an encounter with the Newnham-educated novelist and biographer Mary Agnes Hamilton (b. 1882), known as Molly, who went on to become a Labour MP in the late 1920s and a close friend of the like-minded Ray Strachey (Grenier; Holmes 261–62). Characterized after a first meeting as "a working brain worker" without "a penny of her own," but with "the hard working brain of a professional," Hamilton seemingly recalled Clifford, in that Woolf identified them as belonging to the same type (*Diary* 1: 174). Her remarks testify to her dual attraction to and distaste for the "little bits of literary gossip" that she had just been over-hearing (from the next room) about Murry's editorship, within the context of a broader reflection on authorship:

> They point perhaps to one's becoming a professional, a hack of the type of Mrs W. K. Clifford, who used to know exactly what everyone was paid, & who wrote what, & all the rest of it. I can see father listening with disapproval but secret enjoyment. Mrs Hamilton made me feel a little professional, for she had her table strewn with manuscripts, a book open on the desk, & she began by asking me about my novel; & then we talked about reviewing, & I was interested to hear who had reviewed Martin Schüler [by Romer Wilson], & was a little ashamed of being interested. . . . She has 2 or 3 sisters, all artists according to her, . . . one is a poet, who surrounds herself with sketches of projected books on every conceivable subject, & has written a long poem which she wants us to consider publishing. "She is a poet—certainly a poet", she said, which roused my suspicions. The truth is that Molly Hamilton with all her ability to think like a man, & her strong serviceable mind, & her independent, self-respecting life is not a writer. (*Diary* 1: 254–55)

Woolf's identification with Leslie Stephen here mediates the association of Hamilton with Clifford. Recalling her father's response to Clifford's conversation—both overtly disapproving and covertly enjoying—seemingly enables Woolf to analyze her feelings about her own subsequent exchange of "literary gossip" with Hamilton, in being both "interested" and "a little ashamed of being" so. If engaging in such gossip renders "becoming a professional" equivalent to becoming "a hack of the type" of Clifford, then

Woolf, too, like her father, is implicated in and by the exchange, lacking the desired or desirable distance on this aspect of their shared work.

The immediate move from this response to a description of "feel[ing] a little professional" herself as she talked shop with Hamilton, surrounded by the tools of their joint trade, also marks Woolf as "suspicious" in a few different ways. She appeared to mistrust Hamilton's advocacy of her sister as "certainly a poet" in the context of the Woolfs' work on the Hogarth Press, which eventually became a successful commercial endeavor "in spite of the Woolfs' original intentions not to make money out of it" (Dubino, introduction, 5).[36] And she also suspects Hamilton's own credentials, to conclude that despite her qualifications, she "is not a writer." Over the course of the passage, as first Clifford, then Hamilton comes to exemplify the "type," Woolf sorts through the various categories that she might use not simply to characterize others, but to classify herself: "writer" unmodified is the term at which she arrives. By contrast, a week or so later, she compares her tea with Hamilton to tea with Mansfield, with whom, "as usual," she finds "a sense of ease & interest, which is, I suppose, due to her caring so genuinely if so differently from the way I care, about our precious art. Though Katherine is now in the very heart of the professional world—4 books on her table to review—she is, & will always be I fancy, not the least of a hack. I don't feel as I feel with Molly Hamilton that is [to] say, ashamed of the inkpot" (*Diary* 1: 258). Although she would waffle about Mansfield again and again—especially after her review of *Night and Day*—Woolf here identifies with her without noticeable ambivalence, even though she is at "the very heart of the professional world," affiliating herself with her, as against Hamilton, in their shared "caring" for their "precious art." Ironically, while awaiting news about the publication of her second novel, Woolf "was actually writing primarily for money as journalist more often than her younger, poorer counterpart" Mansfield, whom "by 1918 both Woolfs were apparently associating . . . with 'Grub Street'" (Macnamara 95).

After a later meeting with Hamilton that seems to reflect an awareness of her material circumstances—permanently separated from her husband and responsible for making her own living—Woolf wrote that Hamilton's "courage impresses me," as Clifford's did so many of her peers (Grenier). And she noted as well "the sense [Hamilton] gives of a machine working at high pressure all day long—the ordinary able machine of the professional working woman" (*Diary* 1: 312). While the association of the "professional" with the "machine" anticipates Woolf's skeptical critique of professional training for men in both *Three Guineas* and "A Sketch of the Past," she here accords "the professional working woman" of her own generation a modicum of respect. And even at Woolf's most jaded moments, Hamilton never evokes the "feeling of repulsion" that Woolf had shared with Elena Richmond in January 1920, just a few days after she and Leonard had gone to Clifford's Paddington lodgings for tea. Describing her then as "the whole figure of the nineties—black velvet—morbid—intense, jolly, vulgar—a hack to her tips, with a dash of the stage," Woolf's sole comment on the précis Clifford apparently gave Leonard over tea of the circumstances of her husband's death, and the financial straits in which she found herself thereafter, is that "the pathetic is not her line," that "she talks it to fill up space" (*Diary* 2: 12).

Significantly, references to the reception of her own work and its impact on her opportunities and, perhaps, her ego frame Woolf's rather lengthy account of that meeting with Clifford. She recalls hearing *Night and Day* praised a few nights before by a Heinemann employee whom she met at a party (*Diary* 2: 11–12). Near the close of the entry, she mentions that "a 2nd edition of the Voyage Out [is] needed; & another of Night & Day shortly," while a publisher has offered her "£100 for a book" even as she announces that she will "never write for publishers again anyhow" after the publication of *Night and Day*—as indeed she never did, at least when it came to fiction (12–13). Between these two items, however, she describes the "visit to Mrs Clifford," in which "this talk of novels"—that is, her own novels—"is all turned sour & brackish." At about seventy-five years of age, Clifford has changed her appearance by "false teeth," and her hair "is surely browned by art; but she remains otherwise the same" as the last time Woolf had seen her, approximately "20 years ago" (12).

And as what really interests Clifford, on Woolf's account, are the professional aspects of literary life, that stance takes on a monitory function for Woolf, arguably heightened by her own disavowed interest in such matters:

> If I could reproduce her talk of money, royalties, editions, & reviews, I should think myself a novelist; & the picture might serve me for a warning. I think one may assume it to be more a product of the 90ties than of our age. . . . Having years ago made a success, she's been pulling the wires to engineer another ever since, & has grown callous in the process. . . . She has a review of herself in the Bookman & a portrait, & a paper of quotations about Miss Fingal. I assure you I can hardly write this down— Moreover, I had a feeling that in these circles people do each other good turns; & when she proposed to make my fortune in America, I'm afraid a review in the Times was supposed to be the equivalent. Brave, I suppose, with vitality & pluck—but oh the sight of the dirty quills, & the scored blotting paper & her hands & nails not very clean either—& money, reviews, proofs, helping hands, slatings—what an atmosphere of rancid cabbage & old clothes stewing in their old water! (12)

Casting Clifford's talk as "more a product of the 90ties than our age"—despite her own self-documented participation in "literary gossip" over the preceding several months—Woolf's somewhat "callous" portrait of Clifford's wire-pulling self-promotion accords her bravery, "vitality & pluck," but emphasizes in large part the "dirty" business of her literary labor. Suspecting Clifford, as she had suspected Hamilton, of wanting to trade on their relationship, she also seems once again to suspect herself: for if it were otherwise, why would she need the "warning" that "the picture" would provide? Momentarily implying an audience for her diary writing in protesting to the imaginary "you" that she "can hardly write this down," she practices the facetiously self-critical stance she would later take, in a letter of 1929 to Vanessa Bell, about Hugh Walpole. Describing him as a "brother under the skin . . . of Rose Macaulay and the late Lucy Clifford," who had died just a few months earlier, she derisively comments, "He will talk about reviews and sales and dingy dirty literary shop, and drags me in, who am naturally so pure" (*Letters* 4: 60). Clearly, she knew that she was not, and that no one in her line of work actually could be a purist if aiming to make a living at it.

In her subsequent debate with Logan Pearsall Smith later in the 1920s about her writing for *Vogue*, Woolf claimed she preferred "money" to "prestige" while articulating a strong rationale for publishing in (feminized) middlebrow venues (*Letters* 3: 154; qtd. in Wood, "Made" 12). But in identifying Clifford with gossip, publicity, and the mechanisms of exchange, and locating that "type" as "a product of the 90ties," she differentiated herself from such contemporaries as Walpole, Maugham, and Macaulay even as she disparaged one of the paradigms for literary professionalism that she would have liked to relegate to the prior generation. In belittling Clifford because she wrote for money and talked of "fees," Woolf generated an image of dirt and decay that she identified with the conditions of the turn-of-the-century literary marketplace. The stink of "rancid cabbage & old clothes" insinuates that the poverty of the hack clings not only to Clifford's person and her home but also to her work. In simultaneously attributing to Clifford "a dash of the stage" and claiming "the pathetic is not her line," Woolf also constructed that persona as informed by theatricality, shaped by and for its repeated public performances: having been made "callous" in and by the process, Clifford now lets "the wires" show. And Woolf still recurred to that "warning" even five years later, in a diary entry that refers to Clifford's "hanging lips & clamorous vanity," presumably provoked by a letter from her father's old friend that puffs "an article on George Eliot which she wrote for a special fee": "That is where I shall end," she writes, "if I dont [sic] take care—talking always of 'fees'" (*Diary* 3: 150).[37]

The Compromises of Mary Augusta Ward

About a year before her visit to Clifford, Woolf commented at length on Mary Augusta Ward's *A Writer's Recollections* (1918) in a diary entry that also frames Ward's representation of her career, a very different career than Clifford's, as an object lesson for Woolf herself.[38] Paraphrasing Mark and Matthew, she prefaces her "reflection" by asking, "What would it profit me to gain the praise of the whole world & lose that single voice?" (*Diary* 1: 299):

> I could not resist Mrs Ward, & I stand in her unconscionably long hours, as if she were a bath of tepid water that one lacks the courage to leave. But she set me thinking after tea about fame. No one has had a deeper draught of it. The poor woman, now conscious of a little chill, brings out her old praises & hangs them out of her front windows. "See what Henry James said of me—Walter Pater—George Meredith." And indeed these poor old grandees, solicited I suppose by presentation copies & the rest, do seem to have perjured themselves cheerfully, though I can see them winking. My point is however, that all this blare & pomp has no kind of effect upon the sensitive reader, as I claim to be. . . . The enormous sales, the American editions, the rumble & reverberation— Piccadilly placarded with posters "Marcella out!"—seem like the drum & cymbals of a country fair. No, nothing of this counts—She herself, setting out to write an intimate account of feelings & thoughts, gives nothing but bills of fare & pass books. At what point did she cease thinking? Long Long [*sic*] ago, I should say; & then came to believe implicitly in the mummery: names of the great serve as umbrellas covering vacancy. But all tea table talk to admonish the young, who are, I suppose, now becoming inquisitive & objectionable. What a picture though of the highest life in intellectual circles in London! What a portrait of the Servants Hall; with Mrs H. W. for housekeeper, & Uncle Matt. the master. A Detestable [*sic*] assembly, as she paints it. Literature served up on plate before them. (300)

Anticipating the bodily shock on stepping out of the "tepid" bath of the memoirist's prose, Woolf yet cannot "resist" it, implying the fascination and revulsion she felt for Ward, which both pre- and postdated this moment in time. Describing her, too, as chilled, she interprets Ward's quotation of her "old praises" by James, Pater, and Meredith as her means of protecting herself from the cold blast that has penetrated her house:[39] the decline of Ward's reputation among the "inquisitive & objectionable" younger generation, whose chief representative that year was Lytton Strachey.[40] Woolf discounts the testimonials from the three "great" men—not incidentally, three of her own favorite late-Victorian writers—by doubting their sincerity, attributing their positive comments to "presentation copies & the rest," practices she also associated with Clifford.

Ward did of course deploy such tactics, most famously by sending a copy of *Robert Elsmere* (1888) to Gladstone, who reviewed it for *The Nineteenth Century* and thereby insured its success—a move that Clifford emulated, as noted above, albeit without similarly spectacular results. James subsequently described the publication of *Robert Elsmere* as "a momentous public event," significantly commending the novel for "accomplish[ing] the feat, unique so far as I remember in the long and usually dreary annals of the novel with a purpose, of carrying out her purpose without spoiling her novel" ("Mrs. Humphry Ward" 254, 256). But once Woolf concludes of Ward's popular and, to some extent, critical success and the praise she earned from her late-Victorian peers that "nothing of this counts," she goes on to describe the "nothing" she finds in the memoir itself as "all tea table talk," a phrase she later echoed in describing the impact of her own "tea-table training" on her persona as a *TLS* reviewer ("Sketch" 150).

Recasting Ward as a "housekeeper" who serves up "Literature . . . on plate" to her uncle and "master," Woolf impugns the "intellectual circles" traveled by "the great Mary"—the snide phrase with which James purportedly shocked Pound, as memorialized in "I Vecchii" (1919)—during her ten years as a don's wife in Oxford and ten subsequent years living in Russell Square. These were the decades in which Ward not only aspired to and achieved popular success but also became a leading contender for the place George Eliot had vacated on her death in 1880 as the most "serious" woman writer of her day. As in her comments on Clifford's untidy rooms with their rancid smell, Woolf metaphorically locates Ward in a domestic context, albeit at the higher end of late-Victorian literary life, where her career is portrayed as a matter of enormous amounts of money earned and spent rather than old cabbage and dirty laundry. Notably, when she later reviewed Janet Penrose Trevelyan's biography of her mother for the *Nation and Athenaeum* in 1923, Woolf repurposed the domestic metaphor from her diary as her opening gambit: "None of the great Victorian reputations has sunk lower than that of Mrs Humphry Ward. Her novels, already strangely out of date, hang in the lumber room of letters like the mantles of our aunts, and produce in us the same desire that they do to smash the window and let in the air, to light the fire and pile the rubbish on top" ("The Compromise," *Essays* 3: 380).[41]

Coming on the verge of the publication of her own second novel, Woolf's private "reflection" might serve as her mode of steeling herself against reviews and sales figures yet to come, which would deem *Night and Day* an aesthetic and/or commercial success and/or failure; yet from the point of view she inhabits here, any outcome would be a bad one. Another monitory figure of the literary marketplace, Ward had tasted the very deepest "draught" of "fame" before losing her "originally high prestige in the literary field" (Hipsky 19). Weighing that success in the balance against what she perceives Ward to have lost, Woolf resolves instead to keep "the single voice," clearly loathing what she takes as the memoir's sham invocations of Ward's greatness, its inflated authorial perspective, and the writer's commercial value(s). Yet the comments also tacitly acknowledge this author's status in the 1890s, when a new novel by the best-selling Ward was indeed a mass-media cultural event: "The fact of [*Robert Elsmere's*] success was as indisputable as the celebrity which its authoress . . . acquired"—although, to be fair, Ward wrote of the placards in Piccadilly heralding the publication of *Marcella* that such a thing "never happened to me before or since" (Courtney 3; *Writer's* 2: 162). So, too, for Woolf to ask at what point Ward ceased thinking implies a belief that at some point in the past, Ward *did* think: for how else would she have won the prestige she no longer possesses?

As in her representation of Clifford's worn-out performance of an old part in which "the wires" now show, Woolf casts herself, in an ironically charged phrase, as the "sensitive reader." Unaffected by the pomp, she can see past and through Ward's performance of her role, draped in "mummery" and sheltering behind great names that shield her "vacancy" from downpours. The mocking tone she takes in discussing Ward's memoir—which indeed makes the most of her relatively limited access to all manner of "great" Victorians, from Arnold and Tennyson to Charlotte Brontë and Harriet Martineau—registers Woolf's awareness of and resistance to both one available model for her own career and one manner of making use of a multigenerational literary inheritance. The satire and mockery she directs at Ward's domestic service to her "great" uncle, at the "bills of fare & pass books" that constitute her writing history, and at her record of rampant (over)production all constitute elements in her view of the late-Victorian mode of women's authorship that Ward came to embody. Thus Ward features throughout Woolf's writings as an "example of the compromised woman writer," in the words of Emily Blair, "who . . . lived life within the boundaries of nineteenth-century descriptions of femininity and," like Oliphant, "compromised her artistic integrity for the demands of the marketplace" (18–19). A closer look at Ward's career and how Woolf imagined and represented it also suggests, however, that particular biographical and cultural links to this writer of the "maternal generation" made Ward's example especially charged for Woolf, given their parallel circumstances and other connections between them.

Taken on its own terms, *A Writer's Recollections* leads up to and away from the fabulous success of *Robert Elsmere*. Ward concludes the extended narrative of her literary career with the publication of her eighth novel, *Eleanor* (1900), even though she went on to publish more than a dozen additional ones in the new century (including several that we know Woolf read and/or reviewed), perhaps signaling her sense that the turn of the century put a period to her wavering claim on posterity.[42] While the epilogue covers eighteen years and mentions eight additional novels more or less in passing, the part of the memoir that focuses on her career emphasizes the twelve-year period in which Ward's work both sold extremely well and received generally respectful although not universally positive reviews. That she is the first of the contemporary novelists that Courtney discusses at length in *The Feminine Note in Fiction* (albeit in an uncomplimentary way) suggests the pride of place Ward held at the turn of the century as England's most prominent woman novelist, frequently compared to Charlotte Brontë, on the one hand, and George Eliot, on the other. "Only later in her career . . . did Ward's evolving approach to fiction" make her understandable less as a "serious" novelist of ideas and more as a writer of popular romance (Hipsky 18).

By the time Virginia Stephen began recording her thoughts about Ward, the cooling of her reputation had already begun; Ward's young reader nonetheless took her father's friend's work as something of a provocation. In a 1902 letter to Dickinson about a visit to the London Library in which she complains that "too many books have been written already—its [sic] no use making more," she relays what she has either read or heard about the stage adaptation of *Eleanor* (perf. 1902), in which Robins made her final theatrical appearance: "Eleanor is said to be a worse Prig acted than written—all talk"; then she ambitiously announces, "I'm going to write a great play which shall be all talk too" (Gates 134; *Letters* 1: 60). The following year, again to Dickinson, she sighs, "I wish Providence were a better judge of literature and then we would be spared Humphrey [sic] Wards, or she might publish them in Paradise" (*Letters* 1: 71). That Ward's pace of publication only quickened thereafter, even as both sales and reviews became less and less impressive over time, no doubt contributed to the younger writer's subsequent characterization of Ward as "that old mangy hack" who crowded others out of an already overcrowded market (*Letters* 2: 68). Despite the hostility and contempt Ward aroused as a person, a writer, and a precursor, Virginia Stephen nonetheless continued reading her work as it appeared, the fascination perhaps intensified by a sense of rivalry. In 1906, reading (and perhaps reviewing) *Fenwick's Career*, which anachronistically "inveighs against the newfangled corruption of French impressionist painting," her reading notes call it "a flimsy book: held together by the spun web of words" (Hipsky 56; *Essays* 1: 376n1).[43] Almost ten years later, she described another Ward title, *Eltham House* (1915)—which she read while recovering from the breakdown that coincided with the publication of *The Voyage Out*—as "a vile book": Ward's writing was "as great a menace to health of mind as influenza to the body" (*Letters* 2: 68; *Diary* 1: 211).

Yet, for all that, Woolf still continued to read it. She and her sister appear to have dipped into Ward's memoir more than once, with Woolf facetiously telling Ka Arnold-Forster that *A Writer's Recollections* "was the last Nessa read before the birth [of Angelica Bell on Christmas Day, 1918]—the first she asked for afterwards. She and Duncan [Grant] can talk of nothing else. They knew several passages by heart—the Memoirs, I mean, not the last novel . . . the insight it gives one into the recesses of the human heart. And what a heart!" (*Letters* 2: 309). Almost two decades after the publication of *A Writer's Recollections*, Vanessa Bell called Ward "fascinating in a horrid kind of way" and "as pretentious as anyone could be"; "no doubt she got enough compliments from all the intellectuals of her day to encourage her to think herself a great genius" (*Selected Letters* 386–87). Indeed, Ward's memoir contains nothing like the "intimate account of feelings & thoughts" that both does and does not characterize Woolf's own autobiographical writings.[44] Nor does it in any way reveal the personal or material circumstances under which Ward labored toward the unanticipated success of *Robert Elsmere*. As a thirty-seven-year-old married mother of three, she was then precisely the same age as Woolf was at the moment of first reading and writing about *A Writer's Recollections* while awaiting the publication of *Night and Day*.

John Sutherland's biography of Ward only cinches Woolf's point that the memoir is "tea table talk." *A Writer's Recollections* reveals little of her childhood, adolescence, early career, and family circumstances—none of which could be construed as particularly fortunate or happy, even though (or perhaps because) like Woolf, Ward had indisputably "great" family connections. Sutherland remarks that being "an Arnold was the most important single fact" of her life and that media accounts of her work "routinely identified her . . . as the granddaughter of Thomas Arnold of Rugby and the niece of Matthew Arnold" (*Mrs. Humphry* 1). This lineage was no doubt highly meaningful and, at times, useful to Ward, as Woolf's own descent from the Stephens and the Pattles was to her. But if Ward had some of the cachet associated with the male exemplars of early- and mid-Victorian high-mindedness, she does not seem to have experienced all that many other benefits from her family ties. Born in the colonial outpost of Tasmania, the eldest daughter of the famous schoolmaster's infamous second son, who betrayed his dead father's legacy and impoverished his family by his conversions and reconversions to Newman's Catholicism, Mary Augusta Arnold "had no childhood in the usual sense" (13). On the family's return to England, she was shuttled between her grandmother's home at Fox How and a series of boarding schools, the best of which was run by Anne Jemima Clough (b. 1820); her parents paid almost no attention to her during what Ward herself calls "starved and rather unhappy years" (Writer's 1: 134). She was long "entirely invisible to important male Arnolds like Matthew," whom she did not see on anything like a regular basis until she and her family moved to Bloomsbury in the 1880s, after her husband's academic career had stalled out at Brasenose (J. Sutherland, Mrs. Humphry 13). While Woolf's childhood had been disrupted by death and loss, Ward, too, suffered a series of traumatic dislocations.

Being born a girl also constituted a disadvantage that Ward aimed to overcome. While a number of her brothers (almost all doomed to worldly failure) went to public schools and Oxford colleges, the limitations of her own "training" were ever obvious to Ward, just as inadequate as the educations of those Victorian women whose lives Woolf would go on to cite in Three Guineas, most notably Mary Kingsley (b. 1862). On rejoining her family in Oxford at sixteen, she nonetheless set out on a "great voyage of discovery, organized mainly by myself, on the advice of a few men and women very much older" (Writer's 1: 137): Mark Pattison and his then-wife, the future Emilia Dilke (b. 1840), who represented one model for what a learned woman could be and was "already a scholar, even as her husband counted scholarship"; the philosopher T. H. Green, friend of Leslie Stephen, husband of Symonds's sister Charlotte (b. 1842), and one of the dedicatees of Elsmere; the celebrated Master of Balliol, Benjamin Jowett; and the discriminating Pater, who reviewed Elsmere at Ward's request (140). Each encouraged her to pursue the intellectual ambitions she never quite achieved. "Surrounded all her adult life by the best-trained minds of her time," Sutherland writes, Ward "was always bitter at the institutional neglect of her brain, simply because it was a female brain," in a way that recalls Woolf's own antagonism to the patriarchal system that robbed Victorian daughters so as to beef up what Thackeray's Pendennis called Arthur's Education Fund (Mrs. Humphry 29; cf. Writer's 1: 129–30, 133). No wonder, then, that despite her general antagonism to Ward, Woolf turned back to the Oxford chapters of A Writer's Recollections years later, as Jane Marcus has noted, as a source for the "1880" chapter of The Years ("The Years" 46–47; "Pargetting" 70–71).

Married at twenty-one, Ward managed to avoid excessive childbearing, yet by the end of her first decade as a wife, she had accomplished none of the scholarly tasks she had set for herself. Although the Wards had to borrow most of the £900 deposit, the move to a home at 61 Russell Square in 1881 provided her with space and scope at the very reasonable rent of £100 a year. No doubt chosen for some of the same reasons Vanessa Bell chose 46 Gordon Square a generation later, it was an "altogether grander establishment than Bradmore Road" in Oxford, where Pater and his sisters Clara and Hester had been their neighbors (J. Sutherland, *Mrs. Humphry* 83). London proved congenial to Ward's aspirations. Drawing on her own and her husband's Oxford contacts, she made inroads with editors and publishers like John Morley and Frederick Macmillan and newspapers and periodicals such as the *Pall Mall Gazette*, *Macmillan's*, the *Athenaeum*, and both the *Saturday* and *Quarterly Reviews*. Sutherland estimates her journalistic output over a four-year period at a "million words" (90). Her husband eventually gained a permanent albeit not especially lucrative post as an art critic for the *Times* even as he developed over the course of twenty-five years an expensive taste for speculating in the art market. Entertaining on as regular but larger a scale as Julia Stephen or Lucy Clifford, the Wards had guests for dinner two or three times a week, in addition to holding a weekly Thursday afternoon salon that continued right up until the First World War (82, 92).

Such networking tactics no doubt prepared the ground for *Elsmere*'s runaway popular success. While a children's book and her first novel, *Miss Brotherton* (1884), made little to no public impact, *Elsmere* earned over £4,000 in its first year, and was even more outrageously successful in the United States, where "no book since *Uncle Tom's Cabin*," one of her American correspondents told her, "has had so sudden and wide a diffusion among all classes of readers" (qtd. in *Writer's* 2: 91): some comfort, perhaps, for lost income, since international copyright had not yet been put into place. Her publisher, George Smith, sold the U.S. copyright of her next novel, *The History of David Grieve* (1892), to Frederick Macmillan for £7,000, so that Ward received almost £9,500 for that novel even before "the first library copy . . . was sold to Mudie in January 1892" (J. Sutherland, *Mrs. Humphry* 138). Ward is generally credited with helping to break the economic hold of the circulating libraries by striking the death blow to the three-volume novel when Smith issued a cheap edition of *Marcella* just three months, rather than the typical twelve, after it first appeared; she earned £6,500 on that novel by the end of the year (Hipsky 57–60). She went on to sell the copyright for *Sir George Tressady* (1895–96), a sequel to *Marcella*, to Smith for £10,000 (J. Sutherland, *Mrs. Humphry* 149). All told, Sutherland estimates, "in the ten years between *Robert Elsmere* and *Helbeck of Bannisdale*" (1898), which many consider her last "good" or "serious" novel, Ward earned close to £45,000 from her fiction (159). Making that kind of money required a good deal of labor in addition to that of writing the novels themselves, as Martin Hipsky indicates: with the help of a sister-in-law and a daughter, "Ward kept up a voluminous correspondence with her publishers" on "royalties, serial rights, prospective markets, cheap editions, copyright complexities, translations, dramatizations, illustrations, author's right of veto, and so forth" (37).

Earning such enormous sums led Ward and her family to live well beyond their means, a fact which, in one of Woolf's private analyses, "partly explained" the increasing badness of her novels yet "deepen[ed]" "the mystery of her character" (*Diary* 1: 62). The proceeds from *Elsmere* first financed the move in 1891 from Russell Square to a "palace," as Vanessa Bell called Ward's upscale home in Grosvenor Place, where she attended a few parties with George Duckworth and where her hostess "tried, I suppose, to continue the George Eliot tradition" ("Life" 77). Profits from the next few books, and the expectation of more, enabled Ward to purchase a country estate in 1895. By this point, "her life hardened into life-style" (J. Sutherland, *Mrs. Humphry* 132). Owing to the "increasing financial pressure" of running expensive homes, traveling to improve her always-failing health, supporting various impecunious Arnold relatives, financing her husband's ill-advised art speculations, and paying her only son's gambling debts, she "became a money-generating fiction machine" (133).

As Woolf states in "The Compromise," Ward wrote for money and she earned lots of it—for who could "refuse . . . cheques for £7,000" from George Smith?—which she spent "as the great ladies of the Renaissance would have spent it, upon society and entertainment and philanthropy" (*Essays* 3: 382). And Woolf also implies that Ward brought her troubles on herself, as her upwardly mobile move from Bloomsbury to Belgravia indicates: "Why desert the charming old house in Russell Square for the splendour and expenses of Grosvenor Place? Why wear beautiful dresses, why keep butlers and carriages, why give luncheon parties and weekend parties, why buy a house in the country . . . when all this can only be achieved by writing at breathless speed novels which filial piety calls autumnal, but the critic, unfortunately, must call bad" (381–82). Although she knew from a conversation in 1917 with Ward's nephew Aldous Huxley that his cousin Arnold, a graduate of Eton and Balliol, had "brought [the Wards] near bankruptcy 4 years ago, & she rescued the whole lot by driving her pen day & night" (*Diary* 1: 62)—details of course never mentioned in Trevelyan's biography of her mother—Woolf attributes to Ward alone a desire to possess the trappings of worldly success that led her to "compromise" her art.

At one level, Woolf here turns up the volume on the "crashing and smashing of . . . the strong rose-coloured glass" that Molly MacCarthy made audible in her memoir, *A Nineteenth-Century Childhood* (1924), which began to appear in installments in *The Nation and Athenaeum* during the same month in which Woolf's review of Trevelyan's biography was published (MacCarthy 18). The trashy "rubbish" that once raised the great house, but now provides the tinder for burning it down, paid for those very windows.[45] Yet "The Compromise" also stages an imaginary conversation between the younger Mary Augusta Arnold and the older Mrs. Humphry Ward that goes well beyond mockery in its tone and tenor. Twice quoting the same passage from Ward's early essay "A Morning in the Bodleian" (1872), which Ward coauthored with her future husband and from which her daughter includes lengthy excerpts in the biography, Woolf invites her readers to consider the story that Trevelyan has told, one which "like all good biographies so permeates us with the sense of the presence of a human being that by the time we have finished it we are more disposed to ask questions than to pass judgements" (*Essays* 3: 381).[46]

"A Morning in the Bodleian" draws on Ward's experience as a researcher at that most illustrious of libraries, to which Pattison had secured her admission: given access to an "inner chamber of Bodley," as John Sutherland remarks in alluding to Mary Beton's or Seton's effort to visit that institution in *A Room of One's Own*, Ward "located her room inside, not outside the male-dominated library" ("A Girl" 176). "Priggish but burning" words convey the young "scholar's enthusiasm" for the study of literature (*Essays* 3: 381). And Ward differentiates this naïve "enthusiasm" from the aims and effects of "the young man reading for his pass, the London copyist, or the British Museum illuminator," thus anticipating one of the personae Woolf would create in the undereducated female "I" working in the Reading Room among much better-schooled men ("Morning" qtd. in Trevelyan 22 and in *Essays* 3: 381). With what Woolf implicitly characterizes as an idealizing attitude—albeit one that differs not very much from her own attitude as an earnest beginner thirty years later, in apprenticing herself to Pater—Ward writes that "literature has no guerdon for 'bread-students'": "Only to the silent ardour, the thirst, the disinterestedness of the true learner, is she prodigal of all good gifts" ("Morning" qtd. in Trevelyan 22 and in *Essays* 3: 381, 382).

The subsequent compromises with that Arnoldian disinterestedness form the focus of the questions Woolf poses in lieu of judgments that the reviewer, unlike the diarist, chooses to suspend. "With such an inscription above the portal," she asserts, Ward's "fate seems already decided," going on to sketch first the key facts of her Oxford life, but then emphasizing her deviation from the path of "unremunerative toil." "The career" as a scholar, "which seemed so likely, and would have been so honourable, was interrupted by the melodramatic success of *Robert Elsmere*," and all that followed: "It is here that we begin to scribble in the margin of Mrs Ward's life those endless notes of interrogation" (381). "It is tempting to imagine," she continues, "what the schoolgirl in the Bodleian would have said to her famous successor" who, in abandoning "unremunerative toil" for "society and entertainment and philanthropy," gave up asking questions as well. For "once you breast the complicated currents of modern life at their strongest, there is little time to ask questions and none to answer them" and "only one half-hour in the whole day left for reading Greek," the study of which Ward took up again in the last decade of her life. On her side of this imaginary conversation, the older Ward defends herself by blaming the younger self she addresses: "Yours was the age for seeing visions; and you spent it in dreaming" of being summoned to Buckingham Palace by the Queen; "It was you who starved my imagination and condemned it to the fatal compromise" (382). The books thus written from an imagination thus starved imply other "startling discrepancies between youth and age, between ideal and accomplishment," even as—having ostensibly made up her own mind on Ward many years before—Woolf publicly leaves the final judgment on the "beloved, famous, and prosperous" woman to her readers: "If to achieve all this implies some compromise, still—but here we reach the dilemma which we intend to pass on" (383).

As scholars frequently note of her essays and reviews, asking questions rather than rendering judgments became over time Woolf's preferred mode of engaging her readers in the process of evaluation and assessment that we call critical thinking. Thus, despite what we can take to be Woolf's own views on "the great Mary" and the somewhat snarky tone even of the review, her last sentence leaves it open to us, as readers, not only to make up our own minds and find our own answers but also to ask different questions. In a passage from "A Morning in the Bodleian" quoted by Trevelyan that Woolf did not cite in her review, the young Mary Arnold poses and answers a question of her own in a way that might have resonated with Woolf: "Which is the sadder image, the dust of Alexander stopping a bung-hole, or the brain and lifeblood of a hundred monks cumbering the shelves of the Bodleian?" "Not the former," she answers, "for Alexander's dust matters little where his work is considered,"

but these monks' work is in their books; to their books they sacrificed their lives, and gave themselves up as an offering to posterity. And posterity, overburdened by its own concerns, passes them by without a look or a word! Here and there, of course, is a volume which has made a mark upon the world; but the mass are silent for ever, and zeal, industry, talent, for once that they have had permanent results, have a thousand times been sealed by failure. And yet men go on writing, writing; and books are born under the shadow of the great libraries just as children are born within sight of the tombs . . . many a seed falls among thorns, or by the wayside, many a bud must be sacrificed before there comes the perfect flower, many a little life must exhaust itself in a useless book before the great work is made which is to remain a force for ever. And so we might as profitably murmur at the withered buds, at the seed that takes no root, at the stretch of desert, as at the unread folios. They are waste, it is true; but it is the waste that is thrown off by Humanity in its ceaseless process towards the fulfilment of its law. (qtd. in Trevelyan 23)

As if anticipating the future fate of much of her own work, young Mary Arnold describes the unread books "cumbering" the shelves of the Bodleian, to which the ascetic monks "sacrificed" their lives and which posterity "passes . . . by without a look or a word": for every one with "permanent results," a thousand are "sealed by failure," a term that does not exactly coincide in meaning with "unremunerative toil." But sadder still, the future novelist and her husband suggest, are those unwritten books—"the withered buds," "the seed that takes no root"—that nonetheless contribute to the "ceaseless process." "Many a little life must exhaust itself in a useless book before the great work is made"— by someone else—"which is to remain a force for ever." Here the essay anticipates, I think, Woolf's own well-known remarks in *A Room of One's Own* on the "thinking in common" that undergirds "the single voice," the collective effort driving a quasi-evolutionary process that only very occasionally issues in "masterpieces" (65). Perhaps Woolf paused over this passage in Trevelyan's biography of her mother; perhaps not. But if, in her judgment, courting "the praise of the whole world" had occasioned Mrs. Humphry Ward's loss of her "single voice," then we might yet suggest that Ward's career still contributed something to Woolf's own.

In a 1933 letter to Walpole that compares a second novel by Derrick Leon, rejected by the Hogarth Press after it had published his first, to "a stillborn bantling dropped out of Mrs Humphry Ward," Woolf appeals to their joint difference from their predecessor. Consoling herself on her "sad disappointment" in Leon's follow-up effort, she describes herself at work on her own novel-in-progress as "spouting ink like a whale . . . too profusely": "But they cant [*sic*] say of Hugh and Virginia that they're Mrs Ward's miscarriages; we are our own begetters anyhow" (*Letters* 5: 264). Here disowning Ward as a progenitor for her fiction during the early phase of writing what would become *Three Guineas* and *The Years*, Woolf nonetheless continued to invoke her. And just a few years earlier, she had located the beginnings of her own career as a reviewer in relation to Ward. In her 1931 "Speech to the London and National Society for Women's Service," one of the successor societies to the London and National Society for Women's Suffrage (LNSWS) then led by her friend Pippa Strachey (b. 1872), she comically represented herself as the novice who enters into literary journalism by reviewing the latest production of "the great Mary":

> You have only got to figure to yourselves a girl sitting and writing in a bed-room with a pen in her hand, a girl who had plenty of pens and paper at [her] command. Then it occurred to her to do what again only costs a penny stamp—to slip an article into a pillar-box to a newspaper; and to suggest to the editor of that newspaper that she might be allowed to try her hand at reviewing a novel. He replied that Mrs Humphry Ward had just written her fifty-sixth masterpiece and that it would not matter a straw to her or anybody else if an uneducated and probably incompetent young woman said what she thought of it. (*Essays* 5: 637)[47]

And so she does, for "what could be easier, simpler and [in] its way more delightful than to review Mrs Humphry Ward's novels and to buy Persian cats"—a luxury item rather than a necessity like "bread and butter" or "shoes and stockings"—"with the proceeds" (638). The reference to Ward was removed from the revised essay, "Professions for Women," first published posthumously by Leonard Woolf; the sarcastic jab at the last of Ward's fifty-six masterpieces forming the topic for the speaker's first book review was replaced by the perhaps more palatable claim that the young journalist's initial article "was about a novel by a famous man" (*Essays* 6: 480). And the revision thus also eliminates a striking juxtaposition, for in the speech, Woolf remarks that the story of entering her own profession "is not quite as simple as all that. There is a villain in the piece. That villain was not, I grieve to say, our old friend the other sex—or at least only indirectly. The villain of my story was a woman"—not Mary Ward, let alone Lucy Clifford—but "the Angel in the House" (*Essays* 5: 638).

During the 1930s, Woolf decisively turned back to Ward's heyday, imaginatively reconstructing in *The Years* the experiences of both Kitty Malone, daughter of the master of an Oxford college, and the amateur social worker Eleanor Pargiter, characters that—despite the claim to Walpole about being "our own begetters"—draw explicitly on late-nineteenth-century "types" Ward and her peers helped to establish. Moreover, the disavowal of Ward as "begetter" implies some strong but unacknowledged link between her and Woolf's actual parents, with Julia Stephen so frequently figured by generations of feminist critics as one very salient model for the domestic angel. Trevelyan's biography notes that "Leslie Stephen . . . wrote to Ward often, especially after his wife's death, and came at intervals to Grosvenor Place for a long *tête-à-tête*," sometimes to consult about Vanessa and Virginia (189). In a letter of July 1897, written immediately after his stepdaughter's death, he specifically requested Ward's assistance with his daughters "in that I have no longer [Stella's] interest & advice to count upon. . . . The youngest, Virginia, touched me deeply a day or two ago by telling one of her friends how much she wanted a *woman* to confide in. Now, if, . . . I can sometimes see you & talk to you about them, it will be a comfort to me. . . . I know well how many other calls there are upon your time; but if you will now & then let me see you and let my children see you I shall be grateful" (*Selected Letters* 2: 482; emphasis in the original).

After Leslie Stephen's death, his daughters sought to avoid Ward as much as they possibly could, so that though the family "travelled with the Humphry Wards" to Venice in 1904, Virginia noted that "happily [they] disappeared"; in later years, Vanessa Bell remembered "dodg[ing Ward] round the columns of the Louvre" (*Letters* 1: 137; *Selected Letters* 387). That the hated Ward was one of the three Victorian women whom Julia Stephen recommended to her daughters as role models—the other two being Octavia Hill (b. 1838) and Florence Nightingale (b. 1820)—perhaps anticipates the ambivalent responses of Prue, Nancy, and Rose Ramsay to their mother's example in *To the Lighthouse* (Darley 153). And that Julia Stephen had signed Ward's "Appeal against Female Suffrage" in 1889—for which her friend George Meredith reprimanded her at length—also leads one to suspect that Woolf might have wanted to repudiate that aspect of her mother, too (Meredith 2: 964).[48] But while Ward's association with the time and place of their parents may have been the chief strike against her for Vanessa Bell, it was not, I think, the central reason for Woolf's persistent and prolonged repudiation of either her or Clifford. As I have argued here, it was instead their doggedly professional approach to the business of literature—Ward phenomenally if ephemerally successful, Clifford much less renowned and today even more forgotten—from which Woolf distanced herself and her generation, in casting it as "a product of the 90ties." The late-Victorian shift "from a small audience of cultivated people to a larger audience of people who were not quite so cultivated"—the transformation of the literary field that strongly affected the shape that modernist ideologies would take—nonetheless created enormous opportunities for some women writers, Clifford and Ward included.

Ultimately, however, Woolf's views coincide quite closely with one Clifford herself expressed in her first memorial essay on George Eliot. She recalls the brief friendship they forged after their husbands' deaths, before the triumph of the mass-publicity apparatus in which Clifford necessarily participated: "Celebrities were not two a penny at that time; a flood of trashy books did not block the way of seekers after good work, nor of its doers, and the Press was more self-respecting than it is to-day: it considered the opinions put forth in its literary columns, and made sure that the right men held them before they were allowed expression; it used to be said then that a review in the *Times* sold an edition of a book, and people longed or were curious to see the writer. George Eliot above all others was put on a pedestal" ("Remembrance" 112). During that "age of giants," Clifford implies, Eliot's carefully crafted and guarded persona, made inaccessible to public view because of her scandalous private life and her extreme abhorrence of publicity, helped her to retain the aura of the uncompromising and uncompromised artist (113). As Susan David Bernstein has demonstrated to great effect in *Roomscape*, it is no coincidence that the two "great" women writers who eschewed the publicity of the British Museum Reading Room are the very same two whose deliberate, conscious tactics preserved their distance from what Eliot called "lady novelists" and their "silly novels," whether during the mid-Victorian moment of high-end realism or in the modernist context.

In recalling her own single meeting with George Eliot, visiting Oxford as a guest of Mark and Emilia Pattison (among the putative models for the Casaubons of *Middlemarch* [1871–72]), Ward represented her as a performer conscious of "the effect she had meant to produce" (*Writer's* 1: 145). She simultaneously suggested not only the tactics Eliot employed but also the conditions under which she necessarily operated in becoming the figure that Elaine Showalter has called "Queen George" (*Sexual* 59–76). Clifford, by contrast with Ward, neither published "silly novels" nor deconstructed the fictions of genius that Eliot, Ward, and Woolf, too, promoted. Instead, she adapted herself to the conditions of the literary field as they shifted over time while helping to shape and sustain the writerly communities that were critical to her own success as well as that of others. Rather than continuing to "forget" or "ignore" and thus destroy these writers, bringing Clifford and Ward back into the foreground helps to reveal the fuller range of women writers that Woolf didn't think back through. It also demonstrates the value of forging professional and personal solidarity with other women writers, across generational divides, a value that Woolf herself never fully embraced.

Duckworth and Company

Generations of critics have wondered why Woolf published her first novels with her half brother's publishing firm, especially as she had her doubts as to whether Gerald Duckworth had even bothered to read them (cf. *Letters* 2: 28). His demeanor over lunch at Hogarth House in March 1918 did not inspire confidence: "There is hardly a gleam of life, let alone intelligence in his eye. . . . He has no opinions, but merely a seaweeds [*sic*] drift in the prevailing current." Worse, "his commercial view of every possible subject depressed me, especially when I thought of my novel destined to be pawed & snored over by him" (*Diary* 1: 129). Though professing dislike for "the Club man's view of literature," Woolf nonetheless quoted to her diary part of the letter in which he accepted *Night and Day* for publication, where he described himself as having read it with "the greatest interest" (261, 269). "As I go to the trouble of copying his words verbatim," she admits, "I was a good deal pleased by them. The first impression of an outsider, especially one who proposes to back his opinion with money, means something; though I can't think of stout smooth Gerald smoking a cigar over my pages without a smile" (269). This dual response—distaste for "the commercial view" held by "an outsider" to Bloomsbury and its values alongside satisfaction at his praise—conveys some of Woolf's lifelong ambivalence about both professional authorship and the Duckworth men. "Boorish," "rustic," and "philistine" her half brothers may well have been, but Woolf nonetheless depended for some years on Gerald's residual sense of family loyalty and his financial commitment to the publication of her novels, which were neither especially suited to his taste nor likely to enhance his bottom line ("Sketch" 97).

"Being Leslie Stephen's stepson," as S. P. Rosenbaum points out, "had obvious advantages when it came to starting up a publishing firm" (149). After working for J. M. Dent and finding it "an occupation suitable for a gentleman," Gerald Duckworth founded his company in 1898 (Beare, "Duckworth"). The family connection was prominently mentioned in items that appeared, for example, in "The Literary News from England" column of May 1898 in *The Book Buyer* and, even ten years later, the comparable "Literary Letter" in the illustrated weekly *The Sphere* (Bulloch 333; S[horter] 228). Among the firm's initial publications were the first two volumes of his stepfather's *Studies of a Biographer* (1898) and Henry James's *In the Cage* (1898); it also published a range of titles by John Galsworthy, to whom Duckworth had been introduced by Ford Madox Ford, "an old acquaintance," and by his brother-in-law Jack Hills (Powell 77).[1] It was probably thanks mainly to the abilities of Constance Black Garnett's husband Edward, chief reader from 1901 to 1915, that the Duckworth list came to include works by writers of note who were not either friends or members of the extended family: D. H. Lawrence and Dorothy Richardson (b. 1873); Hamsun, Ibsen, Strindberg, Gorky, and Chekhov in translation; W. H. Hudson, Hilaire Belloc, Evelyn Waugh, and all three Sitwells (Willis 47; Southworth 8).[2] But alongside the works of these higher-end writers, Duckworth and Company also published the best-selling bodice rippers of Elinor Glyn, including the scandalous *Three Weeks* (1907; Rosenbaum 149). Whereas Garnett's imprimatur guaranteed a certain status, in his being the sort of "publisher's reader who [put] literary merit above commercial value," Glyn's presence on the list alongside "stylists of more serious purpose" provides a counterweight, indicating a complementary emphasis on profit (McDonald, *British* 31; S[horter] 228).

Calling him "one of the last and greatest gentleman publishers," the small volume privately published on the occasion of the firm's fiftieth anniversary, a decade or so after Gerald's death in 1937, commends its founder's "resolution to publish only what he in his personal judgment considered good of its kind" (*Fifty Years* 13). Still, the novelist and memoirist Anthony Powell, who joined Duckworth's in 1926 at the age of twenty-one, implicitly confirms that Glyn's books would have been much more to his boss's taste than those of his other authors. In his view, "the truly extraordinary thing about Gerald Duckworth was that he had chosen to become a publisher at all; much less founded a firm for that purpose. His interest in books, anyway as a medium for reading, was as slender as that of any man I have ever encountered" (6). "If allowed to hobnob with the two or three authors he found possible to tolerate"—Galsworthy, Belloc, and Ford are Powell's chief examples—he "would show little or no interest in what names were added to the firm's list" (9). Powell's remarks tend to corroborate Woolf's view in a good many respects: "He moved gloomily through the office, a haze of port-fumes and stale cigar-smoke in his wake; probably showing greater amiability among cronies at The Garrick, where . . . he undoubtedly earned his half-sister's label as clubman" (5–6). Presenting Duckworth's role in the firm in a thoroughly profit-conscious light, he also characterizes him as "staunchly anti-avant-garde"—even as Powell similarly "regard[ed] Bloomsbury as no less elderly, stuffy, [and] anxious to put the stopper on rising talent" (5).

If Woolf disliked placing her own work in mixed company—beside Galsworthy and Glyn, or even Lawrence and Richardson—she never put that on the record. And if Duckworth was "staunchly anti-avant-garde," that did not stop him from forwarding the efforts of Elizabeth Robins to keep Ibsen's work at the forefront in the 1890s. As Geraldine Beare reports, "Plays were always an important part of the Duckworth list," including all of Galsworthy's over a twenty-year period ("Gerald Duckworth" 104). Yet even before he started his firm, the diaries kept by Stella Duckworth and by Kitty Maxse's sisters, Margaret and Susan Lushington (b. 1870), confirm Gerald's frequent attendance at the theater, including the Ibsen offerings on view.[3] He, Margaret, and Stella saw *The Master Builder* at the Trafalgar Square Theatre on 13 March 1893, an outing on which they were joined by George Duckworth, Jack Hills, and Leslie Stephen (A. Curtis 22; Newman 5). Later that year, a letter to Susan Lushington from Kitty's erstwhile fiancé Charley Howard (then Lord Morpeth, later the tenth Earl of Carlisle) announces that he had "told Gerald Duckworth to fix up a party for the Ibsen," probably a performance of *Hedda Gabler* at the Opéra Comique, where it ran from 29 May to 6 June 1893 (Letter [15 May 1893]).

But Gerald not only attended some of these performances; he also played a small part in making them happen. Over forty years ago, Jane Marcus asserted that he "had been a close friend of Elizabeth Robins in the 1890s," having described her fourth novel, *The Open Question* (1898), as one of the greatest books ever written ("Art" 91, 92). He thought so much of her talent that in an undated letter written on Dent stationery, he suggested that he take an unspecified "share in the production" of Robins's projected (though not completed) adaptation of Dante Gabriel Rossetti's "Sister Helen" for the stage. With Robins at the helm and Duckworth acting as a sort of treasurer, the 1893 Ibsen series at the Opéra Comique was financed by subscription "on a noncommercial basis" (Joannou 181). A few years later, Duckworth "calculated that at least two hundred pounds was pledged or anticipated" for Robins's production of *Little Eyolf* in November to December 1896 (Gates 96). When Robins and William Archer initiated the New Century Theatre, he served as treasurer (John 232; cf. A. Curtis 23). Fifteen years later, G. C. Ashton Jonson still recalled Duckworth's collaboration with Robins and Archer in this same endeavor (128). And even after the demise of the New Century Theatre, Duckworth's went on to publish Archer and Harley Granville-Barker's clarion call for a national theater in 1907. Robins herself described her friend as "the most generous of all in his gift of time and influence expended on the subscription list" for the Ibsen productions (qtd. in Newman 5). Yet, even in the face of this well-documented involvement, Woolf scholars have generally failed to notice the behind-the-scenes support the publisher provided to Robins's Ibsen productions or to inquire into its meanings.

No doubt it would be wrong to infer from Gerald's contribution to managing the finances of Robins's productions anything like ideological support in the Stephen-Duckworth circle for the New Woman politics we typically associate with Ibsen's reception in England. When Stella and George Duckworth saw Robins perform in a matinée of *A Doll's House* in March 1893, using tickets given them by Lucy Clifford, Stella called the play "raving mad" (qtd. in A. Curtis 22, and Newman 4). When some unspecified family members and friends "went to the Dolls [*sic*] House" later the same month, Margaret Lushington reported to her diary that there was "rather a family fracas" thereafter (20 March 1893). And in terming *Hedda Gabler* "a satire on advanced women" in a letter to Susan Lushington, the future Earl of Carlisle—eldest son of one of the best-known "advanced women" of the day, the temperance and suffrage activist Rosalind Howard (b. 1845), another associate of Emily Massingberd and Isabel Somerset—implies that some of their circle may have attended as much for a laugh as anything else (Letter [15 May 1893]).

Although we can only speculate about his motives, it is striking that someone represented not just by his younger half sister but also by a much younger employee as resolutely "anti-avant-garde" would have been a part of the Ibsen scene at all. Perhaps it was his "liking for the Theatre" alone that inspired Gerald Duckworth to take up this role in helping Robins to secure the resources to mount the Ibsen productions and thus play the parts she wanted to play—or perhaps he just liked Robins (Powell 6).[4] Or perhaps Robins's brief but apparently deep friendship with his mother generated the sense of loyalty that extended beyond Julia Stephen's death—the same sense, however conflicted on her end, that may have led Woolf to publish with the family firm.

CHAPTER 4

"To Serve and Bless"

Julia Stephen, Isabel Somerset, and Late-Victorian Women's Politics

> "You are behind the times. Do not you know that philanthropy is the *fashion?*"
>
> —Rhoda Broughton, *Dear Faustina*, 1897

> You impressed me so much the other night with the wrongness of the present state of affairs that I feel that action is necessary. . . . The only way to better it is to do something I suppose. How melancholy it is that conversation isn't enough!
>
> —Virginia Stephen to Janet Case, 1 January [1910]

> Do you ever take that side of politics into account— the inhuman side, and how all the best feelings are shrivelled? It is just the same with philanthropy, and that is why it attracts the bloodless women who dont [*sic*] care for their own relations.
>
> —Virginia Stephen to Janet Case [December? 1910]

Two of the epigraphs to this chapter, taken from letters written about a year apart, provide much of the extant evidence for Virginia Stephen's first foray into political advocacy, her short-lived involvement with the People's Suffrage Federation (PSF), which was inaugurated sometime in 1909 and housed for the first year of its relatively brief existence at 34 Mecklenburgh Square.[1] Persuaded as to "the wrongness of the present state of affairs" by Janet Case, who served on the PSF's executive board, she volunteered for "the humbler work," like addressing envelopes. Given that she did not feel herself qualified to "do sums or argue, or speak," she yet felt compelled "to do something" in the belief, "melancholy" though it may have been, that "conversation isn't enough," that "action is necessary" (V. Woolf, *Letters* 1: 421). Perhaps surprisingly to her, the experience yielded some literary fruit:

writing to Violet Dickinson in late February 1910, she described "the office, with its ardent but educated young women, and its brotherly clerks," as "just like a Wells novel" (422).[2] This short sojourn in a building just down the block from her final London home no doubt shaped at least some of those scenes set in the Russell Square suffrage society office in *Night and Day* that I will examine in chapter 5. But within a year of signing on "to do something"—thus anticipating the stance of Evelyn M. in *The Voyage Out*—we find Woolf expressing disenchantment not so much with "action," as we might expect, as with "the inhuman side" of politics, evident in the claim that it shrivels "all the best feelings." She compares it to "philanthropy," somewhat jokingly portrayed as another refuge for "bloodless women" who turn away from caring for "their own relations" toward strangers.

Woolf's stance here supports Hermione Lee's claim that she was "ambivalent all her life about women philanthropists," those mainly of her own class who pursued causes and activities that extended bourgeois women's "proper" sphere of influence beyond their own individual homes to workhouses, refuges, hospitals, prisons, and the dwellings especially of the urban poor (*Virginia Woolf* 121). Clara Jones argues that Woolf also "remained ambivalent about the value of her [own] political and social action throughout her career" (5). But if she came to respect those contemporaries who addressed "practical evils," as I will further demonstrate in the next chapter, then she maintained and perhaps even intensified her hostility to what she perceived as the politics of philanthropy among her late-Victorian foremothers (*Letters* 4: 333).

The association of philanthropic activity with the desire to exercise control over others, frequently characterized in imperial terms, makes a chief point in the case against it. Woolf's 1912 *TLS* review of a biography of the U.S. temperance reformer and suffrage advocate Frances Willard (b. 1839) written by her friend Ray Strachey criticizes those whose "mission is not to create new ideas"—as "Johnson, Shelley, [and] Rousseau" did—"but to popularize, to make people practice as far as practicable the ideas of others, old ideas for the most part, ideas that have become rather dull and rather vague to most people." While the charge of coercion is apparent, perhaps worse, the books such people write are "horrible" because of that coercive imperative: "Could they fulfill their mission if they were not? You must have bold phrases to slip in under people's doors, to force into their hands, to bawl into their faces. They must be phrases, too, about the most private of emotions. You must be ready to share all with crowds in the streets" ("Frances Willard," *Essays* 2: 5). Much of a piece with her resistance to fiction with a purpose, perceived as privileging the polemical over the properly aesthetic, Woolf constructs the "mission" of philanthropy—"to make people practice . . . the ideas of others"—as a violation of autonomy and privacy that mandates "bold" and ugly crowd-speak. She suggests that both a will to power and a failure of originality in thought and language underlay and, perhaps, undermined Willard's program. And we can hear, too, an echo of the idea that the practice of both politics and philanthropy depends on the willingness of the "bloodless" to sacrifice their own privacy and individual interests to "their mission."

As Woolf came to know, mid- and late-Victorian "philanthropists" were a much more varied lot than this review indicates, including a whole host of female elders, Julia Stephen among them. Ruling, organizing, and moralizing were activities associated not only with the public work of Willard and other reformers, or with late-Victorian women's domestic mission, but also with middle-class women's role in promoting the imperial mission at home and abroad, in a mode that Barbara N. Ramusack has named "maternal imperialism."[3] "The close connection between feminism and philanthropy," Barbara Caine affirms, "established the framework through which feminism expanded to incorporate imperial projects and ideals" (*English* 127). If such public power for women was desired by some, it was at the same time feared by others, in that ruling and organizing entails the kind of coercion against which Woolf repeatedly protested, whether in the public or the private sphere, throughout her life and career. In *Mrs. Dalloway, To the Lighthouse,* and other writings, she rightly invokes an explicitly imperial frame for understanding the political and philanthropic work of her female—and sometimes feminist—predecessors. In suggesting in 1909, for instance, that "with help and opportunity," her aunt Caroline Stephen "might have ruled and organised," she identified the chief ground of her ambivalence about both politics and philanthropy in the ideological formation that united the Empress of India with her white, female, middle-class and elite English subjects ("Caroline Emelia Stephen," *Essays* 1: 268).

Although Woolf implies that most women of her parents' generation did not have the chance to remake the world along what they took to be better lines, my analysis in this chapter will focus in part on a woman who did, in considering aspects of the political and philanthropic career of Isabel Somerset. She and her maternal cousin Julia Stephen had come of age in a milieu in which women's "mission" was predicated on their subjection to ideals promulgated especially by their mothers, including strong commitments to serving god and men. As I will illustrate in consulting life writing by and about the Pattle sisters and their second- and third-generation female descendants, Woolf understood those commitments even if, at times, she failed to contextualize them as fully as she might have. By juxtaposing the private views and philanthropic activities of Woolf's mother with Somerset's political career, I show how one of the dominant models for feminist activism in those decades partakes of the coercive elements that Woolf came to disavow in both of these elders: as demonstrated in previous chapters by her attitudes to female writers, she largely discounted the work of the women of that generation and turned instead to the one before it in order to identify and promote more congenial and (or because) more distant precursors. Indeed, we might hypothesize that both her later rejection of the word "feminism" itself and her ongoing ambivalence about political action owe much to the underacknowledged impact of the social purity movement of the second generation on Woolf's views. While older activists like Josephine Butler and the housing reformer Octavia Hill protested against the state's increasing interventions in the lives of its poorest citizens—as did Julia Stephen—Somerset and her allies such as Willard and Grand rejected that libertarian emphasis in favor of an approach antithetical to the particular strand of mid-Victorian feminism that Woolf was subsequently to recover and to valorize.

Julia Stephen

For all her hostility to philanthropy, Woolf did on one occasion exempt her mother from her critique of the colonizing, coercive power that many, then as now, would assign to efforts to moralize the poor in particular. A quick aside in "Reminiscences," drafted from 1907 to 1908, differentiates her mother's "service" (or commitment to "doing good," as she referred to it thirty years later) from "the mischievous philanthropy which other women practice so complacently and often with such disastrous results" ("Sketch" 90; "Reminiscences" 34). In her *DNB* entry on Julia Stephen, Jane Garnett remarks that Woolf here shows herself "keen to distinguish" her mother's work from mischief. But where does the distinction lie? Salient differences between Willard's work and that of Julia Stephen would at a glance include the scope, scale, and explicitly Christian ethos of the former. The public performances that characterized Willard's activities as president of the Women's Christian Temperance Union (WCTU) and, later, of the World's Women's Christian Temperance Union (WWCTU)—activities that Woolf casts in the review as "philanthropy" instead of according them the status of "politics"—would contrast sharply with Julia Stephen's ministrations to suffering individuals. Her "service" would be figured as the good works of one of those "Forgotten Benefactors" whom Leslie Stephen was to celebrate in an address by that name delivered and published after his wife's death, whose "little, nameless, unremembered acts / Of kindness and of love" enrich the private domestic world and matter as much as or more than all the doings of "great" men ("Tintern Abbey," ll. 34–35). By contrast with both Willard's political activism and the myriad philanthropic organizations and institutions that emerged on the late-Victorian scene to evangelize and reform "the people," such as the Salvation Army and the settlement house movement, and despite the fact that her own writing about sickrooms and servants sometimes takes a highly moralizing tone, Julia Stephen's individual, personal "mission" to the poor and the sick presumably appeared far less invasive and complacent to her daughter, at least in the early phase of her career.

That mission forms only part, however, of how Woolf fictionalized her mother's work. Twenty years after "Reminiscences," *To the Lighthouse* positions Mrs. Ramsay's social service in relation to the aspirations and insecurities of her houseguest, Charles Tansley, who accompanies her on a "dull errand in the town" to visit an ailing villager (13). He talks on and on about the work he plans to do, "about settlements, and teaching, and working men, and helping our own class" (16)—the kind of work popularized by Stephen's contemporaries Samuel and Henrietta Barnett (b. 1851) at Toynbee Hall, which was founded in 1884; and by Mary Augusta Ward, first at University Hall in Gordon Square in 1890, then at the nearby Passmore Edwards Settlement in 1897. In the fictional case, however, as the son of a man who keeps a chemist's shop, Tansley claims an ongoing affiliation with "our" class, which he aims to serve. Mrs. Ramsay, by contrast, engages in the one-on-one ministry by the privileged to the poor and the sick that constituted a particularly feminized mode of philanthropy—the "unsalaried, self-instructed kind" appropriate to ladies of her generation—which we might also associate with the early career of Butler or Grand's streetwalking Lady Fulda (Nord, *Apprenticeship* 119).

Yet, such work does not fully satisfy Mrs. Ramsay. Before she goes on her errand with Tansley, the narrative samples her thoughts, about her own "slightly mythical" family background, about "rich and poor, high and low," and her ambition to mend "the things she saw with her own eyes, weekly, daily, here or in London" (*Lighthouse* 12, 13). These musings give rise to an otherwise unarticulated wish, a "hope that thus she would cease to be a private woman whose charity was half a sop to her own indignation, half a relief to her own curiosity," and instead take up a more public role so as to "become what with her untrained mind, she greatly admired, an investigator, elucidating the social problem" (13). On a par with the self-trained Charles Booth, that figure is thus not the equivalent of either the historical Julia Stephen or the derided "mischievous" philanthropist. Woolf links Mrs. Ramsay's slum visiting and sick nursing, that is, as much to her unfulfilled, quasi-professional aspirations as to her missionary zeal for open windows and closed doors. In assigning this "hope" to Mrs. Ramsay in the novel's retrospective look at the prewar years, Woolf thus acknowledges the opportunities for social action that had opened up for some women of her mother's generation, illustrating the role that Stephen occupied as well as specifying ones she did not actually fill, such as settlement worker and social investigator. The emphasis on the role of "investigator" in particular, we might speculate, exempts Mrs. Ramsay from the charge of mischief-making by aligning her aspirations with those of the putatively disinterested student of social science, like Beatrice Webb, carrying "a note-book and pencil with which she wrote down . . . wages and spendings, employment and unemployment" (13)—with the objective analyst that she might have liked to become, in other words, rather than with the sympathetic but unsystematic home or workhouse visitor that Julia Stephen might have been.

Private, individualized service to the poor of the sort that both the actual and the fictional mother conducted was still a going concern even in the early twentieth century, having yielded some ground first to entities such as the Charity Organization Society (COS), founded in 1869, and ultimately to the institutions of the welfare state. By contrast with these increasingly system-atized and bureaucratic practices, or with Lillah Harrison's work with "ine-briate women" in *The Voyage Out*, Mrs. Ramsay's home visiting seems amateurish, even to her. Significantly, though, it is portrayed as neither ugly nor intrusive. Indeed, when Tansley glimpses Mrs. Ramsay "[standing] quite motionless for a moment against a picture of Queen Victoria wearing the blue ribbon of the Garter" and perceives her as "the most beautiful person he had ever seen," Woolf both indicts the mode of the female elders, in light of its imbrication with Victoria's global empire, and implicitly claims that the phil-anthropic or professional urge is not necessarily inimical to beauty, as she sug-gested in her review of the Willard biography, but may rather coexist with it (*Lighthouse* 17–18; Phillips 95–96).

This iconic moment in *To the Lighthouse*, itself "slightly mythical," thus brings together in a single image multiple aspects of Woolf's critique: the im-age of Queen Victoria against which Mrs. Ramsay is momentarily posed sug-gests the implication of the latter in the rule of the former, establishing a continuity between them that evokes their shared mission beyond the confines of the home as well as its coercive impetus. The twin impulse to philanthropy and to professionalism identified in Mrs. Ramsay's character is one that Woolf typically disparages in others—there is nothing even remotely pleasing in how she portrays Willard's work, for example—yet it also forms part of the family inheritance on which she draws. Indeed, the link between personal beauty and social beautification has strong roots among the late Victorians, including Oc-tavia Hill, whom young Virginia Stephen recorded meeting on her fifteenth birthday in January 1897 at Hill's home in Marylebone Road, where she listened to Stella Duckworth, their cousin Jo Fisher the architect, and Hill herself "learnedly argue over" the cottages Stella planned to build, the kind of housing for the poor that Eleanor Pargiter does build in *The Years* (*Passionate* 21).[4]

Far from being "worldly in the thoroughgoing Victorian way" that would have made a marketable asset of her beauty, Mrs. Ramsay aims disinterestedly to put her beauty to use, as Stephen and some of her female relations did, so as "to serve and bless" ("Sketch" 88; Troubridge 40). It is beauty more than service, however, that Woolf typically highlights when she reviews or composes life writings that evoke the interpersonal networks of the first and second generations on her mother's side of the family. Woolf was always "intensely conscious," as Alex Zwerdling writes, "of how partial (in both primary senses of the word) any account of one's family history is sure to be" ("Mastering" 169). As for Katharine Hilbery in *Night and Day*, Woolf's accounts depend on evidence she derives in part from her elders' view of that past—immediate for them, but highly mediated for her. Yet, the keynote of such descriptions almost always centers on the aesthetic quality of an irrecoverable past. In reviewing Henry James's posthumously published memoir *The Middle Years* (1917), for example, Woolf professes not only to experience "pleasure at the mere sight" of "vanished dignity and faded fashions" but also to feel the "thrill with which we recognize, if not directly then by hearsay, the old world of London life" ("The Old Order," *Essays* 2: 168). Interestingly, she draws her primary example of this not from James's text, but from her own family history: "Groups of people would come together at Freshwater, in that old garden where the houses of Melbury Road now stand, or in various London centres, and live as it seems to us for months at a time, . . . in the mood of the presiding genius," be that G. F. Watts at the Prinseps' Little Holland House in Kensington or, out of London, Julia Margaret Cameron (b. 1815) at Dimbola. The divinities that ruled this world "imposed their laws upon a circle which had spirit and beauty to recommend it as well as an uncritical devotion" (170). A few years later, Woolf would represent Mrs. Hilbery, looking through an album of family photographs, recalling the women of such a circle as "so calm and stately and imperial . . . as if nothing mattered in the world but to be beautiful and kind" (*Night* 117; ch. 9).

Twenty years after that, in an imagined scene from "A Sketch of the Past," Woolf conjures up Little Holland House a generation or so before her own birth by reference not solely to its visual artists but also to those women who formed a living picture. Depicting a mid-Victorian picnic very different from the one she more or less simultaneously created for the parodic historical pageant in *Between the Acts* (1941), to which I will return in the afterword, Woolf sketches Little Holland House in Kensington "about 1860," the site of the "education" afforded Julia Jackson under the tutelage of her Anglo-Indian aunts, as "an old white country house, standing in a large garden. Long windows open onto the lawn. Through them comes a stream of ladies in crinolines and little straw hats; they are attended by gentlemen in peg-top trousers and whiskers" ("Sketch" 86).[5] The tea tables "are 'presided over' by some of the six lovely [Pattle] sisters; who do not wear crinolines, but are robed in splendid Venetian draperies" (87). With a gently ironic touch, Woolf envisions her mother's role as "to take such part as girls did then in the lives of distinguished men; to pour out tea; to hand them their strawberries and cream; to listen devoutly, reverently to their wisdom; to accept the fact that Watts was the great painter; Tennyson the great poet; and to dance with the Prince of Wales" (88). All the Pattle sisters were "worldly in the thoroughgoing Victorian way" except for Woolf's grandmother Mia (b. 1818), a distinction that set apart her three daughters—Adeline (b. 1837), Mary (b. 1841), and Julia—from their female cousins. Some of them mingled with royalty, like Alice Prinsep Gurney (b. 1844) and her daughters Laura (b. 1866) and Rachel (b. 1868), and made aristocratic marriages, like the daughters of Virginia Somers (b. 1827) or the Gurney sisters themselves.

But as opposed to the somewhat more credulous tone she takes in "The Old Order," Woolf's later-life remarks register the fictive quality of her own representation of a past she did not know, largely based as it is on her reading. "How easy it is," she concludes, "to fill in the picture with set pieces that I have gathered from memoirs," like James's or Anne Ritchie's (87). Her father, too, had described Little Holland House in similar terms as having "a character of its own. People used to go there on Sunday afternoons; they had strawberries and cream, and played croquet, and strolled about the old-fashioned garden, or were allowed to go to Watts' studio and admire his pictures" (*Mausoleum* 30). And others confirmed that image: in a memoir we know Woolf to have read late in 1939, the artist Will Rothenstein remarks, "Each time one went to Melbury Road was an exhilarating privilege. The memory of these visits to Little Holland House remains as something rich and precious, unlike any other experience" (1: 34).[6] "Set pieces" of this sort typically represent the Pattle sisters as eccentrically dressed and aesthetically ravishing; at odds with mid-Victorian conventions owing to their French descent and Anglo-Indian upbringing; and intensely invested in displaying the beauty that they and many of their daughters possessed, which artists such as Watts and Edward Burne-Jones repeatedly sought to capture. Woolf drew most directly on such material in *To the Lighthouse* when she described Mrs. Ramsay's maternal ancestry in similar terms, attributing "all her wit and her bearing and her temper" to "the blood of that very noble . . . Italian house, whose daughters, scattered about English drawing-rooms in the nineteenth century, had lisped so charmingly, had stormed so wildly" (12–13).

Creating a scene based on other people's memories, Woolf constructs her own access to that past as "based upon one fact" alone, a memory of a day when "my mother took us to Melbury Road; . . . and cried 'That was where it was!' as if a fairyland had disappeared" ("Sketch" 87).[7] And so it did when Thoby and Sarah Prinsep (b. 1816; née Pattle) left London for Freshwater in 1874, and Little Holland House itself was demolished a few years later (Dakers 152, 26). Described as "a hero worshipper, simple, uncritical, enthusiastic," Julia Stephen maintained, in her daughter's mind, a romantic "devotion" to those who peopled the vanished world many other memoirists would represent ("Sketch" 87). Because James had seen aspects of that world "with the detachment of the stranger and the critical sense of the artist," his "hearsay" is legitimized in 1917 (*Essays* 2: 171). Through his good offices Woolf is enabled to perceive "in retrospect a glamour of adventure, aspiration, and triumph such as seems for good or for evil banished from our conscious and much more critical day" (171–72). "But if I turn to my mother," she wrote two decades later, "how difficult it is to single her out as she really was; to imagine what she was thinking, to put a single sentence into her mouth! I dream; I make up pictures of a summer's afternoon" ("Sketch" 87).

When aiming to retrieve a past that she did not experience, then, Woolf finds it hard not to simplify, difficult not to romanticize, even as she remains on guard against that tendency, both early and late in her career. In a 1915 letter to Nelly Cecil criticizing Ward's *Eltham House*—"the writing of a woman who has been accidentally locked in to the housekeeper's room of Longleat say for the past 20 years; and has done nothing but absorb family portraits and family plate"—she confesses her desire to draw "family portraits" of her own (*Letters* 2: 68).[8] "I always mean to write a history of my Great Aunts, who are said in the family to have been incomparably beautiful and romantic," further asking Cecil if "you find any charms in the 1860's? They seem—my mother's family I mean—to float in a wonderful air—all a lie, I daresay" (69). When on reading *Jacob's Room* in 1922 Lytton Strachey reported that he thought the novel "very romantic" (*Letters* 523), Woolf responded, "You put your infallible finger upon the spot—romanticism. How do I catch it?" As if it were an infectious disease, she traces the source of contagion to "my Great Aunts," adding that owing to "the effort of breaking with complete representation . . . one flies into the air": "Next time," she concludes, "I mean to stick closer to facts" (*Letters* 2: 568–69). If here Woolf "prioritises the claims of the imaginative or 'figurative' engagement with the world," both in sketching the unknown Jacob

Flanders largely through the perceptions of other people and in reading and writing about her great-aunts, then she also maintains the sense that the stories about real people that she tells and retells depart from, or replace, or compete with the "facts" (Ellis 24).[9] Both fascinated by the circles in which her mother had moved as a young woman and aware of the limits on accessing her mother's past, Woolf's recognition that family lore may indeed be "all a lie" nevertheless did not stop her from furthering the myths surrounding the Pattle sisters.[10]

Pattledom

Other extended family members also seem to have felt the powerful pull of that lore, and a memoir by Laura, Lady Troubridge (née Gurney), grand-daughter of Sarah and Thoby Prinsep, provides a case in point. Two decades younger than Julia Stephen and about fifteen years senior to Woolf, Troubridge published *Memories and Reflections* in 1926. Her second cousin promptly reviewed it for the *Nation and Athenaeum*, of which Leonard Woolf was then literary editor, just a year before publishing her most autobiographical novel, which draws on Troubridge's memoir in unacknowledged ways.[11] As Woolf would do in drafting "A Sketch of the Past," Troubridge retails the Pattle reputation for beauty as "a family inheritance, missing some of the descendants," such as Cameron, "and reappearing in others, notably in my mother and her first cousin, Julia Jackson" (7). She, too, calls Little Holland House, where she spent much of her own itinerant childhood, "a place of enchantment," "a kind of earthly Paradise, with its dim rooms full of artistic and beautiful objects" (8, 9).[12] Describing the Pattle sisters en masse, Troubridge compares their past to her present: "These women lived on a higher plane than most women seem to now. They cared nothing for the feminist movement and the rights and wrongs of their sex. But they knew that they were here to serve and bless" (40). And that image fits some daughters of the next generation as well. When "our childish life at Freshwater was ended by my grandfather's death, which broke up the mixed household" early in 1878, Troubridge recalls that Julia Duckworth, on the verge of her second marriage, "came to take charge of the paralysed household" as her beloved uncle Thoby lay dying, even as cousin Isabel was fleeing her failed marriage (43). Like Mrs. Ramsay's, Julia Duckworth's "manner was reserved and authoritative, so that she rather frightened" twelve-year-old Laura and her younger sister, whose father's family's business reverses had already created a difficult situation for his then-wife and children; but Troubridge nonetheless describes Woolf's mother as "a great and good woman" who "lived for others" (44).[13]

To be sure, *Memories and Reflections* has relatively little to say about the Pattles and much more about Troubridge's professional career—as a writer of Mills and Boon romance fiction. But Woolf's review never acknowledges either her relationship to Troubridge or her cousin's writing career. It focuses instead on Troubridge's brief account of being "brought up in the very heart of the sisterhood in the Prinseps' home at Little Holland House" ("Pattledom," *Essays* 4: 281). The memoir itself gives precedence to relations Woolf chooses not to consider: Troubridge's sister Rachel, the second Countess of Dudley, whose husband was Lord Lieutenant of Ireland from 1902 to 1905 and to whom Woolf comically refers in *Freshwater* (75); and, in the prior generation, Julia Jackson's aristocratic cousins Isabel and Adeline Somers-Cocks (b. 1852), who opened their homes to Laura and Rachel when their parents' marriage broke up. Leaving aside much of what the memoir is actually about, Woolf instead titled her review "Pattledom," the term Thackeray had coined for the seven Anglo-Indian sisters, of whom he especially admired Virginia, who married the art patron Charles Somers-Cocks and became a countess; Sophia, who likewise made an aristocratic marriage, though of lesser brilliance, in becoming the wife of the baronet Sir John Warrender Dalrymple; and Julia's mother Mia. Indeed, Thackeray's biographers speculate that had he not lost his inheritance in the Bengal bank crash of 1832, he might himself have married Mia Pattle; Vanessa Bell even asked her sister in 1907 if it were "true that Thackeray was in love with Granny" (*Selected Letters* 53).[14] Woolf's grandmother became instead a doctor's wife and, in an irony that seems to have escaped most commentators on "the Angel in the House," a close friend of Coventry Patmore, whose poem first popularized the figure that any woman writer, according to Mia Pattle's granddaughter, would have to try to slay.[15]

Here again Woolf dwells on the "slightly mythical" dimensions of her family background. She repeats stories already in circulation, beginning with the apocryphal anecdote about the fate of her great-grandfather James Pattle's corpse. Although it doesn't even appear in *Memories and Reflections*, Woolf had encountered this particular "set piece" in both Ethel Smyth's 1920 *Impressions That Remained* (2: 251–52) and Kathleen Fitzpatrick's 1923 biography of Isabel Somerset, her review of which I will consider below. And it would feature again in an essay on the Somers-Cocks sisters in a volume of memoirs by E. F. Benson, one of the sons of the Archbishop of Canterbury, Edward Benson, and his wife Minnie, and the best-selling author of the comic roman à clef *Dodo* (1893).[16] Woolf retold the anecdote at least once more herself in her 1926 introduction to a collection of great-aunt Julia's photographs, which draws on a range of memoirists with firsthand experience of both Little Holland House and Freshwater, including Troubridge, Ritchie, Sir Henry Taylor, and Ellen Terry ("Julia Margaret Cameron," *Essays* 4: 375–76). Thus in reviewing Troubridge's recollections she focuses on the larger-than-life, quasi-comic dimensions of that vanished past, picking and choosing the elements that fit into an already established picture; those that do not fit are excluded.

Perhaps more importantly, "Pattledom" further invokes the family's colonial background by casting the "six daughters of surpassing beauty and one daughter of undoubted genius" as women who "ruled a Victorian empire," or what Alison Light has called "the little Empire of home, an *imperium in imperio*" (25). It emphasizes the sisters' rather despotic rule as predicated on their charismatic deportment, being "all of a distinguished presence, tall, impressive, and gifted with a curious mixture of shrewdness and romance. No domestic detail," Woolf concludes, "was too small for their attention" (*Essays* 4: 280). When she created her own comic version of the Little Holland House circle during its island phase in *Freshwater*, such traits reappeared in Cameron's character, to which Woolf assigns an imperious power to command, compose, and represent what she elsewhere called the "agreeable eccentricities" of this singular being's peers ("The Schoolroom Floor," *Essays* 3: 444). Small wonder that Woolf cast her own sister—possessed of both "surpassing beauty" and "undoubted genius," along with a corrosively ironic view of her elders and their ways—to play Cameron's part in the comedy.

The mid- and late-Victorian "empire" under women's rule, however, was not limited to their own households of family and servants, but increasingly extended to the extra-domestic sphere in which the second-generation Pattle descendants—as well as their female friends, acquaintances, and relations—played varied roles. Construed as an aspect of their domestic mission, the mandate "to serve and bless" constitutes a portion of the maternal inheritance that had a definite impact on daughters and granddaughters, nieces and great-nieces. Yet deviations from the norms for femininity were not infrequent. Described by her daughter as having "passed like a princess in a pageant from her supremely beautiful youth to marriage and motherhood," Julia Duckworth renounced her mother's religion after her first husband's sudden death, surely astonishing her family even as she maintained her commitment to caring for others ("Reminiscences" 32). As Woolf later wrote of the interim between her mother's two marriages, "during those eight years spent, so far as she had time over from her children and house, 'doing good,' nursing, visiting the poor, she lost her faith" ("Sketch" 90). If that loss would, in the eyes of some, disqualify her for such service, as Bertha Lathbury argued in "Agnosticism and Women," an essay in the *Contemporary Review*'s April 1880 number, then Stephen, in an unpublished response, begged to differ. She could not "see how [the agnostic woman] has unfitted herself for such work": "Purity of life, sincerity of action, obedience to law, love of our fellow creatures, all those qualities which ennoble life are the stronghold of the Agnostic" (["Agnostic"] 243, 246). Loss of belief in an afterlife—the apostasy that torments Catherine on her husband's behalf in Ward's *Robert Elsmere*—need not, Stephen asserts, alter women's secular mission here on earth. Like Clarissa Dalloway, traumatized by an unexpected and inexplicable death when she saw her sister "killed by a falling tree," as a young widow Woolf's mother began to profess what Peter Walsh calls the "atheist's religion of doing good for the sake of goodness" (*Mrs. Dalloway* 70).

Unlike the worldly Clarissa, however, this agnostic angel subsequently "nursed the dying" not just among her immediate and extended families but also when she "visited the poor" in "London slums" ("Reminiscences" 32, 38). She frequented the "alleys in St. Ives," where "she visited, helped, and started her nursing society," and "the Cancer Hospital in the Brompton Road" ("Reminiscences" 32; "Sketch" 131, 96). "Prompt, practical and vivid," after Herbert Duckworth's death she "spen[t] herself more freely than ever in the service of others" ("Reminiscences" 34). "Also a little imperious," she "took it on herself to dispatch difficulties with a high hand, like some commanding Empress" (39, 35). Although certain aspects of the early "Reminiscences" portrait are value-neutral or even exculpatory, the description of the mother as "imperious," a "commanding Empress," not only encodes the perceived effects of her upbringing under the eye of the Anglo-Indian sisterhood and in service to distinguished men but also implies her coercive power over her own daughters—who, like the Ramsay sisters, went on to "sport with infidel ideas which they had brewed for themselves of a life different from hers" (*Lighthouse* 10). Linking her mother, her aunts, and her cousins to the imperial powers they served most directly in the form of their husbands and sons, Woolf gestures at both their subjection to and complicity with the patriarchal colonial arrangements on which the empire depended at home and abroad.

Another instance of Pattle family life writing, published three years before Troubridge's memoir, provides a complementary angle on the confined and constricted circumstances of one of Julia Stephen's familial contemporaries. Titled "The Chinese Shoe," Woolf's unsigned *TLS* review of Kathleen Fitzpatrick's biography of Isabel Somerset does not associate either its subject or her beautiful mother Virginia with "Pattledom." There is no mention here of Little Holland House, and Woolf did not identify her own relationship to the biographical subject any more than she identified her cousinhood with Troubridge. The orientalizing title conveys instead Woolf's sense of the regime to which Isabel and her sister Adeline were subjected by their mother: she would return to it in "A Sketch of the Past" in alluding briefly (and ethnocentrically) to the "tortures" that her great-aunt Virginia inflicted on her daughters, "compared with which the boot or the Chinese shoe is negligible" (88). For "no woman," Woolf declares, "was ever more completely defrauded of her rights"—by "the Victorian age," her mother, and her husband combined—"in the general conspiracy against her" than Isabel Somers-Cocks: "Each natural desire of a lively and courageous nature was stunted, until we feel that the old Chinese custom of fitting the foot to the shoe was charitable compared with the mid-Victorian practice of fitting the woman to the system" (*Essays* 3: 390).

As the socialist-feminist Margaret Cole (b. 1893) points out in her biographical sketch of Somerset, Lady Somers's eccentric Anglo-Indian "upbringing certainly did not resemble [Somerset's] own" (38). "From the first the beautiful Virginia ruled" with the proverbial iron fist (Fitzpatrick 19). Having lost a four-year-old daughter (also named Virginia) to diphtheria, she kept her surviving girls on a very tight leash and maintained a close eye on every "domestic detail," despite the fact that she spent much of her time traveling across Europe, buying art with her husband, while her daughters remained at home under staff supervision at Eastnor Castle in Herefordshire. In a variation on what Woolf was later to term her own mother's "education" in deference and display at Little Holland House, these two girls "had no education. Their politics, their friendships, their religion, their occupations from morning to night were dictated to them and enforced upon them in letter after letter, and scolding after scolding, by the most beautiful, the most generous, and the most exacting of mothers" (*Essays* 3: 390). (Such details, drawn from letters included in Fitzpatrick's biography, recall Mia Jackson's own voluminous correspondence with her youngest daughter, to which the adult Woolf surely had access.) Subjected to maternal discipline as she was, Isabel nonetheless reacted against the family's politics: Woolf notes that she "read Mill's *Liberty* in secret" and supported the North in the Civil War (390; Fitzpatrick 58). While the only novelists the sisters were purportedly permitted to read were Charlotte Yonge and Walter Scott—dear, as we have seen, to the Stephen daughters a generation later—a 1902 profile mentions that Somerset's favorite novel was *Uncle Tom's Cabin* (Cole 41; Fitzpatrick 63–43; Stoddart 36). Frustrated in her desire "to live in the country and to have fifteen children," she had only one before her marriage ended in 1878; she then temporarily "retired to Eastnor Castle" (*Essays* 3: 390, 391).

In the story Woolf tells, Somerset exemplifies both the state of ignorance in which mid-Victorian young ladies were kept and the lack of options afforded them by socially ambitious mothers who groomed them for a high place in Society. As in her review of Troubridge's memoir, Woolf says little to nothing about the rest of Somerset's life, only alluding near the end of her two columns to the "work among the inebriates for which she is chiefly known." She claims that such work does not "occupy much [space] in her biography," for "when you fit a woman into a shoe, any number of trifles—happiness, work, children—have to be left out" (392). But what Woolf herself leaves out in assessing the biography, which contains a much more substantial amount of information on its subject's social and political work than she implies, provides an important counterpoint to the "slightly mythical" pictures of the female Pattle descendants that she elsewhere relates. If Somerset's life took an unexpected turn when her marriage ended, then her "work among the inebriates," as Woolf calls it here as in *The Voyage Out,* can certainly be construed along the lines of her widowed cousin's workhouse visiting and sick nursing—not exclusively as a compensation for the imagined future each had lost, but as an important element of her adult identity as a woman trained "to serve and bless." The cousins nonetheless departed from Victorian orthodoxies and Pattle myths, albeit in different ways. Subjected to the demands of her mother as well as the needs of her successive husbands and children, one lost her religion but maintained her commitment to service; the other kept and indeed intensified her religious faith, but undertook a public career diametrically opposed to the aristocratic ethos of her upbringing. Isabel Somerset's story sheds light on Julia Stephen's in where they converge and diverge.

Isabel Somerset and Julia Stephen: Private Lives and Public Missions

Excluded from Society upon her separation from her husband and living mainly at Reigate Priory, Surrey (near the town where Katherine Bradley and Edith Cooper also lived for a time), at her father's death in 1883 Isabel Somerset inherited all of his holdings.[17] She "looked after her estates," "visited her tenants, and from that developed her work among women"; "religion and rescue-work were the motives of her life," Benson continues, once she turned her attention to temperance and then "arranged to take the pledge publicly at Eastnor"—since to her mind, "it really was not fair to expect others to practice an abstinence which she did not observe" (82).[18] Her immediate, personal concern for the welfare of her tenants ultimately led her to enter public life and achieve worldwide prominence as a progressive reformer: in Benson's view, Somerset was "one of the pioneers who have won for their sex liberty and the right to work" (76). Unlike Woolf, then, Benson firmly associates her not just with temperance, but with "the woman question" as it was being reconstituted in the 1880s and 1890s.

On inheriting the estate, Somerset began her career as an extension of domestic duties, like Mrs. Ramsay or Julia Stephen, tending to those around her in accord with a hierarchical framework. But over time, she turned to an array of activities associated with the social-purity wing of the women's movement. As I described in the introduction, this effort to moralize the public sphere both legitimated and depended on elite women's intervention in a range of sexually charged issues that I have considered thus far in relation mainly to the conventions of late-century fiction, such as prohibitions on speech about and knowledge of sexuality, and the representation of both prostitution and marriage. As Alan Hunt has argued, for some Victorian women "the ideology of separate spheres . . . provided both the impetus and the legitimation of an expanding engagement with the public life of the wider community"; but the terms of that engagement could and did differ substantially from one woman—and one generation—to the next (95–96). Whereas the fictional Mrs. Ramsay aspires to the public position of "social investigator," and Julia Stephen aimed (in Troubridge's eyes) disinterestedly to put her beauty to use "to serve and bless," Somerset's temperance work led her into forms of participation in the public sphere that would blur any sharp distinction that we, or Woolf, might seek to draw between late-Victorian philanthropy and political advocacy.

How Stephen and Somerset approached the question of temperance provides one indicator of the ideological differences between them. Aside from signing the antisuffrage petition that appeared in *The Nineteenth Century* in 1889, the only other public stance that Woolf's mother is known to have taken consists of two letters published in the *Pall Mall Gazette* (PMG) in October 1879, each signed "Julia Prinsep Stephen," that protested an "experiment in teetotalism." The new medical superintendent of a workhouse in St. George's Union, where "I have visited . . . for many years," had deprived "a number of infirm old women" of "a daily half-pint of beer," one of few comforts available to those "who were making the best of the hard end of a hard life" ("Beer").[19] Stephen was challenged on her grasp of the facts at the workhouse guardians' meeting where her letter came up for discussion: as reported in the PMG, one speaker "believed that she had been misled, and she ought to have better informed herself before sending a letter to the press," while another opined that "the lady had acted very indiscreetly" ("Pauper's Beer"). "With reluctance," Stephen wrote a second letter defending herself against the charge of "deceiving the public," while pressing the veracity of her claims ("Paupers' Beer"). Because she "[felt] passionately" about workhouses, just as Mrs. Ramsay cares deeply for "hospitals and drains and the dairy"—"Milk delivered at your door in London positively brown with dirt . . . should be made illegal"—

Stephen spoke out not once but twice, motivated by her concern for the impoverished elderly women in whom she had come to take a strong charitable interest (*Lighthouse* 61).[20]

Like her cousin, Somerset maintained an ethic of personal service to the sick, poor, and disadvantaged, as in her founding in 1895 of the Duxbury home for female "inebriates"—also known as a "farm colony," along the lines of the model proposed by the Salvation Army leader William Booth's *In Darkest England* (1890)—into which she poured her fortune and where she lived and worked during the last years of her life (Tyrrell, *Woman's World* 247). But in her commitment to the social-purity strand of the contemporary feminist movement, Somerset might well have considered the "experiment" that Stephen protested as a viable and necessary intervention in the lives of the workhouse inmates. Although most analysts of the time would have attributed a pauper's immiseration, at least in part, to excessive alcohol consumption, Somerset would ultimately adopt a medical model in representing alcoholism as a disease. By contrast, Stephen, like Butler or Hill, would have been more inclined to consider the liberty of the subject in thought and action as paramount, with the doctor's "experiment" constituting an infringement of the women's right to do as they pleased.

Stephen's commitments thus lay in another direction than her cousin's. Although she was busy with her growing family, we can safely assume that she indeed carried out her own particular version of what we would now call social work (albeit unpaid) as one of "about half a million women in England . . . involved in philanthropy" by the 1890s, a mass effort facilitated by middle-class and elite women's increasing ease of access to the public sphere (Ross 1). Her activities were thus firmly within "the mainstream of social theory and social action," which "linked the solution of social problems firmly to the family and to social work performed voluntarily by middle-class women who thereby fulfilled their citizenship obligations" (Lewis 1). During the 1870s and 1880s, her London bus journeys took her to and through many districts, rich and poor: Woolf recalled that her "mother did all her immense rounds—shopping, calling, visiting hospitals and work houses [*sic*]—in omnibuses" ("Sketch" 121). When not traveling the provincial legal circuit with Herbert Duckworth or staying with family and friends, she spent the three years of her first marriage living in Bryanston Square, Marylebone, moving to West Brompton only after the death of her mother-in-law in 1872 (Rudikoff 146). Perhaps fortuitously, her first home as a married woman lay at an epicenter of middle-class philanthropic activity in London. In Bryanston Square, she may well have first met Samuel Barnett, who took up a curacy there early in 1867, the year of the

Duckworths' marriage, serving "a parish," in the words of his wife and biographer Henrietta, "whose residents were mainly the rich and the well-to-do, though there were quarters of it inhabited by casual labourers and the feckless, as well as streets occupied by the self-respecting industrial classes" (Barnett 1: 22). Together the Barnetts moved to St. Jude's in Whitechapel in 1873, founding the Toynbee Hall settlement some years thereafter.

Perhaps it was also in Bryanston Square that Julia Duckworth first heard of and met Octavia Hill, who founded the COS in 1869 as part of a group that included John Llewelyn Davies, the Christian Socialist, former tutor of Leslie Stephen, and longtime vicar of another Marylebone parish (Hort and Matthew). Deborah Epstein Nord describes Hill as one "of the generation that formed a bridge between the untrained, upper-class women like Josephine Butler . . . and those women born in the 1850s and 1860s," women somewhat like Margaret Llewelyn Davies, daughter of John and subsequent friend and associate of the Woolfs, "who worked in a trained, salaried and professional way" (*Apprenticeship* 119). Living near Fitzroy Square in the 1850s, by the next decade Hill had begun to manage her first block of houses in Paradise Place, about a mile from the Duckworths' home (Ashton 260). Julia would contribute financially to Hill's efforts, donating £10 every year from 1871 until her death in 1895 (Jones 18). Hill's development of housing for the poor and training of those public-minded women who would superintend it, including Stella Duckworth, also attracted the voluntary labor of Caroline Stephen. Already acquainted with Hill from her research for *The Service of the Poor* (1871), she occupied herself after her mother's death in 1875 by "setting up her own 'model' flats in Chelsea," the Hereford Buildings, "and joining the local committee" of the COS (Bush 37).[21]

While the COS "sought to systematize the provision of relief and embraced bureaucratic methods," Hill simultaneously "insist[ed] on personal and affective interventions" with her tenants, in "close and constant personal contact" (Colón 148; Siegel 116). This provided a model for engagement that Julia Stephen, Caroline Stephen, and no doubt Isabel Somerset, too, would have endorsed. At the same time, Daniel Siegel notes that Hill "straddled conflicting approaches to social work" (117). For example, her "policy of noncoercion in the lives of her tenants," which might seem to differentiate her from the kind of "philanthropist" Woolf was to imagine in her review of Ray Strachey's Willard biography, "depended upon an implicit contract of deferential cooperation on the part of those tenants," as Susan E. Colón observes (157); that latter point would alienate those committed to the socialist critique of class privilege in Hill's own time and in the next generation, including Leonard Woolf.

And the issue of coercion would also mark a fault line in a number of feminist activist projects during the 1880s and 1890s, providing a mixed legacy for those who would follow.

Philanthropy and Feminist Politics

While both Stephen and Somerset undertook their labors without pay, other women of their acquaintance combined philanthropic endeavors with journalism and literary work. At a point on the ideological spectrum close to Stephen's was Mary Augusta Ward, whose increasing involvement throughout the 1890s in founding the Passmore Edwards Settlement, named for its chief benefactor, at the height of her success as a novelist demonstrated that a literary career and a commitment to philanthropic service were not necessarily mutually exclusive. Ultimately built a few blocks from Woolf's later residence at Tavistock Square on land leased from the eleventh Duke of Bedford, the brother-in-law of Somerset's sister Adeline, the settlement's initial Bloomsbury locale in the 1890s was just across the way from what would become the Stephens' first home in Gordon Square. While *Robert Elsmere* includes some attention to the settlement movement, Ward's own most fully realized fictional portrait of a female philanthropist appears in *Marcella*, which I considered in the introduction for its use of a Bloomsbury setting. A South Kensington art student and fledgling Fabian socialist, the title character gives up her aesthetic interests in exchange for politics and philanthropic service, serving a stint as "a rent-collector . . . in the East End" (48). (In the sequel, *The History of Sir George Tressady*, Marcella and her husband, the Conservative politician Lord Maxwell, live for six months in the Mile End Road, Whitechapel.) "It was not in art," the narrator affirms, "that [Marcella] found ultimately the chief excitement and motive-power of her new life—not in art, but in the birth of social and philanthropic ardour, the sense of a hitherto unsuspected social power" (46–47; bk. 1, ch. 2). Although Hill had herself chosen a career in housing reform over pursuing one as an artist decades earlier, for *Marcella*'s author, no such renunciation was necessary. As Jane Lewis writes, Ward's "literary work and social action intertwined in a way that makes the one an essential illumination of the other" (197). The Stephen sisters, however, seem to have ruled out the mingling of social or political work with aesthetic pursuits right from the start: just after they moved to Gordon Square late in 1904, Ward invited them to join in her "Passmore Edwards work," an invitation they were able to refuse, albeit politely, with what Virginia Stephen called "a valid excuse" (*Passionate* 220).

From yet another point on the map, Somerset participated extensively in the print culture of the time, becoming a well-known public figure. In addition to her temperance, suffrage, and social-purity activism, from 1892 to 1895 she owned and edited the successor to the *Women's Penny Paper*, founded by Henrietta Müller (b. 1846) in 1889; subsequently called the *Woman's Herald* starting in 1891, Somerset renamed it the *Woman's Signal* in 1894. The weekly paper was temporarily associated with the Liberal Party and always with feminist causes, while Somerset integrated temperance advocacy into its mix.[22] Beyond her editorial and journalistic work, she authored some short stories first serialized in the *Woman's Signal* and titled *Sketches in Black and White* (1896), issued by T. Fisher Unwin despite its receiving at least one unfavorable reader's report.[23] Taking her title from the opening line of Dante Gabriel Rossetti's "Soul's Beauty" in an indication of her Pre-Raphaelite leanings, she also published a novel, *Under the Arch* (1906). Characterized by Sowon S. Park as suffrage fiction, its preface describes its female protagonist, something of an avatar for Somerset herself, as "an imaginative girl much impressed by the sorrows of the people, who determines when her own happiness is shipwrecked to live for their good" ("Suffrage Fiction" 454; Somerset xiii).[24] She wrote poetry and stories for children, and many, many articles for the press on a large range of topics, including contraception: a piece called "The Welcome Child," published in the U.S. periodical *The Arena*, was summarized in her ally W. T. Stead's *Review of Reviews* under the title "Against Compulsory Motherhood" and characterized by Stutfield in "Tommyrotics" as "a cry of revolt" (836).[25] Owing to her close relationship to Willard, with whom she forged a transatlantic feminist network, she also had a huge following in the United States, where stories about her as well as her own essays frequently appeared in print. Indeed, so well-known and respected was Somerset that "when in 1907 the London *Evening News* . . . polled its readers on their choice for a woman prime minister," she "topped the list of 18 preferred candidates which included such illustrious names" as Fawcett and Hill (Niessen 231). Many years after her death, her first cousin twice removed, Quentin Bell, remarked that Somerset undertook her "reclamation of inebriate women . . . with so much good sense and good humour that she won the affection and admiration, not only of men of charity and good will, but even of the women she assisted" (1: 15).

This limited sampling of the deep and wide commitment on the part of two prior generations of Victorian women to philanthropic and/or political work that could take many different forms, including visiting, nursing, educating, and housing the poor, as well as writing about them, surely suggests the extension of "women's sphere" beyond the household—within limits, that is. "Some advocates of higher education for women did *not* support the vote at this stage," as Laurel Brake remarks, "nor did some women actively engaged in writing for the press, or doing organized and complex philanthropic work" ("Writing" 52). Most notably, Stephen and her sister-in-law Caroline as well as Hill and Ward all opposed the extension of the franchise to women. Although "suffragists and anti-suffragists continued to work together on other social issues," Somerset—a firm and ardent suffragist—developed relationships with women whose politics her cousin would not have supported, even though all arguably shared a maternalist-imperialist ethos (Lewis 6).

Sarah Grand, for example, frequently named Somerset as one of her closest allies in the 1890s. Describing its most prominent members in "The Man of the Moment" (1894), which defended the Pioneer Club against its masculinist detractors, she classified them as "women engaged in philanthropic pursuits, moral and religious"; "as well known for the most part both in public and private as the Archbishop of Canterbury," Grand's named associates include Isabel and Adeline, Willard, and Emily Massingberd (*Sex* 1: 53).[26] Related through her marriage to a Liberal M.P. to the reforming Bright family, Eva McLaren (b. 1852/3), to cite another example, worked both with Hill in Marylebone in the 1870s, perhaps rubbing shoulders with Julia Duckworth, and with Butler on repealing the C. D. Acts. Sister to Henrietta Müller, she served as vice president of the British Women's Temperance Association (BWTA) from 1894 to 1900 and "fully supported Somerset's successful, albeit divisive, attempt to steer the BWTA away from a narrow crusade against drink and towards a broad platform of social reform" (L. Walker). Thirty years later, in the foreword to the reissue of *The Heavenly Twins*, these same names reappear: Grand mentions "Eva McClaren [*sic*], . . . Mrs Massingberd, Lady Henry Somerset, . . . Mrs Oscar Wilde, and many more; all women of high character and great ability" (402). And ten years after that, in an interview with *The Vote*, the list of "particular colleagues" from the 1890s is again much the same: McLaren, Massingberd, Somerset, and the Viscountess Harberton (b. 1843), who founded the Rational Dress Society in 1880 (Priestley McCracken 323). With the exception of Grand herself, and by contrast with the Bloomsbury-based progressive feminist network of the 1880s mentioned in the introduction, all of these women were connected in some way to wealth or political power and/or moved in aristocratic circles. They held overlapping memberships in a range of societies and organizations. All were feminist activists, although they would have used neither word to describe themselves in the 1890s; moreover, while their advocacy was extensive, their feminism probably appears rather conservative to us today.

As for Fawcett, McLaren, Massingberd, and Grand, Somerset's political agenda encompassed a wide range of contemporary issues. In the 1890s, she simultaneously served on the executive of the Women's Liberal Federation; belonged to both the Central National Society for Woman's Suffrage and Butler's Ladies' National Association (LNA); and was a vice president of the National Vigilance Association (NVA). She became both president of the BWTA and vice president of the WWCTU, assuming the presidency of the latter after Willard's death in 1898 and holding it until 1906, when Rosalind Howard succeeded her (Niessen 222; Tyrrell, "Somerset"). Meeting Somerset and Willard together at Friday's Hill, then the country home of Hannah Whitall Smith (b. 1832), grandmother of Ray Strachey and Karin Stephen, Rothenstein found them so formidable that they "overawed me by the ethical and social ideals they preached" in their critique of both male privilege and economic inequality (1: 203).[27]

Under Willard's leadership and in collaboration with Somerset, the WWCTU evolved its "Do Everything" policy in the 1890s.[28] As Ruth Bordin notes, Willard "first used the term 'Do Everything' in her 1881 presidential address" to the American WCTU convention, by which she originally meant trying out a variety of "tactics" rather than achieving a number of goals; "the shift in emphasis"—intended to promote coalitions among individual reform movements—"was gradual," culminating in a speech that Willard delivered to the BWTA at Exeter Hall in 1893 (130, 198). Quite as ambitious as it sounds and criticized as overreaching by those who sought to keep the BWTA focused on temperance, the policy Willard and Somerset promoted aimed to leverage the combined power of single-issue organizations—whether devoted to temperance or suffrage, to ending prostitution or promoting rational dress—into a cohesive reform platform, increasingly moving away from the philanthropic to the more explicitly political.[29]

Becoming president in 1890 of the BWTA, which claimed "50,000 members by 1892," Somerset was already trying to "do everything" even before meeting Whitall Smith, who introduced her to Willard (Hollis 48). An avowed Christian socialist, she may (or may not) have joined the Fabian Society, as Willard did around 1893 (Gifford 377).[30] Somerset by then conceived of poverty as both cause and effect of working-class intemperance—even in the face of the fact that, as numerous critics within and beyond the BWTA delighted in pointing out, her holdings in London's Somers Town, just to the north of Bloomsbury, included a high number of leases to pubs.[31] The 9 January 1889 edition of the *PMG* included a report of her speech on "juvenile drinking in the East End" ("Juvenile" 6). She also "spoke at meetings, both on temperance and on [other] social questions, as far afield as South Wales," while in the aftermath of the Great Dock Strike of 1889, at a meeting held to encourage sweated women workers to unionize, she "shared a platform in the East End with John Burns," Tom Mann, H. H. Champion, and other labor leaders (Cole 56). Among them was Clementina Black, who had recently formed the Women's Trades Union Association in tandem with Burns, and was described by the *PMG* report of that meeting as "indefatigable" in her efforts to organize working women ("Trades" 6).

Although Ian Tyrrell asserts that she "was among the vanguard of those who embraced the cause of labor in the British women's movement," Somerset did not apparently maintain this immediate connection with labor activism any more than Black dedicated her time to temperance (*Woman's World* 243). Nevertheless, the conjunction of their names at this critical moment in organizing working-class women illustrates nonetheless how even feminists traveling in very different circles could and did join together across those differences to promote shared ends.[32] Moreover, this glimpse of a temporary and perhaps strategic alliance between Somerset and Black also suggests another point of contrast and comparison to Stephen, who responded directly to Black's published work in an unpublished essay from the early 1890s.[33] "The Dislike to Domestic Service" appeared in the March 1893 issue of *The Nineteenth Century* as Black's riposte to several earlier pieces in the same venue that had advocated "a certain rearrangement of the present conditions of domestic service . . . from the point of view of the employing householder"; she took up "the same question from the point of view of the servant" (622). Considering "Black's attempts to bring domestic labour to the foreground as labour," Ruth Livesey notes her belief that "material conditions had shaped a great gulf between 'ladies' like herself and working-class women, one that instinctively bred mistrust and misunderstanding" (*Socialism* 63, 64)—a point Woolf was also to make many years later in her controversial introduction to Margaret Llewelyn Davies's edited collection *Life as We Have Known It* (1931). Characterizing domestic work as "a system of total personal subservience," Black also raises the problem of servants being sexually coerced, abused, or assaulted by the men of the households in which they labored, somewhat euphemistically referring to their subjection to "temptations and insults": "It is unquestionable that the very large majority of girls who pass into Homes and Refuges have been servants" ("Dislike" 622, 623, 624).

Stephen's draft essay both contests the charge that "the life of a servant is so subservient" and counters that "to serve is no bad office, and . . . should be no degradation" (["Servant"] 248). "A woman who earns her bread in an honourable calling can hardly be considered as dependent in any sense but the one in which we happily all share, that we cannot do without our fellow creatures" (249), characteristically advocating "a recognition of mutual dependence" as a means of narrowing the class gap (Light 38). Upholding the ideal of "service" as blessing enables Stephen implicitly to connect maids and mistresses within a framework of interdependence. In words that resonate with the rhetoric of coverture, antisuffrage, and the resistance to Home Rule, she argues that as "our interests are united we can best help them by making the union stronger, not by separation" (["Servant"] 252).

Interestingly, however, Stephen does not directly refute what she terms the "far more serious charge . . . that homes and refuges are chiefly filled with girls from the servant class" (249). Rather, she points out that since such institutions "are as a rule supported by ladies," it is only "natural that the servants whom these ladies or their friends have employed should turn to them for help." "The poor factory girl," on the contrary, "has too often no such friend, and if she is also without a home hides her sorrow in the workhouse," another institution—one with which Stephen, as we know, was quite familiar—still largely run entirely by men, as few women could fulfill the elected role of poor law guardian until the property qualification for the office was removed in 1894 (S. King). In other words, Stephen finesses Black's underlying assertion—that domestic service makes working-class women especially vulnerable to "temptations and insults" from men, whether fellow servants or employers—by implying that working women are everywhere subject to men's sexual overtures; at least servants, she implies, would or should have a sympathetic mistress to whom they could turn. On a point that her daughter would later contest in her representation of "street love," Stephen calls it "unnecessary to dwell on the evils to a girl of having to walk night after night from her work" (*Pargiters* 50; ["Servant"] 249).[34] While Black emphasizes the class component of male sexual aggression, Stephen does not; moreover, she implicitly suggests that the antidote to sexual danger lies in strengthening the tie between female employers and female servants, rather than, say, in holding men accountable for their behavior, as so many of her contemporaries were doing at the time. And while Black is willing to name "the evils" working women face, albeit euphemistically, Stephen is not, refusing to participate in the "unprecedentedly frank public discussion of sexual matters, designed to purify family life and promote one standard of morality for men and women," that characterized so much of late-Victorian feminism (Bolt 132).

That is not to say, however, that Stephen did not recognize and deplore those "evils" even as she failed to name them: as Fawcett wrote in "Speech or Silence," published in the immediate aftermath of the "Maiden Tribute" scandal in 1885, "There are probably no men and very few women to whom the statements [regarding child prostitution] were really revelations" (329). Given Stephen's history of workhouse visiting, it seems more than likely that she would have come across a good deal of firsthand evidence of the "insults and temptations" to which working-class women and children were especially exposed. And given, too, that young Virginia Stephen or one of her siblings routinely accompanied Stella Duckworth on her London travels, as a way of "protecting" her from unwanted male attention, their mother obviously believed that women of the upper classes were also subject to such threats ("Sketch" 97). To some extent, Somerset might well have shared her cousin's skepticism about the possibility of ensuring women's sexual safety wherever they might work or live. In "The Welcome Child," for example, she argues that women suffer the consequences of unwanted pregnancy "not only in the garret and cellar, but in homes of opulence and ease. The unwritten tragedy of woman's life is *there*" (43; emphasis in the original). One might further speculate that Somerset would have wholly agreed with the claim, as Stephen put it in her essay on agnosticism among women, that "far from allowing that our work is lower or less important than [men's]," "we ought and do claim the same equality of morals" (["Agnostic"] 246–47). If spheres were (and ought to remain) separate for Stephen, then the phrase "equality of morals" sounds as if a shared ethical stance might yet cut across that separation. Writing in a religious idiom, Somerset expresses a very similar sentiment in an essay titled "Pure Women," in which she asserts that "the moral law is the same for man and for woman, and where it is a sin in woman, it is a sin in man" (9). But in Somerset's case, taking action toward securing women's safety was part of her broader political platform even if she, too, manifested in her practice an imperialist-maternalist stance that would extend "protection" only to some women and only on particular terms. For much of the social-purity work to which she dedicated her time in the 1890s brought Somerset into conflict with those who, like Butler, sought not to regulate and thus in their view to sanction "vice," but to extend legal protections and rights to those women whose life circumstances made them vulnerable to male predation. Given that difference, however, we might also say that the imperializing rhetoric of women's mission still undergirds the approaches of Stephen and Somerset and their elder contemporary Butler.

Somerset and Social-Purity Activism

The tenor of Somerset's feminist activities can best be grasped in relation to three particular controversies of the 1890s, all of which can be understood within the framework of the social-purity advocacy that Woolf was to reject as a basis for sociopolitical change. To "do everything" meant objecting to the sexual double standard across a range of discursive sites: my examples here include contesting the commodification of women's bodies on stage, challenging sexual violence in an international context, and intervening in debates over prostitution in the empire. And Somerset also urged these activities on others, as Olwen Claire Niessen reports: "Her address to the 1896 NBWTA annual council," for example, "had focussed upon the purity question, attacking the sexual double standard of morality, promoting the ethic of chastity for both men and women, and urging her membership to increase their participation in rescue work among prostitutes" (190–91). All of these advocacy efforts were predicated on problematic assumptions about race, class, sexuality, and gender that would continue to shape the women's movement—and Woolf's view of it—into the next generation.

In what Tracy C. Davis calls a "campaign against the official complicity toward public manifestations of female sexuality in middle-class music halls," Somerset initiated in the summer of 1894 the movement to suspend the liquor license of one of London's variety theaters for staging "living pictures," or *tableaux vivants*, as part of the NVA's effort to "purify" the public sphere (42). She used the *Woman's Signal* as her chief medium for contesting the Palace Theatre of Varieties' live staging of artworks, drawn "almost exclusively from paintings by Royal Academy artists," in which female models wore "suggestive flesh-coloured tights" to approximate the nude (Faulk 158; Somerset, "Living" 65; qtd. 168). "Suggestive" as simulated female nakedness might have been to male theatergoers, Somerset argues the case less on that ground than as an "intervention" aimed at rescuing the female performers from "ruin and degradation": "We have, in letting women make public merchandise of the beauty of their bodies, surpassed even the Oriental standard for female degradation" ("Living" 65; qtd. in Faulk 169, 170). Alongside Laura Ormiston Chant (b. 1848), who undertook a better-known protest with Somerset's support against the visible presence of prostitution at the Empire Theatre of Varieties, Somerset, too, "championed an alternative empire, a republican Anglo-American version of empire to be moralized by female activists" (Walkowitz, *Nights* 48).[35] Both elite male sexual conduct and female sexual display were to be curbed and curtailed on grounds of indecency in the interests of raising the metropolis from "the Oriental standard" to which it had regressed. But a letter to the *Dundee Evening Telegraph*, appearing under the signature of "A Living Picture Girl," made a most salient rejoinder to Somerset's most explicit point: "Lady Somerset no doubt means well, but should her appeal succeed and those pictures cease to be produced, many would have to return to employment yielding a pittance of 10s or so a week, with the result that Lady S. [*sic*] would simply have hastened the catastrophe she wished to avoid"—the economic "ruin and degradation" of the performers ("Living" 2).

Inevitably, Somerset's positions were also challenged by a host of male luminaries, including George Bernard Shaw in *The Saturday Review* and Arthur Symons in a forum published by *The New Review*; they mainly argued their cases along aesthetic lines. Yet Somerset also objected on that ground to a *tableau vivant* based on one of Jean-Léon Gérôme's "Moorish Bath" paintings, which was subsequently eliminated from the Palace's nightly fare (Faulk 158).[36] One of several extant Gérôme canvases with this title depicts in the foreground the body of a naked woman with olive-toned skin, seen from behind and illuminated by a light source from above; in the unlit background, a crouching black woman, her hands whitened by the palm oil she is mixing as a body wash, is further shrouded by a headscarf that obscures her face. The painting represents that "Oriental standard" via racialized relations of dominance and submission between mistress and servant established by visual means. Interestingly, Somerset invited readers of the *Woman's Signal* to compare this "living picture" with a painting by a Pattle family intimate not apparently selected for *tableau-vivant* treatment, G. F. Watts's "Psyche" (1880). By contrast with Gérôme's composition, the goddess stands alone, a full-frontal nude with eyes modestly cast down, her blue-veined ivory skin luminously glowing. If Watts's painting is, in Somerset's view, "a glorification of womanly form," with "genius and reverence" for that form "confessed in every touch," then the *tableau* based on Gérôme's canvas—which by contrast with the Watts painting could inspire "unruly thoughts"—presumably demonstrates the debasement of both women's bodies ("Living" 65).

Given Gérôme's predilection for harem scenes, Somerset may also be alluding to without fully articulating her discomfort with the social relations of non-Western life as she understood them, an ethnocentric perspective that emerges as well through her participation in another movement of the time. Reviving British cultural memory of the "Bulgarian atrocities" of the 1870s, the massacres that began in 1894 during the reign of the Turkish ruler Abdul Hamid II inspired strong protests and concerted action among a range of reformers and humanitarians on behalf of Armenian refugees—not Albanian ones, as in Clarissa Dalloway's infamous conflation of the two (*Mrs. Dalloway* 107–8).[37] Indeed, when poor weather cut short their planned cycling trip through Normandy in the late summer of 1896, Somerset and Willard traveled to Marseilles to organize relief efforts for refugees in temporary accommodations, once again using the *Woman's Signal* as a platform for fundraising and organizing (R. Strachey, *Frances* 294–95; Niessen 162–63). As historian Michelle Elizabeth Tusan establishes, "Feminist perspectives on the Eastern question appeared in feature articles, book reviews, and biographical sketches of women activists in all of the major women's papers"; she calls Somerset "a key voice in this campaign" who intervened by using her position to speak for the Christian Armenian women she represented as subjected to religious persecution and sexual exploitation under Muslim rule (*Smyrna's Ashes* 36). In a review of Frederick Davies Greene's *The Armenian Crisis in Turkey* (1895), Somerset makes her overarching position clear, calling "the crescent and the cross" entirely opposed forces: "the one, the radiant beacon light that leads men on to higher civilization and nobler humanity; the other, steeped in blood, represents the degradation of women, and therefore the degradation of mankind" ("Books" 297). This position had a good deal of support among feminists of the time: while Ward and other apologists for the continued disenfranchisement of Englishwomen "argued that masculine rule was almost a condition of Britain's retention of India," for example, "for she would otherwise forfeit the respect of the native population," as Martin Pugh avers, "suffragists repeatedly urged that Islamic societies were failing to progress precisely because of their reluctance to free their women from seclusion, ignorance, and subjection" (54).

Somerset's rhetoric on the question is thus infused with an imperialist-maternalist ethos. As the only woman to address a May 1895 meeting chaired by the Duke of Argyll protesting both the massacres and the failure of the British government to act, she was reported as representing herself as speaking on behalf of both oppressed and empowered Christian women everywhere: "It was fitting that an English woman's voice should be lifted up for the Armenian women in this great circle of England's power, culture, and opportunity. A hundred thousand women wearing the White Ribbon—emblem of purity and peace—were invisibly present with her as she stood there trying to represent their holy indignation and burning love for their sisters in the clutch of the harem-despot at Constantinople" ("Massacres"). On the one hand, in imploring her Anglo-American constituency "to forge a sisterhood with rape victims," Somerset aimed to mobilize a transnational feminist network that would transcend cultural differences to speak with one voice (Tusan, *Smyrna's Ashes* 38). On the other, however, she invoked stereotypical assumptions about "Christian women being killed and raped by Moslem 'infidels'"—also presumed to be polygamists—that entailed the hierarchical privileging of some women over others (Niessen 162). With Willard, too, lamenting the destruction of "Christian families" by the "barbarous Turk," "both women were convinced that Armenians were being victimized primarily because of their religion and their defence of feminine purity and monogamous marriage within an hostile Moslem environment" (Gifford 417; Niessen 162).

Publicly circulating orientalist stereotypes of unbridled male lust, moreover, Somerset also privately drew on the logic of eugenics and invoked the horrors of race mixture, telling Willard by letter that "the children that are being born now, half Turk and half Armenian, . . . are so awful that a race will be created that ought to be destroyed before it is born. Idiots, maimed, and otherwise doomed children" (qtd. in Niessen 165). As in the contemporary conflict between Willard and the U.S. antilynching activist Ida B. Wells, white women's anxieties about interracial sex and its miscegenous outcomes generated a rhetoric of racial purity that Somerset, like many others, would defend on "scientific" grounds.[38] Casting the Turks as purveyors of "uncivilized" marital practices such as polygamy, she draws on the eugenicist thinking and fears of racial degeneration that preoccupied so many New Women, including Grand, at the end of the century. Even more immediately, the maternalist-imperialist position was taken up by younger feminist activists at home, including Alys Russell (b. 1867; née Pearsall Smith), a daughter of Hannah Whitall Smith, aunt of Ray Costelloe, and friend of Virginia Stephen, who worked closely with Somerset in the new century on issues of infant welfare and maternity. An essay on "The Ghent School of Mothers" in *The Nineteenth Century and After*, founded on a Flemish model that provided a basis for a nursery in St. Pancras, describes this training enterprise for working-class mothers as intended, significantly, to eliminate "those causes and conditions which in the long run determine a serious degeneration of race" ("Ghent" 975). Although one historian concludes that Russell's "ideas and activities were radical," another situates this work as part of the "widespread movement in Britain and its colonies to improve scientifically the conditions of motherhood as part of the program of social imperialism and the cult of national efficiency" (Davin 39; Tyrrell, *Woman's World* 248). Some of these ideas would re-emerge in Woolf's own conflicted relationship to eugenic thought.[39]

Perhaps the most contentious and best-known instance of Somerset's social-purity stance, inflected by eugenics, concerns the support she afforded to the revival of the C. D. Acts in India in the late 1890s.[40] After their repeal in England in 1886, Josephine Butler and her LNA allies turned their attention to their operation on the subcontinent. They formed the British Committee for the Abolition of the State Regulation of Vice in India, with Butler working in concert with the leadership of the WWCTU as superintendent of its Social Purity Department, founded in 1885 in the aftermath of the "Maiden Tribute," from 1891 to 1897 (Niessen 194). (Indeed, for a time, Butler, Somerset, and

Willard even shared the same address, all writing letters or journal entries in 1893 from the same location—perhaps a temperance hotel for women—at 57 Gordon Square.)[41] At first, as a member of the executive committee of the LNA, Somerset spoke out against regulation both in addressing the British section of the WWCTU in July 1892 and at the annual council of the Women's Liberal Federation in 1893 (Niessen 192, 193). She drew on the firsthand reports of WWCTU missionaries Elizabeth Andrew and Dr. Katherine Bushnell, subsequently published under the provocative title *The Queen's Daughters in India* (1898), which "revealed not only that regulation was entrenched but also that Indian prostitutes" were abused, deceived, and silenced by military authorities (Niessen 192).

Butler's initial alliance with Somerset and Willard over this shared interest in repeal, however, broke down under a number of factors, which Niessen terms "ideological differences and personal rivalries" (194). As divergent opinions inflected by imperialist biases emerged on the question of regulation in India, with some European WWCTU affiliates suggesting a compromise position, Butler began commenting to correspondents on "the impossibility of working all these women-questions together" (Letter to Mrs. Clark). She expressed her stance in somewhat condescending terms: "The people need one question at a time put before them & this great bouquet of different questions brought together by the WWCTU must rather confuse them I think" (Letter to Miss Forsaith [11 July 1895]). For her part, Butler maintained that the WWCTU leaders lacked sufficient knowledge of and commitment to ending regulation, and she challenged their whole emphasis on "purity." In a letter of 4 April 1895 meant for wide circulation, she asserted that "the Purity workers of Lady H Somerset's WWCTU are going sadly wrong on account of ignorance of the abolitionist question" (Letter to "Dear Friends"). Later, she lamented, "Our cause has not gained, but is suffering sadly from the union with it of the WWCTU" (Letter to the Miss Priestmans [3 May 1895]).

Although one might say that Butler had herself been a major instigator of the turn to social purity within feminist advocacy, in that she was one of the behind-the-scenes inspirations for the "Maiden Tribute" campaign, she insisted on her own movement's difference from it. "The cause for wh[ich] I have worked," she wrote to her son Stanley, "is *not* a 'Purity Crusade' nor a Morality Crusade. These crusades are needed; but they are *educational*, slow & gradual, beginning in the nursery & the schoolroom; our Federation movement is quite another thing. *It was and is a revolt against & an aggressive opposition to a gross political & illegal tyranny.* Lady Henry Somerset & her following never see this, & go on talking eloquently but vaguely about Purity, which is *not* a call to battle" (Letter to Stanley Butler [1896]; emphasis in the original).

Moreover, Butler ultimately resisted the assimilation of the goals of the anti-regulation struggle with those of the temperance movement, denying the claim that they were "twin movements. On the moral side they are; but they are very different in one essential element. The state never *created a slave class* to minister to drunkards. The state never deprived *women* of their civil and natural rights in order that *men* might get drunk more comfortably" (Letter to Miss Forsaith [27 October 1896]; emphasis in the original). Although the historian Antoinette Burton claims that "maintaining distinctions between repeal work and other kinds of reform intervention remained a priority for Butler," Tyrrell takes issue with Butler's assertions here, noting that "the tangled narrative of Butler's conflict with Somerset in the 1890s does not support the straightforward polarization of abolitionist and social purity sentiment that Butler sought to convey," in that Somerset's ultimate withdrawal of her proposals "represented the work of a coalition of social purity and antiregulation forces that persisted well beyond 1885" (Burton 142; Tyrrell, *Woman's World* 210).

While Butler took a hard line, Somerset came to support what she referred to as a "compromise," predicated on the ambiguous notion of protection. She was approached through an intermediary by Lord George Hamilton, secretary of state for India, for her views on his plan to reinstate a modified form of regulation in light of highly contested reports that "more than half of British soldiers on the subcontinent were now infected with venereal disease" (Niessen 196; cf. Fitzpatrick 197–98). Somerset's response, summarized in the *Times* on 21 April 1897 under the title "The Health of the Army in India," suggested some modifications.[42] She accepted the perceived need for some form of regulation, but insisted it ought to apply to English men and Indian women alike: "Soldiers should be strictly supervised and subjected to the same medical examination as the women" (Niessen 199). Casting her concern for the health not only of the empire's fighting men and "the women of India"—"who already bear alone the brunt of an iniquity wrought by two"—but also for English soldiers' current or future wives and children, Somerset repeatedly emphasized that her support for regulation was based on "rational and scientific principle" ("Health" 484). Periodic examination of both men and women was the only "scientifically defensible" method of controlling the spread of the disease and thus of protecting "the unborn from a devastating curse" (482, 484). Considered in this light, her support for access to contraception seems a good deal less enlightened than Stead represented it as being. She must certainly have agreed, then, with Lord Hamilton's claim that "the health of the civil population and of subsequent generations in this country is seriously imperiled by . . . men constitutionally diseased" ("Copy" 453).

Somerset's support for regulation in this modified form created a firestorm in the feminist movement. Though it won the approval of Ward, Nightingale, and Fawcett's sister Dr. Elizabeth Garrett Anderson (who had always supported the C. D. Acts), all of whom signed a memorial in favor of Somerset's position along with a number of other high-profile, mainly aristocratic women, it outraged most of her other allies. Frances Willard did not share her view, which Somerset ultimately retracted just before Willard's death in February 1898; Florence Fenwick Miller (b. 1854) trashed her stance in the *Woman's Signal*, of which she had taken ownership in 1895, following a series of disputes with Somerset over the role of temperance news in the paper once Fenwick Miller became its editor (VanArsdel 187–89, 191–98). And in April 1897, Butler argued privately of Somerset's plan—a "pitiful hybrid monster"—that while "she claims complete equality in the treatment of men & women sinners, [she] arrives by this means at proposing the most rigorous & perfect State regulations of harlotry & fornication that I have ever yet seen proposed" (Jordan and Sharp 5: 490). Butler went on to suggest in a number of letters to her closest allies that Somerset had been possessed by the devil, also telling Willard that she "suspected that [Somerset's] mind had been poisoned by certain men,— men experienced and deeply skilled in the art of poisoning" (Letter [29 November 1897]).

At least part of the dispute between Butler and Somerset, I submit, rested on the generational differences between them. Butler publicly assessed Somerset's stance as a matter of aristocratic bias and class ignorance, writing in the pamphlet "Truth before Everything" (1897), "Men and women alike in the most exalted social classes frequently possess extraordinarily little knowledge of the conditions of life among the poor" (339). But she also justifiably argued that because Somerset "never took part in the old agitation" against the C. D. Acts in England, she "comes fresh into the field, when the old struggle in this country has been so largely forgotten" ("Reply" 527). When those feminists who constituted a second wave of activism at century's end departed from the ways and means of "the old struggle," Butler criticized both their lack of historical memory and the diffuse brief of their campaign. Different sets of tactics between those who kept a single-issue focus and those who aimed to "do everything" might then be read as a generational shift predicated in part on the younger generation's lack of knowledge of even the immediate past, or on a pervasive impatience (during the 1890s in particular) with the "slow & gradual" changes that the introduction of a higher moral standard through early education would only eventually (and only in theory) bring about. Yet, that Somerset, like Grand, owed something to Butler's model of advocacy—

and especially to her brave and canny use of both print and platform—even as she departed from it ideologically suggests that tensions and conflicts over the tactics, rhetoric, and scope of feminist activism at the end of the century have multiple dimensions, including a generational one that would have a shaping effect on subsequent generations as well. That Woolf so highly praised Butler for her egalitarian and libertarian stance—while paying only limited attention to Somerset—no doubt reflects the shifting fortunes of feminism in the postsuffrage period between the two wars. But it also attests to how conflicts between and among feminist generations—arising when a later generation takes up that "old struggle" against a "conspiracy of silence" in a new idiom and with new ends in view—not only lead to gaps in our understanding of such movements, gaps that may never be entirely filled, but also fracture feminist solidarities.

For her part, Somerset defended her compromise along a number of different lines. A letter to Willard of 29 March 1897, on the "prostitute caste" in India, took up a cultural relativist position, suggesting a "difficulty" in "how to deal with those to whom what is sin to us is no sin." Invoking some allies within the antiregulation movement as supporting a new departure in the campaign, she subsequently claimed to Willard that "all the more level-headed see that absolute blank opposition is no way of dealing with it, and that the only way to secure justice to the men and to the women is to be open-minded and fair, and to give those who are trying to do right full mead of praise"; "almost all the Repeal people except a few of the ultras see it in the same light," whereas "Josephine Butler is too old to take in any new situation" (Letter [2 April 1897]). Here Somerset gestures at generational differences, while also defending her position against Butler's "very fierce attacks upon me" as a maternalist intervention. "Of course I am very sorry to differ from a woman whom I respect so much; but every day I live I see more clearly that there is another point of view," she told Willard; "the fact is, the policy of ignoring is impossible; and while I believe in the rights of men and women I also believe in the rights of the unborn," here alluding to what Tyrrell terms "the embarrassing issue of racial contact between Europeans and Indians" (Letter [18 June 1897]; *Woman's World* 199). Perhaps influenced by the contemporary discussion of hereditary vice popularized by Grand and other such second-generation New Woman novelists as Dowie in *Gallia* and Emma Brooke in *A Superfluous Woman* (1894), Somerset aimed both to attack the double standard of sexual morality and to prevent the transmission of venereal disease to children of the next generation, on whose "frail, tiny forms lay heavily the heritage of the fathers. The beaten brows, the suffering eyes, expiated in themselves the crimes and debauchery of generations" (Brooke 270–71). In advocating racial as well as social purity and championing feminist eugenics in the interests of reproductive futurity, Somerset's stance exemplifies the mixed legacy of the late-century women's movement for those who would follow.

The imperialist bias of much feminist advocacy in the 1890s and beyond makes itself felt in Woolf's fiction most crucially not in *To the Lighthouse*, but in *Mrs. Dalloway*. Clarissa's confusion over Albania and Armenia—which Trudi Tate calls an "obvious, even heavy-handed, satiric moment in the novel"— signifies her complicity with the value system, shot through with imperialist practices and beliefs, that the novel unambiguously criticizes (147).[43] "Worshipping proportion, Sir William [Bradshaw] not only prospered himself but made England prosper, secluded her lunatics, forbade childbirth, penalised despair": he undertakes, in other words, the eugenic project closely identified with the medical establishment, and especially with the "rational and scientific principle" on which Somerset had based her own conclusions about the threat to the nation's health posed by the unchecked sexual indulgence of Britain's military men (*Mrs. Dalloway* 89).[44]

Woolf's point of view on the coercive forces *Mrs. Dalloway* associates not just with medical men but also with the philanthropic "mission" has a long genealogy, with a strongly gendered component. Both Virginia and Vanessa felt an intense personal dislike for those of their female relations who engaged in "good works," especially when allied with Christian zeal, as in the efforts of Rosamond (b. 1868) and particularly Dorothea Stephen (b. 1871) to convert their godless younger cousins. Hostility to and/or amusement at said efforts (and, later, bemusement at Dorothea's disapproval of Vanessa's lifestyle)[45] permeated the whole family: as Leslie told Thoby Stephen by letter, "Dorothea is writing to Ginia trying to persuade her to be a Christian. She does not seem to have a very promising disciple thus far: or I should have to intervene" (17 January 1903). Six months later, a letter from Virginia Stephen to Violet Dickinson claims that this same "fat religious cousin . . . is trying to prove that certain sections of her soul are alive and afloat while ours are 'atrophied'" (*Letters* 1: 85). The pressure to conform she associated with these female relations "left Woolf with a lifelong distaste for any kind of coercion" and strongly implies her ongoing hostility to missionary appeals, or what she usually called preaching (McNees, "Woolf's Imperialist" 63). And the Stephen sisters scorned the proselytizing manner even when it lacked the Christian element. Reporting to Dickinson on a visit to cousin Herbert Fisher at Oxford in 1905, Virginia describes how his wife Lettice (b. 1875) "expounded her theories, always proving them in her own person—how, for instance, the ideal life is the married life—the life of a worker—she teaches—the life of a philanthropist—she runs a slum. We had to confess that our lives were *not* after this pattern. Why is virtue so unattractive[?]" (*Letters* 1: 193; emphasis in the original).[46] But her antipathy to the "unattractive" went still deeper. Corresponding in 1931 with her new friend Ethel Smyth, Woolf acknowledges that while "practical evils must be put to the sword . . . votes, wages, peace and so on," what she "can't abide is the man who wishes to convert other men's minds," referring to how their elder Stephen cousins, sounding a bit like Miss Kilman of *Mrs. Dalloway*, "rasped and agonised us as children by perpetual attempts at conversion" (*Letters* 4: 333).

An extract from a long diary entry of 1919 on the two-volume biography of Canon Samuel Barnett, written by his wife Henrietta—in which Woolf dwells on the "peculiar repulsiveness of those who dabble their fingers self approvingly in the stuff of others' souls," "plunged to the elbow" in blood and "red handed if ever philanthropists were"—makes the point most forcefully: "Has this coarseness of grain any necessary connection with labour for one's kind? . . . More & more I come to loathe any dominion of one over another; any leadership, any imposition of the will" (*Diary* 1: 255–56). Such a stance would seem to translate more or less directly into the fierce resistance to the "imposition of the will," as practiced on a global scale, famously evinced by *Mrs. Dalloway*'s narrator:

> Proportion has a sister, less smiling, more formidable, a Goddess even now engaged—in the heat and sands of India, the mud and swamp of Africa, the purlieus of London, wherever in short the climate or the devil tempts men to fall from the true belief which is her own—is even now engaged in dashing down shrines, smashing idols, and setting up in their place her own stern countenance. Conversion is her name and she feasts on the wills of the weakly, loving to impress, to impose, adoring her own features stamped on the face of the populace. At Hyde Park Corner on a tub she stands preaching; shrouds herself in white and walks penitentially disguised as brotherly love through factories and parliaments; offers help, but desires power . . . though concealed, as she mostly is, under some plausible disguise; some venerable name; love, duty, self-sacrifice. (90)

Glossing the psychology and behavior of characters as diverse as Bradshaw, Miss Kilman, and Lady Bruton, Woolf's narrator here identifies the impulses underlying a sense of "mission" with the desire for power over others, articulating deep hostility to those that would violate both the integrity of the body and "the privacy of the soul" (113). "Lov[ing] blood better than brick," Conversion "feasts most subtly on the human will," counting another range of

characters—Lady Bradshaw, Septimus Warren Smith, and even Clarissa Dalloway herself—among her prey (90).

Here Woolf fashions the object of perhaps the most memorable and scath-
ing critique anywhere in her fiction as a shape-shifter: smiling and sinister,
saintly and stern, "concealed . . . under some plausible disguise" of virtue
wherever she appears, whether in the outposts of empire, urban slums, "factories and parliaments," or Hyde Park's Speakers' Corner, once home to the
Tyburn gallows. Given its ubiquity and plasticity, this pointedly feminized
"sister" synthesizes a range of disparate but clearly related instances of domination into a single, totalizing image that links the empire abroad to the empire at home in the form of the "social system . . . at work, at its most intense,"
that *Mrs. Dalloway* anatomizes (*Diary* 2: 248). Within this analysis, Conversion
"offers help"—to the poor, for instance—only because she "desires power." Regarded from this point of view, it would indeed seem that "labour for one's
kind" is necessarily self-seeking, masked in the guise of altruism.

Strikingly, the writer who everywhere else resists "purpose" and abhors
"preaching" verges very closely on both in explicitly indicting imperial and domestic rule through her creation of allegorical figures that are gendered feminine. Although we might read their unmasking as part of a feminist critique
of empire, we might also interpret them as part of Woolf's critique of feminism as she knew it. If personifying conversion in female form may be just a
matter of literary convention, then it may still also imply a rejection of the
imperialist-maternalist "mission" embodied in a figure such as Somerset, as
part of Woolf's movement away from the tenuous and tentative identification
with feminist advocacy that we can glimpse in the first letter to Janet Case of
1910 quoted above, or from her often-quoted assertion in 1916 that she became "steadily more feminist" by reading about the war—that "preposterous
masculine fiction"—every morning in the *Times* (*Letters* 2: 76). In the 17 October 1924 diary entry in which she belatedly records that she has completed
Mrs. Dalloway, Woolf refers to the coming election as "the usual yearly school-
boys [*sic*] wrangle," preparing for the "dose of lies" she will encounter in the
daily newspaper: "If I were still a feminist," she writes, "I would make capital
out of the wrangle. But I have travelled on" (*Diary* 2: 318). Yet, as Zwerdling
writes of the direction she took after the "culminating achievement" of *The
Waves* (1931), "to go on she would have to go back": in the genealogical project of rereading and rewriting women's history that Woolf undertook in the
last decade of her life and career, traveling on would thus require returning to
the past (*Virginia Woolf* 12).

Somerset, Symonds, Stephen, and Sexuality

Like Evadne Frayling and Edith Beale, Isabel Somerset paid a price, though not as high, for her innocence and ignorance. "Accused by his wife of sodomitical crimes" in her petition for custody of their only child, Lord Henry was a younger son of the Duke of Beaufort as well as "an MP, comptroller of the Queen's household, and protégé of Prime Minister Disraeli"; he was also an older brother of that better-known Somerset, Lord Arthur, who would become a key figure in the Cleveland Street affair of 1889 (Kaye 29).[1] According to the available evidence, Lord Henry had engaged in a string of affairs with other men, including one of Julia and Isabel's first cousins, Walter Dalrymple, son of their aunt Sophia (R. Black 23; Kaye 18; Niessen 40–43). This last detail perhaps added some heat to the "family rows" surrounding the end of the Somerset marriage, to which Leslie Stephen alluded almost twenty years after the fact in his *Mausoleum Book*, where he mentions the "terrible scandal" in veiled tones and calls Lord Henry a "blackguard" (64). In reviewing Kathleen Fitzpatrick's biography of Isabel Somerset nearly thirty years after that, Woolf clearly indicates her awareness of the backstory of this long-ago incident. Archly quoting Fitzpatrick in "The Chinese Shoe," she describes Lord Henry as guilty "of a crime 'that was only mentioned in the Bible,'" implying both a behind-the-times prudishness on the part of the biographer and her own knowingness (Fitzpatrick 115; qtd. in *Essays* 3: 391).

Yet Woolf also notes that Somerset's disclosure of her husband's sodomy led her to be "cut by a large section of society" (391). Having belatedly realized that Lord Henry had married her for money rather than love, she had not only ended her marriage but also revealed some of its details: in an unusually public step, apparently taken at the urging of her mother, Isabel secured both a legal separation and primary custody of her son, thus exposing the Somerset family and her own to a degree of public scrutiny. Her "crime" thus lay in publicizing rather than silently sanctioning her husband's sexual practices. By rupturing the code of silence women were supposed to maintain about men's sexual lives, Somerset's act anticipated the reputation she subsequently earned for her political activities: she became, in the words of Margaret Cole, a "traitor to her class" (56). But not to every member of her extended family. Julia Duckworth chaperoned Isabel Somerset for several fraught days early in February 1878, accompanying her back to the marital home from which she had precipitously fled with her child, with an eye not only to propriety but also to strengthening her cousin's claims to custody (Niessen 58).[2]

Whatever else the Stephens may have thought of Lord Henry's behavior and his wife's decisions, the long-standing relationship between the cousins seems to have remained relatively intact. With Julia having attended Isabel's coming-out ball early in 1870, just before her first husband's death, "Julia's cousins," especially Isabel and Adeline, "were also part of her world of widowhood" (Fitzpatrick 85; Rudikoff 150). The Stephens spent their honeymoon at Eastnor Castle, a few months after the scandal broke. Later on, Julia Stephen "often visited her aunt" Virginia there, though "Leslie declined to accompany her"; but they nonetheless accepted Adeline's loan of her house at Chenies, thirty miles or so from London, to recuperate after Julia's mother Mia's death in 1892 (Rudikoff 150; *Mausoleum* 75). Even after Julia Stephen died in 1895, the family connection remained active: Stella Duckworth's 1896 pocket diary records a trip with Gerald "to get a wedding present for Somey," Isabel's son; the next year, she reported to Susan Lushington that "Cousin Isabel has offered us Reigate" for her honeymoon with Jack Hills "& we have half-accepted," though they ultimately made other plans (Letter [n.d.]). Although the political differences between the cousins were considerable, Isabel Somerset nonetheless remained part of Julia Stephen's family.

It seems fair to assume that Woolf, given her adult friendships and experiences, would have shared neither her father's shock at this "terrible scandal" nor Isabel Somerset's anxiety about the potential consequences of her husband's having access to their child. She would have probably perceived the response to the end of the Somerset marriage as an instance of homophobic panic on the part of her immediate and extended family that was congruent with their times. But considering the stance of another member of the Stephen-Duckworth circle might yield a different view. Art historian, poet, apologist for same-sex desire, as well as a professional colleague and friend of Leslie Stephen, John Addington Symonds was acquainted with both Lord Henry and Lord Arthur, each of whom left England for Italy in the aftermath of their respective scandals. When Benjamin Jowett called the elder brother "an unmentionable rascal," as Symonds reported in a letter to Edmund Gosse written at the height of the Cleveland Street affair, Symonds reproved Jowett, telling him that "he ought to be more tolerant" (Younger 3). Would he have said the same to, or of, Leslie Stephen?

As Joseph Bristow has established, Stephen's *Mausoleum Book* opens with an ambivalent allusion to his reading of Horatio Brown's 1895 biography of Symonds; published just at the moment of the Wilde trials, it was based on Symonds's candid memoir, itself not published in full until 2016 (Bristow 127–31). Perhaps not incidentally, there is a snapshot of Brown at St. Ives, dated 1892, in one of Leslie Stephen's photograph albums, where he appears with key members of the Duckworth-Stephen family, including young Virginia herself ("Stephen-Duckworth"). A letter to Gosse from Symonds establishes that the latter also visited the Stephens in Cornwall in September of that year, and without any other discernible links between Brown and Leslie Stephen, we can only assume that Brown was there because Symonds was there (*Letters* 3: 796). Leslie Stephen repaid this particular visit from Symonds by staying with him and his family at Davos in February 1893, just two months before Symonds died in Venice (812). Indeed, Stephen had visited the Symonds family in Switzerland for the better part of a decade, even after he gave up mountaineering, with Julia Stephen sometimes accompanying her husband; several of the Symonds daughters made long stays with the Stephens in London, giving rise to their close friendship with Madge Symonds, one of the models for Sally Seton in *Mrs. Dalloway*, who later married Julia Stephen's nephew, Will Vaughan.[3] All of Symonds's daughters "seem to have been well aware of their father's homosexuality" and so, too, presumably, of his discursive campaign to decriminalize sex between men in the wake of the passage of the Criminal Law Amendment Act in 1885 (Fowler 201). This legislation, introduced by the MP Henry Labouchère and enacted to raise the age of sexual consent from 13 to 16, included the infamous section 11, which penalized sex between men as "gross indecency." "It is scarcely plausible," then, that Symonds's sexuality was a secret from his friend (Broughton 18). Wouldn't Stephen have extended to Symonds, though not to the "blackguard" Lord Henry, the tolerance for which his friend would have pleaded in vain from an antagonist to Greek love such as the Oxford don Jowett?

As both Bristow and Trev Lynn Broughton have noted, Stephen's allusion to Brown's biography casts it as the secret history of an "inner life" that provides a powerful counter-example for the current writer: he described the biography in exactly the terms Brown had provided, calling it "virtually an autobiography" and "an internal history," although sanitized and spiritualized for public consumption (*Mausoleum* 4). While Symonds's "internal history" is writ large, Stephen's own will remain private, buried with him in "the grave" (4). The sort of self-disclosure in which Symonds engaged—even the bowdlerized Symonds of the biography—appears to have struck Stephen as excessive. As Bristow speculates, Symonds's candor, even in muted form, "unsettled a much-needed silence about male sexuality" that Stephen sought to preserve (131). "Some struggles," Woolf might have observed, would be better left unspoken and unwritten from her father's point of view (*Mausoleum* 4).

But the tolerance Symonds sought from Jowett—and perhaps received from Stephen—he also sought, much more importantly, from the state. If indeed "the general interdiction of candid discussion of sexual matters," as Morris B. Kaplan notes, "coexisted with considerable tolerance in some reaches of 'society,'" the Labouchère clause in the 1885 legislation made the actual, tangible limits of that tolerance crystal clear (192). And such limits would remain in place for many years to come, despite some Bloomsbury assumptions about the changing times. Corresponding with Symonds's daughter Katharine Furse in 1939, who was seeking access to her father's manuscript autobiography at the London Library, Woolf congratulates Furse on her projected effort at "telling the truth about your father" and implicitly commends their generation for its candor and frankness about sex (Fowler 210).[4] Yet her confidence in greater freedom of expression among the moderns is simply not sustainable. At the beginning of the decade, Woolf's own project of narrating "the sexual life of women" had foundered, while just a few weeks after the letter to Furse cited above, Woolf wrote, in a somewhat different context, "all books now seem to me surrounded by a circle of invisible censors" (*Diary* 4: 6; 5: 229).[5] Whatever freedoms of private expression the moderns had achieved, the political status of men who had sex with men remained unchanged, in the face of both Isabel Somerset's speech and Leslie Stephen's silence.

CHAPTER 5

"A Different Ideal"

Representing the Public Woman

> It seems to me more & more clear that the only
> honest people are the artists, & that these social
> reformers & philanthropists get so out of hand, &
> harbour so many discreditable desires under the
> disguise of loving their kind, that in the end there's
> more to find fault with in them than in us. But if I
> were one of them?
>
> —Virginia Woolf, *Diary*, 19 July 1919

> No passion is stronger in the breast of man than the
> desire to make others believe as he believes.
>
> —*Orlando*, 1928

> My difficulty always was the political attitude to
> human beings—that some were always right, others
> always wrong. I did hate that. And do still. But as you
> say one gets more sensible.
>
> —Virginia Woolf to Margaret Llewelyn Davies,
> 25 July 1930

In his third volume of autobiography, *Beginning Again* (1963), Leonard Woolf describes how in his first year of marriage he was "induced . . . to join" a Care Committee of the Charity Organization Society (COS) branch in Hoxton—"a typical London east end district," several miles' walk from the Woolfs' lodgings at Cliffords Inn in Fleet Street—by one of his wife's maternal first cousins. "Like many serious, middle class, maiden ladies of the Victorian era engaged in 'good works,'" Marny Vaughan carried on, as Stella Duckworth had, the mission of her mother's generation through her ongoing participation in the COS (99). But having attended a few sessions of that committee and made some "home visits" to applicants in Vaughan's company, Leonard decidedly rejected the group's approach. "Hoxton turned me from a liberal into a socialist," for "in Hoxton one was confronted by some vast, dangerous fault in the social structure, some destructive disease in the social organism, which could not be touched by paternalism," which he associated with his years as a colonial administrator in Ceylon, "or charity or good works," the more feminized branch of the imperial mission at home; and "this led directly to my next political step" (100). He went on to make "a thorough study of the [cooperative] movement, both its principles and its practice" (105). And his guide was Vaughan's differently minded contemporary Margaret Llewelyn Davies—daughter of one of the COS's founders and niece of Girton College's cofounder Emily Davies (b. 1830)—who served as general secretary of the Women's Co-operative Guild (WCG) for more than three decades.

As Leonard moved from working with Vaughan to allying himself with Davies, Virginia simultaneously began to refine her ideas about philanthropy in relation to her husband's emerging political interests and her developing sense of women's political activism. Exposure to his pursuits brought her into much closer contact with the labor politics of the time, enabling her to differentiate further between women's philanthropic service, which she would increasingly designate as an outdated practice, and their political advocacy, a harbinger of "the new." As Ellen Ross notes, "That many middle-class suffragists and other feminist activists had been, or continued to be, what we would now call social workers, is one indication of the relationship between the movement for women's rights and the outpouring of female concern with poverty" (8). But her own qualified support for some feminist causes notwithstanding, Woolf's underlying attitude to those whom she perceived as intervening in the lives of others remained consistent over time. Within a few months' time of reviewing Ray Strachey's biography of Frances Willard in November 1912, for example, she accompanied Leonard on a fortnight's research trip to factories and cooperative stores in Manchester, Liverpool, Leeds, Glasgow, and Leicester. Writing to her friend Ka Cox about the working-class people she observed (and perhaps met), she described them as "perfectly respectable and content, rather like old gentlemen in Clubs, supposing they were worn down and out at elbows." The class condescension in her tone gives way to a highly ironic contrast of her own work with that of the labor organizer: "I see at a glance that nothing—except perhaps novel writing—can compare with the excitement of controlling the masses. The letters you'd get! The jobs you'd be sent on—and then people would always be telling you things, and if you could move them you would feel like a God. I see now where Margaret and even Mary MacArthur get their Imperial tread. The mistake I've made is in mixing up what they do with philanthropy" (*Letters* 2: 19).[1] Although Ruth Livesey asserts that Woolf here shows herself to be "thrilled by the prospect of individual power labour activism offered women of her generation," I think it is more accurate to say that "controlling the masses," whether as a novelist or an activist, held little appeal for her—even if "people . . . telling you things" certainly did (*Socialism* 209). Woolf instead identified that impulse to control with Davies and MacArthur (b. 1880). While by early 1913, Woolf was no longer "mixing up what they do with philanthropy," she nonetheless cast these political organizers, allied with causes that she supported, as having the "Imperial tread": she heard the sounds of what she would later personify as Proportion and Conversion in their very footsteps.

Better known for their work in women's organizations, with Davies taking the helm at the WCG in 1889 and MacArthur serving as secretary of the Women's Trade Union League beginning in 1903, the two also served as joint honorary secretaries for the PSF, the adult suffrage group mentioned at the outset of chapter 4, for which Virginia Stephen volunteered, albeit ambivalently, during 1910.[2] Although Woolf no doubt supported the goals of all three organizations, the maternal-imperialist strain of women's political work continued to exasperate her. In June 1918, after hearing Davies's coworker and companion Lilian Harris (b. 1866) lecture to the Richmond branch of the WCG, which met at the Woolfs' home, she commented on one aspect of the Guild's mission: "I think I should take exception to their maternal care of the women's souls, if I were connected with the movement. . . . I see the terrible temptation of thinking oneself in the right, & wishing to guide & influence" (*Diary* 1: 151). As Sowon S. Park has observed, "Woolf's objections regarding the style of leadership . . . were undoubtedly coloured by class, but they were also observing a serious political issue which was much discussed within suffrage societies" and which led to major divisions within the women's movement ("Suffrage and Virginia Woolf" 126). The autocratic style of such leaders as Emmeline Pankhurst (b. 1858) and her daughter Christabel, that is, threatened to reproduce the very worst aspects of patriarchal domination. As Rebecca West wrote years afterward in an essay included in *The Post Victorians* (1933), "There was no nonsense about democracy in the Women's Social and Political Union" (495). Woolf would especially underline this point in *The Years*, which is also, in the view of Anna Snaith, "Woolf's most sustained representation of anti-colonialism" ("Race" 209).

Throughout the course of her life and career, as I have argued, Woolf consistently identified both the desire for control over others that she perceived in the women around her, whatever their politics, and their tendency to reproduce rather than transform existing structures of domination as chief reasons for her resistance to both philanthropy and turn-of-the-century feminist politics, especially when conducted under the sign of "maternal care." Yet, if her opposition to such structures and the attitudes that enforced them did not change, her point of view on those friends and allies who embodied them nonetheless shifted over time, at least to some extent.[3] In this chapter I thus look closely at the distance Woolf traveled over two decades, between her representations of suffrage politics in *Night and Day* and in *The Years*, both of which decidedly criticize aspects of "the Cause" yet emphatically support some feminist aspirations. For example, as I explore below, Woolf makes *Night and Day*'s Mary Datchet the avatar of the new political woman, implicitly contrasted in the novel with the older Sally Seal, on one hand, and her apolitical contemporary Katharine Hilbery, on the other. Mrs. Seal seeks, albeit ineffectually, the kind of control over the people of England that Woolf persistently criticized. Yet, in a way that befits her position as a daughter of empire, even Katharine, otherwise distanced by birth, class, and temperament from her activist peers, laughingly describes herself as wanting to "beat . . . down" and "trample" the young professionals and politicos who seem to possess something she does not (*Night* 54, ch. 4; cf. Phillips 84–86). Different as these three characters are from one another, elder and younger alike all display what Woolf's narrator calls "lustful arrogance" (175; ch. 14). *The Years*, too, challenges the will to power. When Lady Lassiter (née Kitty Malone) insists to Eleanor Pargiter, "Force is always wrong—don't you agree with me?—always wrong!" and then repeats the very same words again in the final chapter, albeit a little less insistently, we are meant to observe the paradox in coercively arguing against coercion (170, "1910"; 378, "Present Day"). Across time, aging, and change, Woolf persistently resists that "lustful arrogance," no matter who evinces it and what positions they take.

I situate my reading of these works in relation to the generational dynamics I have been tracing throughout this book. Here I consider Woolf's attitudes to her older contemporaries Davies and Janet Case, Girton-educated women descended from progressive activists, who embraced and participated in the new social movements of the 1880s and 1890s. I juxtapose that point of view with the one she took toward her younger friend, Ray Strachey, also college-educated, who belonged to the third generation of the feminist family so intimately associated with Julia Stephen's cousin Isabel Somerset. Two of Woolf's closest associates to occupy the category of "the public woman," Davies and Strachey challenged the norms that had made that term, in Grand's heyday, a euphemism for prostitute. Both were supported largely by private incomes rather than paid work—Strachey had the requisite £500 a year around 1909, though she also went on to earn her living (Holmes 89). Yet, each differed very fully in Woolf's eyes from those "serious, middle class, maiden ladies" of Julia Stephen's day and of Virginia Stephen's childhood and adolescent years, most of whom had taken philanthropy as an unpaid vocation. As a critical interlocutor, Case in particular challenged Woolf's thinking about both politics and aesthetics, bringing perspectives shaped by her own late-Victorian experiences to bear on her former student's work and attitudes. Perhaps most importantly, as her elders aged, Woolf inevitably did, too, and with age came new ways of thinking not only about her own life course—as she aged out of the younger generation and into an older one—but also about differences and continuities between and within generations of women.

Suffrage Generations in *Night and Day*

Even a relatively positively regarded character like Mary Datchet has a decidedly imperial dimension. Early in *Night and Day*, she imagines herself as being "at the very centre of it all, that centre which was constantly in the minds of people in remote Canadian forests and on the plains of India, when their thoughts turned to England" (44; ch. 4). As Kathy J. Phillips has also noted, while viewing the spoils of military adventure that came to be called the Elgin Marbles, Mary "conjured up a scene of herself on a camel's back, in the desert, while Ralph [Denham] commanded a whole tribe of natives" (80; ch. 6). Her imperial dreams notwithstanding, this figure constitutes a far more compelling portrait of a political operative than we find in Woolf's first novel. Much less sardonically than *The Voyage Out*, with its satire on Evelyn M.'s membership in "the Saturday Club," *Night and Day* presents a "meeting of a society for the free discussion of everything" by "people who wished to meet, either for purposes of enjoyment, or to discuss art, or to reform the State" (42; ch. 4). Yet Mary's almost reflexive tendency to understand her own strategies for state reform as the right ones—a position that changes, as she does, over the course of the novel—marks a link between this activist of the third generation and her elders, in their shared desire for domination over others.

One of several scenes set in the women's suffrage society office in Russell Square—which is, significantly, *not* an adult suffrage group (Jones 68–77)—depicts a committee meeting attended by Mary; her coworkers, Mr. Clacton and Mrs. Seal (whose title indicates her age rather than her marital status); and their leader, Kit Markham. (Though it may be just a coincidence, the latter shares the name of a leading member of the National League for Opposing Woman Suffrage, the female imperialist Violet Markham, who—like her colleague, the MP Jack Hills—subsequently converted to a prosuffrage stance during the war [Markham 96].)[4] As Mary aims to curb the unruly thoughts inspired by a recent conversation with Ralph, "without conscious effort, by some trick of the brain," she stops staring out the window and snaps back to attention: "What line was it advisable to take? She found herself strongly disapproving of what Mr. Clacton was saying. She committed herself to the opinion that now was the time to strike hard. Directly she had said this, . . . she became more and more in earnest, and anxious to bring the others round to her point of view" (*Night* 173; ch. 14).[5] Effectively cowing the rest of the committee—"all rather elderly people, . . . inclined to side with her and against each other, partly, perhaps, because of her youth"—Mary does "bring the others round": "Indeed, when she had won her point she felt a slight degree of contempt for the people who had yielded to her" (174–75). Although persuading this small group is by no means equivalent to "controlling the masses," "the feeling that she controlled them all filled Mary with a sense of power." Channeling the perception Woolf had expressed to Cox, minus the irony, Mary "felt that no work can equal in importance, or be so exciting as, the work of making other people do what you want them to do" (174). Notably, the narrator casts Mary's auditors as deferring to her, despite her lack of age and experience, and siding against one another, suggesting that her youth gives her power over them in this respect, too.

Mary's position as a member of the younger generation certainly differentiates her in other ways from her coworkers, starting with her appearance. The narrative's first detailed word portrait depicts her as a solid, sturdy body. She looks older than twenty-five "because she earned, or intended to earn, her own living, and had already lost the look of the irresponsible spectator," a figure we could identify with the author herself, as expressed in the narrator's distanced stance. In its place she had "taken on that of the private in the army of workers": "Her gestures seemed to have a certain purpose; the muscles round eyes and lips were set rather firmly, as though the senses had undergone some discipline, and were held ready for a call on them" (42–43; ch. 4). Having been subjected to "some discipline," extending even to "the senses," so, too, is her mind "already in a groove, capable, that is, of thinking the same thoughts every morning at the same hour" (76; ch. 6). Described in terms that anticipate both Woolf's representation of Rose Pargiter in *The Years* and her critique of the patriarchal machine in *Three Guineas*, Mary's bodily and mental deportment also contrasts sharply with the description of Sally Seal, who appears in the same chapter, during our first view of Mary at work in her Russell Square office on the day Katharine visits for tea. With "a face that seemed permanently flushed with philanthropic enthusiasm," Sally "was always in a hurry, and always in some disorder": "Only her vast enthusiasm and her worship of Miss Markham, one of the pioneers of the society, kept her in her place, for which she had no sound qualification" (78). The differences in demeanor between

Sally and Mary bespeak the changes in opportunity, temperament, and experience from one generation to the next.

Unlike the college-educated Mary, who ultimately leaves her unsalaried post at the women's suffrage society for a paid position elsewhere, Sally is the kind of amateur social worker that Leonard Woolf identified in Marny Vaughan, albeit represented in the novel as somewhat more silly than "serious." Yet, despite Woolf's satirizing the type and her amateurishness—as in the narrator's reference to her "mental ambiguity"—Sally Seal's suffrage work does concentrate her attention on a single goal (78). Her monomaniacal air conveys the narrowing of the feminist agenda brought about by the rise of the Women's Social and Political Union (WSPU) after 1905, in which the multiple commitments and associations of late-Victorian feminists like Somerset and Grand gave way to both a sharper focus on winning the vote and a devaluation of the older generation's nonmilitant or "constitutional" means of promoting political change. In tracing Sally's descent from a late-Victorian line of women's activism, the novel draws quite concretely on this character's second-generation roots.

Sally's discourse and demeanor also contrast sharply with both of the novel's younger heroines. Much to Mary's chagrin, she persists in talking "shop at tea" even in the presence of the very distant and self-conscious Katharine, and explains her zeal for suffrage by reference to her background in philanthropy: "'It's my misfortune to be an enthusiast, . . . my father's daughter could hardly be anything else. I think I've been on as many committees as most people. Waifs and Strays, Rescue Work, Church Work, C. O. S.—local branch—besides the usual civic duties which fall to one as a householder. But I've given them all up for our work here, and I don't regret it for a second,' she added. 'This is the root question, I feel; until women have votes—'" Here Mary abruptly cuts her off, fines her sixpence for talking "shop" over tea, and tells her, "We're all sick to death of women and their votes" (84). The narrative thus similarly truncates our view of Sally's prior history, although even just the short list of her "committees" and the "civic duties" associated with being a "householder"—and thus property owning—probably tells us what we need to know (Jones 81).

Daunted by Mary's bluntness, Sally goes on to allude to some mysterious "domestic circumstances" (never clarified, but presumably attendant on being "[her] father's daughter") that prevented her from "giving her youth" to the cause as she sees Mary doing (*Night* 85; ch. 6). This detail anticipates the very different portrait of a late-Victorian single woman, Eleanor Pargiter, that Woolf would fashion in *The Years*; it fits Davies's circumstances as well, in that she lived with and cared for her father, after her mother's death, for the final twenty years of his life, facts that first led Jane Marcus to suggest Davies as a model for Eleanor (*"Years"* 45). But even Sally the ineffectual enthusiast has designs on others: Katharine's "unlikeness to the rest of them . . . had subtly stimulated Mrs. Seal to try and make a convert of her" (*Night* 86). "Demand[ing]" to know why their visitor is not "a member of our society"—a question Katharine never answers directly, although she goes on to describe herself as "a convert already"—Sally "could not classify [Katharine] among the varieties of human beings known to her" (87, 93, 86). The narrator describes Sally's final extended speech in this chapter as "a tirade against party government," thoroughly apropos to the circumstances of the suffrage movement during the time at which the novel is set. She makes a further reference to her dead father as having been, like Kit Markham, "one of the pioneers": "But reflecting that the glories of the future depended in part upon the activity of her typewriter, she bobbed her head, and hurried back to the seclusion of her little room, from which immediately issued sounds of enthusiastic, but obviously erratic, composition" (89).

While Woolf certainly parodies the character's zeal, the narrative does suggest via Mary's point of view that there is something valuable in Sally's single-minded commitment to "the Cause." After the committee meeting in which Mary dominates the other members of the executive and feels as well "a sort of pity for the enthusiastic ineffective little woman," she is brought up short when Sally voices a version of Mary's own desire to command (175; ch. 14). Typically, "when Mrs. Seal said anything, even if it was what Mary herself was feeling, she automatically thought of all that there was to be said against it" (176). Thus in hearing Sally say, as she looks down from her window into the square below, "If only one could . . . make them understand. . . . If only one could *make* them see," Mary's "arrogant feeling that she could direct everybody, dwindled away," even as she begins to consider the end her colleague has in view (175–76; emphasis in the original). Grandiose though it is, Sally's belief that the coming of the vote will be "a great day, not only for us, but for civilization" impresses Mary, who "could not help looking at the odd little priestess of humanity with something like admiration. While she had been thinking about herself, Mrs. Seal had thought of nothing but her vision"—a statement that anticipates the view readers take of Lily Briscoe as she works on her painting in the face of Charles Tansley's misogyny, her own lack of confidence, and, ultimately, the absence of Mrs. Ramsay (*Lighthouse* 176–77). Though parodied throughout, as the artist's perseverance is not, Sally's intensity and integrity are not completely derided.

The fulfillment of her "vision," however, does not depend on Sally alone. In a later turn of events, Mary returns from the Christmas holiday with Ralph at her family home "to find that by some obscure Parliamentary manoeuvre the vote had once more slipped beyond the attainment of women." The implications for her coworkers are readily predictable: "Mrs. Seal was in a condition bordering upon frenzy. The duplicity of Ministers, the treachery of mankind, the insult to womanhood, the setback to civilization, the ruin of her life's work, the feelings of her father's daughter—all these topics were discussed in turn, and the office was littered with newspaper cuttings branded with the blue, if ambiguous, marks of her displeasure" (*Night* 268; ch. 20). In the crisis at hand, both Sally and her male colleague emphasize the need to persuade their apathetic fellow citizens of the righteousness of their goal. "We want to know what people all over England are thinking," Mr. Clacton declares; "we want to put them in the way of thinking rightly" (269). Fearing that Mary will defect from the office in favor of married life, Sally "set her mind to work at once to make the prospects of the cause appear as alluring and important as she could." And she ends her "harangue" by stumbling into "a perpetual source of bewilderment to her—the extraordinary incapacity of the human race, in a world where the good is so unmistakably divided from the bad, of distinguishing one from the other, and embodying what ought to be done in a few large, simple Acts of Parliament, which would, in a very short time, completely change the lot of humanity" (277). These last overblown sentiments about the transformative effects of legislation aside, it is Sally's rigid notion of good and bad as "unmistakably divided"—which recalls the conversation among Katharine's aunts about "the rights and wrongs of the affair" in which cousin Cyril is involved—that catches Mary's attention. She "begins to doubt the campaign because of its unquestioning rigidity," which ultimately brings her closer not to Sally's, but to Katharine's position (Snaith, *Virginia Woolf* 32).

Recalling the earlier episode in which "she had spent the whole of a committee meeting in thinking about sparrows and colours, until . . . her old convictions had all come back to her," Mary reflects that "they weren't, rightly speaking, convictions at all": "She could not see the world divided into separate compartments of good people and bad people, any more than she could believe so implicitly in the rightness of her own thought as to wish to bring the population of the British Isles into agreement with it. She looked at the lemon-coloured leaflet, and thought almost enviously of the faith which could find comfort in the issue of such documents; for herself she would be content to remain silent for ever if a share of personal happiness were granted her" (*Night* 271; ch. 20). Mary here explicitly repudiates the desire to convert others, the desire Woolf so distrusted. Moreover, in opposing political gain to "personal happiness," she winds up abjuring even the latter: "She saw to the remote spaces behind the strife of the foreground, enabled now to gaze there,

since she had renounced her own demands, privileged to see the larger view."
As for Katharine, "there remained a hard reality, unimpaired by one's personal
adventures, remote as the stars, unquenchable as they are." In "this curious
transformation from the particular to the universal" (275), Mary joins Katharine's quest for impersonality—"so lofty and so painless"—to the "different
spirit" she achieves by her "renunciation" (286; ch. 21). Yet, the narrator nonetheless uses the problematic military metaphor to describe Mary's change in
status: "She had enlisted in the army, and was a volunteer no longer" (278;
ch. 20).

To be sure, there is something melancholy in Mary's sense that she now
belongs, as do Sally Seal and Mr. Clacton, to the "shadow people, flitting in
and out of the ranks of the living—eccentrics, undeveloped human beings,
from whose substance some essential part had been cut away" (279). Yet her
fuller commitment to her now-salaried political work—which, by the end of
the novel, no longer involves women's suffrage—suggests a third-generation
rearticulation of the visionary ideals of the prior generation that discards both
enthusiasm and conventional moral categories in favor of a less programmatic
approach to the matters at hand. This rearticulation indeed bridges "the gulf
between the world of high culture and the world of suffrage, as represented
respectively by Katharine and Mary," in that "the inevitable clash of aesthetic
and political principles" is mitigated by the subordination of both to another
end (Park, "Suffrage and Virginia Woolf" 129). As Snaith asserts, "Neither
Mary nor Katharine can achieve a totality of both public and private fulfillment"; yet, we should add that the appreciation of "hard reality," "remote"
and "unquenchable," to which both characters aspire is much less a matter of
doing or having than of being, more a question of attitude and orientation
than achievement (*Virginia Woolf* 33). As Woolf reflected on her construction
of Katharine's character in January 1915, in the very early stages of composing *Night and Day* just before her breakdown, "I want to see what can be said
against all forms of activity" (*Diary* 1: 22; emphasis in the original).

Politics, by contrast, partakes of the unreal, to both Woolf and her character-
avatar. Reporting on a Fabian Society meeting she attended early in 1915, at
which Beatrice Webb and others discussed "The Conditions of Peace," Woolf
mockingly describes the crowd of "earnest drab women, who are thought
'queer' at home, & rejoice in it" and the "broad nosed, sallow, shock headed
young men," all of whom "looked unhealthy & singular & impotent." Taking novelist's notes, she narrows her focus by means of "a pun": "The interest
was watching Mrs Webb, seated like an industrious spider at the table; spin-
ning her webs . . . incessantly," clearly a favorite in-joke as Leonard Woolf used
it, too, in referring to the "Fabian spider-web" (*Diary* 1: 26; *Beginning Again* 114).

Recurring to the quip in deeming "the idea that these frail webspinners can affect the destiny of nations . . . fantastic," Woolf nonetheless concludes her remarks by claiming "it was well worth going,—& I have now declared myself a Fabian," while Katharine will support the aims of the suffrage society and yet refuse to work for it: "Oh dear no," she tells Ralph, "that wouldn't do at all" (*Diary* 1: 26; *Night* 93, ch. 6).

Once again shaped by her creator's experience, Katharine's point of view on the women's suffrage society office also uses the web-spinning metaphor to convey her sense of its distance from what the narrator calls "the normal world":

> The view she had had of the inside of an office was of the nature of a dream to her. Shut off up there, she compared Mrs. Seal, and Mary Datchet, and Mr. Clacton to enchanted people in a bewitched tower, with the spiders' webs looping across the corners of the room, and all the tools of the necromancer's craft at hand; for so aloof and unreal and apart from the normal world did they seem to her, in the house of innumerable typewriters, murmuring their incantations and concocting their drugs, and flinging their frail spiders' webs over the torrent of life which rushed down the streets outside. (*Night* 92)

Neither Katharine nor her author ever quite loses her sense that the "frail" enchantments incapable of containing "the torrent of life," and the "impotent," shadowy character of those who devise them, constitute an alternative to "the normal world," on one hand, and "hard reality," on the other. This "bewitched" world and its denizens function metaphorically along the lines of the solitary lady weaving her tapestry atop a "tower" in Tennyson's Shalott: contact with "the torrent of life" would release them, but only into the "hard reality" of death.

Even though Mary is subsequently represented as further disciplined, this time by her unhappiness over Ralph rather than by ambition or vocation, she still retains something of a magical, "enchanted" quality. When Katharine arrives at Mary's rooms in search of Ralph late in the novel, the narrator comments on the transformation "which had left its traces for ever upon [Mary's] bearing. Youth, and the bloom of youth, had receded, leaving the purpose of her face to show itself in the hollower cheeks, the firmer lips, the eyes no longer spontaneously observing at random, but narrowed upon an end which was not near at hand. This woman was now a serviceable human being, mistress of her own destiny" (471; ch. 31). And so, having realized she is "in love no longer," she warms herself metaphorically by "the steady glow which had seemed lit in the place where a more passionate flame had once burnt" (476).

In *Night and Day*'s celebrated last glimpse of her, Katharine and Ralph gaze up at Mary's window from the street, where "they stood for some moments, looking at the illuminated blinds, an expression to them both of something impersonal and serene in the spirit of the woman within, working out her plans far into the night—her plans for the good of a world that none of them were ever to know" (536; ch. 34).

In pursuit of "an end . . . not near at hand," the making of a better world for subsequent generations, Mary becomes something of a heroic figure. As Judith Wilt has observed, Woolf "award[s] her some of that elusive cachet of the 'impersonal,'" suggesting her awareness of and appreciation for what she was to call, in describing Ray Strachey, "a different ideal" (170; *Diary* 1: 156). By novel's end, Mary still perceives herself as part of a collective movement in her new position as an organizer for a society on the labor question, and thus "believ[es] that 'our' views, 'our' society, 'our' policy, stood for something quite definitely segregated from the main body of society in a circle of superior illumination" (*Night* 377; ch. 26). Yet, by transmitting second-generation ideals into a new idiom, the "impersonal and serene" commitment she makes to a version of Sally Seal's "vision" clearly identifies her as worthy of respect and even admiration from the narrator's point of view—even if those ideals bear the stamp of the imperial context in which they arose.

Janet Case, Margaret Llewelyn Davies, and Generational Differences

After what appears to have been their first meeting in March 1909 at the Hampstead home of Janet Case and her sister Emphie, ten years before the publication of *Night and Day*, Virginia Stephen composed a portrait of Margaret Llewelyn Davies that lends further credence to the idea that she was one of the originals for Mary Datchet (e.g., Briggs, *Virginia* 53; Marcus, "Pargetting" 73).[6] As importantly, the sketch also suggests that she took Davies—two decades older than herself—as representative of a particular type, one much closer in kind to Mary Datchet than to Sally Seal. Comparing the guest to her hosts, she concludes, "Miss Davies comes of a sterner stock":

Her features are sharper, her eyes burn brighter; once she must have had something of the beauty of a delicate Greek head. Now, being also past forty years of age, she has the same look of having passed a strenuous life in toil of some kind for others. Women who have worked but have not married come to have a particular look; refinement, without sex;

tending to be austere. Miss Davies, it is clear, has far less tolerance than her friends; and has done what she has done through the force of conviction. . . . I imagine that she might be stern and even bigoted; but that she is also fervent to uphold her lofty views. ("Hampstead" 9–10)

As in the repeated focus on Mary's physiognomy and how it is transformed over the course of *Night and Day*, this portrait emphasizes the "particular look" of those women "who have worked but not married"—still a very possible life outcome for Virginia Stephen in 1909—and depicts the visible signs of Davies's circumstances. Her "strenuous life" has, perhaps, sharpened her features and brightened her eyes, making her refined, sexless, and "austere." (In his memoirs, Leonard Woolf similarly describes Davies as "serious, austere, dynamic" [*Beginning* 104].) Presumably assessing her as well on the basis of their discussion, the writer deems her less tolerant than the Case sisters, with whom Davies attended Girton, and definitely a person of "conviction": possibly "stern" or "bigoted," but certainly "fervent" in "her lofty views." And she goes on to give a glimpse of their conversation, decidedly different from what Virginia Stephen's own was at the time: "They drop easily into what is I suppose their shop; they describe the last problem play; they discuss the last development in the fight for the franchise. It is all admirably sane, altruistic, and competent" ("Hampstead" 11).

At this early moment in her own career—this sketch being roughly contemporary with her remarks on her only recorded meeting with Alice Meynell—Virginia Stephen begins to constitute Davies as what she would call ten years later, in reference to Ray Strachey, "the public woman": "a type, after all, no less marked than the literary type, though not yet so fully observed & recorded" (*Diary* 1: 159). Davies is not subjected to the sort of critique that Meynell, Lee, Clifford, and Ward regularly receive, belonging as she does to a slightly younger cohort than theirs and constituting an alternative to "the poetess" or "the literary type." Moreover, although there is substantial evidence of connections between members of the extended Davies clan and her own birth family, that Woolf forged her relation to Davies during early adulthood rather than in adolescence gives a different quality to their association.[7] Mediated more by her relation to Case, on one hand, and to Leonard Woolf, on the other, their friendship was always shaped by the substantial support that Davies offered to both Leonard and Virginia during the mental breakdowns of the 1910s. Most importantly, this woman is no relic from the South Kensington past. As a figure of and in the present, Davies's interest in both "the last problem play" and "the fight for the franchise" yet signifies the continuity of her descent from the reformers of the prior generation, such as her aunt

Emily, the woman's educationalist, and her Christian Socialist father. Born and raised in Marylebone—Julia Duckworth's home during her first marriage—Llewelyn Davies left it in 1889, when her father's anti-imperialism exiled his family to Kirkby Lonsdale in the Lake District after a sermon on that subject allegedly offended the most important member of his audience: the aging Queen Victoria, Empress of India, who was by no means amused (V. Woolf, *Letters* 6: 250n2).

Yet, by contrast with *Night and Day*'s admiring final image of Mary Datchet, Woolf's attitude to Davies—akin to Sally Seal in this respect in being very much "her father's daughter"—and her "lofty views" is always predicated on a certain ambivalence. For example, when she wrote to Case in December 1910, after her year's involvement with the PSF, of seeing "Miss LL. [*sic*] Davies at a lighted window in Barton St" in Westminster, where Davies's brother Crompton had a home, "with all the conspirators round her, and cursed under my breath," we have to wonder what provokes the curse (*Letters* 1: 442). Davies's figure appears, but she is not alone: Does the writer flair up at the sight of "all the conspirators," who crowd round their leader? Or is the conspiracy itself something to distrust? While it is hard to know quite how to take this comment—it could be, as Naomi Black suggests, just another in-joke that is re-purposed less satirically in *Night and Day*; or, as Snaith writes, "a subtle critique . . . of organized political campaigns"—the vision of Davies as part of a collective body of workers, drawing on a multigenerational family legacy of political and social action, rather than as the solitary and somewhat isolated woman Mary Datchet becomes, seems to inspire Woolf's laughing hostility (N. Black 38; Snaith, *Virginia Woolf* 33).

Good friends to one another as to Woolf, Davies and Case also constitute an important and critical audience for their younger contemporary in the first decades of her career. As living and engaged representatives of the late-Victorian world, their aesthetic and political commitments, shaped by those times, persisted into the present, generating conflict between old and young. In a letter from January 1916 to Davies, for example, Woolf pronounced that she did not "see that there's much good in [attending] Lectures—clever people go home and gossip about them, and thats [*sic*] about all. But then, my dear Miss Davies, what does do good? You say sitting on Town Councils and upholding one's ideals." Striking a Wildean note, she adds, "I incline to think that that merely improves one's own soul." Admitting nonetheless in a complimentary tone that "the Women's Guild has done something," she went on in the years following to host meetings of the local branch of the WCG at her home in Richmond, serving for a time on its executive and arranging for speakers who would provide such "lectures" for the guildswomen (*Letters* 2: 76).

But later in 1916, Davies turned the tables on Woolf, during a joint Cornwall holiday, when Woolf's own stance as an artist came under discussion. As Woolf reported to her sister, "I have had several arguments about art and morality with Margaret, and I hope I have done some damage"—presumably to Davies's view of the relationship between the two. "But a life rooted in good works is hard to injure," she concludes, "especially as she always assumes that I think what Oscar Wilde thought in the 80ties" (*Letters* 2: 119). Here Woolf implicitly protests the evocation of late-Victorian aestheticism as the proper analogue for her own practice, even in the face of her earlier allusion to the critique of philanthropy Wilde made in "The Soul of Man under Socialism" (1891). She distances herself both from Davies, who seems to have upheld the necessity of a conscious moral purpose for art—and whose own literary tastes in later life tended to Dickens and the romance novelist Ethel M. Dell (b. 1881), as Woolf noted in her diary in May 1925—and from Wilde, who famously declared in the preface to *The Picture of Dorian Gray* (1891) that "all art is quite useless" (*Diary* 3: 23; Preface 236). Although we don't know if or when Davies read *The Voyage Out*, with its construction of politically engaged late-Victorian works as "behind the times" and its other digs at those who would conjoin literature and politics, her identification of Woolf with *l'art pour l'art* and Woolf's rejection of that association constitute generationally marked readings of recent literary, social, and cultural history.

A conflict of this kind recurs even more sharply in Woolf's sparring with Case a few years later during tea at her Hampstead home in November 1918, as the war was ending and Woolf was finishing *Night and Day*. To be sure, even in the first phase of their relationship, the student had made a point of baiting her "cheerful & muscular" tutor, as she described Case in a diary sketch from July 1903: "After a time I found out her line of teaching, & rather set my back against it—at least I discovered certain opinions which she held very vigorously—& which when contradicted, were worth a good half hours [*sic*] discussion. I contradicted them; . . . & to my delight she took me quite seriously" (*Passionate* 182). Even then, Virginia Stephen noted what would continue to be a major point of contention between her and her teacher. Schooled in the classics at Girton, Case had not only "published several scholarly articles on Greek literature" but also produced a translation of Aeschylus's *Prometheus Unbound* "designed for readers with little or no background in classical literature" (Prins 40). Shaped by her investments in the literary and political debates of the 1880s, Case "read with a less purely literary interest in the text than I did," Woolf wrote; "she was not by any means blind to the beauties of Aeschylus and Euripides (her two favourite writers) but she was not happy till she had woven some kind of moral into their plays" (*Passion-*

ate 183). Here Virginia Stephen clearly locates Case's position within the purpose versus pleasure contests of the fin de siècle, and that Case read literature with an eye to the political or "moral" should not surprise us. As a niece of Sir James Stansfeld—Radical MP, cabinet member, and the chief parliamentary advocate of Josephine Butler's campaign to repeal the C. D. Acts—she would presumably have been much closer to Grand than to Wilde in her textual politics.

Although she commended her teacher in 1903 for possessing "the rare gift of seeing the other side" of the argument, Woolf was less willing fifteen years later to engage with Case's position (*Passionate* 184). A diary entry of September 1918 contrasts Case's way of reading, which Woolf posits as typical of her friend's times, with her own. "All her generation use their brains too scrupulously upon books, seeking meaning rather than letting themselves run on for pleasure," the latter being the readerly stance Woolf would advocate in such essays as "On Not Knowing Greek" (1925) and "How Should One Read a Book?" (1932) (*Diary* 1: 192). Meeting up with Case about two months later, she afterward deplored "the depressing effect of talking to some one [*sic*] who seems to want all literature to go into the pulpit; who makes it all infinitely worthy & safe & respectable. I was led into trying to define my own particular search—not after morality, or beauty or reality—no; but after literature itself" (*Diary* 1: 213–14). She felt that "effect" even on the next day and tried to roust it, noting how "Janet's chill falling upon the last pages of my novel still depresses me. . . . Praise? fame? Janet's good opinion? How beside the mark they all are!" (*Diary* 1: 214).

And she was still thinking and writing about it ten days later in a letter to Vanessa Bell, in which she criticizes the fifty-five-year-old Case's taste as behind the times: "I had a fearfully depressing talk with old Janet Case the other day; at the end of which I came to the conclusion that when nice educated people who've spent their lives in teaching Greek and ought to know something about it, have less feeling for modern fiction, including my own which she advised me to give up and take to biography instead since that was 'useful,' than a stranded jelly fish on which the flies have already settled, its [*sic*] high time for us writers to retire to the South Seas." The recommendation of biography as a "useful" genre suggests the tenor of Case's aesthetics, while her lack of "feeling for modern fiction" means that in this context, at least, she could not—or could no longer—see "the other side," the argument Woolf was making. This has a lamentable impact on her former student: "There's practically no one in London now," she complained to Bell, "whom I can talk to either about my own writing"—as Katherine Mansfield had decamped to San Remo several months earlier, owing to poor health—"or Shakespeares [*sic*]. I'm beginning to think that I'd better stop writing novels, since no one cares a damn whether one writes them or not" (*Letters* 2: 293).

A year later, just after the publication of *Night and Day*, the dispute was renewed; this time, Davies took up the cudgel on Case's behalf as well as her own. Recounting a visit to what she sardonically terms "the immaculate & moral heights of Hampstead," where both Davies and the Case sisters lived at the time, Woolf describes an extended "scene of revelation & explanation with Margaret":

> Tentatively she began it—how Janet & she felt that perhaps—they might be wrong, but still in their view—in short my article on Charlotte Brontë was so much more to their liking than my novels. Something in my feeling for human beings—some narrowness—some lack of emotion—here I blazed up & let fly. So you go on preaching humanity, was the gist of what I said, when you've withdrawn, & preserve only the conventional idea of it. But its [*sic*] *you* that are narrow! she retaliated. On the contrary, I shiver & shrink with the oncoming contest as I step up your stairs. I? But I'm the most sympathetic, the most human, the most universal of people. You grant that Janet moralises? I said. O yes, she granted that readily. But the idea of herself as a forcible intense woman, excluding the greater half of the human heart staggered her. She took the blow well. (*Diary* 1: 312–13; emphasis in the original)

Woolf seems to believe she has gotten the better of the exchange, in holding up a mirror to Davies that shows her an image at odds with how she sees herself. Rather than "sympathetic," "human," and "universal," Woolf deems her "forcible" and "intense," lacking the full comprehension of "the human heart" to which she pretends. Having "withdrawn" from ordinary human life, Woolf alleges, and substituted in its place "only the conventional idea of it," Davies stands accused of loving "humanity" in the abstract, all the while maintaining her distance from it.

Here Woolf makes a point that clearly underlies her own developing critique of "the public woman," which first Davies, then Ray Strachey, came to embody for her. Such claims recall her remarks to Case eight or nine years earlier, quoted at the outset of chapter 4, about "the inhuman side" of politics, how it "shrivel[s]" "all the best feelings." Interestingly, however, the faults Woolf attributes to Davies are quite similar to those that Davies and Case purportedly find in Woolf's fiction, a "narrowness" and "lack of emotion" that distorts or limits her characters. We might take this as an indictment of the impersonal narrator that Woolf deployed in her first two novels, with their pervasive irony and satire on conventional manners and morals, including their criticism of heterosexual marriage, middle-class philanthropy, and political advocacy. Moreover, just as Case had, a year earlier, advocated biography as a "useful" genre, Davies seeks to persuade Woolf to turn away from fiction to nonfiction, this time to the practice of literary journalism, with which Woolf had become, as we know, increasingly disenchanted.

The quarrel may have been mended, but the conflict continued, even as Woolf came to own an underlying likeness between herself and her friend in spite of their different pursuits and positions. Her subsequent letter to Davies refers to the "atmosphere" that "all incorruptible and dominating characters have": "They suffer for their insight with one eye by being blind with t'other," generously adding, "I think thats [sic] the case with me too." She simultaneously reasserted the differences between their respective lines of work and how their preferences made each "blind" to the other's values: "You'll never like my books, but then shall I ever understand your Guild? Probably not" (Letters 2: 399). And she aimed, as she had with Case, to articulate even more precisely "where we differ": "Its [sic] a question of the human heart, and cutting out the rotten parts according to ones [sic] convictions. That's what I want to do" (400). Still, the criticisms must have rankled, as this letter goes on to reference those positive reviews of Night and Day (though not Mansfield's more ambivalent one) that praised the novelist for having the sympathetic imagination Davies and Case perceived her to lack. And some months later she parenthetically informed Case that her fiction was not quite so insular or inaccessible to common readers as her elders may have thought: "(did I make it plain to you and Margaret who say I'm no novelist, and only write for the parish of Bloomsbury[,] that such is the demand among the lower middle classes for my work that new editions of the V.O. and N. and D. have to be prepared at once?)" (Letters 2: 420–21).

From this exchange, we can see Woolf certainly understood the differences between herself and her older friends as generationally marked, with a specific focus on their divergent aesthetics. Case's views in particular nonetheless continued to command her unwilling attention. Five years later, in response to her friend's letter on the more or less simultaneous publication of The Common Reader and Mrs. Dalloway, Woolf noted (at the age of forty-three), "Everyone over 40 prefers the C.R: everyone under 40 Mrs. D. I find myself torn between the two" (Letters 3: 201). From the context, we can infer that her next letter to Case further responds to written criticisms the teacher had made of her former student's fictional work, to which Woolf replies by implicitly linking one's age to one's tastes. Here she challenges her correspondent's preference for her criticism over her fiction, first repeating back to Case her perceived disdain for the novel's "matter" and simultaneous praise of its "style":

Woolf asserts that this not-so-common reader found *Mrs. Dalloway* "shallow and uninteresting and unreal in matter but . . . so lovely and clever and dashing and brilliant in style that one cant [*sic*] help reading every word." Woolf defends her own position by disparaging the late-Victorian Stevenson ("One can always separate his technique from his matter, and the pleasure is so thin that I, for one, can't read a single thing of his . . . a second time") and praising the Romantic Lamb ("not one of his essays, which are, of course, technically perfect, can be split into two like that") (211).

Despite her firm rejection of Case's distinction between "style" and "matter"—a distinction that, as we have seen, held particular weight in the debates of the 1890s—she still remembered her teacher's strictures a year later. As she remarked while completing *To the Lighthouse* in September 1926, "Odd how I'm haunted by that damned criticism of Janet Case's 'it's all dressing . . . technique. (Mrs Dalloway). The C. R. has substance.'" She concludes that "in ones [*sic*] strained state any fly has liberty to settle, & its [*sic*] always the gadflies," thus registering the psychic and bodily unease that accompanied her completion of any deeply felt project; indeed, she fell ill with the flu just a few days later (*Diary* 3: 109). But the implication that her essays were solid, serious, and substantial, whereas her fiction was not, lodged in her mind. Even in identifying Case as one who reads for "meaning" rather than "pleasure," albeit without probing the possibility of a way of reading that would entail both, Woolf finds it hard simply to discount the views of these elders, whom she mainly respected even as, or when, she differed from them.

Aging into the Older Generation

In the later stages of her relationships with Davies and Case, Woolf's attitude took a turn, as her own generation came to the fore. She began to observe her older friends aging out of active involvement and into the final phases of their lives. After a talk with Case late in 1918 when Woolf posited "60 as an age limit," in which she perceived her friend as "so anxious to be in the front, to share what the young feel," she characteristically represented the temporal distance between them by a spatial metaphor: "If I represent the young, my feelings tend to develop on such different lines that I can only wave my hand over leagues of Sea [*sic*]" (*Diary* 1: 215). At one moment imagining that "for [Case] age will be a profitable season" while at another deeming it "a melancholy" one for her, Davies, and Harris, by the early 1920s Woolf was associating the end of one's working life with the approach of death (*Diary* 1: 262, 271). "One ought to work—never to take one's eyes from one's work; & then if death should interrupt, well, it is merely that one must get up & leave one's stitching—one won't have wasted a thought on death. Margaret says in her work one gets superannuated. One must give it up. A very cruel work then" (*Diary* 2: 142). Ten years later, Woolf's new friend of the 1930s, the hard-working Ethel Smyth, would provide a sharp contrast with Davies, impressing Woolf with a vision of "an old age entirely superior in vitality to Margaret's"—in part, perhaps, because Smyth gave no signs of retiring—by enacting a different model of what later life could be (*Diary* 3: 306). Ultimately, Woolf would refigure the careers of these elders in *The Years* in ways that speak especially to her own shifting point of view as she self-consciously aged out of one generation and into another.

Yet, we should note that the experience of watching others age—and so, by implication, watching herself do so as well—makes its way into the very novel Case found so unsatisfactory. Glimpsing from her window "the old lady opposite climbing upstairs" after her unpleasant encounter with the proselytizing Miss Kilman, Clarissa Dalloway celebrates the distance from others, here made literal, that she finds essential to maintaining "the privacy of the soul" (*Mrs. Dalloway* 113). When a few hours later she looks out the window once more, having heard of Septimus Warren Smith's death and intuitively deeming Sir William Bradshaw responsible, in that she believes him "capable of some indescribable outrage—forcing your soul," she again sees "that old woman, quite quietly, going to bed alone" (165, 166). The "terror" that has been haunting her all day subsides, quelled by the fifth and final repetition of the touchstone line from *Cymbeline*, "Fear no more the heat of the sun" (IV. ii, 258; qtd. 166). As Elfi Bettinger perceptively observes from an age studies perspective, "A moment of contact with the old lady in the room opposite, going to bed, with dignity, quietly, alone—offers a fleeting glance into a (possible) future" (182). As a woman in her early fifties, in a distant but uncannily intimate relation to both the younger Septimus and that old lady, Clarissa meets and to some extent masters her fear, both of coercion by others—Miss Kilman, Sir William—and of approaching death. One of the many Woolf characters who consciously consider their own aging even as they imaginatively travel back to the past, Clarissa bears the imprint of her creator's elder contemporaries, as they, too, wonder (like Peter Walsh in this novel, or Mrs. Ramsay in *To the Lighthouse*) what they have made of their lives.

As Clarissa Dalloway contemplates aging and death in the comparative context the novel establishes, Woolf marked the end of Case's and Davies's careers by adopting a retrospective lens that doubled as a window on her own possible future. As "the heart of the woman's republic" began to falter (*Diary* 1: 147), by 1931 Woolf felt "the pathos when our teachers become our learners," especially in relation to Case, who unlike Davies or Woolf had never had the luxury of a private income. "She has had I suppose a far harder life than I knew—illness, poverty, & all the narrowness of living," Woolf wrote. "How I used to wait for her lesson: & then the arguments, the excitements" that Virginia Stephen had noted even in 1903; "I was 17 she said when she came," adding that Case "clings to youth" and "felt unsuccessful" (*Diary* 4: 11). Writing her former teacher's obituary at Davies's request six years later, Woolf repeated some of these details, having already channeled others into the character of Kitty Malone's tutor, Lucy Craddock, first in *The Pargiters* and then, in a more concentrated fashion, in *The Years*, which appeared in print just a few months before Case's death in July 1937. As Jane Marcus has noted, Woolf's work on both the novel and *Three Guineas* informed the portrait of Case she drew for the *Times* obituary even as it also recalls Woolf's earliest remarks about her teacher ("*Years*" 47–48).

The obituary makes a firm and unqualified link between Case's literary and political interests, that perennial bone of contention between teacher and student: "Her Greek was connected with many things. It was connected, naturally, seeing that she was the niece of Sir James Stansfeld, the reformer, with the life, with the politics of her day. She found time for committees, for the suffrage, for the Women's Cooperative Guild, . . . for all the causes that were then advanced and in dispute." The memorial tribute also suggests that Case would have been an excellent candidate for a post at the new women's college imagined in *Three Guineas*: "So sound a scholar and so fine and dignified a presence[] never held any of those posts that might have given her an academic position," because "she enjoyed too many things . . . to concentrate upon one ambition" ("Miss Janet Case," *Essays* 6: 112). Implying that to achieve such a position at male-dominated Oxbridge, as Jane Harrison (b. 1850) did at Newnham starting in 1898, would have required the narrowing of attention that constitutes specialization, Woolf defends and even celebrates the amateur while also establishing that Case "was no dilettante; she could edit a Greek play and win praise from the great [A. W.] Verrall himself" (111). Sealing her subject's posthumous membership in the Society of Outsiders, she concludes that Case "wanted no prominence, no publicity. She was contemplative, reticent, withdrawn"—characteristics and attitudes that Woolf would identify as her own preferred tactics and enduring traits in her last decade (112).

She represented Davies, by contrast with Case, as "the public woman" whose loss of an active career affected her much more negatively, in that her retirement revealed the narrowness of her life's scope. Having suffered defeat in her effort to persuade the WCG to adopt a wide-ranging peace platform in June 1918, three years before she stepped down from her post after thirty-one years, Davies gave voice over tea and dinner with the Woolfs to "lamentations, aspirations & too sanguine expectations; all exaggerated, so I felt, in comparison with their real value." Woolf went on to sum up in her diary what she perceived as the leader's mixed legacy: "The directness and superb vigour of her character always overcome me with admiration. Given a keener mind, or a subtler, or some sort of discipline that"—a bit like Sally Seal—"she's never had, she might have done marvels. I sometimes guess that she thinks her work less good than it should have been. Or it may be only the terrific shadow of old age" (*Diary* 1: 159). Having quoted Davies earlier in 1918 as saying "'my lifes [*sic*] a compromise—all a compromise,'" Woolf further glossed that statement in 1925, confessing herself "sorry for her, since how awful it would be to 'retire' at 60: to sit down & look at poplar trees? Moreover, she once said she had 'compromised'; her father making entire work impossible; & she now regrets things, I imagine; has seen so little of the world, & carried nothing to the extreme" (*Diary* 1: 147; 3: 23). Five years later, she viewed Davies's old age as "a tragedy in its way," describing both her and Harris as "flabby & bloodless," and Davies as "pathetic to me now—conciliatory & nervous where she used to be trenchant & severe." The (negative) prospect of later life that Davies enacted led Woolf to forge plans for her own future: "Must old age be so shapeless? The only escape is to work the mind. I shall write a history of English literature, I think, in those days. And I shall walk. And I shall buy clothes, & keep my hair tidy, and make myself dine out" (*Diary* 3: 297).

New Public Women

Woolf's view of Davies's public career as a factor in determining the contours of her old age perhaps reinforced her ambivalent outlook on those closer contemporaries who extended the pioneering work of second-generation activists but dedicated their efforts primarily to improving the political and economic lot of women of their own class. A decade younger than Davies and older than Woolf, Pippa Strachey had organized the famous Mud March of 1907 and formed the putative model for one of the honorary treasurers to whom Woolf responds in *Three Guineas*. She continued her work for women's causes into the 1920s and 1930s, as the "superannuated" Davies retired and the women's movement struggled to maintain its momentum even as it divided over tactics and goals. On the verge of the granting of the vote to women over thirty, Woolf recorded her friend's forecast of the future of the movement: it "will turn now into a campaign for equality, by day & night," a campaign from which Strachey did not retire until she was well into her seventies (*Diary* 1: 118).

Despite Strachey's association with the vanguard of the women's movement, in February 1918 Woolf nonetheless termed her "an older fashioned type then we're used to," who "spoke of old days of parties, . . . George Duckworth, Jack Hills & Christmases at Corby," thinking "those people so 'civilised' compared with our cropheads," Barbara Bagenal and Dora Carrington (both b. 1893), self-consciously modern artists rather than late-Victorian–style aesthetes or activists (117–18). Valuing Strachey's work—as she did that of Pippa's sister Pernel (b. 1876), who became principal of Newnham in 1924—Woolf still saw her as "an older fashioned type." Generationally speaking, she identified Pippa with the men of the Stephen-Duckworth circle, even though her politics differed dramatically from theirs.

But Pippa's closest friend Ray Strachey, who married Pippa's brother Oliver in 1911 and thus became a member of a second "multigenerational feminist family," represented a newer, younger breed of the public woman (Holland 76). With an "immediate and impressive feminist heritage" tinged by a maternal-imperialist stance, she belonged to a third generation of activists and reformers (Caine, "Mothering" 296). After their father's death in 1899, Ray and her sister Karin Costelloe—who became Woolf's sister-in-law in 1914—were virtually raised by their grandmother, Hannah Whitall Smith, the U.S.-born suffragist, temperance activist, and close ally of Frances Willard, to whom she first introduced Isabel Somerset. Neglecting to mention her feminist political connections and focusing instead on her religious interests, Virginia Stephen compared this exact contemporary of Leslie Stephen to his younger sister: "A very spruce and practical edition of the Quaker," she told Dickinson upon meeting her in 1910, "without any mysticism about her, though she too is a great light! I imagine they might have been rivals, for [she] also writes books upon the soul, and hers are translated into Chinese" (Letters 1: 436).[8] Reading them in relation to their religious leanings, however, Woolf missed one rather large difference between the two. In the years immediately preceding her death in 1909, Caroline Stephen published three antisuffrage essays in The Nineteenth Century (Bush 43–44). By contrast, Whitall Smith wrote in 1888 that without equal citizenship, "I do not see how women can ever feel like anything but aliens in whatever country they may live" (qtd. in B. Strachey 102; emphasis in the original). As a woman, she might have said, she had no country.

Whitall Smith's daughters carried on their mother's political legacy to different extents and in different ways. One of two women of the younger generation who replied to "The Revolt of the Daughters" (1894), an essay by Blanche Althea Crackanthorpe (b. 1846/7) that appeared in The Nineteenth Century, Alys Pearsall Smith argued that what a girl wants is "the right to belong to herself" so as to pursue her "individual development" even against her parents' wishes (447, 449). At the moment when women began to hold offices in local government, she decided to run for the Westminster Vestry in 1894 with the support of her family's friends and London neighbors, Sidney and Beatrice Webb. She even arranged her wedding to Bertrand Russell—announced in the *Woman's Herald* and for which Isabel Somerset designed her dress—just in advance of the election in order to secure British citizenship, her mother's strictures on women's status as perpetual "aliens" notwithstanding (Turcon 117, 115).[9] Associated in the twentieth century with the artists and intellectuals of Chelsea, where she lived for many years with her brother Logan Pearsall Smith after her separation and divorce from Russell, yet still a familiar figure to the Bloomsberries, she was active in a range of feminist and temperance undertakings in the 1890s and beyond; indeed, of the three Smith children who survived to adulthood, she alone took up her mother's commitments to progressive reform for an extended period of time. Despite Somerset's concerns about her agnosticism, she ran a club for working-class girls in London and became the Youth Branch organizer for the BWTA (B. Strachey 134, 127). A member of the WCG, she also came to share and promulgate the eugenicist principles that inflected so much late-Victorian feminist activism, as I discussed in chapter 4.

While Alys remained closely tied to her birth family, her sister Mary (b. 1864) enacted her own daughterly revolt, which affected her daughters in multiple ways. An active New Woman, she emigrated to England, after attending Smith and Radcliffe, to marry the lawyer and political activist Frank Costelloe; there she took up the political activities of her elders, writing the "plan of work for the [WWCTU]" in 1886, which "made [social] purity equal in importance to temperance as the 'twin causes' of WWCTU reform" (Tyrrell, *Woman's World* 194).[10] Serving in 1890 as president of the Westminster, Chelsea, and Guildford Women's Liberal Association, she was interviewed late that year by the *Women's Penny Paper*, which described her as "one of our hardest workers in the cause" ("Interview with Mrs. Costelloe" 113). She nonetheless abandoned both feminist politics and her first marriage, leaving her husband and daughters and going to live and work in Italy with the art historian Bernard Berenson. That her earliest interests were literary is borne out in comments by her brother, who credited her with his own first exposure to literary culture: she "knew the whole of *In Memoriam* by heart; she could chant pages of Swinburne and Mrs. Browning by the hour" (L. Smith 8). She also introduced her family to the risqué and radical Walt Whitman, first by her passion for *Leaves of Grass* (1855) and then by making the poet's acquaintance in person.[11]

Looking back on her earlier life after breaking away from the political involvements of her family and first husband, Mary Berenson honored those commitments but represented her real interests as antithetical to them. In a 1904 letter to Ray, she described herself at the time of her marriage as "terribly in earnest over the Woman Question, and my wild dreams were to have a child who would overpass the usual feminine limits and prove conclusively that the female brain, if properly trained, could surpass (as I firmly believed it could) all the achievements of the inferior male brain. . . . It wasn't so much of my daughter I dreamed but of the Cause of Woman. How much of this Cause has descended to thee as birthright, who can say?" (Berenson 119). Writing to Karin in 1912, she defended her decision to end her marriage as a matter of contrasting desires between husband and wife, in terms that reproduce the familiar division between the active and the contemplative, the political and the aesthetic: he "wanted bustle and activity, he was ambitious and loved people and power and influence, and I wanted a quiet life, out of the world, with one's real adventures in books and art" (179).

Ray Strachey's family history thus combined the putatively divergent threads of Victorian aestheticism and activism. While Woolf certainly emphasized her friend's embrace of the latter—a path that did not please Mary Berenson, who "would have preferred her daughter . . . to have pursued the more cultured route"—it is nonetheless somewhat inaccurate to say that Strachey "rejected her mother's ideas and values entirely" (Fraser 29; Caine, *Bombay* 311). For instance, following in the wake of other women involved in the late-Victorian labor and women's movements—including Fawcett, Ford, Somerset, and Clementina Black—she, too, tried her hand at fiction.[12] In addition to her biographies of Willard, Whitall Smith (*A Quaker Grandmother* [1914]), and Fawcett, Strachey published three novels between 1907 and 1927 that draw on personal experience, family background, and historical material.[13] And of the three, the first, *The World at Eighteen* (1907), published by T. Fisher Unwin when she was just twenty years old, directly engages with recognizably topical issues for educated young women of the time.[14]

Set in Italy and "clearly autobiographical," *The World at Eighteen* details a young and inexperienced woman's resistance to the marriage plot into which her expatriate mother aims to insert her, and concludes with the daughter's break from her American cousin-suitor, a character based on "a second cousin from Pittsburgh" (Holmes 49, 44). Although the mother is no villain, the novel's somewhat open ending turns away from the narrative closure that marriage had typically provided, and implies this daughter's third-generation revolt against maternal expectations. Biographically speaking, it sheds an ironic light on Mary Berenson's attitude to a daughter's right to determine her own course, which she confided her to her diary in 1892: "Poor old people everywhere . . . try to make over young people's lives according to their pattern—and poor young people! What an awful institution for hypocrisy and oppression the family is! Honesty is the one *personal* virtue. . . . I shall *never* oppress my daughters" (Berenson 48–49; emphasis in the original). While her sentiments clearly anticipate not only Bloomsbury's critique of the family but also its interpersonal ethics, whether or not Ray and Karin's mother lived up to those standards is an open question. Her daughter's first novel surely suggests otherwise: it gives the heroine's mother the same surname that Grand had given to the parallel character in *Babs the Impossible*, a fictional figure described by Strachey's recent biographer as "mainly preoccupied with her own comfort" (Holmes 50).

Although narrated in a formally conventional way, *The World at Eighteen* eschews the tragic ending that so many New Woman novelists had fabricated and that Woolf would also construct in the dénouement of her first novel. Appearing in print well before *The Voyage Out* and seemingly before the two women had even met, there is a copy of it in what remains of the Woolfs' library, given to Virginia Stephen by Ray's future sister-in-law Marjorie (King and Miletic-Vejzovic 218). But nowhere in her letters or diaries does Woolf mention Ray Costelloe's novel, which took up the Jamesian plot of a young woman's entrance into "the world," one that Woolf, too, would refashion. Instead, she represents her slightly younger friend solely through the lens of her suffrage activism and public advocacy on women's issues. Even though Ray Strachey's pursuits were not exclusively political—she was also a prolific portrait painter—and even though her politics were recognizably different from those of Davies, especially on the matter of England's involvement in the war, Woolf nonetheless predicted that she would develop along similar lines over time.[15]

On the occasion of Strachey's 1918 lecture to the Richmond WCG at the Woolfs' home, Woolf remarked that Leonard "likes [Ray] better than [he does] the cropheads" and depicted her as a spiritual sister under the skin to their older friend. Perhaps drawing on the sense she derived from the conversation with Davies quoted above, she surmised that the younger woman, too, would quickly become "superannuated":

How strange it is to see one's friends taking their fixed shape! How one can foretell middle age for them, & almost see them with the eyes of the younger generation! "Rather a terror," I think they'll say of Ray. She has the look of conscious morality which is born of perpetual testifying to the right. She has grown heavier, more dogmatic; her attitudes are those of the public speaker & woman used to knocking about the country. She speaks in all the counties of England. She has lost such feminine charm as she had; she seems mature. But she is made of solid stuff; & this comes through & pleases me. . . . R. tends to think us a set of gifted but good for nothing wastrels. Her days [*sic*] work gives her some claim to look down upon us; but it would be unfair to say that she condescends or judges. She merely makes one aware of a different ideal. (*Diary* 1: 155–56)

Here again, Woolf articulates many of her perceptions in bodily terms: it is not only that her friend repeatedly makes public speeches that urge the righteousness of her cause, but also that she has "the look . . . born of" doing so, which results in her taking on a "fixed shape." While here she mentions Strachey's putting on weight in a relatively neutral way, a letter to Vanessa Bell written six months later is more censorious, describing her as "floppy, fat, untidy, clumsy" (*Letters* 2: 357). (Mary Berenson had noted some years earlier that her daughter "distinctly wants *not* to be attractive" [qtd. in Holmes 44; emphasis in the original].) The implied contrast of Strachey's body type with Woolf's own also implies other oppositions, between her "fixed shape" and Woolf's liquidity. She had already compared herself to her younger friend in an August 1915 letter to Davies in which she asserted that Strachey "makes [her] feel like a faint autumnal mist—she's so effective, and thinks me such a goose" (*Letters* 2: 63). Here, Woolf's perception that Ray "is made of solid stuff"—like *The Common Reader*, perhaps, in Case's estimation—suggests that she has another kind of weight, a utility Woolf feels herself to lack as one of the "gifted but good for nothing wastrels." A later diary description of "Ray sitting impassive in the arm chair, rotund, massive, a little surly, in the style of Widow [Louise] Creighton"—a highly ironic comparison to the Stephen-Duckworth family friend who coauthored the 1889 "Appeal against Woman's Suffrage"—also associates her weightiness with her political pursuits and interests. "She disapproves of abstract questions in a world," Woolf writes, "where there are so many concrete ones" (*Diary* 2: 81).

Ray Strachey's loss of "feminine charm," implicitly equated with the advent of maturity and her public career, might be said to confirm Woolf's own continued possession thereof, yet it also betrays another distinction between these contemporaries. In the letter to Vanessa Bell quoted above, written six months before the publication of *Night and Day*, Strachey's "becoming more and more the public woman" also means that she "mak[es] fewer concessions than ever to brilliancy, charm, politeness, wit, art, manners, literature and so forth." Possessing such qualities and affinities would presumably counter the "conscious morality" and "perpetual testifying to the right" that Woolf had both labeled "dogmatic" and referred to as "a different ideal"—different, that is, from her own. Strachey was "full of news upon women's future," Woolf told her sister: "But, my God, if *thats* [sic] the future whats [sic] the point in it?" (*Letters* 2: 357; emphasis in the original). Here and elsewhere, Woolf represents the publicly engaged woman as something of a gender hybrid, as in the *Night and Day* narrator's description of Mary Datchet, in whom "all the feminine instincts of pleasing, soothing, and charming were crossed by others in no way peculiar to her sex" (43; ch. 4); or in the bodily characterization of Rose Pargiter in *The Years*, which was further inflected by Woolf's intimacy with Ethel Smyth in the 1930s. But in the diary entry of 1918 quoted above, Woolf also conveys the non-normativity of Strachey's gender performance through a temporal lens. Claiming the power to see her "almost . . . with the eyes of the younger generation," Woolf aligns her vision with those whom, she imagines, will in time view Strachey as "a terror." Yet it may be as much the onset of her own "middle age" as Strachey's "fixed shape" that terrorizes the writer. For by asserting that (the younger) Strachey will (soon) appear older (than her) in the eyes of others, Woolf makes herself younger—at just around the moment when she was criticizing the aging Case for showing herself "so anxious to be in the front, to share what the young feel." For Woolf, in this context, being a public woman appears to entail becoming old before one's time.

To be sure, such a fate might as readily befall a man as a woman, an aesthete as an activist. The Edward Pargiter of the "1880" chapter of *The Years*, for example, presumably takes his "fixed shape" long before we meet him again in the "Present Day" chapter of the novel, having learned to suppress the erotic feelings, for men and for women, that his study of classical Greek both arouses and feeds.[16] Woolf presents the effects of this choice, if we can call it that, in bleak terms. Having achieved academic success, Edward "had the look of an insect whose body has been eaten out, leaving only the wings, the shell"; most damningly, he resembles "a blue-eyed horse whose bit no longer irked him. His movements were from habit, not from feeling" (365; "Present Day"). As Woolf saw it, the primary task of aging would be to avoid that kind of end. Comparing Smyth to the late Vernon Lee in a letter from July 1940, Woolf praised the former for being "not a finished precious vase, but a porous receptacle that sags slightly, swells slightly, but goes on soaking up the dew, the rain, the shine, and whatever else falls upon the earth"; by contrast, "Vernon Lee, I daresay, completed her shape, and was sun dried and shell like" (*Letters* 6: 406). Reflecting two decades earlier on Pippa Strachey's generationally marked preference for Duckworths over cropheads, which she decidedly did not share, Woolf mused that "age consists not in having a different point of view, but in having the same point of view, faded," an insight about how *not* to live one's life that resonates not only with her outlook on Davies, Case, or Pippa

Strachey but also with her own varied experiments in fiction, literary criticism, and cultural critique, in which a shift of audience or perspective generates a new and different form and style (*Diary* 1: 118). But in Woolf's case, avoiding the advent of a "fixed shape" in the future—yet without becoming entirely "shapeless" in "old age," as she perceived Davies, Strachey, or any other "public woman" as likely to become—meant turning back to the past, in works that reassessed the women's movement from the vantage point of a later-life perspective.

Woolf's Historicist Turn

The "public women" who populate *The Years* bear little outward resemblance to either Mary Datchet or Sally Seal. But it is not really the case that "in the twenty years between *Night and Day* and *Three Guineas*, [Woolf's] satire on suffragism has turned to satire on the anti-suffragists," while "her own 'sour deprecation'"—a phrase from *Three Guineas*—"of the conspirators has been forgotten" (*Three* 78n17, ch. 2; qtd. in Lee, *Virginia Woolf* 277–78). I contend instead that whereas *The Voyage Out* and *Night and Day* bear the imprint of Woolf's early ambivalence about feminist politics, Victorian philanthropy, and the circle of like-minded "conspirators" led by Davies, her last projects return to the mid- and late-Victorian past in ways influenced by ever-increasing temporal distance, by Woolf's growing knowledge about what we have come to call women's history, and by her determination to remain open, as she aged, to "having a different point of view." To be sure, the tone has changed—it is much more serious than satirical—but why it has changed is the real question.

Rather than consider this backward glance as revisionist, as does Hermione Lee, or nostalgic, as does Steve Ellis, we might instead see it as an act of invention that depends on reconceiving the past in new terms. All those major works left unfinished at Woolf's death—the literary-historical essay "Anon," *Between the Acts*, and "A Sketch of the Past"—intertwine a strong emphasis on the "now" of the time of writing with an equally pervasive awareness of "then." Becoming more attuned to the historical past means, in the first place, learning a good deal more about it. Both Barbara Green and, in greater detail, Anna Snaith have demonstrated the importance of Woolf's support for and creation of archives of women's history, whether in her reading, research, and material contributions to the Women's Library in Marsham Street— another initiative of Pippa Strachey's LNSWS—or in her own voluminous notebooks of press cuttings, which were so critical to the evidence-based argument she made in *Three Guineas* (Snaith, "'Stray'"; Neverow; Pawlowski). The educational work of Pernel Strachey at Newnham, the political activism of Pippa and Ray, and their print advocacy of women's issues, past and present, clearly provided some of the underpinning for this new departure in Woolf's career; Kathryn Holland calls the Strachey women "major sources for Woolf's conceptualization of British women's liberties and the history of the [suffrage] movement" and casts them as her "principal feminist interlocutors" (75). These women had carried on the work of the older generation—including that of Pernel and Pippa's mother, Jane (b. 1840), a longtime suffragist—and helped to transmit its import to Woolf.

In what we might consider a foundational moment of Woolf's historicist turn, the early pages of *The Pargiters* posit that "we cannot understand the present if we isolate it from the past."[17] The first pages of the text thus immediately encourage readers to make an imaginative leap: in order to understand how "we" arrived at this present, "we must become the people that we were two or three generations ago." Choosing the more distant ancestor, the narrator moves back beyond the limits of personal memory in an effort to reconstruct the shaping force of history on the here and now. "Let us be our great-grandmothers," she declares, thus implying unawareness on the part of her audience regarding the struggles of those earlier generations (8). If we assume that Woolf was consciously aiming to address younger women in her speech to the Junior Council of the LNSWS, then the great-grandmothers of those listeners-turned-readers would be mid-Victorians, rough contemporaries of not only the seven Pattle sisters but also Josephine Butler and Octavia Hill.

Woolf thus returns, at the outset of *The Pargiters*, to a past that she knew only very imperfectly and selectively; in order to transmit any knowledge of it to the next generation, she had first to learn about it, and imagine it, for herself. Indeed, the extended time scheme of *The Pargiters*—a multigenerational, even multicentury project, initially designed to present "a faithful and detailed account of a family . . . from the year 1800 to the year 2032"—implies from the outset a belief in the ongoing impact of a past that exceeds our capacity to remember or know it, or to know fully how it has shaped us (9). Yet we can also infer from the long chronological sweep of the projected work a conception of the historicist imagination as dialectically forged in the very effort to do so. Simultaneously, the extended temporal dimension also enables a representation of character over time, as it does or does not change, in ways that speak to the problematic of aging as Woolf came to conceive it.

In representing women's educational and political activism in *The Pargiters*, *The Years*, and *Three Guineas*, Woolf thus conscientiously drew on a wide range of sources, including all manner of books—like *"The Cause"* (1928), Ray Strachey's history of the suffrage movement, as well as her *Careers and Openings for Women: A Survey of Women's Employment and a Guide for Those Seeking*

Work (1935)—to expand the limits of her own subjective experience and "correspondingly applied to friends for accurate information to support her new work" (Wood, *Virginia Woolf's Late Cultural Criticism* 52). To take just a few salient examples, she consulted memoirs and histories of the movement to found and sustain Oxbridge colleges for women, including a biography of Anne Jemima Clough, the first principal of Newnham, by her niece Blanche Athena Clough (b. 1861), and *Emily Davies and Girton College* (1927) by her cousin-in-law Barbara Stephen (b. 1872), who had married one of Fitzjames Stephen's sons. Strikingly, the "Fifth Essay" of *The Pargiters* even quotes an old nemesis's remarks on how "worthless" her education had been, noting that Mary Augusta Ward, a former student of Anne Jemima Clough, had paid "tribute to the woman teacher of later days, the women who teach women, as Miss Craddock taught Kitty [Malone]" (*Writer's* 1: 96; qtd. in *Pargiters* 112). She asked Davies in November 1932 for another look at a letter to her aunt Emily from Walter Bagehot—whom Leslie Stephen had praised in *Studies of a Biographer* for his "clear insight into fact"—in which he had refused his help in founding Girton (L. Stephen, "Walter Bagehot" 173; *Letters* 5: 125). Woolf cited that letter in both *The Pargiters* (34) and *Three Guineas* (37n23; ch. 1).

She also set out to learn more about the WSPU and the suffragettes, imploring Smyth late in 1932 to "tell me all about your suffrage life one of these days" (*Letters* 5: 137). She repeated her request a week later, eager to know "all about Mrs Pankhurst and the suffrage. And why did you militate? I am turning over [*The Pargiters*] in my mind; and want to know a few facts" (*Letters* 5: 141). An inveterate reader of Smyth's memoirs well before they became friends, Woolf commented on the manuscript chapter of *Female Pipings in Eden* (1934) dedicated to Smyth's two years' involvement in the suffrage campaign and her intimacy with Emmeline Pankhurst that "the Pankhurst paper is by far the most convincing suffrage argument there can be" (*Letters* 5: 211). From her relationship with Smyth, she thus gained a wider point of view on "the Cause" in that unlike the Strachey women—but like Elizabeth Robins, who had become the Woolfs' Sussex neighbor—Smyth had been aligned with the militant rather than constitutional wing of the suffrage movement.[18] After meeting Emmeline Pankhurst and succumbing to her charisma, she put aside her musical career for two years in order to contribute her services to the cause, and spent three weeks in Royal Holloway Prison for her militancy; moreover, like Ray Strachey in relation to Millicent Garrett Fawcett, she joined her leader in fully supporting Britain's involvement in the war.

The underlying continuity between most suffragists and suffragettes on this point no doubt gave Woolf pause, especially in light of the approach of another global conflict. For on her analysis in *Three Guineas*, whether they were for or against women's suffrage, a significant majority of "the daughters of educated men" had in 1914 both "consciously . . . desired 'our splendid Empire'" and "unconsciously . . . desired our splendid war" (49; ch. 1). Thus, just a month or so after asking Smyth, "Why did you militate?" Woolf wanted to know the background to Smyth's criticism of one pacifist in particular, asking "Why do you think Vernon Lees [sic] views on the war detestable? What would you say to mine? And what are yours?" to which Smyth replied, "I hate her utter lack of patriotism" (Letters 5: 146 and n).[19] As I suggested in chapter 1, Lee's critique of patriotism provides an important antecedent to Woolf's own, being as much or more a product of her aesthetic and philosophical commitments as of her cosmopolitan upbringing and affiliations. We might also read this older contemporary's relative indifference to feminism, as it was articulated in her day, as providing a parallel to Woolf's ambivalent relation to the movement. The more explicit emphasis in both The Years and Three Guineas on issues of force and coercion thus reveals a particularly problematic aspect not only of Victorian domestic life but also of late-Victorian and Edwardian feminist politics, with both spheres instantiating the logic of imperial domination from which Lee and Woolf consistently dissented.[20]

In this light, we can compare the strand of Night and Day that registers and to some extent indicts the will to power of all those characters involved in "the Cause" with companion scenes from The Years that explore different characters but similar events from a range of vantage points. By setting the scenes that focus most closely on the workings of the suffrage movement during the year 1910—even though "all direct references to suffrage were cut from the published version of '1910'" in The Years—Woolf alludes to her one year of direct involvement in the movement (Wood, Virginia Woolf's Late Cultural Criticism 48). As Snaith establishes in her exhaustively annotated edition of the novel, this chapter is set at a precise moment in time: the very day of Edward VII's death. More importantly in terms of Woolf's narrative, it takes place during the nine-month period in which the WSPU called a halt to militancy pending the negotiations surrounding the potential passage of the Conciliation Bill, which would have granted suffrage only to some women. "During this truce, the WSPU joined with other suffrage societies in supporting the Conciliation Bill," which explains why Rose Pargiter, clearly associated with the suffragettes, attends the same meeting as her suffragist sister Eleanor and their cousin Kitty, who putatively abjure the use of force (Years 465; cf. Tickner 110–11). So, too, might this temporary lull in militancy and the concomitant rapprochement between different factions enable us to gloss another feature of this chapter, a motif that both unites and differentiates Rose and Eleanor, two sisters born almost fifteen years apart, whose relation to one another as eldest and youngest sisters of a "long" family approximates that between Virginia Stephen and Stella Duckworth.[21]

Already ruminating on her past as she looked down at the Thames from the Embankment, when forty-year-old Rose lunches with her cousins Sara and Maggie and hears them discuss the Pargiter family "as if Abercorn Terrace were a scene in a play," she experiences a curious doubling of her own identity: "They talked as if they were speaking of people who were real, but not real in the way in which she felt herself to be real. It puzzled her; it made her feel that she was two different people at the same time; that she was living at two different times at the same moment. She was a little girl wearing a pink frock; and here she was in this room, now" (150; "1910"). This "odd feeling" points to both continuity and discontinuity in Rose's sense of her own identity over time, an effect also registered in part through her physical appearance (152). Some of the first perceptions the narrator attributes to Rose in this chapter concern her lack of confidence in what she wears and how she looks, which Eleanor, too, disparages in the "1908" chapter (140). Having "caught a glimpse of her own figure in a tailor's window," Rose thinks it "a pity . . . not to dress better, not to look nicer" (145; "1910"). These details recall her father's repeated description of her in "1880" as a "grubby little ruffian" who wears a stained pinafore over her "stiff pink frock," a detail her brother Martin also recalls years later (11, 10, "1880"; 142, "1908"). That frock provides a trace of the traumatic incident from "1880" in which a man exposes his genitals to her.[22] "More like a man than a woman" in her cousin Maggie's eyes, Rose appears throughout this section to be suspended not only between the child she was then and the adult she is now but also between two gender constructs, signified by the feminized frock of childhood and the mannish "coats and skirts from Whiteley's"; the latter function as an outward emblem of the "fixed shape" she has apparently attained, while the "pink frock" lingers in memory, connoting gendered and sexual trauma (153, 145; "1910"). Her clothing contributes to the overall impression she makes on others throughout the novel, stemming from her identification with her father, Colonel Abel Pargiter: "She ought to have been the soldier, Eleanor thought," since she appears "as if she were leading an army," "as if she were a military man" (141, 145, "1910"; 323, "Present Day"). Although *Three Guineas* concentrates exclusively on how men's fashion signifies their patriarchal status, Rose's costume is also something like a uniform, one that simultaneously indicates her sex/gender nonconformity and obscures an unacknowledged but persistent strand of her identity.

The tension between gendered identifications—as between past and present, inward consciousness and external performance—holds the two in a kind of suspense, at least temporarily leaving open the possibility of some new or different configuration of identity in the future. Although Margaret Homans writes of Rose that after her childhood trauma, "her character had become . . . frozen in a single reactive posture, a single preoccupation," we might instead read her appearances in both "1908" and "1910," each of which mixes present sensations with past recollections, as threshold moments in which breaking through that "frozen" state and shattering that "fixed shape" is still possible (417–18). Certainly by the time the character reappears, in the long chapter that concludes the novel, such a possibility has not come to pass. Rose does not escape the structures, in place from the outset of the novel, that still exert their force in "Present Day."

Instead, she has become like her sister Delia, whose youthful "political fervor" for Home Rule "leads to neither justice nor liberty" (Thomas Davis 15). At the outset of the novel, Delia imagines herself as both Abel Pargiter's "favorite daughter" and the fantasy lover of Charles Stewart Parnell, the "great" advocate of Home Rule who would be publicly exposed as an adulterer in 1891, as readers of *The Years* already know Delia's father to be from its opening scene (12, 13; "1880"). Yet Delia wants as much or more to *be* Parnell as to stand beside him, feeling herself far more "suppressed," to use Peggy Pargiter's word, than Eleanor ever does (302; "Present Day"). Delia fantasizes a release from her mother's sickroom and the family home by imagining herself on the platform, Parnell "by her side"; he listens to her "speaking in the cause of Liberty, . . . in the cause of Justice," as Josephine Butler and others were doing at the historical moment in which this scene is set (20; "1880"). But with her psychic development "undermined by her entrapment in her sexualized fantasy of liberation," she had gotten precisely the reverse fate, having mistakenly "married the most King-respecting, Empire-admiring of country gentlemen" instead of the "wild rebel" for whom she'd hoped (Weihman 42; 359, "Present Day").[23]

Indeed, through her participation in the militant movement, Rose, too, has come to embody the very structures she sought to overturn: they both inhabit and inhibit her. From their niece Peggy's perspective, both Rose and Martin, still quarrelling after fifty years, "had a certain line laid down in their minds, . . . and along it came the same old sayings"; they do not alter, they simply repeat, having attained their "fixed shape" (323; "Present Day"). In the final extended passage of the novel in which she appears, Rose "brandish[es] her [butter] knife" in her brother's face, professing her patriotism, even as holding the knife enables her fleetingly to recall but not fully to process the childhood trauma she associates with "wearing a pink frock" (374, 375). The novel thus demonstrates the context in which Rose's complicity with militarist institutions develops, displays the damage it incurs, and yet also challenges the idea that it is inevitable.

For if both Rose and Delia attain their "fixed shape" partially through their participation in political activism, their eldest sister, the differently active and aware Eleanor, does not. In one of the letters she wrote to Stephen Spender that responded to his reading of the novel, Woolf indicated that while all the other characters, save the very youngest of the first generation of Pargiter cousins, Maggie and Sara, "were crippled in one way or another," "Eleanor's experience though limited partly by sex and the cramp of the Victorian up-bringing was meant to be all right; sound and rooted" (*Letters* 6: 122). The novel partially registers these qualities through her limited tolerance for repetition. Already at the suffrage meeting in "1910" when Rose and Sara arrive, Elea-nor, too, fathoms a division within herself. She comes across as impatient with talk while listening to Miriam Parrish read a letter: "I've heard all this, I've done all this so often," she reflects. The faces around the table "even seemed to re-peat themselves" and she can anticipate the speeches others will make before they make them ("I know what he's going to say, I know what she's going to say"): "There's no other way, I suppose, she thought, taking up her pencil again. She made a note as Mr Spicer spoke. She found that her pencil could take notes quite accurately while she herself thought of something else. She seemed able to divide herself in two. One person followed the argument—and he's put-ting it very well, she thought, while the other, for it was a fine afternoon, and she had wanted to go to Kew, walked down a green glade and stopped in front of a flowering tree" (*Years* 158). The situation and setting definitely recall that scene from *Night and Day* in which the much younger Mary Datchet succeeds in focusing on the business of the committee meeting despite being distracted by thoughts of Ralph Denham. It also recalls the meeting that Eleanor attends in the "1891" chapter, which Snaith's notes to the novel identify as one "simi-lar to Octavia Hill's Society of Women Housing Managers," the sort of meet-ing that we know Stella Duckworth to have attended in taking up and continuing the work her mother had done, albeit in a more systematic way, as appropriate to women of her generation (*Years* 441). But the older Eleanor, over fifty and bored by the predictable repetitions, can both attend to the meet-ing out of habit and entertain an alternative to it, imagining herself doing something else, something she values positively, at that very moment. Unlike Rose, who involuntarily feels like "two different people at the same time," or Mary, who quells her distraction only by "some trick of the brain," Eleanor can willfully "divide herself in two," even as she remains stationed in the pre-sent. Indeed, it may be that capacity for imaginative flight that enables the older Eleanor in particular, "sound and rooted," to persist and even to prosper de-spite her unpropitious circumstances as the dutiful eldest daughter of a de-manding father who had lived long past his time, well into the new century.

In that last detail, Eleanor Pargiter most definitely recalls Margaret Llewe-lyn Davies, whose father did not die until he was ninety and she was fifty-five. But in other respects, Eleanor's character bears the traces of a range of women senior to Woolf. Her commitments outside her family, as *The Years* demonstrates from its very beginning, lie in social service, whether by visiting the poor and advising them on birth control or building cottages as "part of a wider movement for the improvement of working-class housing" (*Years* 409). Such activities closely resemble ones that Stella Duckworth, following in her mother's footsteps, had carried out as a young unmarried woman. These were the sort of practices that the younger Woolf had typically derided, as in her representation of Sally Seal in *Night and Day*, or Evelyn M. and her friend Lil-lah Harrison in *The Voyage Out*, and in her remarks on a whole host of older friends and relatives, some but by no means all of which I have referenced.

What changes, then, in Woolf's portrait of what she calls "a well-known type; . . . philanthropic" is that the passionate (or enthusiastic) devotion to principles is presented without ridicule (90; "1891"). Eleanor's angry response to a photograph of Mussolini, "the usual evening paper's blurred picture of a fat man gesticulating," suggests her ongoing commitment to the ideals that she, like her sister Delia or Josephine Butler half a century earlier, names "free-dom and justice" (298, 299; "Present Day"). "Odd" and "queer" as it seems to her niece Peggy, at almost eighty years of age Eleanor still cares for "the things that man had destroyed" (298). Perhaps paradoxically, it is the character who has filled the most conventional late-Victorian roles for the "daughters of ed-ucated men"—tending to her younger siblings and her father, joining commit-tees, visiting the homes of the poor—who, as she ages through the novel, evinces the greatest capacity for growth and change and the greatest optimism for a different future.

Twenty years on from *The Voyage Out* and *Night and Day*, then, Woolf's own commitments remain intact—the opposition to force and coercion persists, as does the resistance to the simple binary of "right" and "wrong"—but her point of view on both the philanthropic and political work undertaken by some of her elders, including Case and Davies, has changed. Working as they did—and as at times it seems that we, too, do—for "the good of a world that none of them were ever to know," those who came before Woolf, practicing their dif-ferent pursuits, did not always proceed along the lines she picked out for her-self. Yet, with age, I think, she did finally become "more sensible" of the value of their commitment to "a different ideal" from her own.

Afterword

The final chapter of *The Years* stages a series of conversations between members of the older and younger Pargiter generations as they gather for a family party, and one in particular offers a key to thinking about how Woolf's relationship to the late-Victorian past changed as she aged over time. In an early scene, Eleanor's niece Peggy, a physician in her mid-thirties, shows herself to be both curious about and oddly nostalgic for her aunt's experiences. Discussing the portrait of Peggy's grandmother Rose that hangs in Eleanor's flat—one of the "solid objects" that appears off and on throughout the novel—Peggy asks her aunt if it is "like her" (31, "1880"; 293, "Present Day"). "'Not as I remember her,' said Eleanor," who keeps changing the subject, "thinking of something else," even as Peggy keeps returning to the topic of "Eleanor's childhood" and to "how things had changed" (294). Knowing little of her aunt's experiences, Peggy wants to think of Eleanor's past in fixed terms, and so Eleanor obligingly points out the still-visible signs of a late-Victorian world on their way to the family reunion—"Abercorn Terrace" and "the pillar-box," a house "where we used to dine" (299, 300). Sounding much like the younger Woolf did in romanticizing the 1860s, Peggy relishes the fragments she gathers: "It seemed to her so peaceful and so safe"; "so interesting; so safe; so unreal—that past of the 'eighties; and to her, so beautiful in its unreality" (294, 300). Peggy expresses nostalgia for a world she never knew, one for which most members of her aunt's generation, who lived through it, are by no means nostalgic. Resisting those demands for pictures of a "peaceful" and "safe" past that was anything but, Eleanor silently frames her desires in terms of "here and now," one of *The Years'* early titles (*Diary* 4: 6): "I do not want to go back into my past, she was thinking. I want the present" (303; "Present Day"). As for Kitty, another member of the late-Victorian generation, "the present; the future; that was what she wanted" (379).

As her aunt intuits, Peggy's questions about the past ultimately derive from "bitterness," a radical postwar cynicism about the present and the future as well as a lack of satisfaction with her lot in life that she cannot shake (303). Her effort to do so leads to an uncanny, perhaps deliberate repetition-with-a-difference of the scene from *Night and Day* that I analyzed in chapter 1: as Katharine Hilbery had gazed at her grandfather's portrait in hopes of finding answers to her difficulties and dilemmas, Peggy Pargiter "looked at the picture of her grandmother as if to ask her opinion"—but in this case with very different results (295). In that earlier scene of communion with the dead, the living descendant had felt a "kinship of blood" that connected past and present, "mak[ing] it seem possible . . . to believe that they look with us upon our present joys and sorrows" (*Night* 338; ch. 24). By contrast, this representation of Peggy's grandmother has no answers to offer, no shared perspective to provide: she "had assumed the immunity of a work of art; she seemed as she sat there, smiling at her roses, to be indifferent to our right and wrong" (295; "Present Day").

The differences between these remarkably similar moments in two novels published almost twenty years apart, each what Woolf called a "novel of fact" rather than "vision," have many determinants, one being the immediate circumstances of the female descendant who seeks something from the ancestor's portrait (*Pargiters* 9). As I argued above, Katharine's relationship to the "great" past, present as it is in her daily life, usually weighs on her. But in the portrait scene she successfully reanimates the long-dead poet: whether or not she indulges in mere projection, she feels herself able to achieve intergenerational communion. By contrast, the contours of Peggy's life are not defined by or confined to a daughterly or granddaughterly role, as Katharine's had been: a practicing physician with more than one room of her own, Peggy leads the kind of life Woolf would attribute to the women she addressed in her 1931 speech to the LNSWS. Yet, the life of the new professional woman, no longer housebound, has its stresses and strains as well.[1] The complexities of her present presumably shape Peggy's desire for a simpler past.

It is also the case, of course, that whereas Katharine Hilbery aims to make contact with a "great" man, thereby circumventing the mediation of her mother, Peggy Pargiter seeks the "opinion" of an ordinary woman, the grandmother she never knew, marking the sort of shift that we can see, I believe, in Woolf's own trajectory over time: from the ambivalent "ancestor worship" of *Night and Day* to the historical fact-finding in which she engaged throughout the 1930s. There is nonetheless still ambivalence about the late-Victorian past, both as it was lived and as it is later recollected. To Peggy's aunt Delia in "1880," for instance, the portrait had represented a "girl in white . . . presiding over the protracted affair of her own death-bed with a smiling indifference that outraged" her daughter (40–41). That both Delia and Peggy read "indifference" in their female predecessor's image suggests a transtemporal link between the elder and the younger: each is dissatisfied in her own time, if for different reasons; each seeks something from the mother/grandmother, or her aestheticized image, that is beyond her, or its, capacity to provide. By contrast with Alardyce of *Night and Day*, the dying mother or dead grandmother who has become "a work of art" in *The Years* has nothing to offer either her first- or second-generation descendants; the smiling silence of the image underwrites its "immunity" to "our" human concerns.

Very different from Lily Briscoe's abstract "tribute" to mother and child, which she describes in painterly terms as "the relations of masses, of light and shadow," the stereotypically sentimental "Victorian" portrait of Rose Pargiter—which depicts "a red-haired young woman in white muslin holding a basket of flowers on her lap"—opens a representational gap between the aestheticized and the actual, a gap that death exposes and exploits (*Lighthouse* 56; *Years* 9, "1880"). Although readers learn very little about Rose the elder, dying as she does at the outset, the only scene in which she lives and speaks presents her in strikingly un-idealized terms. The few details we receive of the "silly simpering picture" coexist uneasily with the decidedly unsentimental view of the dying woman's body, mediated by her daughter Delia's vision (*Pargiters* 23): her "pouched and heavy" face; the "brown patches" on her skin and the "queer yellow patches" in her hair; "the white and wasted hand" (19, 22; "1880"). Shrouded in "the sour-sweet smell of illness," Rose's memories of her own past, conveyed in "broken" sentences, have no coherence or pattern to them (19, 22). Twenty-year-old Delia sees her only as "an obstacle, a prevention, an impediment to all life": even when she "tried to whip up some feeling of affection, of pity," by turning to memory—recalling "that summer . . . at Sidmouth, when she called me up the garden steps"—"the scene melted as she tried to look at it" (20). Unlike Mrs. Ramsay, who leaves behind the memories of scenes on which Lily Briscoe can draw, which "stayed in the mind affecting one almost like a work of art," this mother persists only as a visual image that neither represents nor communicates what her descendants want or need to know (*Lighthouse* 164). Here we might conclude that the ideal that has really been "destroyed" by *The Years*—rather than "laid . . . to rest," as in *To the Light-house*—is the aestheticized version of the mother and her times (298, "Present Day"; "Sketch" 81).

In its portrayal of the image of the mother, *The Years* turns away from an idealized maternal past, particularly in that Delia's view in "1880"—as hostile to the portrait as to her mother's protracted dying—looks to be predicated on her identifications with men: as Thomas S. Davis remarks, "It is not her father . . . but her mother who represents antiquated and constraining late Victorian feminine roles" (13). Like her sister Rose, Delia takes up the position of "the public woman" who leaves the private home for political life and dedicates herself to a cause or causes, be it women's suffrage, Home Rule for Ireland, temperance, or social purity. Such an opportunity for the women of the 1880s and 1890s was pioneered not only by Butler, whose commitment to "Liberty and Equality and Justice" Woolf placed at the center of her analysis in *Three Guineas*, but also by Fawcett, Grand, and the women of their intersecting networks, including Massingberd, Dilke, and Somerset, as well as so many of the Bloomsbury-based women of those decades. In identifying themselves with activist causes, however, both Delia and Rose also share some of the highly problematic commitments of most feminist reformers of their time: they embrace models for public action that, in Lisa Weihman's words, "expose women's complicity in the production of a fantasy of the national home through their support of the institutions that maintain and perpetuate nationalism as a positive value" (31). Significantly, it is not Peggy, who has joined a profession and thus also "the procession" led by "the sons of educated men," but her brother North who explicitly rejects this mindset as "not for him, not for his generation. . . . Not halls and reverberating megaphones; not marching in step after leaders, in herds, groups, societies caparisoned" (*Three* 77, ch. 2; 369, "Present Day"). The evocation of fascist rallies bespeaks both the approach of another war and Woolf's continuing dissent from the politics that both lead to war and aim to oppose it, whether specifically feminist politics or not.

If those politics might be said to have their roots in the Victorian era, they still continued to flourish in the present day, as a final return to the Victorian past in the third playlet of Miss La Trobe's pageant in *Between the Acts* illuminates. Woolf here casts her parodic representation of empire in deadly comic terms that continue to critique its ideological project at home and abroad. Transformed by his costume, makeup, and truncheon into "a huge symbolical figure," the local publican Budge is "eminent, dominant" (115, 117), words used earlier to describe the pageant's Queen Elizabeth (61). "Directing the traffic of 'Er Majesty's Empire" in the heart of London, he "take[s] under [his] protection and direction the purity and security of all Her Majesty's minions; in all parts of her dominions; insist[s] that they obey the laws of God and Man" (116–17). "But mark you," Budge intones, "our rule don't end there": "Over thought and religion; drink; dress; manners; marriage too, I wield my truncheon. Prosperity and respectability always go, as we know, 'and in 'and. The ruler of an Empire must keep his eye on the cot; spy too in the kitchen; drawing-room; library; wherever one or two, me and you, come together. Purity our watchword; prosperity and respectability" (117). In what immediately follows, domesticity is further aligned with the imperial project in a scene set "about 1860" (118).[2] "The Picnic Party" depicts lovers who become engaged on the basis of their mutual desire "to convert the Heathen" (119).[3] Songs, prayers, and an elaborate repast give way to a gramophone recording of "Home Sweet Home." When it ends, Budge offers his own version of domestic bliss around the tea table, modeled on that of "our widowed Queen"— Prince Albert died in 1861—as she "calls the Royal orphans round her knee" (124). This mid- rather than late-Victorian scene in La Trobe's pageant is discernibly unambivalent about the past in that it conveys the deep, ongoing "resistance" to patriarchal imperialist values, whether evinced by men or women, that characterizes all of Woolf's work including *The Years* (125).

But in its cartoonish representation of "1860," *Between the Acts* aims not just to discredit the nineteenth-century ideologies of empire and domesticity as they shaped the lives of the subjects of "the White Queen Victoria," but to incite her readers to register the persistence of those 'Victorian' ideologies into "present time" (117, 129). Constructing yet challenging firm distinctions between past and present, Woolf registers both continuity and change, identifying perspectives on the past as variable depending on the age and experience of those who witness and respond to the pageant. Before the playlet begins, for instance, Mrs. Lynn Jones shares her memories of a less-than-perfect past, when "you couldn't walk—Oh, dear me, no—home from the play" because of the "loose women," like those who haunt Piccadilly in *The Voyage Out* or Regent Street in *The Heavenly Twins* (114). And she recalls that past from a new vantage point: "Was there, she mused, . . . something—not impure, that wasn't the word—but perhaps 'unhygienic' about the Home? Like a bit of meat gone sour, with whiskers, as the servants called it?" All the same, "'it was beautiful,' Mrs. Lynn Jones protested. Home she meant," even if it was not only beautiful (124). Whiskered meat, like whiskered men or ladies in petticoats, has gone spoiled or rotten, while the clock's hands, like the record on the gramophone, continue "round and round and round" without stopping (125).

But that clock marks not only change, or the passage of time, but also continuity. "Were they like that?" asks Isa Oliver, born in 1900, of Lucy Swithin, who "had lived in the reign of Queen Victoria." Mrs. Swithin's response, quoted at the outset of this book, denies the difference between them and us. But it's not the case that she doesn't "believe in history," as William Dodge asserts (125); it is Lucy Swithin, after all, who is reading a book called "an Outline of History" on her first appearance in the novel, early on the morning of the pageant, musing on dinosaurs and "rhododendron forests in Piccadilly" (6). Given that long view of deep time, one that Woolf, too, acquired over the course of her life, it is no wonder Lucy perceives a likeness between "them" and "us."

Woolf's belief that the values La Trobe's pageant indicts had *not* changed, or had not changed enough, inspired much of her writing and research in the 1930s; those values she had once taken to be quintessentially "Victorian" turned out to be active still in the contemporary moment, evident "in herds, groups, societies caparisoned." Anticipating "present time," the playlet holds up a mirror of the Victorian past to viewers (and readers), inviting them (and us) to gaze on a past that, spoiled though it may be, isn't even now really over. As the audience members await the pageant's final scene, they inhabit the liminal space and time between the acts: "They were neither one thing nor the other; neither Victorians nor themselves" (127). "Dressed differently" though members of the pageant's audience assuredly are from their Victorian antecedents, Woolf suggests that the mirror of historical retrospect reflects not just how they looked then, but how we look now. Yet she also encourages us to enact how we might become, in the present and the future, not just "dressed differently," but actually different.

Notes

Introduction

1. For a fuller analysis of this passage and the anthropological terms Woolf deploys throughout this portion of the memoir, see Corbett, *Family Likeness* 183–87.

2. I am by no means first to argue this: see, for example, Ezell; Booth, *How to Make It*; E. Blair; and Hite, *Woolf's Ambiguities*.

3. See Ingleby 23–24 and 249–50 for additional incisive comments on Woolf's construction of this divide in relation to the Phyllis and Rosamond text.

4. Millicent Vaughan went on to marry a baronet, Sir Vere Isham, in 1895.

5. In the 1890s, George Duckworth interacted with the Booths professionally as well as socially. By walking the city, he helped to generate the data for the famous Booth poverty maps. In contrast with Woolf's representations of him, Mary Booth called Duckworth one of her husband's "most efficient and zealous colleagues" (20–21). O'Day and Englander, dating the first wave of his involvement from late 1891 to 1893, have pointed to his "highly individual reports" as "of singular importance to the Booth inquiry," in his being "curious and responsive to Londoners and their problems" (19, 107). Charles Booth himself described this junior colleague as having "a quick eye observant of details, a cool counsel, judgement, plenty of determination and"—sounding rather more like the George Duckworth we think we know—"very conciliatory manners" (qtd. in O'Day and Englander 107). To access additional information on Duckworth's work with Booth, see the online project *Charles Booth's London*.

6. After Kitty's sister-in-law Violet married Nelly's brother-in-law Edward, the two women met and became close friends (A. Curtis 45).

7. Two of the Massingberd sisters, Mary and Diana, married brothers named Montgomery, which perhaps accounts for Woolf's mistake.

8. Even now, rumor has it that Cust fathered the woman who gave birth to Margaret Thatcher.

9. For more on Fawcett's campaign, see Caine, *Victorian* 213, 231–33; Kent 153–55; Rubinstein 87–89; and R. Strachey, *Millicent* 118–20, which discusses the whole incident but without using Cust's name.

10. Despite her agential role in the "Maiden Tribute" controversy, Josephine Butler also repeatedly articulated the belief that the state should keep out of the private affairs of its citizens. As her most recent biographer notes, "there were a number of sexual scandals involving public men in which [Butler] took a close interest, but about which she was rarely judgmental": "she had distanced herself from the 'leaders of the war against impurity' . . . over the issue" of Parnell's adulterous relationship with

Katharine O'Shea (Jordan, *Josephine Butler* 276–77); she was not keen on the 1892 efforts to block Charles Dilke's return to public life; and she even expressed some limited sympathy for Oscar Wilde's fate. While she privately deplored both "the Oscar Wilde madness," which "has spread like a plague thro' London fashionable & artistic society," and the values she associated with this fraction of the aristocratic sphere—"What fools people are who worship art & beauty & perfumes & poetry & nonsense in place of God"—she tended to assess the sexual lives of men not from the standpoint of "purity," but as a matter of the liberty of the subject (Letter to Stanley Butler [24 April 1895]).

11. Though inaccurate on some of the details, Virginia Stephen referred to this event in 1909, when she complained to Violet Dickinson about having to write "a d—d dull review of a book by a woman who had a child before she married—Mrs Henry Cust" (*Letters* 1: 387).

12. When Dilke aimed to stand for election to the London County Council in 1889, "in an incredibly short time a protest against the attempt . . . was got up and signed by 1604 ladies," including Fawcett and her sister Elizabeth Garrett Anderson, Elizabeth Blackwell, Annie Besant, Eva McLaren, Margaret Bright Lucas, Anna Swanwick, Laura Ormiston Chant, and Mrs. Samuel Barnett ("Women's Protest"). For details, see Demoor, *Their Fair Share* 62; and Israel 212.

13. The Stephen-Duckworth family connections to the Dilkes both preceded and continued after their years as next-door neighbors. The mother of Maye Dilke and Virginia Crawford, Martha Mary Eustace Smith was a distant cousin of Sophia Pattle's husband, Sir John Dalrymple, through whom she "gained an entrée to Little Holland House" in the 1850s (Wilcox). In later life, Maye's son married Lucy Clifford's daughter, Ethel; Woolf referred twice to one of Maye's daughters, Sybil, who died in a fire in 1931, as "my oldest friend" (*Letters* 4: 291, 293). Perhaps most importantly, Leslie Stephen and Henry Fawcett had been tutors at Trinity Hall during Dilke's tenure there and exerted a considerable influence on him; no doubt the Crawford divorce case and its protracted aftermath attracted Stephen's interest. For further analysis of this scandal, see Corbett, "On *Crawford*."

14. My use of the term "public women" follows Hite, *Woolf's Ambiguities*, and is informed as well as by Evans, who uses it "to signal the primacy of their public presence for both their celebrants and their critics, and to reference their contradictory associations with both the 'new woman' and the original 'public woman,' the prostitute" (5).

15. "The wealth of the Dilkes in real life compared with our own moderate means impressed us," Woolf recalled. "We noticed how many new clothes Mrs Dilke wore; how seldom my mother bought a new dress"; and young Virginia Stephen invented "wild stories of the Dilke family," who "dug under the floor and discovered sacks of gold; and held great feasts and ate fried eggs" ("Sketch" 79).

16. A front-page profile titled "Mrs Ashton Dilke" in the *Women's Penny Paper*, reporting on her candidacy for a position on the West Lambeth School Board (which she won), characterizes her as active and energetic while also noting her sympathy for Home Rule. But not everyone thought so highly of her "eloquence." Complaining to a friend about a conversation on "women's rights questions," in November 1889 Rudyard Kipling described this new female acquaintance as "mild and merciful compared to the Mrs. Assheton [*sic*] Dilke whom I met at Macmillan's last night. . . . Her mission in life is to set all mankind right about female education. She manages to do

this in a tone that makes you long ardently to kick her round the room forty times" (1: 355).

17. One of the complicating factors in the scandal was that Charles Dilke was alleged to have had an affair, after his first wife's death, with Martha Mary Eustace Smith that preceded his relationship with her daughter (Jenkins 236–37, 239).

18. "Why should Bloomsbury be singled out from all other districts? Why not Hampstead or Chelsea? Chelsea has always been the home of painters and writers and highbrows generally. There were George Moore and his circle, universally admired and respected, with Logan Pearsall Smith round the corner and painters, of course, by the hundred" (V. Bell, "Notes" 114).

19. Rumpelmayer's did Clarissa Dalloway's catering (*Mrs. Dalloway* 3); Jane Goldman calls its London and Paris tea shops "a haunt of the chic and the famous" ("1925" 71).

20. Livesey focuses on Woolf's links with the next generation of the Bloomsbury socialists of the 1880s, with particular attention to her close contemporaries David Garnett, Dollie Radford, and Noel Olivier, as well as Rupert Brooke and Jacques Raverat.

21. Herself a veteran of progressive social movements such as the Fellowship of the New Life, a trades-union activist and organizer in her native Leeds, a member of both the Pioneer Club and the Independent Labour Party as of 1893, and a suffragist with whom Ray Strachey came to travel on a speaking tour, Ford sets her fiction in Bloomsbury and keeps it there: with the single exception of a bus ride to Chelsea via Regent Street in the novel's last chapter, West Central constitutes the sole site of the novel's action (Hannam 69; Waters 30; Holmes 88).

22. See Ingleby 64–74 on Bloomsbury's position in *Vanity Fair*.

23. Bernstein notes the way in which the space itself changed over time: first in 1857, when the domed room opened; then with the rapid demise of the two rows designated "For Ladies Only"; and then again in 1907, when its redecoration included for the first time the names of members of "the male literary canon emblazoned underneath the dome," to which Woolf's narrator reacts so forcefully in *Room* (157).

1. Gender, Greatness, and the "Third Generation"

1. Whitworth notes that "Woolf alludes to the unearned increment in *Night and Day* [35; ch. 3], where Katharine Hilbery benefits from a metaphorical increment in the value of the poetic works of her grandfather," connecting this to the contemporary debate on land values (38). More recently, in the explanatory notes to his edition of the novel, he also references the proto-eugenicist discourse of hereditary genius visible in some lines from James Russell Lowell's poem, "Verses Intended to Go with a Posset Dish to My Dear Little God-daughter, 1882": "I simply wish the child to be / A sample of Heredity / Enjoying to the full extent / Life's best, the Unearned Increment" (ll. 44–47; cf. *Night* 561).

2. Kuper argues that "elite kin marriages . . . contributed to the formation of a new social stratum in England," which Annan first called "the intellectual aristocracy" in a 1955 essay ("Changing" 721). He further demonstrates the breadth, range, and diversity of that stratum in *Incest and Influence*, which includes sections on the Darwins, the Stephens, and Bloomsbury. For a critique of Annan's original formulation, see Whyte.

3. As in the letter to Vanessa Bell from 1911, in which she describes the grounds for her depression: "To be 29 and unmarried—to be a failure—childless—insane too, no writer" (*Letters* 1: 466).

4. Of the first cousins on both sides of her family, Woolf could have pointed to her much older first cousin Katharine Stephen (b. 1856), who became principal of Newnham in the early twentieth century, as a single woman distinguished for her professional achievements. Others married men of some distinction. Among Woolf's eight female first cousins on her mother's side of the family, Adeline Fisher (b. 1870) married the well-known composer Ralph Vaughan Williams, who was related to both the Wedgwoods and the Darwins. Florence Fisher (b. 1864) married twice, first Leslie Stephen's biographer, the historian F. W. Maitland (a match brokered by Julia Stephen), then Darwin's son Francis; Cecil Sharp published a volume of her plays after her death in 1920. Cordelia Fisher (b. 1879) married a journalist while another Vaughan sister, Augusta (b. 1861), had "innumerable penniless children" (really only four) with her husband, whose farming venture failed (*Diary* 1: 88n19; "22 Hyde" 169). The other three maternal first cousins—Marny Vaughan and her sister Emma (b. 1874), who lived together in Kensington, and Emmeline Fisher (b. 1868)—never married.

5. Perhaps recalling this encounter almost thirty years later, Woolf told Stephen Spender that James "loomed up in my young days almost to the obstruction of his works"; in an interview after Woolf's death, Elizabeth Bowen stated that Woolf "had rather a horror of HJ as an influence" (*Letters* 5: 392; Bowen 48). Woolf had reviewed *The Golden Bowl* in 1905, *Portraits of Places* in 1906, and was reading *The American Scene* (1907) just before this meeting (*Essays* 1: 22–24, 124–27).

6. See Hite's discussion of this review in *Woolf's Ambiguities* 78–79.

7. For a groundbreaking discussion of historicism in Woolf studies, see Cuddy-Keane, "Virginia Woolf."

8. For more information on Pennell, who was a close friend of Rosamond Marriott Watson, see Hughes, *Graham R.*, passim.

9. Harold Williams also makes this claim in his lengthy survey of *Modern English Writers*, which Woolf reviewed in 1918, where he "does his best to insist," in Woolf's words, that 1890 "was the year in which the Victorianism of the Victorian age virtually, or practically, or to some extent, passed away. . . . It was replaced gradually by a patchwork of influences" ("Caution and Criticism," *Essays* 2: 303).

10. Also see E. Blair's discussion of Bourdieu's argument, to which my own is indebted (16–17).

11. Here as elsewhere, Woolf represents her older and younger contemporaries "in animal images in a kind of literary bestiary": Trodd cites similar descriptions of Edith Sitwell, Stella Benson, Elizabeth Robins, Rose Macaulay, and Rebecca West (178, 178–80).

12. As Parejo Vadillo points out, "there are substantial similarities between Julia Stephen and Meynell, and Lily [Briscoe] and Meynell," only some of which I detail here ("Generational" 132).

13. Some years after this, however, in 1931, Woolf was still harping on the "hard boiled aridity" of Meynell's style, which in writing to Smyth she contrasts with the fluidity and fire of her own: "My veins run liquid language, and red hot rum" (*Letters* 4: 361).

14. Her review of Meynell's *Hearts of Controversy* (1914) demonstrates respect even in disagreement: "She, much more than most of us, knows what her standards are,

and applies them as she reads. Her criticism, therefore, has a character and a definiteness which make it worth considering, worth testing, and worth disagreeing with" (*Essays* 2: 176). Interestingly, Vita Sackville-West went on to edit and publish a centenary edition of Meynell's poetry and prose in 1947.

15. To take one salient example, see my analysis in "The Great War" for more on Woolf and Lee's shared antiwar sympathies and their critique of patriotism.

16. Also see Vanessa Bell's letter to Margery Snow from Florence, dated 25 April 1904: "We went one day to see Miss Paget who writes under the name of Vernon Lee" (*Selected Letters* 15). Resident mainly in Italy although she considered herself English, Lee spent the war years in Britain, unable to return to her home outside Florence. It was at the end of this period that Woolf met her for the third and seemingly final time in 1920 "at the 1917 Club," founded by Leonard Woolf and others, where political and aesthetic radicals mixed (*Letters* 2: 550). A letter to Violet Dickinson from July 1926, the year in which the Hogarth Press published Lee's *The Poet's Eye* in its pamphlet series, reports that Woolf passed up another opportunity to see her in favor of visiting Thomas Hardy (*Letters* 3: 283).

17. The novel thus anticipates the replacement in *Jacob's Room* of "the daughter-father relationship with the sister-brother relationship as the paradigm for female-male social relations" (Swanson 46).

18. For Shakespeare, see Fox 120–26; for Fielding, Squier 71–90; and for Dostoevsky, Rubenstein 19–59.

19. The identification of Mrs. Hilbery with Ritchie is firmly established in the scholarship; see Zuckerman, who points to the many details of both Thackeray's circumstances and Ritchie's life that Woolf adapts for her characters. Writing to C. P. Sanger in December 1919, Woolf acknowledged her model but minimized the likeness: "Of course there are touches of Lady Ritchie in Mrs Hilbery; but in writing one gets more and more away from the reality, and Mrs Hilbery became to me quite different from any one in the flesh" (*Letters* 2: 406). A slightly later letter to Ka Arnold-Forster claims that "some old creatures have crept from what I supposed to be their graves to hiss at me" about the book, which Kitty Maxse, for one, did not like (410; also see Woolf's subsequent letters to Vanessa Bell and Margaret Llewelyn Davies, 411–13). A letter to Vanessa Bell written over a year later recounts as a "triumph that the Ritchies are furious with me for Mrs Hilbery; and Hester is writing a life of Aunt Anny to prove she was a shrewd, [*sic*] and silent woman of business" (474). For more on Woolf's attitude to Ritchie, see A. Holton.

20. After finishing the obituary for the *Times Literary Supplement* in 1919, Woolf reported in her diary Ritchie's remark that "the pleasant thing" about a childhood such as her own "was to know them all as ordinary people, not as great men" (*Diary* 1: 248).

21. Woolf knew Ritchie's novels well: in a 1931 exchange with the publisher Jonathan Cape, she claimed to "have a great admiration for the early ones" (*Letters* 4: 310). Some critics have considered *The Village on the Cliff* (1867) and *Old Kensington* as intertexts for *Night and Day*; the latter, for example, draws heavily on Ritchie's childhood memories of her Kensington home and adopts the two-suitor plot that Woolf uses in that novel. For further discussion, see Zuckerman; De Gay, *Virginia Woolf's Novels* 44–66; A. Holton; and McCail.

22. Indeed, Gérin concludes that "outside her own family," Oliphant "was perhaps the person that [Ritchie] loved and admired most" (246). See E. Blair 116–21 for an analysis of their personal and professional relationship.

23. For a reading of this aspect of the novel in the context of the Stephen family history of writing domestic biography, see Tolley 122–31.

24. More speculatively, this passage of roman à clef may also subtly reference Ritchie's own brush with marital disaster, her husband (and cousin) Richmond's affair (ca. 1886) with Lionel Tennyson's widow, Eleanor Locker (Gérin 213–15). For a time, the affair strained Ritchie's close relationship with the entire Tennyson family, but it was resolved when Richmond chose to stay married and Eleanor went on to marry Augustine Birrell, whom Woolf first met in 1923 owing to her friendship with his son Francis.

25. For excellent brief overviews of Stephen family relations with the Carlyles, see McNees, "Legacy"; and Bradshaw, Carlyle's House 25–29.

26. "J.O.B.," as she was typically known, was a cousin to Arthur Henry Hallam and thus also a close associate of the Tennyson family. Blanche Warre-Cornish, Molly Mac-Carthy's mother and a Thackeray/Ritchie relation, dedicated her only novel, Alcestis (1873), to J.O.B., who also published several novels of her own, including Only George (1866), Influence (1871), and Not a Heroine (1873). Considering their roman-à-clef elements, D. J. Taylor describes Brookfield's novels in relation to Henry Esmond, 321–22; see also Peters 183.

27. Although Thackeray died suddenly in 1863, his wife lived on until 1894.

28. Having reviewed Lewis Melville's The Thackeray Country (along with another book on Dickens in the same series) in 1905—her very first TLS review—Woolf may have read about Thackeray's Bloomsbury past at 13 Great Coram Street in Russell Square and would certainly have recognized the large number of references to Bloomsbury in his novels. See "Literary Geography" (Essays 1: 32–36); and Zemgulys's discussion of this review, 162–64.

29. Commenting on the question of "our 'lives'" in the context of discussions over who would write Fry's, Woolf remarked, "The EMF. [sic] Goldie thing to me quite futile" in its bowdlerized form (Diary 4: 247). Earlier conversations among Blooms-berries about the possibility of Woolf's writing the life of Lytton Strachey had foundered on the supposition that his life story could not be told at that moment, either.

30. See Fowler for the correspondence between Furse and Woolf regarding Furse's efforts to access the manuscript and to write a "true" biography of her father.

31. "'Knowledge' and 'sex' become conceptually inseparable from one another—so that knowledge means in the first place sexual knowledge; ignorance, sexual ignorance" (Sedgwick 73).

32. For more on James in this respect, see Leckie 158–69.

33. For an analysis of the development of the division between reform literature, or fiction with a purpose, and the impersonal stance evinced by James and associated with early modernism, see Claybaugh, esp. 134–51.

34. See Fogel for a very thorough account, constructed from Woolf's letters, diaries, and reviews, of her complex "two-sided" attitude to James (79).

35. Silver implies that Woolf also read The Story of an African Farm for this review (Reading Notebooks 226).

36. She repeats Hardy's remark verbatim in a letter of 1932 to Harmon H. Goldstone, perhaps thinking of her own project in The Pargiters (Letters 5: 91). Jude is probably in this respect more definitely "marred by a flaw" than Tess, owing to its explicit critique of the divorce laws of its time.

37. Courtney's second wife, Janet Hogarth Courtney, was a close friend to the novelist May Sinclair and, for a time, an active antisuffragist, but she later recanted that position (G. Thomas).

38. In "Forster and Women," Goldman discusses as well the differences between the "two versions of his paper, one addressed to his exclusively male Cambridge colleagues, the other to the mixed company of Bloomsbury" (122).

39. For the definitive study of nineteenth-century women's education in this key, see Prins.

40. For example, she was caught off guard by Vanessa Bell's initial response to *Night and Day*, which Woolf characterized as having given her sister "the horrors" by reminding her of "our particular Hell" at 22 Hyde Park Gate (*Letters* 2: 393). A few months later, reflecting on a conversation with her friend Marjorie Strachey about her novel-in-progress concerning her unhappy love affair with a married man, Woolf wondered to her diary if "I too, deal thus openly in autobiography & call it fiction?" (*Diary* 2: 7).

41. Courtney's attribution of responsibility to Hardy for the excesses of "problem novels" is all the more ironic in light of Schaffer's findings concerning the indebtedness, bordering on plagiarism, of *Jude the Obscure* to Malet's 1890 *The Wages of Sin* (216–41).

42. Hyman correctly notes that, as a critic, Woolf "uses the same terms of decay and disease" that her father employed "to characterize bad books" ("Late" 147). But it was not Leslie Stephen alone who found aestheticism so threatening: as Grand's Ideala comments in *The Beth Book*, implicitly drawing on the associations of such aesthetes as Swinburne, Pater, and Wilde with sexual dissidence, "The works of art for art's sake, and style for style's sake, end on the shelf much respected, while their authors end in the asylum, the prison, and the premature grave" (460; ch. 47).

43. Squier argues that this episode in *Night and Day* serves as "a metatextual gloss upon Woolf's dilemma" in writing the novel, in that by Katharine's "choosing the modern novel, she runs the risk of being mocked or condemned as tasteless," while in "choosing the safer classical alternative, she runs another risk—of losing her audience" (73).

44. Whitworth identifies Woolf as at times both a Day's and a Mudie's subscriber (*Night* 592).

45. Fielding died in Lisbon in 1754; his *Journal of a Voyage to Lisbon* was not published until 1913, just two years before *The Voyage Out*. Woolf visited his tomb with her brother Adrian on 7 April 1905 (*Passionate* 262).

46. Just a year or so before the publication of *Night and Day*, Woolf recorded a conversation with the elderly Lady Strachey, born in 1840, who told her that at "the age of 18 her father gave her leave to read Tom Jones (I think) on condition she never said she'd read it" (*Diary* 1: 107).

47. Hite considers Dostoevsky's influence on Woolf in *Woolf's Ambiguities* 23–24.

48. Somewhat ironically given the context of "Cyril's misbehavior," Wells fathered a child out of wedlock with Amber Pember Reeves—on whom he based the heroine of *Ann Veronica* (1909)—then brought about a marriage between her and George Rivers Blanco White. I would assume that Woolf knew these details, at least at second hand.

49. On a related note, Garrity "wonders how different the map of British modernism would have looked had Woolf organized a literary salon for women" of her own generation (*Step-daughters* 19).

I. Grand Reads Woolf

1. For Grand's familiarity with *Time and Tide*, see *Sex* 2: 131. Bosanquet was herself a Hogarth Press author, having published *Henry James at Work* with the Woolfs in 1924.

2. As with *A Room of One's Own*, perhaps Grand read Bosanquet's 13 March 1937 review of *The Years* in *Time and Tide*. Given the novel's runaway success, this appears likely.

2. New Women and Old

1. Notably, Terence himself reads aloud to Hirst from Hardy's "He Abjures Love" (qtd. 111–12; ch. 9), dated by Hardy to 1883 but not published in *Time's Laughingstocks* until 1909. Unless otherwise noted, all references to *The Voyage Out* are to the 1992 Oxford World's Classics edition, which reprints the 1915 version of the novel published in the U.K. by Duckworth and Company.

2. Based on their physical description alone, Ardis identifies these unnamed books as "Bodley Head publications . . . bound volumes of the *Savoy* . . . touchstones in the British debates about New Women, New Hellenism, and the cultural work of literature in the 1880s and 90s" (*Modernism* 1). Fogel suggests that Rachel's reading also recalls James's Nanda Brookenham in *The Awkward Age* (1899) reading a French novel covered in blue paper (125). For a fuller discussion of all the readers and reading in *The Voyage Out*, see Schlack 1–28; and, more briefly, Flint 271–73.

3. For an intriguing analysis of Woolf's relation to Austen as established in *The Voyage Out*, see Wollaeger, esp. 38–43.

4. This sentence and the one that immediately follows, also quoted below, were omitted from the 1920 U.S. edition. Marshik notes Woolf's use of the word "purpose" to refer to authorial intention in one of the early drafts of *The Voyage Out* (100).

5. In addition to Hite, "Public Woman," and *Woolf's Ambiguities* 110–33, see John 184–92 for more about *My Little Sister* and its genesis.

6. No books by Grand, Egerton, or Caird are catalogued in the library Leonard Woolf left at his death in 1969 (King and Miletic-Vejzovic). There is also no evidence that she read and discussed them with her Cambridge-educated male friends—although such books would have been staple fare for her older feminist contemporaries.

7. See Moretti's further discussion of what he calls the "very questionable concept" of generations in *Graphs, Maps, Trees*, which posits the possibility of "a particularly significant 'destabilization'" as "[giving] rise to a clearly defined generation" as a way of explaining why genres rise and fall, or appear and disappear, at roughly twenty-five-year intervals (22, 22n11).

8. Woolf is responding somewhat ironically to Clive Bell's recommending a range of French fiction to her. "La Maison Tellier" (1881), by Guy de Maupassant, significantly concerns a madam who closes her place of business for the weekend and takes her "girls" with her on a visit to her brother's village to attend her niece's confirmation.

9. As Hite shows, Woolf consistently revised the character of Rhoda in successive drafts of *The Waves* (1931) to eliminate her polemical voicing of "her creator's own antipolemical views." More broadly, as she notes, "polemic against polemic (and po-

lemicists) is characteristic of Woolf in her literary essays and informal writing" (*Woolf's Ambiguities* 52).

10. It is worth noting here that Rachel's ignorance parallels Woolf's subsequent representation of her own. She wrote in "A Sketch of the Past" that it was her brother-in-law Jack Hills who "first spoke to me openly and deliberately about sex—in Fitzroy Square" when she was about twenty-five, or roughly the same age as the protagonist of *The Voyage Out*: "He opened my eyes on purpose, as I think, to the part played by sex in the life of the ordinary man," describing herself at the time as "incredibly, but only partially innocent" (103–4). That is, she had "known since I was sixteen or so, all about sodomy, through reading Plato," but much less about the sexual behavior of the so-called ordinary man, affirming the bookish origins of some of her sexual knowledge (104).

11. "The King's records show Virginia's sustained enrollment in a range of subjects at the Ladies' Department, including History (Continental and English), Greek (Intermediate and Advanced), Latin and German," but not English literature (Kenyon Jones and Snaith 6–7).

12. Exceptions to that rule among painters would include Phillip Burne-Jones (b. 1861), Arthur Studd (b. 1863), and Will Rothenstein (b. 1872).

13. Recent scholarship by Mullin (*James Joyce*) and Backus further demonstrates how broadly and deeply Joyce read in late-Victorian popular and periodical literature and how well-informed he was about the sexual scandals and controversies of those decades.

14. Yonge was a favorite for multiple generations of the extended Stephen-Duckworth family. Ritchie told Yonge in 1891 that *The Daisy Chain* rested on her young daughter's bedside table, as it had on her own when she was around the same age (Ritchie, *Anne* 242). Woolf chose to read Yonge's *The Heir of Redclyffe* (1853) on her honeymoon (*Letters* 2: 2, 6). And in reminiscing about her grandmother, Henrietta Garnett recalls that while they posed for Vanessa Bell, her sister Amaryllis would "read aloud from the works of Miss Charlotte M. Yonge": "Nessa and her sister, Virginia, had been brought up on them. Amaryllis and I inherited their addiction for the writings of Miss Yonge and we enjoyed them for very much the same reasons. We adored the death scenes. We relished them. They made us cry and they made us laugh. And Nessa laughed too" (156).

15. My admittedly partial source for these conclusions is the short-title catalogue compiled by King and Miletic-Vejzovic. See Daugherty, "Learning" for her speculations regarding the contents of Leslie Stephen's library.

16. Bonnell cites Grand's more appreciative comments on Zola: "There is much that is objectionable and even hateful, that does not obscure the noble service he has done in brushing aside the merely conventional, and showing life as it is, not merely as we fancy it ought to be" (qtd. in "Sarah Grand" 130).

17. Both Hite and Chan suggest in their respective analyses of Rachel Vinrace, who also receives little formal schooling, that this may have been more of a mixed blessing than an unmitigated curse for her reading history. Hite contends that "the mediocrity of [Rachel's] education paradoxically fosters the aesthetic capacity that gives her a more intense and ontologically valuable reality" (*Woolf's Ambiguities* 124). Chan notes that a lack of formal education "has allowed her to exercise her intrinsic talent to the full" (4). One could perhaps say something similar of Rachel's author.

18. On meeting Hardy in 1926, however, Woolf recorded his remark that he and Leslie Stephen "stood shoulder to shoulder against the British public about certain matters dealt with in" *Far from the Madding Crowd* (*Diary* 3: 97). See also Marshik 88–89.

19. As editor of the *Cornhill*, for instance, Thackeray rejected Barrett Browning's "Lord Walter's Wife" in 1861, in deference to the presumed sensibilities of his readers, because of its "account of unlawful passion felt by a man for a woman" (Thackeray, *Letters* 226–27). Her gracious if pointed response accepts the judgment, but protests the censorship: "I am deeply convinced that the corruption of our society requires, not shut doors and windows, but light and air—and that it is exactly because pure & prosperous women choose to *ignore* vice, that miserable women suffer wrong by it everywhere" (228).

20. Mangum discusses some additional contributions to this debate by Janet Hogarth (later the wife of W. L. Courtney), Hugh Stutfield, and James Ashcroft Noble, all published in the 1890s and some of which refer explicitly to Grand's fiction (30–35). See also Arata, esp. 169–78; and Ardis, *New* 29–58.

21. William Hepworth Dixon was no stranger to controversy around the representation of sexuality, having sued the *Pall Mall Gazette* in 1872 for libel in its characterization of his *Spiritual Wives* (1868), a two-volume work that described the workings of Mormon polygamy (Mullin, "Poison" 23–25).

22. Leonard's correspondence with Lytton Strachey during their Cambridge years also reports his reading of Balzac, Zola, Huysmans, Wilde, and Flaubert, to whose works his future wife did not have such access, it seems, until after her father's death (*Letters* 22–29).

23. For a more extended consideration of Evadne's reading than I can offer here, see Mangum 101–9.

24. For more on how Smollett and Fielding figure in the reviews of the novel, see Bonnell, "Sarah Grand" 131–33, and "Legacy" 473–75. Stutfield's position in "Tommyrotics" is representative: "I would much rather see a boy or girl reading 'Tom Jones' or 'Roderick Random' than some of our 'modern' works of fiction" (Stutfield 836; qtd. in Bonnell, "Sarah Grand" 132n28).

25. Youngkin also makes the point that from the narrator's perspective, "Evadne would have benefited more fully had she talked about these books with other people rather than just writing about them" (46).

26. For a very thorough treatment of Grand's engagement with eugenics, see Richardson 95–155.

27. Evadne goes on to compare her first marriage to the marital situation in Balzac's *A Woman of Thirty* (1842).

28. Although I disagree with Heilmann's claim that neither Evadne nor Ideala, in the book of that name, "suffers any physical or mental harm" because of her "conscious decision[s] to frustrate [her] sexual desire," her careful contextualization of Evadne's diagnosis as hysterical is exemplary (74). For other readings of Evadne's hysteria, see Hetherington; and Pykett, *"Improper"* 173–74.

29. For further discussion of this passage, see Eberle 211–12. Critics and historians generally identify Butler's reading of *Ruth* as a decisive moment that initiated her involvement in rescue work: for just one example, see Walkowitz, *City* 87–88. In a claim I will further consider below, Walkowitz also notes that Butler's sketches of the pros-

titutes she rescued took the form of "literary melodramas, evocative of *Ruth* and the fallen-women fiction of the 1850s and 1860s" (88).

30. Grand no doubt came across these comments in J. W. Cross's *George Eliot's Life* (1885).

31. E. Blair argues on the basis of this passage, which moves from Gaskell's writing to Woolf's own novel-in-progress, *Mrs. Dalloway*, that "thinking about Gaskell's fiction leads Woolf to her discovery"—or at least the description—of the "'beautiful caves behind my characters'" (*Diary* 2: 263; qtd. in E. Blair 72). While I would not assign quite this level of agency to Woolf's rereading of Gaskell, the point supports her larger argument, with which I fully agree: "As Woolf works to establish a break with the generation preceding her, she returns selectively to the traditions of the next generation back from them" (17).

32. This speech is quoted in full in the *Personal Reminiscences*, which we know Woolf to have read at the time of researching and composing *Three Guineas*. For a selection of the growing scholarship on Victorian women and the periodical press, see Beetham; Brake, *Subjugated Knowledges*; Demoor, *Their Fair Share*; Tusan, *Women Making News*; and Youngkin.

33. Mangum adapts and extends Hadley's argument, which focuses on Butler and *Diana of the Crossways*, to Grand's work by noting that Meredith had rejected *The Heavenly Twins* as a reader for Chapman and Hall (86–87).

34. Eberle further suggests a shift in Grand's own terms from the time of writing *Ideala* (1888) to *The Beth Book* (1897): In the former, "the heroine actually does interact with 'fallen women'" while ten years on, "Beth necessarily remains at a careful remove from actual scenes of reclamation. Her place is at the podium and her proper sphere is one of solitude, abstract thinking, and inspired oratory" (230–31). I will return to this point below in considering the care Lady Fulda shows to "fallen" women in *The Heavenly Twins*. For more on Gaskell's reticence about the details of Ruth's sexual experience, see D'Albertis 93–94.

35. By contrast with what I take to be Grand's and Woolf's disparaging views of Gaskell, contemporary feminist critics find a very progressive tenor in *Ruth*, and in Gaskell's work more generally. See, for example, D'Albertis's reading of the novel, which calls it "a manifesto—both for women activists and for women writers—for shaping and even directing the course of social debate about women's sexuality in the nineteenth century" (101).

36. In 1922 Grand became mayoress of Bath, which was not an elected position; the widowed mayor invited her to serve this ceremonial function.

37. For more on this aspect of *The Pargiters* and *The Years*, see Corbett, *Family Likeness* 187–91.

38. Grand subsequently returned to Kensington after she left her husband, living first at Sydney House, 24 Sinclair Road, Kensington from 1891 to 1894, then at 60 Wynnstay Gardens—neither very far from 22 Hyde Park Gate (*Sex* 2: 4).

39. Eberle argues that "*The Beth Book* cannily evokes 'old' narratives of social reform and sexual transgression in order to establish a 'new' narrative that charts the ascent of the 'woman of genius'" such that "Butler's crusade" takes a back seat to "the text's primary evocation of the heroine's rise to power" (224). But she also concludes that "Grand's response to Butler is further complicated by her reluctance to acknowledge

her predecessor as a 'mother'" while resisting "an alternative model of 'sisterhood'" with prostitutes (203). I would find Eberle's argument, while parallel in some respects to my own, more viable if it accounted for *The Heavenly Twins* as well as *The Beth Book*.

40. For the biographical basis of this character in Grand's life and additional analysis of her role in the novel, see Mangum 140–41. Bonnell describes both Grand's objections to *l'art pour l'art* and the hostile responses of male reviewers who considered Grand's realism improbable ("Sarah Grand").

41. On Gaskell's anxiety about the scandal attached to her writing the novel, see, for example, Nord, *Walking* 159–60. Regarding Grand, Denney notes, "In two articles in the *Quarterly Review* from 1894, for example, she was attacked for 'aiming at sexual laxity' which the anonymous author concluded linked her with radicals. . . . She was defended against these charges in the pages of *Literary World* and *Christian World*, her friends intimating that the anonymous author was none other than the anti-suffrage leader, Mrs. Humphrey [*sic*] Ward" (198; also cited in Mangum 112–13).

42. In words spoken by Beth Maclure, the writer-heroine of *The Beth Book*, that resonate with Evadne's response to French fiction, "Manner has always been less to me than matter. When I think of all the preventable sin and misery there is in the world, I pray God give us books of good intention—never mind the style!" (460; ch. 47). Here Grand's view contrasts sharply with the attitudes of Henley's circle to what McDonald calls "the moral mode of reading, which judged art by ethical standards and focused on *what* was represented rather than the *manner* of representation" (*British* 41).

43. Though frequently attributed to Tennyson himself in conversation, the phrase first appears in print, as far as I can tell, in a review of *Gareth and Lynette*, signed C. A. L. G., in the February 1873 issue of the *Victoria Magazine* (qtd. in McCauley, para. 19).

44. See Mangum 95–96 for some discussion of Edith's parents' responsibility for her fate.

45. First, as a Catholic Frenchwoman, Marie is arrested by the Tenor's singing of "The Litany of the Blessed Virgin," and recalls singing it herself as a girl; then all three hear the bells that chime throughout the book, which intone that God is "watching over Israel" (376; bk. 4, ch. 3). Marie is moved to pray as the Tenor departs, while the Boy stands watching her, without "any movement of pity or kindly compassion for the girl; . . . he would have left her there to any fate that might await her, and would have expected all right-minded people," perhaps including Edith's mother, "to do the same" (376–77).

46. That in the process of fulfilling her mission Lady Fulda also saves herself, in some way, by turning her disappointment in love to account—for she had loved the Tenor, her brother's college friend, as a younger woman—seems implicit in how Grand connects these incidents. It is also highly conventional: D'Albertis, for example, follows Poovey in identifying *Ruth* with those "popular fictions that variously described a woman's turn to nursing as a compensation for thwarted love" (97).

47. Marshik goes on to argue that Woolf's "texts engage in dialogue with social purity concerns," as, for example, in the South American setting of *The Voyage Out*, with South America apparently constituting a major site of anxiety over white slavery in the first decades of the twentieth century, comparable to Brussels a few decades earlier (92).

48. While contextualizing prostitution in *Mrs. Warren's Profession* in relation to stage censorship and Shaw's own ambivalent relation to social purity, Marshik does not at-

tend in any concerted way to the important role which women of Grand's stripe played in that movement.

49. Lytton Strachey's letters about the Friday Club make it sound rather dreary. In one, he reports that he went with his sister Pippa on Friday, 1 December 1905, to a meeting at the flat of Walter Creighton, son of Mandell and Louise Creighton: "The whole place depressed me by its air of third-rate incompetence blindly aiming at it knew not what"; referring to the Stephen siblings, he thought "the Gothic family seemed strangely out of place. Poor people! They so hate propriety that they're driven out into this wretched sort of groove" (*Letters* 98). A few years later, his future sister-in-law Ray Strachey found it marginally more interesting: "They don't seem to do very much, these people, but they talk with surprising frankness. One of their greatest joys seems to be to tear their friends limb from limb" (qtd. in Holmes 99).

50. Woolf's choice of name for the minister may not be accidental. Although she did not review his memoirs until 1918, she no doubt had heard of E. Belfort Bax, socialist, lawyer, and author of *The Fraud of Feminism* (1913). The review sardonically comments, "We feel ourselves exalted almost to the rank of that impartial observer to whom the England of the nineteenth century will appear as the Rome of the year 116 appears to an observer of the present day" and emphasizes "the drastic moral tone of Mr Bax's generation. No words seem to have been more often upon their lips than 'humbug', 'cant', 'sentimentalism' and 'superstition.' No generation has ever put more trust in reason, or rated more highly the powers of pure intellect" ("A Victorian Socialist," *Essays* 2: 261, 262).

51. For another perspective, see Childs's reading of the representation of prostitution in *Mrs. Dalloway* in the context of eugenics (42–46).

52. In "Going Public," Walkowitz points out that during the last quarter of the nineteenth century, "in the elegant shopping districts around Regent Street, prostitutes, dressed in 'meretricious finery,' could and did pass as respectable, while virtuous ladies wandering through the streets, 'window gazing at their leisure,' often found themselves accosted as streetwalkers" (7). Far more famously and securely, Clarissa Dalloway does her morning errands in Regent Street several decades after Evadne's streetwalking.

53. For alternative readings of this passage, see Heilmann 76–77; and Hetherington 160.

54. This phrase appears only in the U.S. edition (81; ch. 6), which Woolf revised for publication in 1920.

55. In an article that appeared in *Vote* in August 1933, Grand named Fawcett as one of her "particular colleagues" in the suffrage movement (Priestley McCracken 323).

56. Perhaps Oliphant wouldn't have had to be quite so productive as a novelist had she edited a periodical: though she "tried repeatedly to achieve the regular employment and steady income of an editorship such as [Leslie] Stephen, William Thackeray, Charles Dickens, and Anthony Trollope, the best paid literary men of her generation, enjoyed," she never got one (E. Blair 118).

II. Disinterestedness

1. Craig argues that "it is birth control that opens up the discursive space for Woolf to claim that mental chastity . . . has replaced physical chastity as a chief virtue for

womankind," but without noticing that for Woolf the "vice" lies less in the fact of prostitution than in sexually transmitted disease (134).

2. Although Chan sees Woolf as "building" on this rhetoric, I do not think her use of the metaphor is "an attempt to highlight how these women writers were . . . victims of participation in professional society in the twentieth century" (90). It is certainly the case that Woolf "delimit[ed] the group of women to whom the guidelines . . . applied" at her time of writing *Three Guineas*: "They had to be in a good enough financial position to have the freedom to write what they wanted" (90–91). But as Woolf of course knew, this would be a very small group indeed.

3. Woolf's first example draws on the recently discovered journal of the nineteenth-century governess Ellen Weeton, published in 1936, which laments the writer's lack of access to education. The second consults the memoir of one of Ward's teachers and the first principal of Newnham, Anne Jemima Clough, written by her niece Thena [Blanche Athena] Clough and published in 1897. The latter not only worked closely with Woolf's first cousin Katharine Stephen at Newnham but also, in an incident Woolf mentions in *Three Guineas*, had "to stand and watch on the night of 20 October 1921 when male undergraduates celebrating the defeat of one of the schemes for improving the women's position used a handcart as a battering ram against the bronze gates constructed as a memorial" to her aunt (38, ch. 1; G. Sutherland).

4. She returns one more time to Butler in the third chapter of *Three Guineas*, in the course of her meditation on the word "free," just after she burns that "word without a meaning," that "dead" and "corrupt" word, "feminist" (121). One might infer, among other things, that in torching the term "feminist," Woolf aims also to incinerate the group identity it called into being insofar as it effaces individual identity, via the selflessness that she takes Butler as celebrating.

5. "Justice and Equality and Liberty" is the epigraph to Millicent Garrett Fawcett and E. M. Turner's biography of Butler (14–15).

3. "Ashamed of the Inkpot"

1. While Collier argues that "in her fiction and journalism of the mid to late twenties, Woolf repeatedly dramatized this conflict with reference to three distinct but related sets of oppositions: art vs. commerce, private vs. public writing, and amateurism vs. professionalism," I would suggest that the tensions arise much earlier in her private writing ("Virginia Woolf" 363).

2. Simpson argues that the establishment in the 1910s of "what might be called Bloomsbury gift-spheres, particularly the Omega Workshops and the Hogarth Press," helps us to gloss "Woolf's attempts to negotiate the central dilemma for artists in a capitalist society: how to make a living without capitulating to market forces and compromising their artistic gift," correctly noting that "she distinguished between writing produced explicitly to make money," like literary journalism, "and that not intended for specific commercial ends," "such as her essays and especially her fiction" (171). By contrast, Cucullu contends that the press's "success signaled an alliance between art and market, between elitist modernism and consumer capitalism that was openly and actively pursued within and without the Woolf home," describing the Woolfs as "materially bound to the very consumer-based economy against which both the idea of an aristocratic way of life and the aesthetic practices of an avant-garde defined them-

selves" (45, 46). My stance here draws on elements of both positions, but does not fully coincide entirely with either one.

3. For Ritchie as a model of literary professionalism for Woolf, see Dell 40–41; and Daugherty, "'Young Writers.'"

4. For early extant examples of Virginia Stephen practicing, see her Cornwall diary from 1905, or from Giggleswick in 1906, in *Passionate* 281–308.

5. Much later on, in "The Modern Essay" (1925), a review of Ernest Rhys's five-volume collection *Modern English Essays 1870–1920* that singles out Pater as a "true writer" of "extravagant beauty," the earlier judgment on Stevenson still stands: "It is admirably done, but we cannot help feeling anxious, as the essay proceeds, lest the material may give out under the craftsman's fingers. The ingot is so small, the manipulation so incessant. And perhaps that is why the peroration . . . has the sort of insubstantiality which suggests that by the time he got to the end he had left himself nothing solid to work with" (*Essays* 4: 218, 223, 219).

6. Woolf reviewed this book for *The Guardian* in July 1906, which appears to invalidate the conjectural dating of the letter to Nelly Cecil quoted just below as January 1905 (*Essays* 1: 116–17; *Letters* 1: 176).

7. In line with Woolf's critique of reviewing as articulated in the 1920s, most scholars of Woolf's literary journalism have focused very little on what Woolf read for these earliest reviews. In Cuddy-Keane's words, "the trenchant point" of that critique concerns "the conditions of the reviewer's task": "having to read too many books too quickly and having to make definitive pronouncements in a meager few lines of print" (*Virginia Woolf* 169). In addition to Dubino, see Collier, *Modernism* 71–105.

8. As it happens, W. E. Forster was not only a great-uncle to Will Arnold-Forster, husband of Woolf's good friend Ka Cox, but also an uncle by marriage to Mary Augusta Ward.

9. For more detailed analyses, see Beetham 115–30; Brake, *Print* 145–70; McDonald, *British* 22–53; and especially Stetz.

10. For more on Lyttelton and *The Guardian*, see Rudikoff 95–100. Unlike other commentators, who mainly emphasize the journal's Anglo-Catholic orientation, Rudikoff identifies this periodical as "close to the center of new thought" (100).

11. By contrast, the letter to Vanessa Bell that reports on this meeting focuses much less on Elena Richmond's literary interests and rather more on how Woolf came to tell "this gigantic mass of purity" the details of "the story of George," to which Richmond responded that neither she nor her husband had ever liked him: "I couldn't resist applauding her, and remarking that if she had known all she would have hated him" (*Letters* 2: 505).

12. One can only wonder if Lucy Clifford had pressured Elena Richmond for support in her career, but in any event, the *TLS* did review her final novel, *Miss Fingal*, on 3 April 1919 (Demoor, "'Not'" 241).

13. The best sources for information about Lucy Clifford are Chisholm, *Such*; Dawson 162–89; and Demoor, "'Not'" and "Self-Fashioning."

14. Bicknell points out that Annan misdated and mischaracterized this passage as Clifford's response to Julia and Leslie's wedding (Stephen, *Selected Letters* 1: 192n3).

15. "The Senate of University College set up a Public Testimonial Fund. Led by Huxley, Tyndall and Leslie Stephen, over 200 friends and colleagues made financial contributions and signed a tribute to [W. K. Clifford] which was hurried through so that

he would know of it before he died. The list of famous names stands as an indicator of how much he was loved and respected" (Chisholm, "Science" 663–64).

16. See Dawson regarding Lucy Clifford's negotiations with Karl Pearson, who edited her husband's unfinished manuscripts for publication as *The Common Sense of the Exact Sciences* (1885), and for discussion of the hostile reviews the work attracted. Dawson also shows that she used her connection to MacColl to plant information in the *Athenaeum*; promoted "the work of her husband's allies" in the "Science Gossip" column; and "seems to have used her position and contacts at the anonymous *Athenaeum* to ensure favourable coverage of him" (177, 178).

17. For information on *The Quiver*, see Cooke, who describes it as "for a brief period (1865–69) a serious competitor to *Good Words* and *The Cornhill*" (para. 9); and Brake and Demoor 524–25. Clifford published another serial, titled *Their Summer Day*, in this periodical in 1887, as well as some travel essays on Austria in 1902 (Chisholm, *Such* 188–89).

18. Chisholm includes a bibliography of Clifford's works in her dual biography of husband and wife (*Such* 188–90).

19. According to Jane Garnett's entry in the *Oxford Dictionary of National Biography* (*ODNB*), Julia Stephen left over £5,000 at her own death. This information derives from the National Probate Calendar, now available online via the National Archives.

20. Bicknell suggests that these stories might have been part of a projected collection, to be illustrated by Leslie Stephen, in which the publisher of Clifford's *Children Busy, Children Glad, Children Naughty, Children Sad* (1881) had expressed interest (see Stephen, *Selected Letters* 2: 324n2). For Julia Stephen's published and unpublished writing, see Gillespie and Steele.

21. Chisholm demonstrates that Clifford not only fictionalized her birthdate and birthplace but "was always secretive about her family roots" and "expunged all tangible links with the maternal side of her family"; her maternal grandfather Thomas Gaspey, with whom she grew up in London, "was a most successful journalist, poet, writer," and two of his sons were also writers (*Such* 9). Her mother lived until 1903 (Demoor and Chisholm 36–37). Clifford worked as a book reviewer for *The Standard* for fourteen years while her brother John Lane was its society correspondent, but she "never spoke to him or acknowledged him as her brother" (Chisholm, *Such* 81; cf. Pollock 80–81).

22. While Julia Stephen held her "at homes" on Sundays, her daughters chose Thursday for theirs at Gordon Square.

23. "Among those who remained cold towards Vernon Lee after the publication of her novel were Watts Dunton, the Rossettis and Madox Brown, the Humphry Wards, Oscar Wilde, and Mathilde Blind. As time passed most of them ceased to cut her, but she was always regarded with suspicion and distaste" (Ormond 147). Diedrick calls the split with Blind "temporary" (170).

24. She did not become close to Henry James until the 1890s—her correspondence with his brother William, who was interested in her late husband's work, actually precedes the friendship with Henry—but their relationship lasted until the end of his life. Clifford was "one of only three people to inherit money from James" at his death (Demoor, "'Not'" 239). For one version of the backstory on the Lee-James conflict, see Murphy.

25. Lowndes writes that Clifford "threw all her influence into making [Kipling's] work known" (64). She also mentions the details of the quarrel (64–65), as do Pollock 91; Seymour-Smith 153–54; and Chisholm, *Such* 73–78.

26. For more on Clifford's advocacy of Blind's novel, ultimately published by T. Fisher Unwin in 1884, see Diedrick 188–89. In a discussion of Blind's poem "Perfect Union" (1881), which was dedicated to the memory of W. K. Clifford, Diedrick suggests that Blind "and Lucy Clifford became influential progressive voices in the 1880s and '90s, adapting W. K. Clifford's positivism to their own feminist ends" (169).

27. See Demoor for more on Clifford's use of the gossip column to puff her own work as well as her daughter Ethel Clifford's poetry ("Women Authors" 62). Having published two volumes with John Lane (*Songs of Dreams* [1903] and *Love's Journey* [1905]), Ethel Clifford gave up her career as a poet on marrying Fisher Wentworth Dilke on 7 June 1905. While the Stephen siblings may well have been invited to and/or attended the wedding, because of their ties to both the Cliffords and the Dilkes, I have found no evidence of that.

28. Albeit published anonymously, her first great success, *Mrs. Keith's Crime*, went into "several reprints which revealed the author's name and which made sure she would have a publisher" in the near future (Demoor, "Self-Fashioning" 276).

29. For a reading of the infanticide theme in the novel, see C. Hancock, esp. 308–12.

30. Stetz considers Watson's review, one of two significant mentions of Clifford in the October 1892 number of the *Bookman*, as an example of the "strategic alliances between and among the men who ran publishing businesses and periodicals" in which Clifford figured as "little more than an object of exchange" (127). We might qualify that conclusion somewhat by reference to Clifford's own active participation in a range of publicity tactics.

31. On Bennett's acknowledged debt to Clifford, see [Burstein], "*The Old Wives' Tale*." Subsequent correspondence between the two, however, shows a less-than-appreciative tone on the part of Bennett (Demoor, "'Not'" 244).

32. The letter continues: "In fact I shd have done so if only the *thinking responsible* women had asked for the vote: I can't stand the silly rabble of women who don't care tuppence for the thing itself—only for the lark or the excitement—& the women who were born to lead sheltered lives & wd only vote as they menfolk told them & not care a damn which side it was—I *dont* want to give these the vote" (emphasis in the original).

33. Blind also pursued the strategy of engaging Gladstone's interest in her work; see Diedrick 201–2.

34. This letter to Vanessa Bell, which recounts Clifford's return visit to the Woolfs, also contains some of Woolf's crueler remarks about her; see *Letters* 2: 426–27. It announces as well the death and funeral of Mary Augusta Ward, which Clifford purportedly attended.

35. After Clifford's death, she wrote, again to Vanessa, "All that remains of her in my mind is a cows [sic] black blubbering cunt: why that image persists I know not" (*Letters* 4: 52).

36. By contrast with Dubino, Simpson suggests that the Hogarth Press "represents a resistance to a capitalist ethos" in that "it was never driven by conventional economic goals of achieving commercial success and making a profit" (173–74). And by contrast with Simpson, Chan asserts, "the Woolfs consistently professed the 'disinterestedness' of the press in their stated goals, yet also consistently profited from this" (84).

37. While Woolf writes that Clifford was going to publish this essay in *The Nineteenth Century and After*, either she misunderstood the information or Clifford conveyed

it incorrectly; the essay to which Clifford referred actually appeared in *The Bookman* within a few months of this letter, while she had already published another memoir of Eliot in *The Nineteenth Century and After* in 1913.

38. She asked John Middleton Murry at the end of 1918 to send a copy to Vanessa Bell, to whom she sardonically commented that "it seemed to me a masterpiece without rival" (*Letters* 2: 307).

39. In actuality, the comments quoted from Pater and Meredith on Ward's fiction are quite minimal (*Writer's* 2: 87, 138, 183). Only James, with whom Ward had a long-standing personal and professional relationship, is quoted and described at any length (2: 16–20, 88–89, 195–98, 201–10, 223–25).

40. For Woolf's remarks on the kerfuffle that ensued from Strachey's portrait of Ward's grandfather Thomas Arnold in *Eminent Victorians*, see *Diary* 1: 166; *Letters* 2: 261, 281. For representative criticisms of Ward by other writers of Woolf's time—Pound, Wilde, Wells, Bennett, and even Ward's nephew Aldous Huxley—see J. Sutherland, *Mrs. Humphry* 200–1; cf. West, "Gospel." Bindslev cites an unpublished letter to Louise Creighton in which Ward writes, "The success of [*Eminent Victorians*] especially with the young, seems to me a melancholy business. However, as that very able person Ernest de Sélincourt said to me here last week—'Attacking the Victorians has become a bore! We shall soon be booming them again. The wheel comes round'" (qtd. 5n10).

41. Woolf may be not-so-subtly alluding here to Ward's antisuffrage novel *Delia Blanchflower* (1914), in which a venerable mansion is burned to the ground.

42. Along with a copy of *A Writer's Recollections*, the only other book by Ward that remained in the Woolfs' library at the time of Leonard's death, a signed presentation copy belonging to Leslie Stephen, was *Helbeck of Bannisdale*, published in 1898 (King and Miletic-Vejzovic 237).

43. Appendix II of *Essays* 1: 374–76 includes a *Guardian* review of this novel, but stops short of attributing it to Woolf.

44. For a discussion of this aspect of *A Writer's Recollections*, see Corbett, *Representing Femininity* 102–4.

45. Jaffe might connect the rhetoric of "breaking and falling, crashing and destruction" that Woolf deploys to the violence of the suffragettes "in late 1910," "as the women's movement intensified into a campaign of destruction following the Black Friday riots in November" ("Character in Fiction," *Essays* 3: 434; Jaffe 185).

46. J. Sutherland notes that "A Morning in the Bodleian" was privately printed by Humphry Ward the year before their marriage and signed "By Two Fellows," indicating their joint authorship. It appeared with the same signature in *The Dark Blue* in 1872 and also in a U.S. periodical, slightly modified and with no signature, under the title "A Morning in the Bodleian Library."

47. Woolf is not, however, entirely fictionalizing here. She told Violet Dickinson in April 1906, "I sent my H[umphry] Ward to the Speaker, but I see they have a review already, longer and even more vindictive than mine. They call her a snob, and a sentimentalist, with no knowledge of art, or humanity. So the honor of English literature is saved, and I can meet Mrs Ward unblushing" (*Letters* 1: 219).

48. Among other things, Meredith accused Julia Stephen of demonstrating an "irrational obstructiveness" in her objection to women's suffrage, and compared England's treatment of Ireland to Englishmen's treatment of Englishwomen.

III. Duckworth and Company

1. One token of their friendship is that Galsworthy dedicated *The Inn of Tranquility: Studies and Essays* (1912) to Hills (Gindin 315).

2. We can speculate here that family connections might also have facilitated his hiring of Edward Garnett. As Victorian men of letters, Leslie Stephen and Edward's father Richard were well acquainted with one another. Each man's library contains signed presentation copies from the other (King and Miletic-Vejzovic; *Catalogue*). And Garnett wrote almost two hundred entries for the *Dictionary of National Biography* (A. Bell).

3. Selections from the diaries of Margaret Lushington, Mildred Massingberd, and Stella Duckworth appear in Anthony Curtis's edited volume *Before Bloomsbury*. In my further research in the Surrey History Centre archives, I found Margaret Lushington's diaries in particular to be useful in gaining a sense of the social life, including visits to the theater, in which all three Duckworth siblings participated.

4. Powell asserts that Gerald Duckworth had been disappointed in love by someone associated with the theater, calling it a "legendary love affair" but without providing additional details (6). Perhaps it is a bridge too far, but it does seem possible that Robins was the focus of Gerald Duckworth's erotic interest, as of so many other men's in the London theater world of the 1890s.

4. "To Serve and Bless"

1. Hermione Lee incorrectly identifies both Virginia Stephen and Mary Datchet of *Night and Day* as working for the National Union of Women's Suffrage Societies (NU-WSS) (*Virginia Woolf* 275, 276). See, most recently, Jones for a compelling argument for understanding Woolf instead as an adult suffragist (65–68).

2. More precisely, the Wells novel in question would be *Ann Veronica*, which if only because of the uproar its publication occasioned we can safely assume that Woolf read, or at least read about. See Evans's comparative analysis of this novel with *Night and Day* and *The Years*, which includes useful mappings of character movements throughout London in all three novels (88–130).

3. For a more recent historical analysis of the imperialist underpinnings of late-century feminism, see Burton as well as Caine, *English* 168–72.

4. See Maltz, who uses the term "missionary aestheticism" to refer to the activities of Octavia Hill, the Barnetts at Toynbee Hall, and others.

5. Cf. Lily Briscoe imagining Mr. Ramsay "stretch[ing] out his hand and rais[ing Mrs. Ramsay] from her chair. It seemed somehow as if he had done it before; as if he had once bent in the same way and raised her from a boat which, lying a few inches off some island, had required that ladies should thus be helped on shore by the gentlemen. An old-fashioned scene that was, which required, very nearly, crinolines and peg-top trousers" (*Lighthouse* 201).

6. Woolf notes that she is reading Rothenstein's memoirs in *Letters* 6: 368.

7. For the centrality of scene making to Woolf's art, see Squier 7–8.

8. Longleat was the Wiltshire childhood home of Beatrice Thynne and Katie Cromer, sisters to the Marquess of Bath and mutual friends of both Cecil and Woolf.

9. At the same time, however, she also came to resent the misrepresentations of others, calling Rothenstein's memoirs "mendacious" for the way in which she, Vanessa,

Stella, and their Jackson grandmother were portrayed on the basis of his visits to Hyde Park Gate in the 1880s and 1890s (*Letters* 4: 294).

10. To be sure, in some of the books she reviewed, Woolf used insider knowledge to correct misapprehensions. Considering a Meredith biography written by one of his distant relatives, she writes, "Meredith's character will differ according to the temperament of the reader and the opportunities he may have had for knowing Meredith in the flesh, or seeing him through the eyes of those intimate with him," as Woolf's parents were: "To his friends, we have reason to know, he was a man to be loved, not merely a writer to be admired" ("Small Talk About Meredith," *Essays* 3: 5, 6). Nevertheless, she, too, presents the women of the first maternal generation in terms of canonical stories about them that depend as much on myths as on facts.

11. As Dell notes, "Woolf appropriates other people's first-hand memories, seemingly at pains to suppress just how much material she has taken": and "it is mostly the female sources whom she renders anonymous" (8).

12. For an extended account of the Little Holland House set, see Dakers 21–40.

13. Thoby and Sarah's daughter Alice had married Charles Henry Gurney in 1864, just two years before the catastrophic collapse of Overend and Gurney. Gurney's father Daniel expressed concern to protect the marriage settlements into which he had entered, fearing that other liabilities would not enable him to remain "quite honourable to the families into which my children have married" (qtd. in Elliott 166). Charles and Alice subsequently separated and later divorced.

14. For Thackeray's infatuation with Mia—whom he had nicknamed "Theodosia"—see Beaumont 475; Peters 72; and D. Taylor 108, 310.

15. Vanessa Curtis takes note of Mia Jackson's relationship to Patmore in *Virginia* 32–33, as do Parejo Vadillo, "Generational" 124–25; E. Blair 37; and Dell 125. In her memoir of her mother, Viola Meynell quotes a letter from Alice to her husband that refers to Mia Jackson as "Coventry Patmore's first friend" (198). A selection of Patmore's letters to Jackson appears in Champneys (2: 189–218). In a letter of condolence addressed to Woolf's aunt Mary Fisher, Patmore calls her mother "the dearest friend I had" (218). The Woolf library holdings at Washington State University include a presentation copy from Patmore to Julia Jackson of the fourth edition of *The Angel in the House*. Leslie Stephen hated Patmore's poetry and offended his future mother-in-law by saying so: see the letter from 1877 to Mia Jackson included in Maitland 314–15. Although he apologized to Mrs. Jackson, he maintained his opinion in an unpublished letter to Julia of 23 July 1877, in which he declared George Sand "as much better than Miss Martineau as, say, Swinburne is superior to C.P. . . . Swinburne is worth a dozen of your popish friend."

16. We know Woolf to have read Benson's memoir from a postscript to a letter of 1938 to Vanessa Bell in which she mentions that it includes "an account of Cousin Isabel and Adeline" (*Letters* 6: 300). The memoir also contains a humorous portrait of Ethel Smyth, who was the model for one of Benson's characters in *Dodo* (Kertesz).

17. Along with other members of their family, Cooper and Bradley moved to Reigate in 1888, living there for about a decade until resettling in Richmond (Donoghue 46, 103).

18. According to Cole, Somerset became involved in the temperance movement because "one of her dearest friends had committed suicide under the influence of

drink" (54). I have seen this view repeated elsewhere (e.g., Tyrrell, "Somerset"), but I have not been able independently to verify it.

19. "St George's Union was formally constituted on 28th March, 1870" and "initially inherited several existing workhouses from its member parishes including the St Margaret and St John workhouse on Wright's Lane, and the St George Hanover Square's Mount Street and Fulham Road premises" (Higginbotham). It appears from the context of the guardians' discussion, as reported in the *PMG*, that Julia Stephen was not visiting in Mount Street at the time of this discussion (that workhouse was just a mile from her former Bryanston Square home), but rather at the Union's Fulham Road facility in Little Chelsea, very close to her later home in West Brompton (D. Walker). According to Vanessa Curtis, it is "likely that the workhouse visited by Julia Stephen and Stella Duckworth during the 1880s and 1890s was the original Kensington Workhouse" (*Hidden* 23).

20. Dirty milk was a major "source of alarm" to British consumers "from the 1880s to the First World War" (Atkins 233). Childs notes that since Mrs. Ramsay has inquired into milk production, "she has also entered the eugenics debate," because a lack of access to milk obviously affects the health of the nation's children (33). See also Dekter.

21. Her brother commented on her action in somewhat condescending tones, describing Caroline Stephen as "taking to a charitable enterprise after the fashion of Miss Hill, building some lodging houses, from wh[ich] she is to extract rent—I hope it will answer. Any way it will amuse her" (*Selected Letters* 1: 203).

22. For the women's advocacy press of the 1890s, see Tusan, *Women Making News* 99–139. One of Somerset's coadjutors at the *Woman's Herald* was Christina S. Bremner (Tusan 122). Her main staffers at the *Woman's Signal* were Edwin Stout, a Stead associate, and Annie E. Holdsworth, author of *Joanna Traill, Spinster* (1894) and the future sister-in-law of Vernon Lee (Niessen 114; VanArsdel 183). When Holdsworth fell on hard times after Eugene Lee-Hamilton's death, Somerset helped to secure a pension for her from the Royal Literary Fund (Lee-Hamilton). As I will return to below, relations with Florence Fenwick Miller, the successor to Holdsworth whom Somerset appointed in 1895, were not so smooth, and Somerset relinquished control of the paper to her in September 1895 (Niessen 141–43; VanArsdel 179–212). For a comparison of the relatively conservative feminist politics of the *Woman's Signal* with the more progressive *Shafts*, see Caine, *English* 140–43.

23. Unwin's reader Wilfred Hugh Chesson grants that "both stories reach a respectable level in point of style," but concludes of Somerset's manuscript that "*the salient all-redeeming authentic touch is wanting*, and to prove our point we need only suggest that doubters should read Arthur Morrison and *then* read Lady Henry Somerset. The difference lies in this: the man has lived and studied *among* the people he describes"; "Morrison's low-born Londoners say exactly what they would say: Lady Somerset's low-born Londoners say just what we would expect an intelligent person writing at Reigate to imagine they would say" (emphasis in the original).

24. As Koven remarks of Beatrice Potter's turn to the East End after her failed romance with Joseph Chamberlain, "The cultural link forged in late Victorian London between 'disappointment' and slumming achieved the status of the conventional wisdom in the decades ahead" (199). But Somerset's characterization of her heroine's shipwreck no doubt also draws from her personal experience.

25. Somerset appears to have had a fairly close relationship with Stead. For example, Robinson reports that Stead learned about the details of the Tranby Croft affair—a royal baccarat scandal involving the Prince of Wales that originated at a house party in September 1890—"while staying at Eastnor Castle" and that Stead and Somerset met through "his diligent and highly respected solicitor, George Lewis" (180). A character sketch of Somerset, presumably by Stead, appeared in the June 1893 number of *The Review of Reviews*. The prior month, an opinion piece that strongly supported her re-election to the presidency of the BWTA appeared under Stead's byline in Somerset's *Woman's Herald*.

26. Adeline's career as a social reformer is reviewed in Forsythe. Of particular note is his finding that "early in her married life she led a movement to rescue women who were street dwellers or prostitutes around Victoria Station, London."

27. Although she never remarks on Hannah Whitall Smith's connection to cousin Isabel in writing, Woolf actually stayed at Smith's home in Iffley, outside of Oxford, more than once, reporting her visit of October 1910 to "a remarkable family—Costelloes and Pearsall Smiths" to Violet Dickinson (*Letters* 1: 436). I will consider Woolf's relation to some of her contemporaries among the "Costelloes and Pearsall Smiths" in chapter 5.

28. Bordin credits that "shift in emphasis" in part to Willard's reading of Edward Bellamy's utopian fiction *Looking Backward* (1887) and her subsequent correspondence with him, which led her toward her effort "to create a united reform coalition in 1892," the year after Willard and Somerset first met (148). Niessen disputes this view (136–37).

29. For conflicts within the BWTA during 1893 and 1894 over Somerset's efforts, see Niessen 129–41.

30. R. Strachey, *Frances* 289; Bordin 200; Niessen 136–37. Epstein asserts that "through [Somerset Willard] was introduced to and joined the Fabian Society" (142). Tyrrell writes that the two "became Fabian socialists and preached against the gospel of wealth, which they claimed was destroying Anglo-American society" ("Somerset"). Despite the repeated assertion in the scholarship, I have not identified any specific evidence that Somerset joined the Fabian Society: for instance, while Willard's name appears in the Society's *List of Members* (1894), Somerset's does not.

31. See Niessen on Somerset's pub ownership issues, which were widely reported (81, 120). Gifford states that "in her 1894 annual address" to the BWTA, Somerset "announced that she had come to the conclusion that poverty caused intemperance as well as the reverse—at that time still a somewhat startling declaration" (391). Willard made a similar claim at a WWCTU congress held in London in 1895 (Epstein 144–45).

32. Interestingly, Willard some years later interviewed Black for the *Woman's Herald* on women's trades-union organizing efforts, which may imply some continued association between the two (Youngkin 103).

33. Koven includes some brief remarks on Black's essay (164).

34. For an analysis of "street love" in *The Pargiters*, see Corbett, *Family Likeness* 187–91.

35. The fullest description of Somerset's move against the Palace is in Faulk. Most scholarship concentrates on the Empire Theatre of Varieties, where Chant called attention to the number of prostitutes strolling the promenade section of the theater. See Stokes 54–93; T. C. Davis; Bland 95–97, 114–15; Marshall, *Actresses* 131–36; Walkowitz, *Nights* 44–63; and Donohue.

36. Since multiple Gérôme paintings bear some version of that title, it is difficult to say which of them provided the model (*Jean-Léon Gérôme*). But as the "living pictures" were noted for "reproduc[ing] paintings with realism," it seems safe to assume that the tableau represented a white female bather and a black female servant, which is the focus of all three paintings (Faulk 155).

37. For an analysis of how Clarissa's confusion would have been interpreted in the 1920s, see Tate 147–70. Her analysis makes only a passing reference to the longer historical context for the massacres, which predates the temporal setting of the novel by almost fifty years.

38. Niessen 183–90; Bordin 216–18. For an extended analysis of the conflict between Willard and Wells, see Ware 169–224. For Wells's response to Willard, see Wells-Barnett 138–48.

39. See Childs 22–74.

40. For a fuller history of the agitation over the C. D. Acts in the 1890s than I can offer here, see Tyrrell, *Woman's World* 191–220; Ware 147–58; and Burton 127–69.

41. The stationery on which Somerset wrote to Florence Nightingale on 3 February 1893, as well as a letter by Josephine Butler to Mary Priestman from 2 June 1893, is embossed with this address.

42. In a letter to Willard dated 29 November 1897, Butler claimed she had "much difficulty in accepting the idea that [Somerset] originated those six horrible propositions."

43. While we can only speculate as to how much Woolf knew about Somerset's activism on behalf of Armenian women, her own writings suggest not much interest in the genocide. Although in 1911 she visited Broussa, one site of the 1894 to 1896 massacres, by 1919 she wrote in her diary "she could not mind" whether the number of Armenians murdered in the 1915 genocide was "4,000 or 4,000,000," as "the feat is beyond me" (*Diary* 1: 271; qtd. in Barrett, "Virginia Woolf's Research" 107). Even if, as Barrett points out, "her critical stance on imperialism in her fiction pre-dates her marriage to Leonard Woolf," this diary entry gives me pause (113).

44. On the contemporary medical support for eugenics, see Greenslade 227–33.

45. For Dorothea Stephen's disapproval of Vanessa Bell, see Woolf's letters to her and to Bell regarding one of Dorothea's visits (*Letters* 2: 488–89, 492).

46. In addition to cofounding the Oxford Sanitary Aid Association in 1902, a few years after her marriage to H. A. L. Fisher, Lettice Fisher earned a first in modern history at Somerville, tutored modern history at St. Hugh's College, "and was among the university women whom Millicent Fawcett co-opted onto the national executive of the NUWSS," chairing the executive from 1916 to 1918; she went on to "found the National Council for the Unmarried Mother and her Child" in 1918, and chaired that group until 1949 (Moyse).

IV. Somerset, Symonds, Stephen, and Sexuality

1. Kaye has recently offered a comprehensive account of the end of the Somerset marriage in his introduction to *A Marriage below Zero* (1889) by Alan Dale (pseud. Alfred J. Cohen), 17–26. For details on Lord Arthur's involvement in the Cleveland Street scandal, see Kaplan 166–223; Cocks 144–52; K. Thomas 39–69.

2. The crisis in the Somerset marriage came just around the time of Julia Duckworth's second engagement: even as she was nursing her beloved uncle Thoby through his final illness at Freshwater in February 1878, Leslie Stephen reported she was also "call[ed] in . . . to help" her cousin (*Mausoleum* 64). Although Niessen refers only to "a Mrs. Duckworth" as Somerset's chaperone, my close reading of the letters Leslie Stephen wrote to her during this period (held at the Berg Collection) counters the claim that "Julia spent all the time between the engagement and the marriage on 26 March 1878 nursing her beloved uncle Thoby Prinsep" (Niessen 58; Reid 339). At least some of that time, I believe, she was in London with her cousin.

3. The family friendship faded over time, especially after Vanessa Bell rebuked Vaughan in 1920 for her moralizing disapproval of the Bells' unorthodox marriage and concern over Angelica Bell's parentage. Calling her "incredibly impertinent," Bell told Vaughan, "If you cannot accept me as I seem to you to be, then you must give me up, for I have no intention of confessing my sins or defending my virtues to you" (*Selected Letters* 235). In a later letter to David Garnett, Woolf called Vaughan "an incredible figure from the Victorian past" (*Letters* 3: 27); at Vaughan's death in November 1925, she remarked that "[t]hey buried a faggot of twigs at Highgate, as far as I am concerned" (*Diary* 3: 46). Despite her provincial life in a Manchester suburb with five sons, the once rather unconventional Sally Seton of *Mrs. Dalloway* is treated much more sympathetically.

4. See Heidt, and also Fowler for additional context on Furse's project.

5. For discussion of this remark in context, see Zwerdling, "Mastering" 179–81.

5. "A Different Ideal"

1. Livesey incorrectly characterizes this letter of March 1913 as "Woolf's response to [the Newcastle WCG] congress"—to which Woolf recurred years later in her "Introductory Letter" to *Life as We Have Known It*—which actually took place in June 1913, while Park mistakenly interprets this quotation as referring to suffragists (*Socialism* 209; "Suffrage and Virginia Woolf" 120).

2. "Most of the leading women in the pre-1914 Labour Movement," including MacArthur "campaigned for adult suffrage rather than for a separate women's bill" (Pugh 28). The fullest account of Woolf's involvement with the PSF is Jones 65–107.

3. Here I differ from Naomi Black's contention that "Woolf's writings demonstrate a constant and consistent pattern that is both feminist and recognizably the same over time" and agree with Park that "there is a thread of constant revision" in Woolf's relation to suffrage (N. Black 2; "Suffrage and Virginia Woolf" 133).

4. Both Whitworth, in his explanatory notes to *Night and Day*, and Jones also note the potentially motivated choice of "Markham" as the name of the leader Sally Seal worships (580; 83).

5. In a speculative reading, Bradshaw suggests that Mary's distraction in chapters 14 and 20 implies "specific connections between sparrows and suffragettes" ("'Wretched Sparrows'" 46).

6. The discovery of the sketches collected in *Carlyle's House* corrects the claim that "Virginia Stephen was not yet acquainted with Davies when, in January 1910, she wrote to offer her services to Janet Case," as the "Hampstead" sketch is dated 19 March 1909 (N. Black 37).

7. For example, Margaret's father had been Leslie Stephen's coach during his years at Cambridge (*Passionate* 6n10; Stephen, *Selected Letters* 1: 141n1). One of his sons, Arthur Llewelyn Davies, spent his honeymoon at Talland House in St. Ives with his wife Sylvia du Maurier in 1892 (A. Curtis 11).

8. Woolf refers here to *The Christian's Secret of a Happy Life* (1875), an international best seller inspired by Whitall Smith's association with the Holiness evangelical movement in the United States.

9. The wedding was rather a challenge, thanks to Russell's aristocratic family's disapproval of the match. An account of it was published in the *Woman's Signal*, 27 December 1894. For details, see Turcon.

10. Frank Costelloe was a key player in the ultimately unsuccessful effort to validate the election of Lady Sandhurst and Jane Cobden (daughter of the Radical politician Richard and future wife of the avant-garde publisher T. Fisher Unwin) to the London County Council, in a case that provided a rallying point in 1889 for women seeking to expand their involvement in local government. See the memoir by L. Smith for a brief account of Costelloe and his impact on young Mary Smith (110–12; 138–39).

11. Mary Smith had started corresponding with the poet on reading *Leaves of Grass*, thus forming a relationship that her mother worried would make her appear "impure" in the eyes of marriageable men (L. Smith 92–108; Mary Berenson qtd. in B. Strachey 67).

12. Fawcett published the novel *Janet Doncaster* in 1875.

13. Her other novels are *Marching On* (1923) and *Shaken by the Wind* (1927), the latter of which became "an instant popular success" (Holmes 233).

14. Strachey herself studied mathematics at Newnham, somewhat to her mother's chagrin. Karin excelled in the moral sciences at the same college and also studied at Bryn Mawr starting in 1906, where Ray enrolled as a postgraduate student and where their cousin, M. Carey Thomas, served as president.

15. Unlike the pacifist Davies, or her sister Karin—who labored alongside Adrian Stephen and other Bloomsberries in groups such as the No-Conscription Fellowship and the Union of Democratic Control—Ray Strachey shared Fawcett's position on the war, throwing herself into the wartime work that almost all of her Bloomsbury contemporaries eschewed.

16. See McCoskey and Corbett 468–69 for more on this character.

17. So, too, she wrote a few years later in "A Sketch," is "this past . . . much affected by the present moment"; indeed, "the present when backed by the past is a thousand times deeper than the present when it presses so close that you can feel nothing else" (75, 98).

18. However, Robins resigned in late 1912 from the WSPU in protest at the Pankhurst split with the Pethick-Lawrences, amid growing qualms about increasing militancy (John 166).

19. Smyth and Lee had met in England in 1893 and the friendship between them survived until Lee's death in 1936, despite their disagreement over the war and the issue of patriotism (Gunn 132). Smyth's last memoir, *What Happened Next* (1940), contains a portrait of Lee.

20. To be sure, Woolf's own present in the early 1930s also fueled her preoccupation with politics. As Wood has established, she was beset by the consciousness of her

difference and distance from the younger male writers of her time—the so-called Auden generation—and of the increasing militarization of Europe, which seemed inevitably to be leading to another war; Wood thus argues that "it was the development of Woolf's feminist politics while writing [*The Years*] . . . which necessitated the production of a new critical work suitable for expounding her late feminist-pacifist stance" (*Virginia Woolf's Late Cultural Criticism* 66).

21. On the genealogical tree Leaska included in his edition of *The Pargiters*, the year of Eleanor's birth is given as 1856, while Rose, the youngest of the family, is born in 1870 (V. Woolf, *Pargiters* 2).

22. See my discussion of this incident in *Family Likeness* 193–98.

23. As Snaith points out, "Delia's 'Cause' in the manuscript is suffrage and not Home Rule," indicating "a recognition of the links between the two causes" ("Race" 211).

Afterword

1. We can gloss Peggy's "bitterness" by reference to Woolf's analysis in *Three Guineas*, with its pervasive, overarching concern that those "daughters of educated men" who have entered into the male-dominated universities and professions should not merely follow the predetermined patriarchal route that would lead, in Woolf's view, to destruction.

2. While in the earlier typescript of "Pointz Hall," "The Picnic Party" is set "about 1880," the later typescript dates it as "1860" (*Pointz* 150, 381). For someone who is not a Victorianist by training, or not all that historically minded, the substitution of the earlier for the later date, with just twenty years' difference between them, might seem insignificant. I contend, however, that even if this is not a verifiably motivated choice, it is all the same a meaningful one insofar as it tacitly constructs a difference between mid- and late-Victorian norms.

3. Mitchell et al. point out that "the Victorian proposal scene in *Between the Acts* . . . draws on Norman's proposal to Meta in *The Daisy Chain*" by that favorite author of the Stephen girls, Charlotte Mary Yonge ("Introduction to the 1890s," n1).

WORKS CITED

Alexander, Christine. "Play and Apprenticeship: The Culture of Family Magazines." *The Child Writer from Austen to Woolf*, edited by Alexander and Juliet McMaster, Cambridge UP, 2005, pp. 31–50.

Anderson, Amanda. *The Powers of Distance: Cosmopolitanism and the Cultivation of Detachment*. Princeton UP, 2001.

Annan, Noel. "The Intellectual Aristocracy." *Studies in Social History: A Tribute to G. M. Trevelyan*, edited by John Harold Plumb, Books for Libraries Press, 1969, pp. 241–87.

——. *Leslie Stephen: The Godless Victorian*. Weidenfeld and Nicolson, 1984.

Aplin, John. "'A True Affection': Anne Thackeray Ritchie and the Tennysons." The Tennyson Society, 2006.

Arata, Steven. "Realism." Marshall, *Cambridge Companion*, pp. 169–87.

Archer, William, and H[arley]. Granville-Barker. *A National Theatre: Scheme and Estimates*. Duckworth, 1907. *Internet Archive*, archive.org/details /nationaltheatres00archuoft/page/n6. Accessed 7 Sept. 2019.

Ardis, Ann L. *Modernism and Cultural Conflict, 1880–1922*. Cambridge UP, 2002.

——. *New Women, New Novels: Feminism and Early Modernism*. Rutgers UP, 1990.

Ashton, Rosemary. *Victorian Bloomsbury*. Yale UP, 2012.

Atkins, Peter. *Liquid Materialities: A History of Milk, Science and the Law*. Ashgate, 2010.

Atkinson, Damian. "Cust, Henry John Cockayne [Harry]." *Oxford Dictionary of National Biography*. Oxford UP, 6 Jan. 2011, doi.org/10.1093/ref:odnb/32683. Accessed 26 Feb. 2020.

Avery, Todd P. "Ethics Replaces Morality: The Victorian Legacy to Bloomsbury." *English Literature in Transition, 1880–1920*, vol. 41, no. 3, 1998, pp. 294–316.

Backus, Margot Gayle. *Scandal Work: James Joyce, the New Journalism, and the Home Rule Newspaper Wars*. Notre Dame UP, 2013.

Badeni, June. *The Slender Tree: A Life of Alice Meynell*. Tabb House, 1981.

Baring, Maurice. *The Puppet Show of Memory*. Little, Brown, 1922.

Barnett, Dame Henrietta. *Canon Barnett: His Life, Work, and Friends*. Houghton Mifflin, 1919. 2 vols.

Barrett, Michèle. Introduction. *Women and Writing: Virginia Woolf*. Harcourt Brace Jovanovich, 1979, pp. 1–39.

——. "Virginia Woolf's Research for *Empire and Commerce in Africa* (Leonard Woolf, 1920)." *Woolf Studies Annual*, vol. 19, 2013, pp. 83–122.

Barrie, J. M. Letter to Lucy Clifford. 31 Oct. 1920. British Library. Manuscript.

Beare, Geraldine. "Duckworth, Gerald L'Étang." *Oxford Dictionary of National Biography*. Oxford UP, 23 Sept. 2004, doi.org/10.1093/ref:odnb/47451. Accessed 26 Feb. 2020.

——. "Gerald Duckworth and Company Limited (London: 1924–); Gerald Duckworth and Company (London: 1898–1924)." *British Literary Publishing Houses, 1881–1965*, pp. 103–7. *Dictionary of Literary Biography*, vol. 112, Gale Research, 1991.

Beaumont, John. "Thackeray in 'Pattledom.'" *Notes and Queries*, vol. 52, no. 4, 2005, pp. 474–76.

Beer, Gillian. "The Dissidence of Vernon Lee: *Satan the Waster* and the Will to Believe." *Women's Fiction and the Great War*, edited by Suzanne Raitt and Trudi Tate, Clarendon Press, 1997, pp. 107–31.

——. "The Victorians in Virginia Woolf: 1832–1941." *Virginia Woolf: The Common Ground*, U of Michigan P, 1996, pp. 92–111.

Beetham, Margaret. *A Magazine of Her Own? Domesticity and Desire in the Woman's Magazine, 1800–1914*. Routledge, 1996.

Bell, Alan. "Garnett, Richard." *Oxford Dictionary of National Biography*, Oxford UP, 23 Sept. 2004, doi.org/10.1093/ref:odnb/33334. Accessed 26 Feb. 2020.

Bell, Quentin. *Virginia Woolf: A Biography*. Harvest, 1972. 2 vols.

Bell, Vanessa. "Life at Hyde Park Gate after 1897." *Sketches in Pen and Ink*, pp. 67–81.

——. "Notes on Bloomsbury." *Sketches in Pen and Ink*, pp. 95–114.

——. *Selected Letters of Vanessa Bell*, edited by Regina Marler, Pantheon, 1993.

——. *Sketches in Pen and Ink*, edited by Lia Giachero, Pimlico, 1998.

Bennett, Arnold. "Meredith." *Books and Persons: Being Comments on a Past Epoch, 1908–11*, George H. Doran, 1917, pp. 134–39.

——. Preface. *The Old Wives' Tale*. 1908. Penguin, 1983, pp. 31–35.

——. *Journalism for Women: A Practical Guide*. The Bodley Head, 1898. *Internet Archive*, www.archive.org/details/journalismforwo00benngoog. Accessed 23 Dec. 2017.

Benson, A. C. "Two Sisters." *As We Were: A Victorian Peep Show*. Longmans, 1930, pp. 75–90.

Berenson, Mary. *Mary Berenson: A Self-Portrait from her Letters and Diaries*, edited by Barbara Strachey and Jayne Samuels. Norton, 1983.

Bernstein, Susan David. *Roomscape: Women Writers in the British Museum from George Eliot to Virginia Woolf*. Edinburgh UP, 2013.

Bettinger, Elfi. "'The Journey, Not the Arrival, Matters'—Virginia Woolf and the Culture of Aging." *Journal of Aging, Humanities, and the Arts*, vol. 1, no. 3–4, 2007, pp. 177–90.

Bindslev, Anne M. *Mrs. Humphry Ward: A Study in Late-Victorian Feminine Consciousness and Creative Expression*. Almqvist and Wiksell International, 1985.

Black, Clementina. *An Agitator: A Novel*. London, 1895.

——. "The Dislike to Domestic Service." *The Nineteenth Century*, vol. 33, no. 193, 1893, pp. 454–56. *Prose by Victorian Women: An Anthology*, edited by Andrea Broomfield and Sally Mitchell. Garland, 1996, pp. 621–24.

Black, Helen C. *Notable Women Authors of the Day*. MacLaren, 1906.

Black, Naomi. *Virginia Woolf as Feminist*. Cornell UP, 2004.

Black, Ros. *A Talent for Humanity: The Life and Work of Lady Henry Somerset*. Antony Rowe, 2010.

Blair, Emily. *Virginia Woolf and the Nineteenth-Century Domestic Novel*. State U of New York P, 2007.

Blair, Sara. "Local Modernity, Global Modernism: Bloomsbury and the Places of the Literary." *ELH*, vol. 71, no. 3, 2004, pp. 813–38.

Bland, Lucy. *Banishing the Beast: Sexuality and the Early Feminists*. The New Press, 1995.

Blau DuPlessis, Rachel. "Feminist Narrative in Virginia Woolf." *NOVEL: A Forum on Fiction*, vol. 21, no. 2–3, 1988, pp. 323–30.

Bolt, Christine. *The Women's Movements in the United States and Britain from the 1790s to the 1920s*. U of Massachusetts P, 1993.

Bonnell, Marilyn. "The Legacy of Sarah Grand's *The Heavenly Twins*: A Review Essay." *English Literature in Transition, 1880–1920*, vol. 36, no. 4, 1993, pp. 467–78.

———. "Sarah Grand and the Critical Establishment: Art for (Wo)man's Sake." *Tulsa Studies in Women's Literature*, vol. 14, no. 1, 1995, pp. 123–48.

"The Books of 1892." *The Publishers' Weekly*, vol. 43, no. 4, 28 Jan. 1893, pp. 169–90. *HathiTrust Digital Library*, hdl.handle.net/2027/hvd.32044093010239 ?urlappend=%3Bseq=183. Accessed 7 Sept. 2019.

Boone, Joseph Allen. *Tradition Counter Tradition: Love and the Form of Fiction*. U Chicago P, 1987.

Booth, Alison. *Greatness Engendered: George Eliot and Virginia Woolf*. Cornell UP, 1992.

———. *Homes and Haunts: Touring Writers' Shrines and Countries*. Oxford Scholarship Online. Oxford UP, 2016, doi:10.1093/acprof:oso/9780198759096.001.0001. Accessed 7 Sept. 2019.

———. *How to Make It as a Woman: Collective Biographical History from Victoria to the Present*. U of Chicago P, 2004.

[Booth, Mary]. *Charles Booth: A Memoir*. Macmillan, 1918.

Bordin, Ruth. *Frances Willard: A Biography*. U of North Carolina P, 1986.

Bourdieu, Pierre. "The Field of Cultural Production, or: The Economic World Reversed." *The Field of Cultural Production: Essays on Art and Literature*, edited by Randal Johnson, Polity Press, 1993, pp. 29–73.

———. *Masculine Domination*. Translated by Richard Nice, Stanford UP, 2001.

Bowen, Elizabeth. Interview. Noble, pp. 47–52.

Bowlby, Rachel. *Feminist Destinations and Further Essays on Virginia Woolf*. Edinburgh UP, 1997.

Bradshaw, David. "'Wretched Sparrows': Protectionists, Suffragettes, and the Irish." *Woolf Studies Annual*, vol. 20, 2014, pp. 41–52.

———, editor. *Carlyle's House and Other Sketches*. Hesperus Press, 2003.

Bradshaw, David, and Rachel Potter, editors. *Prudes on the Prowl: Fiction and Obscenity in England, 1850 to the Present Day*. Oxford UP, 2013.

Brake, Laurel. "Pater the Journalist: Essays from *The Guardian*." *English Literature in Transition, 1880–1920*, vol. 56, no. 4, 2013, pp. 483–96.

———. *Print in Transition, 1850–1910: Studies in Media and Book History*. Palgrave, 2001.

———. *Subjugated Knowledges: Journalism, Gender and Literature in the Nineteenth Century*. New York UP, 1994.

———. "Writing Women's History: The 'Sex' Debates of 1889." *New Woman Hybridities: Femininity, Feminism, and International Consumer Culture, 1880–1930*, edited by Margaret Beetham and Ann Heilmann, Routledge, 2004, pp. 51–73.

Brake, Laurel, and Marysa Demoor, editors. *Dictionary of Nineteenth-Century Journalism*. Academia Press and The British Library, 2009.

Briggs, Julia. *Virginia Woolf: An Inner Life*. Harcourt, 2005.

Bristow, Joseph. *Effeminate England: Homoerotic Writing after 1885*. Columbia UP, 1995.

Brooke, Emma. *A Superfluous Woman*. New York, 1894. *HathiTrust Digital Library*, hdl.handle.net/2027/uc2.ark:/13960/t4kk96c4s. Accessed 8 Oct. 2018.

Brooker, Peter. *Bohemia in London: The Social Scene of Early Modernism*. Palgrave Macmillan, 2004.

Brosnan, Leila. *Reading Virginia Woolf's Essays and Journals: Breaking the Surface of Silence*. Edinburgh UP, 1997.

Broughton, Rhoda. *Dear Faustina: A Novel*. New York, 1897. *HathiTrust Digital Library*, hdl.handle.net/2027/uva.x001132252. Accessed 7 Sept. 2019.

Broughton, Trev Lynn. *Men of Letters, Writing Lives: Masculinity and Literary Auto/Biography in the Late-Victorian Period*. Routledge, 1999.

Bulloch, J. M. "The Literary News in England." *The Book Buyer: A Review and Record of Current Literature*, vol. 16, no. 4, May 1898, pp. 333–35. *HathiTrust Digital Library*, hdl.handle.net/2027/pst.000019139005?urlappend=%3Bseq=349. Accessed 6 Oct. 2019.

[Burstein, Miriam E.]. "*The Old Wives' Tale*: A Brief Note." *The Little Professor*, 10 Nov. 2006, littleprofessor.typepad.com/the_little_professor/2006/11/. Accessed 7 Sept. 2018.

Burton, Antoinette. *Burdens of History: British Feminists, Indian Women, and Imperial Culture, 1865–1915*. U of North Carolina P, 1994.

Bush, Julia. "Caroline Stephen and the Opposition to British Women's Suffrage." *Quaker Studies*, vol. 15, no. 1, 2010, pp. 32–52.

Butler, Josephine. Letter to Stanley Butler. 24 April 1895. Josephine Butler Letters Collection, London School of Economics, The Women's Library. Manuscript.

——. Letter to Stanley Butler. [1896]. Josephine Butler Letters Collection, London School of Economics, The Women's Library. Manuscript.

——. Letter to Mrs. Clark. 6 May 1895. Josephine Butler Letters Collection, London School of Economics, The Women's Library. Manuscript.

——. Letter to "Dear Friends." 4 Apr. 1895. Josephine Butler Letters Collection, London School of Economics, The Women's Library. Manuscript.

——. Letter to Miss [Fanny] Forsaith. 11 July 1895. Josephine Butler Letters Collection, London School of Economics, The Women's Library. Manuscript.

——. Letter to Miss [Fanny] Forsaith. 27 Oct. 1896. Josephine Butler Letters Collection, London School of Economics, The Women's Library. Manuscript.

——. Letter to Miss [Fanny] Forsaith. 26 Apr. 1897. Jordan and Sharp, vol. 5, pp. 490–91.

——. Letter to Mary [Priestman]. [2 June 1893]. Josephine Butler Letters Collection, London School of Economics, The Women's Library. Manuscript.

——. Letter to the Miss Priestmans. 3 May 1895. Josephine Butler Letters Collection, London School of Economics, The Women's Library. Manuscript.

——. Letter to Frances Willard. 29 Nov. 1897. Josephine Butler Letters Collection, London School of Economics, The Women's Library. Manuscript.

——. *Personal Reminiscences of a Great Crusade*. London, 1896. *HathiTrust Digital Library*, hdl.handle.net/2027/hvd.rslerk. Accessed 8 Oct. 2018.

——. *Recollections of George Butler.* 5th ed., Bristol, 1896. *HathiTrust Digital Library,* hdl.handle.net/2027/uc1.31175006879608. Accessed 8 Oct. 2018.

——. "Reply to Lady Somerset's Scheme for Dealing with Disease in the Indian Cantonments." 1897. Jordan and Sharp, vol. 5, pp. 523–34.

——. "Truth before Everything." 1897. Jordan and Sharp, vol. 3, pp. 334–58.

Caine, Barbara. *Bombay to Bloomsbury: A Biography of the Strachey Family.* Oxford UP, 2005.

——. *English Feminism, 1780–1980.* Oxford UP, 1997.

——. "Mothering Feminism/Mothering Feminists: Ray Strachey and *The Cause.*" *Women's History Review,* vol. 8, no. 2, 1999, pp. 295–310.

——. *Victorian Feminists.* Oxford UP, 1992.

Carter, Mia. "History's Child: Virginia Woolf, Heritage, and Historical Consciousness." *Alif: Journal of Comparative Poetics,* vol. 27, 2007, pp. 68–95. *JSTOR,* www.jstor.org/stable/30197973. Accessed 7 Sept. 2019.

Catalogue of the Library of the Late Dr. Richard Garnett, C.B. . . . Comprising a Large Collection of Modern Poetry, Books and Pamphlets Relating to the British Museum. Sotheby, 1906. *HathiTrust Digital Library,* hdl.handle.net/2027/uc2.ark:/13960/t4pk09j39. Accessed 7 Oct. 2018.

Cecil, Hugh, and Mirabel Cecil. *Clever Hearts: Desmond and Molly MacCarthy, a Biography.* Gollancz, 1990.

Champneys, Basil. *Memoirs and Correspondence of Coventry Patmore.* George Bell and Sons, 1900. 2 vols.

Chan, Evelyn Tsz Yan. *Virginia Woolf and the Professions.* Cambridge UP, 2014.

Charles Booth's London: Poverty Maps and Police Notebooks. London School of Economics and Political Science, 2016, booth.lse.ac.uk. Accessed 5 June 2017.

Chesson, Wilfred Hugh. Reader's Report on Lady Henry Somerset, *Sketches in Black and White.* 24 Sept. 1895. Berg Collection, New York Public Library. Manuscript.

Childs, Donald J. *Modernism and Eugenics: Woolf, Eliot, Yeats, and the Culture of Degeneration.* Cambridge UP, 2001.

Chisholm, Monty. "Science and Literature Linked: The Story of William and Lucy Clifford, 1845–1929." *Advances in Applied Clifford Algebras,* vol. 19, nos. 3–4, 2009, pp. 657–71. *SpringerLink,* doi:10.1007/s00006-009-0188-x. Accessed 11 Mar. 2017.

——. *Such Silver Currents: The Story of William and Lucy Clifford 1845–1929.* Lutterworth Press, 2002.

Clay, Catherine. *British Women Writers 1914–1945: Professional Work and Friendship.* Ashgate, 2006.

Claybaugh, Amanda. *The Novel of Purpose: Literature and Social Reform in the Anglo-American World.* Cornell UP, 2007.

Clement, Mark. "Massingberd, Emily Caroline Langton." *Oxford Dictionary of National Biography,* Oxford UP, 24 May 2007, doi.org/10.1093/ref:odnb/53060. Accessed 26 Feb. 2020.

Clifford, Lucy Lane. Application to the Royal Literary Fund. Apr. 1875–15 Mar. 1879. British Library. Manuscript.

——. Letter to William Ewart Gladstone. 14 Nov. 1895. British Library. Manuscript.

——. Letter to Frederick Macmillan. N.d. [ca. 1883]. British Library. Manuscript.

——. Letter to Frederick Macmillan. 12 Aug. 1909. British Library. Manuscript.

——. Letter to Elizabeth Robins. 27 Nov. 1911[?]. Elizabeth Robins Papers, Fales Library, NYU. Manuscript.

Clifford, Mrs. W. K [Lucy Lane]. *Aunt Anne*. London, 1892.

——. *A Flash of Summer*. Boston, 1896.

[——]. *Mrs Keith's Crime: A Record*. 2 vols. London, 1885.

——. "A Remembrance of George Eliot." *The Nineteenth Century and After*, vol. 74, 1913, pp. 109–18.

Clodd, Edward. *Memories*. 2nd ed., Chapman and Hall, 1916. *HathiTrust Digital Library*, hdl.handle.net/2027/uc2.ark:/13960/t1xd0v613. Accessed 7 Oct. 2018.

Cocks, H. G. *Nameless Offences: Homosexual Desire in the Nineteenth Century*. I. B. Tauris, 2003.

Colby, Vineta. *Vernon Lee: A Literary Biography*. U of Virginia P, 2003.

Cole, Margaret. *Women of To-Day*. 1938. Books for Libraries Press, 1968.

Collier, Patrick. *Modernism on Fleet Street*. Ashgate, 2006.

——. "Virginia Woolf in the Pay of Booksellers: Commerce, Privacy, Professionalism, *Orlando*." *Twentieth Century Literature*, vol. 48, no. 4, 2002, pp. 363–92.

Colón, Susan E. *The Professional Ideal in the Victorian Novel: The Works of Disraeli, Trollope, Gaskell, and Eliot*. Palgrave Macmillan, 2007.

Cooke, Simon. "Periodicals: *The Quiver*." *The Victorian Web*, 2 May 2013, www.victorianweb.org/periodicals/quiver/cooke.html. Accessed 7 Sept. 2019.

"Copy of a Despatch to the Government of India Regarding the Measures To Be Adopted for Checking the Spread of Venereal Disease among the British Troops in India (Lord Hamilton's Despatch)." *Parliamentary Papers*, vol. 63, 1897, pp. 617–23. Jordan and Sharp, vol. 5, pp. 449–58.

Corbett, Mary Jean. "On *Crawford v. Crawford and Dilke*, 1886." *BRANCH: Britain, Representation and Nineteenth-Century History*, edited by Dino Franco Felluga, branchcollective.org. Accessed 7 Feb. 2020.

——. *Family Likeness: Sex, Marriage, and Incest from Jane Austen to Virginia Woolf*. Cornell UP, 2008.

——. "The Great War and Patriotism: Vernon Lee, Virginia Woolf, and 'Intolerable Unanimity.'" *Virginia Woolf Miscellany*, no. 91, Spring 2017, pp. 20–22.

——. *Representing Femininity: Middle-Class Subjectivity in Victorian and Edwardian Women's Autobiographies*. Oxford UP, 1992.

Costelloe [Strachey], Ray. *The World at Eighteen*. T. Fisher Unwin, 1907. *Google Books*, books.google.com/books/?id=KVFTAAAAYAAJ. Accessed 7 Oct. 2018.

Courtney, W. L. *The Feminine Note in Fiction*. Chapman and Hall, 1904.

Craig, Layne Parish. *When Sex Changed: Birth Control Politics and Literature between the World Wars*. Rutgers UP, 2013.

Cross, J. W. *George Eliot's Life, as Related in Her Letters and Journals, Arranged and Edited by Her Husband*. Edinburgh, 1885. 3 vols.

Cucullu, Lois. *Expert Modernists, Matricide, and Modern Culture: Woolf, Forster, Joyce*. Palgrave Macmillan, 2004.

Cuddy-Keane, Melba. *Virginia Woolf, the Intellectual, and the Public Sphere*. Cambridge UP, 2003.

——. "Virginia Woolf and the Varieties of Historicist Experience." Rosenberg and Dubino, pp. 59–77.

Curtis, Anthony, editor. *Before Bloomsbury: The 1890s Diaries of Three Kensington Ladies*. The Eighteen Nineties Society, 2002.

Curtis, Vanessa. *The Hidden Houses of Virginia Woolf and Vanessa Bell*. Robert Hale, 2005.

——. *Virginia Woolf's Women*. U of Wisconsin P, 2002.

Dakers, Caroline. *The Holland Park Circle: Artists and Victorian Society*. Yale UP, 1999.

D'Albertis, Deirdre. *Dissembling Fictions: Elizabeth Gaskell and the Victorian Social Text*. St. Martin's, 1997.

Darley, Gillian. *Octavia Hill*. Constable, 1990.

Daugherty, Beth Rigel. "Learning Virginia Woolf: Of Leslie, Libraries, and Letters." *Virginia Woolf and Communities: Selected Papers from the Eighth Annual Conference on Virginia Woolf*, edited by Jeanette McVicker and Laura Davis, Pace UP, 1999, pp. 10–16.

——. "Reading, Taking Notes, and Writing: Virginia Stephen's Reviewing Practice." Dubino, pp. 27–41.

——. "'Young Writers Might Do Worse': Anne Thackeray Ritchie, Virginia Stephen, and Virginia Woolf." *Aesthetic Theory and Literary Practice*, edited by Gina Potts and Lisa Shahriari, pp. 20–36. *Virginia Woolf's Bloomsbury*, vol. 1. Palgrave Macmillan, 2010.

Davidoff, Leonore. *Thicker than Water: Siblings and Their Relations, 1780–1920*. Oxford UP, 2012. *Oxford Scholarship Online*, doi:10.1093/acprof:oso/9780199546480.001. Accessed 7 Oct. 2018.

Davin, Anna. "Imperialism and Motherhood." *History Workshop Journal*, no. 5, 1978, pp. 9–65. *JSTOR*, www.jstor.org/stable/4288158. Accessed 5 Apr. 2015.

Davis, Thomas S. "The Historical Novel at History's End: Virginia Woolf's *The Years*." *Twentieth-Century Literature*, vol. 60, no. 1, 2014, pp. 1–26.

Davis, Tracy C. "The Moral Sense of the Majorities: Indecency and Vigilance in Late-Victorian Music Halls." *Popular Music*, vol. 10, no. 1, 1991, pp. 39–52.

Dawson, Gowan. *Darwin, Literature and Victorian Respectability*. Cambridge UP, 2007.

Debenham, Helen. "The *Cornhill Magazine* and the Literary Formation of Anne Thackeray Ritchie." *Victorian Periodicals Review*, vol. 33, no. 1, 2000, pp. 81–91. *JSTOR*, www.jstor.org/stable/20083712. Accessed 7 Sept. 2019.

De Gay, Jane. "Exploring Leonard and Virginia Woolf's Personal Library: Mirrors of the Soul?" *International Journal of the Book*, vol. 9, no. 2, 2012, pp. 41–50. *EBSCOhost*, doi:10.18848/1447-9516/CGP/v09i02/36932. Accessed 7 Sept. 2019.

——. *Virginia Woolf's Novels and the Literary Past*. Edinburgh UP, 2006.

Dekter, Gregory. "'Perishable and Permanent': Industry, Commodity, and Society in *Mrs. Dalloway* and *To the Lighthouse*." *Virginia Woolf Miscellany*, no. 88, Fall 2015/Winter 2016, pp. 14–16.

Dell, Marion. *Virginia Woolf's Influential Forebears: Julia Margaret Cameron, Anny Thackeray Ritchie and Julia Prinsep Stephen*. Palgrave Macmillan, 2015.

Demers, Patricia. "Toys and Terror: Lucy Clifford's *Anyhow Stories*." *The Nineteenth-Century Child and Consumer Culture*, edited by Dennis Denisoff, Ashgate, 2008, pp. 190–200.

Demoor, Marysa. "'Not with a Bang but a Whimper': Lucy Clifford's Correspondence, 1919–1929." *Cambridge Quarterly*, vol. 30, no. 3, 2001, pp. 233–56.

OhioLINK Electronic Journal Center, doi:10.1093/CAMQTLY/30.3.233. Accessed 7 Sept. 2019.

——. "Self-Fashioning at the Turn of the Century: The Discursive Life of Lucy Clifford (1846–1929)." *Journal of Victorian Culture*, vol. 4, no. 2, 1999, pp. 276–91. *Oxford Academic*, doi.org/10.1080/13555509909505993. Accessed 7 Oct. 2018.

——. *Their Fair Share: Women, Power and Criticism in the* Athenaeum, *from Millicent Garrett Fawcett to Katherine Mansfield, 1870–1920*. Ashgate, 2000.

——. "Where No Woman Fears to Tread: The Gossip Column in the *Athenaeum*, 1885–1901." *BELLS: Barcelona English Language and Literature Studies*, vol. 7, 1996, pp. 33–42. *Open Access Journals (RACO)*, www.raco.cat/index.php/Bells/article/view/102769/149174. Accessed 7 Sept. 2019.

——. "Women Authors and Their Selves: Autobiography in the Work of Charlotte Yonge, Rhoda Broughton, Mary Cholmondeley, and Lucy Clifford." *Cahiers Victoriens et Edouardiens*, no. 39, 1994, pp. 51–63.

Demoor, Marysa, and Monty Chisholm, editors. *"Bravest of Women and Finest of Friends": Henry James's Letters to Lucy Clifford*. English Literary Studies Monograph Series no. 80. U of Victoria P, 1999.

Denney, Colleen. *Women, Portraiture and the Crisis of Identity in Victorian England*. Ashgate, 2009.

DeSalvo, Louise. "Virginia Woolf's Revisions for the 1920 American and English Editions of *The Voyage Out*." *Bulletin of Research in the Humanities*, vol. 82, 1979, pp. 338–66.

DiBattista, Maria, and Lucy McDiarmid, editors. *High and Low Moderns: Literature and Culture, 1889–1939*. Oxford UP, 1996.

Dickens, Mary Angela. "A Chat with Mrs. W. K. Clifford." *The Windsor Magazine*, vol. 9, Mar. 1899, pp. 483–85. *Google Books*, books.google.com/books/?id=fw48AQAAMAAJ. Accessed 7 Oct. 2018.

Diedrick, James. *Mathilde Blind: Late-Victorian Culture and the Woman of Letters*. U of Virginia P, 2016.

Dolman, Frederick. "Women Speakers in England." *The Cosmopolitan: A Monthly Illustrated Magazine*, vol. 22, no. 6, Apr. 1897, pp. 676–80. *HathiTrust Digital Library*, hdl.handle.net/2027/hvd.hnycht?urlappend=%3Bseq=706. Accessed 7 Sept. 2019.

Donoghue, Emma. *We Are Michael Field*. Absolute Press, 1998.

Donohue, Joseph. *Fantasies of Empire: The Empire Theatre of Varieties and the Licensing Controversy of 1894*. U of Iowa P, 2005.

Dowie, Ménie Muriel. *Gallia*. 1895, edited by Helen Small, Dent, 1995.

Dubino, Jeanne. Introduction. *Virginia Woolf and the Literary Marketplace*, edited by Dubino, Palgrave Macmillan, 2010, pp. 1–23.

——. "Virginia Woolf: From Book Reviewer to Literary Critic, 1904–1918." Rosenberg and Dubino, pp. 25–40.

Duckworth, Gerald. Letter to Elizabeth Robins. N.d. Elizabeth Robins Collection, Fales Library, NYU. Manuscript.

Duckworth, Stella. Letter to Susan Lushington. N.d. Lushington Family Archive, Surrey History Centre. Manuscript.

——. Pocket Diary for 1896. Berg Collection, New York Public Library. Manuscript.

Eberle, Roxanne. *Chastity and Transgression in Women's Writing, 1792–1897: Interrupting the Harlot's Progress.* Palgrave, 2002.

Eliot, George. *The George Eliot Letters,* edited by Gordon S. Haight, vol. 2, Yale UP, 1954.

Eliot, T. S. Obituary of Virginia Woolf. Noble, pp. 119–22.

Elliott, Geoffrey. *The Mystery of Overend and Gurney: A Financial Scandal in Victorian London.* Methuen, 2006.

Ellis, Steve. *Virginia Woolf and the Victorians.* Cambridge UP, 2007.

England and Wales, National Probate Calendar (Index of Wills and Administrations), 1858–1995. Find a Will, probatesearch.service.gov.uk/#wills. Accessed 8 Sept. 2019.

Epstein, Barbara Leslie. *The Politics of Domesticity: Women, Evangelism, and Temperance in Nineteenth-Century America.* Wesleyan UP, 1981.

Evans, Elizabeth F. *Threshold Modernism: New Public Women and the Literary Spaces of Imperial London.* Cambridge UP, 2018.

Ezell, Margaret J. M. *Writing Women's Literary History.* Johns Hopkins UP, 1993.

Fabian Society (Great Britain). *List of Members.* Fabian Society, 1894. *HathiTrust Digital Library,* hdl.handle.net/2027/inu.30000126302391. Accessed 28 Aug. 2019.

Faulk, Barry J. *Music Hall and Modernity: The Late-Victorian Discovery of Popular Culture.* Ohio UP, 2004.

Fawcett, Millicent Garrett. "Speech or Silence." *The Contemporary Review,* vol. 48, Sept. 1885, pp. 326–31. *HathiTrust Digital Library,* hdl.handle.net/2027/ mdp.3 9015078140699?urlappend=%3Bseq=336. Accessed 8 Sept. 2019.

Fawcett, Millicent Garrett, and E. M. Turner. *Josephine Butler: Her Work and Principles, and Their Meaning for the Twentieth Century.* 2nd ed., The Association for Moral and Social Hygiene, 1928.

Felski, Rita. *The Gender of Modernity.* Harvard UP, 1995.

Fifty Years, 1898–1948. Duckworth, 1948.

Fitzpatrick, Kathleen. *Lady Henry Somerset.* Jonathan Cape, 1923.

Flint, Kate. *The Woman Reader, 1837–1914.* Clarendon Press, 1993.

Fogel, Daniel Mark. *Covert Relations: James Joyce, Virginia Woolf, and Henry James.* U of Virginia P, 1990.

Ford, Isabella O. *On the Threshold.* London, 1895.

Forsythe, Bill. "Russell [née Somers-Cocks], Adeline Mary, Duchess of Bedford." *Oxford Dictionary of National Biography.* Oxford UP, 3 Jan. 2008, doi.org/10 .1093/ref:odnb/48836. Accessed 26 Feb. 2020.

Fowler, Rowena. "Virginia Woolf and Katharine Furse: An Unpublished Correspondence." *Tulsa Studies in Women's Literature,* vol. 9, no. 2, 1990, pp. 201–28.

Fox, Alice. *Virginia Woolf and the Literature of the English Renaissance.* Clarendon Press, 1990.

Francis, Emma. "Why Wasn't Amy Levy More of a Socialist? Levy, Clementina Black, and *Liza of Lambeth.*" *Amy Levy: Critical Essays,* edited by Nadia Valman and Naomi Hetherington, Ohio UP, 2010, pp. 47–69.

Fraser, Hilary. *Women Writing Art History in the Nineteenth Century: Looking Like a Woman.* Cambridge UP, 2014.

Freedman, Jonathan. *Professions of Taste: Henry James, British Aestheticism, and Commodity Culture.* Stanford UP, 1990.

Froude, James Anthony. *My Relations with Carlyle.* Longmans, Green, 1903.

Froula, Christine. "On French and British Freedoms: Early Bloomsbury and the Brothels of Modernism." *Modernism/modernity*, vol. 12, no. 4, 2005, pp. 553–80. *Project Muse*, doi:10.1353/mod.2005.0111. Accessed 7 Oct. 2018.

——. *Virginia Woolf and the Bloomsbury Avant-Garde.* Columbia UP, 2005.

Gagnier, Regenia. *Individualism, Decadence, and Globalization: On the Relationship of Part to Whole, 1859–1920.* Palgrave Macmillan, 2010.

Gallagher, Catherine. "George Eliot and *Daniel Deronda*: The Prostitute and the Jewish Question." *Sex, Politics, and Science in the Nineteenth-Century Novel*, edited by Ruth Bernard Yeazell, Johns Hopkins UP, 1986, pp. 39–62.

Galsworthy, John. *The Inn of Tranquillity: Studies and Essays.* Heinemann, 1912.

Galton, Francis. *Hereditary Genius: An Inquiry into Its Laws and Consequences.* London, 1869.

Garnett, Angelica. Prologue. *Sketches in Pen and Ink*, by Vanessa Bell, pp. 1–39.

Garnett, Henrietta. "Visits to Charleston: Vanessa." *Charleston Past and Present*, Harvest/HBJ, 1987, pp. 153–60.

Garnett, Jane. "Stephen [*née* Jackson], Julia Prinsep." *Oxford Dictionary of National Biography.* Oxford UP, 23 Sept. 2004, doi.org/10.1093/ref:odnb/46943. Accessed 26 Feb. 2020.

Garrity, Jane. "Selling Culture to the 'Civilized': Bloomsbury, British *Vogue*, and the Marketing of National Identity." *Modernism/modernity*, vol. 6, no. 2, 1999, pp. 29–58. *Project Muse*, doi:10.1353/mod.1999.0016. Accessed 11 Mar. 2017.

——. *Step-daughters of England: British Women Modernists and the National Imaginary.* Manchester UP, 2003.

Gaskell, Elizabeth. *Ruth.* 1853, edited by Angus Easson, Penguin, 2004.

Gates, Joanne E. *Elizabeth Robins, 1862–1952: Actress, Novelist, Feminist.* U of Alabama P, 1994.

Gérin, Winifred. *Anne Thackeray Ritchie: A Biography.* Oxford UP, 1981.

Gifford, Carolyn De Swarte, editor. *Writing Out My Heart: Selections from the Journal of Frances E. Willard, 1855–96.* U of Illinois P, 1995.

Gillespie, Diane F., and Elizabeth Steele, editors. *Julia Duckworth Stephen: Stories for Children, Essays for Adults.* Syracuse UP, 1987.

Gindin, James. *John Galsworthy's Life and Art: An Alien's Fortress.* U of Michigan Press, 1987.

Gissing, George. *The Collected Letters of George Gissing*, edited by Paul F. Mattheisen et al., vol. 5, Ohio UP, 1994.

Gladstone, W. E., et al. "The Question of Divorce." *The North American Review*, vol. 149, no. 397, Dec. 1889, pp. 641–52. *JSTOR*, www.jstor.org/stable/i25101901. Accessed 21 Jan. 2018.

Glage, Liselotte. *Clementina Black: A Study in Social History and Literature.* C. Winter, 1981.

Goldman, Jane. "Forster and Women." *The Cambridge Companion to E. M. Forster*, edited by David Bradshaw, Cambridge UP, 2007, pp. 120–37.

——. "1925, London, New York, Paris: Metropolitan Modernisms—Parallax and Palimpsest." *The Edinburgh Companion to Twentieth-Century Literatures in English*, edited by Brian McHale and Randall Stevenson, Edinburgh UP, 2006, pp. 61–72.

——. "Virginia Woolf and Modernist Aesthetics." *The Edinburgh Companion to Virginia Woolf and the Arts*, edited by Maggie Humm, Edinburgh UP, 2010, pp. 35–57.

Goldman, Lawrence. "Woodhull, Victoria Claflin." *Oxford Dictionary of National Biography*, Oxford UP, 1 Sept. 2017, doi.org/10.1093/ref:odnb/98231. Accessed 26 Feb. 2020.

Grand, Sarah. *Babs the Impossible*. New York, 1901. *HathiTrust Digital Library*, hdl .handle.net/2027/uc2.ark:/13960/t1vd6qh14. Accessed 7 Oct. 2018.

——. *The Beth Book*. 1897. Thoemmes Press, 1994.

——. Foreword. *The Heavenly Twins*. 1923. Grand, *Sex, Social Purity and Sarah Grand*, vol. 1, pp. 397–408.

——. *The Heavenly Twins*. 1893. U of Michigan P, 1992.

——. "The Man of the Moment." *North American Review*, vol. 158, no. 450, 1894, pp. 620–27. Grand, *Sex, Social Purity and Sarah Grand*, vol. 1, pp. 50–57.

——. "The Modern Young Man." *The Temple Magazine*, vol. 2, September 1898, pp. 883–86. Grand, *Sex, Social Purity and Sarah Grand*, vol. 1, pp. 58–63.

——. *Sex, Social Purity and Sarah Grand*, edited by Ann Heilmann and Stephanie Forward, Routledge, 2000. 4 vols.

Green, Barbara. *Spectacular Confessions: Autobiography, Performative Activism, and the Sites of Suffrage, 1905–1938*. St. Martin's Press, 1997.

Greenslade, William. *Degeneration, Culture and the Novel, 1880–1940*. Cambridge UP, 1994.

Grenier, Janet E. "Hamilton [*née* Adamson], Mary Agnes." *Oxford Dictionary of National Biography*. Oxford UP, 24 May 2007, doi.org/10.1093/ref:odnb/39455. Accessed 26 Feb. 2020.

Gualtieri, Elena. *Virginia Woolf's Essays: Sketching the Past*. St. Martin's, 2000.

——. "Woolf, Economics, and Class Politics: Learning to Count." Randall and Goldman, pp. 183–92.

Gunn, Peter. *Vernon Lee: Violet Paget, 1856–1935*. Oxford UP, 1964.

Hadley, Elaine. *Melodramatic Tactics: Theatricalized Dissent in the English Marketplace, 1800–1885*. Stanford UP, 1995.

Haight, Gordon S. *George Eliot: A Biography*. Oxford UP, 1968.

Hancock, Catherine R. "'It Was Bone of Her Bone, and Flesh of Her Flesh, and She Had Killed It': Three Versions of Destructive Maternity in Victorian Fiction." *LIT: Literature, Interpretation, Theory*, vol. 15, no. 3, 2004, pp. 299–320. *Taylor and Francis Online*, doi:10.1080/10436920490489687. Accessed 11 Mar. 2017.

Hancock, [Ernest] La Touche. "The Railway Novel." *Desultory Verse*, Neale, 1912, p. 22. *Internet Archive*, www.archive.org/details/desultoryverse00hanc. Accessed 10 Mar. 2017.

Hannam, June. *Isabella Ford*. Basil Blackwell, 1989.

Hardy, Thomas. Preface [to the 5th and later eds.]. *Tess of the d'Urbervilles*, edited by Juliet Grindle and Simon Gatrell, Clarendon Press, 1983, pp. 3–8.

"The Health of the Army in India." *Times*, 21 Apr. 1897, p. 10. Jordan and Sharp, vol. 5, pp. 482–84.

"The Heavenly Twins: Bath's Mayoress Tells Their Story—Josephine Butler Centenary." *Bath and Wilts Chronicle and Herald*, 19 June 1928, p. 7. Grand, *Sex, Social Purity and Sarah Grand*, vol. 1, pp. 317–22.

Heidt, Sarah J. "'Let JAS Words Stand': Publishing John Addington Symonds' Desires." *Victorian Studies*, vol. 46, no. 1, 2003, pp. 7–31.

Heilmann, Ann. *New Woman Strategies: Sarah Grand, Olive Schreiner, Mona Caird*. Manchester UP, 2004.

Hensley, Nathan K. "What Is a Network? (And Who Is Andrew Lang?)." *Romanticism and Victorianism on the Net*, no. 64, 2013, doi:10.7202/1025668ar. Accessed 11 Mar. 2017.

Hepworth Dixon, Ella. *"As I Knew Them": Sketches of People I Have Met on the Way*. Hutchinson, 1930.

——. *The Story of a Modern Woman*. 1894, edited by Steve Farmer, Broadview Press, 2004.

Hetherington, Naomi. "The Seventh Wave of Humanity: Hysteria and Moral Evolution in Sarah Grand's *The Heavenly Twins*." *Writing Women of the* Fin de Siècle: *Authors of Change*, edited by Adrienne E. Gavin and Carolyn W. de la L. Oulton, Palgrave Macmillan, 2012, pp. 153–65.

Higginbotham, Peter. *The Workhouse: The Story of an Institution*. www.workhouses.org.uk. Accessed 1 Jan. 2018.

Hill, Katherine C. "Virginia Woolf and Leslie Stephen: History and Literary Revolution." *PMLA*, vol. 96, no. 3, 1981, pp. 351–62.

Hipsky, Martin. *Modernism and the Women's Popular Romance in Britain, 1885–1925*. Ohio UP, 2011.

Hite, Molly. "The Public Woman and the Modernist Turn: Virginia Woolf's *The Voyage Out* and Elizabeth Robins's *My Little Sister*." *Modernism/modernity*, vol. 17, no. 3, 2010, pp. 523–48. *Project Muse*, doi:10.1353/mod.2010.0011. Accessed 7 Oct. 2018.

——. "Virginia Woolf's Two Bodies." *Genders*, no. 31, 2000. *Genders 2008–2013*, www.colorado.edu/gendersarchive1998-2013/2000/01/10/virginia-woolfs-two-bodies. Accessed 7 Oct. 2018.

——. *Woolf's Ambiguities: Tonal Modernism, Narrative Strategy, Feminist Precursors*. Cornell UP, 2017.

Holland, Kathryn. "Late Victorian and Modern Feminist Intertexts: The Strachey Women in *A Room of One's Own* and *Three Guineas*." *Tulsa Studies in Women's Literature*, vol. 32, no. 1, 2013, pp. 75–98. *Project MUSE*, muse.jhu.edu/article/536393. Accessed 24 Aug. 2019.

Hollis, Patricia. *Ladies Elect: Women in English Local Government, 1865–1914*. Clarendon Press, 1987.

Holmes, Jennifer. *A Working Woman: The Remarkable Life of Ray Strachey*. Matador, 2019.

Holton, Amanda. "Resistance, Regard and Rewriting: Virginia Woolf and Anne Thackeray Ritchie." *English: The Journal of the English Association*, vol. 57, no. 217, 2008, pp. 42–64. *Oxford Academic*, doi:10.1093/english/efn009. Accessed 7 Oct. 2018.

Holton, Sandra Stanley. *Suffrage Days: Stories from the Women's Suffrage Movement*. Routledge, 1996.

Homans, Margaret. "Woolf and the Victorians." Randall and Goldman, pp. 410–22.

Hort, A. F., and H. C. G. Matthew. "Davies, (John) Llewelyn." *Oxford Dictionary of National Biography*. Oxford UP, 25 May 2006, doi.org/10.1093/ref:odnb/32739. Accessed 26 Feb. 2020.

Howard, Charles James Stanley. Letter to Susan Lushington. 15 May 1893. Lushington Family Archive, Surrey History Centre. Manuscript.

Hughes, Linda. "A Club of Their Own: The 'Literary Ladies,' New Women Writers, and *Fin-de-Siècle* Authorship." *Victorian Literature and Culture*, vol. 35, no. 1, 2007, pp. 233–60.

——. *Graham R.: Rosamond Marriott Watson, Woman of Letters*. Ohio UP, 2005.

Hunt, Alan. *Governing Morals: A Social History of Moral Regulation*. Cambridge UP, 1999.

Huyssen, Andreas. "Mass Culture as Woman: Modernism's Other." *After the Great Divide: Modernism, Mass Culture, Postmodernism*. Indiana UP, 1986, pp. 45–62.

Hyman, Virginia R. "Concealment and Disclosure in Sir Leslie Stephen's *Mausoleum Book*." *Biography*, vol. 3, no. 2, 1980, pp. 121–31.

——. "Late Victorian and Early Modern: Continuities in the Criticism of Leslie Stephen and Virginia Woolf." *English Literature in Transition, 1880–1920*, vol. 23, no. 3, 1980, pp. 144–54.

Ingleby, Matthew. *Nineteenth-Century Fiction and the Production of Bloomsbury: Novel Grounds*. Palgrave Macmillan, 2018. *Springer Link*, doi.org/10.1057/978-1-137-54600-5. Accessed 8 Sept. 2019.

"Interview with Mrs. Costelloe." *Women's Penny Paper*, vol. 2, no. 112, 13 Dec. 1890, pp. 113–14. Microfilm.

"Interview with Mrs. Massingberd." *Women's Penny Paper*, vol. 1, no. 12, 12 Jan. 1889, p. 1. Microfilm.

Israel, Kali. *Names and Stories: Emilia Dilke and Victorian Culture*. Oxford UP, 1999.

Jackson, Holbrook. *The Eighteen Nineties: A Review of Art and Ideas at the Close of the Nineteenth Century*. Mitchell Kennerley, 1913.

Jaffe, Aaron. *Modernism and the Culture of Celebrity*. Cambridge UP, 2005.

James, Henry. "The Art of Fiction." *The Art of Fiction and Other Essays*. Oxford UP, 1948, pp. 3–23.

——. *The Complete Notebooks of Henry James*, edited by Leon Edel and Lyall H. Powers, Oxford UP, 1987.

——. "Mrs. Humphry Ward." *Essays in London and Elsewhere*, New York, 1893, pp. 253–58. *Internet Archive*, www.archive.org/details/essaysinlondonan00jameiala. Accessed 12 Mar. 2017.

Jean-Léon Gérôme (1824–1904). Introduction and commentaries by Gerald M. Ackerman. Dayton Art Institute, 1972.

Jefferson, George. *Edward Garnett: A Life in Literature*. Jonathan Cape, 1982.

Jenkins, Roy. *Victorian Scandal: A Biography of the Right Honourable Gentleman Sir Charles Dilke*. Chilmark Press, 1965.

Joannou, Maroula. "'Hilda, Harnessed to a Purpose': Elizabeth Robins, Ibsen, and the Vote." *Comparative Drama*, vol. 44, no. 2, 2010, pp. 179–200. *JSTOR*, www.jstor.org/stable/23038111. Accessed 8 Sept. 2019.

John, Angela V. *Elizabeth Robins: Staging a Life, 1862–1952*. Routledge, 1995.

Jones, Clara. *Virginia Woolf: Ambivalent Activist*. Edinburgh UP, 2017.

Jonson, G. C. Ashton. "A London Theatre Libre." *The Drama: A Quarterly Review of Dramatic Literature*, vol. 1, no. 1, 1911, pp. 123–30. *HathiTrust Digital Library*, hdl.handle.net/2027/mdp.39015048884913?urlappend=%3Bseq=135. Accessed 7 Oct. 2018.

Jordan, Jane. *Josephine Butler*. John Murray, 2001.

Jordan, Jane, and Ingrid Sharp, editors. *Josephine Butler and the Prostitution Campaigns: Diseases of the Body Politic*. Routledge, 2003. 5 vols.

Jusová, Iveta. *The New Woman and the Empire*. Ohio State UP, 2005.

"Juvenile Drinking in the East End: Lady Somerset Speaks Out." *Pall Mall Gazette*, 9 Jan. 1889, p. 6. *British Newspaper Archive*, www.britishnewspaperarchive.co.uk/viewer/bl/0000098/18890108/015/0006. Accessed 29 Sept. 2018.

Kaplan, Morris B. *Sodom on the Thames: Sex, Love, and Scandal in Wilde Times*. Cornell UP, 2005.

Kaufmann, Michael. "A Modernism of One's Own: Virginia Woolf's *TLS* Reviews and Eliotic Modernism." Rosenberg and Dubino, pp. 137–55.

Kaye, Richard A. Introduction. *A Marriage below Zero*, by Alan Dale [pseud. Alfred J. Cohen]. Broadview Press, 2018, pp. 9–43.

Keating, Peter. *The Haunted Study: A Social History of the English Novel 1875–1914*. Secker and Warburg, 1989.

Kelly, Serena. "Lyttelton [*née* Clive], (Mary) Kathleen." *Oxford Dictionary of National Biography*. Oxford UP, 23 Sept. 2004, doi.org/10.1093/ref:odnb/50712. Accessed 26 Feb. 2020.

Kent, Susan Kingsley. *Sex and Suffrage in Britain, 1860–1914*. Princeton UP, 1987.

Kenyon Jones, Christine, and Anna Snaith. "'Tilting at Universities': Woolf at King's College London." *Woolf Studies Annual*, vol. 16, 2010, pp. 1–44.

Kersley, Gillian. *Darling Madame: Sarah Grand and Devoted Friend*. Virago, 1983.

Kertesz, Elizabeth. "Smyth, Dame Ethel Mary." *Oxford Dictionary of National Biography*. Oxford UP, 25 May 2006, doi.org/10.1093/ref:odnb/36173. Accessed 26 Feb. 2020.

King, Julia, and Laila Miletic-Vejzovic, editors. *The Library of Leonard and Virginia Woolf: A Short-Title Catalogue*. Washington State UP, 2003.

King, Steven. "'We Might be Trusted': Female Poor Law Guardians and the Development of the New Poor Law: The Case of Bolton, England, 1880–1906." *International Review of Social History*, vol. 49, no. 1, 2004, pp. 27–46.

Kipling, Rudyard. *The Letters of Rudyard Kipling*, edited by Thomas Pinney, U of Iowa P, 1990–2004. 6 vols.

Koven, Seth. *Slumming: Sexual and Social Politics in Victorian London*. Princeton UP, 2004.

Kucich, John. "Curious Dualities: *The Heavenly Twins* (1893) and Sarah Grand's Belated Modernist Aesthetics." *The New Nineteenth Century: Feminist Readings of Underread Victorian Fiction*, edited by Barbara Leah Harman and Susan Meyer, Garland, 1996, pp. 195–204.

——. *The Power of Lies: Transgression in Victorian Fiction*. Cornell UP, 1994.

Kuper, Adam. "Changing the Subject: About Cousin Marriage, among Other Things." *Journal of the Royal Anthropological Institute*, vol. 14, no. 4, 2008, pp. 717–35. *JSTOR*, www.jstor.org/stable/20203737. Accessed 8 Sept. 2019.

——. *Incest and Influence: The Private Life of Bourgeois England.* Harvard UP, 2009.

Laity, Cassandra. *H. D. and the Victorian Fin de Siècle: Gender, Modernism, Decadence.* Cambridge UP, 1996.

Lathbury, Bertha. "Agnosticism and Women." *The Nineteenth Century*, vol. 7, no. 38, 1880, pp. 619–27.

Leckie, Barbara. *Culture and Adultery: The Novel, the Newspaper, and the Law, 1857–1914.* U of Pennsylvania P, 1999.

Ledger, Sally. "The New Woman and Feminist Fictions." Marshall, *Cambridge Companion*, pp. 153–68.

——. *The New Woman: Fiction and Feminism at the Fin de Siècle.* Manchester UP, 1997.

Lee, Hermione. "'Crimes of Criticism': Virginia Woolf and Literary Journalism." *Grub Street and the Ivory Tower: Literary Journalism and Literary Scholarship from Fielding to the Internet*, edited by Jeremy Treglown and Bridget Bennett, Clarendon Press, pp. 112–34.

——. *Virginia Woolf.* Knopf, 1997.

Lee, Vernon. *Vernon Lee's Letters.* N.p., 1937.

Lee-Hamilton, Eliza-Ann [Annie E. Holdsworth]. Application to the Royal Literary Fund. 22 July 1909–19 Oct. 1909. British Library. Manuscript.

Le Gallienne, Richard. *The Romantic '90s.* Doubleday, Page, 1925.

Leighton, Angela. *On Form: Poetry, Aestheticism, and the Legacy of a Word.* Oxford UP, 2007.

Lewis, Jane. *Women and Social Action in Victorian and Edwardian England.* Stanford UP, 1991.

Light, Alison. *Mrs. Woolf and the Servants: An Intimate History of Domestic Life in Bloomsbury.* Bloomsbury, 2008.

Lilienfeld, Jane. "'The Gift of a China Inkpot': Violet Dickinson, Virginia Woolf, Elizabeth Gaskell, Charlotte Brontë, and the Love of Women in Writing." *Virginia Woolf: Lesbian Readings*, edited by Eileen Barrett and Patricia Cramer, New York UP, 1997, pp. 37–56.

Linton, E[liza] Lynn. "Candour in English Fiction." *The New Review*, vol. 2, 1890, pp. 10–14. *HathiTrust Digital Library*, hdl.handle.net/2027/njp.32101076519535?urlappend=%3Bseq=22. Accessed 7 Sept. 2019.

Livesey, Ruth. "Socialism in Bloomsbury: Virginia Woolf and the Political Aesthetics of the 1880s." *Yearbook of English Studies*, vol. 37, no. 1, 2007, pp. 126–44.

——. *Socialism, Sex, and the Culture of Aestheticism in Britain, 1880–1914.* Oxford UP, 2007.

"A Living Picture Girl." *Dundee Evening Telegraph*, 8 Aug. 1894, p. 2. *British Newspaper Archive*, www.britishnewspaperarchive.co.uk/viewer/bl/0000453/18940808/011/0002. Accessed 29 Sept. 2018.

"The Living Pictures." *The New Review*, vol. 11, no. 66, 1894, pp. 461–70. *HathiTrust Digital Library*, hdl.handle.net/2027/hvd.hw3qe2?urlappend=%3Bseq=497. Accessed 7 Sept. 2019.

"London's Woman Club: The Pioneer Is Run on Principles Very Masculine." *The Washington Post*, 26 Apr. 1896, p. 21. *ProQuest*, proxy.lib.miamioh.edu/login?url=https://search-proquest-com.proxy.lib.miamioh.edu/docview/143777316?accountid=12434. Accessed 21 May 2018.

Lorimer, Adam [pseud. William Lorimer Watson]. *The Author's Progress; or, The Literary Book of the Road*. Blackwood and Sons, 1906. *Google Books*, books .google.com/books/?id=x2ZDAQAAMAAJ. Accessed 28 May 2018.

Lovell, Terry. "Thinking Feminism with and against Bourdieu." *Feminist Theory*, vol. 1, no. 1, 2000, pp. 11–32.

Lowell, James Russell. "Verses Intended to Go with a Posset Dish to My Dear Little God-daughter, 1882." *Last Poems of James Russell Lowell*, Boston, 1895, pp. 38–40.

Lowndes, Marie Belloc. *The Merry Wives of Westminster*. Macmillan, 1946.

Lushington, Margaret. Diary. Lushington Family Archive, Surrey History Centre. Manuscript.

MacCarthy, Molly. *A Nineteenth-Century Childhood*. Doubleday, 1924. *HathiTrust Digital Library*, hdl.handle.net/2027/mdp.39015002996828. Accessed 12 Mar. 2017.

Macnamara, Katie. "How to Strike a Contemporary: Woolf, Mansfield, and Marketing Gossip." Dubino, pp. 91–106.

Mahoney, Kristin. "Vernon Lee at the Margins of the Twentieth Century: World War I, Pacifism, and Post-Victorian Aestheticism." *English Literature in Transition, 1880–1920*, vol. 56, no. 3, 2013, pp. 313–42. *Project Muse*, muse-jhu -edu.proxy.lib.miamioh.edu/article/510815. Accessed 8 Sept. 2019.

Maitland, Frederic William. *The Life and Letters of Sir Leslie Stephen*. G. P. Putnam's Sons, 1906.

Maltz, Diana. *British Aestheticism and the Urban Working Classes, 1870–1900: Beauty for the People*. Palgrave Macmillan, 2006.

Mangum, Teresa. *Married, Middlebrow, and Militant: Sarah Grand and the New Woman Novel*. U of Michigan P, 1998.

Mannheim, Karl. "The Problem of Generations." *Essays on the Sociology of Knowledge*, edited by Paul Kegskemeti, Oxford UP, 1952, pp. 276–320.

Mansfield, Katherine. Review of *Night and Day*. *Virginia Woolf: The Critical Heritage*, edited by Robin Majumdar and Allen McLaurin, Routledge and Kegan Paul, 1975, pp. 79–82.

Marcus, Jane. "Art and Anger." *Feminist Studies*, vol. 4, no. 1, 1978, pp. 68–98. *JSTOR*, doi: 10.2307/3177626. Accessed 31 July 2017.

———. "Pargetting *The Pargiters*." *Virginia Woolf*, pp. 57–74.

———. *Virginia Woolf and the Languages of Patriarchy*. Indiana UP, 1987.

———. "*The Years* as Götterdämmerung, Greek Play, and Domestic Novel." *Virginia Woolf*, pp. 36–56.

Marcus, Laura, et al. Introduction. *Late Victorian into Modern*, edited by Marcus et al., Oxford UP, 2016, pp. 1–18.

Markham, Violet R. *Return Passage: The Autobiography of Violet R. Markham*. Oxford UP, 1953.

Marshall, Gail. *Actresses on the Victorian Stage: Feminine Performance and the Galatea Myth*. Cambridge UP, 1998.

———, editor. *The Cambridge Companion to the Fin de Siècle*. Cambridge UP, 2007.

Marshik, Celia. *British Modernism and Censorship*. Cambridge UP, 2006.

"The Massacres in Armenia: Great Meeting at St. James's Hall." *London Evening Standard*, 8 May 1895, p. 3. *British Newspaper Archive*, www

.britishnewspaperarchive.co.uk/ viewer/BL/0000183/18950508/007/0003. Accessed 29 Sept. 2018.

McCail, Ronald. "A Family Matter: *Night and Day* and *Old Kensington.*" *The Review of English Studies*, vol. 38, no. 149, 1987, pp. 23–39. *JSTOR*, www.jstor.org /stable/517035. Accessed 8 Sept. 2019.

McCauley, Anne. "Brides of Men and Brides of Art: The 'Woman Question' of the 1860s and the Photographs of Julia Margaret Cameron." *Études Photographiques*, vol. 28, 2011. *Directory of Open Access Journals*, journals .openedition.org/etudesphotographiques/3469. Accessed 7 Sept. 2019.

McCoskey, Denise Eileen, and Mary Jean Corbett. "Virginia Woolf, Richard Jebb, and Sophocles' *Antigone.*" *A Companion to Sophocles*, edited by Kirk Ormand, Wiley-Blackwell, 2012, pp. 462–76.

McDonald, Peter D. *British Literary Culture and Publishing Practice, 1880–1914.* Cambridge UP, 1997.

——. "Modernist Publishing: 'Nomads and Mapmakers.'" *A Concise Companion to Modernism*, edited by David Bradshaw, Blackwell, 2003, pp. 221–42.

McNees, Eleanor. "The Legacy of the Writing Desk: Jane Welsh Carlyle to Virginia Stephen Woolf." *Virginia Woolf Miscellany*, no. 68, 2005, pp. 8–9.

——. "The Stephen Inheritance: Virginia Woolf and the Burden of the Arnoldian Critic." *Cambridge Quarterly*, vol. 44, no. 2, 2015, pp. 119–45.

——. "Woolf's Imperialist Cousins: Missionary Vocations of Dorothea and Rosamond Stephen." *Virginia Woolf and Her Female Contemporaries: Selected Papers from the Twenty-Fifth Annual International Conference on Virginia Woolf*, edited by Julie Vandivere and Megan Hicks, Clemson UP, 2016, pp. 62–68.

Meisel, Perry. *The Absent Father: Virginia Woolf and Walter Pater.* Yale UP, 1980.

Meredith, George. *The Letters of George Meredith*, edited by C. L. Cline, Clarendon Press, 1970. 3 vols.

Meynell, Viola. *Alice Meynell: A Memoir.* Charles Scribner's Sons, 1929.

Miller, Jane Eldridge. *Rebel Women: Feminism, Modernism and the Edwardian Novel.* U of Chicago P, 1997.

Mitchell, Charlotte, et al. "Introduction to the 1890s." *Letters of Charlotte Mary Yonge*, edited by Mitchell et al., University of Newcastle, Australia, c21ch.newcastle .edu.au/yonge/letters-1890-1901. Accessed 6 Oct. 2019.

Moi, Toril. *Sexual/Textual Politics: Feminist Literary Theory.* Methuen, 1985.

Moretti, Franco. *An Atlas of the European Novel.* Verso, 1998.

——. *Graphs, Maps, Trees: Abstract Models for a Literary History.* Verso, 2005.

Morgan, Charles. *The House of Macmillan (1843–1943).* Macmillan, 1944.

Moyse, Cordelia. "Fisher [*née* Ilbert], Lettice." *Oxford Dictionary of National Biography.* Oxford UP, 8 Jan. 2009, doi.org/10.1093/ref:odnb/41132. Accessed 26 Feb. 2020.

"Mrs Ashton Dilke." *Women's Penny Paper*, vol. 1, no. 3, 10 Nov. 1888, pp. 1–2. Microfilm.

Mullin, Katherine. *James Joyce, Sexuality and Social Purity.* Cambridge UP, 2003.

——. "Poison More Deadly than Prussic Acid: Defining Obscenity after the 1857 Obscene Publications Act (1850–1885)." Bradshaw and Potter, pp. 11–29.

Murphy, Geraldine. "Publishing Scoundrels: Henry James, Vernon Lee, and 'Lady Tal.'" *The Henry James Review*, vol. 31, 2010, pp. 280–87.

Neverow, Vara. "'Tak[ing] Our Stand Openly under the Lamps of Piccadilly Circus':
Footnoting of the Influence of Josephine Butler on *Three Guineas*." *Virginia
Woolf and the Arts: Selected Papers from the Sixth Annual Conference on Virginia
Woolf*, edited by Diane F. Gillespie and Leslie K. Hankins, Pace UP, 1997,
pp. 13–24.

Newey, Kate. "Women's Playwriting and the Popular Theatre in the Late Victorian
Era, 1870–1900." *Feminist Readings of Victorian Popular Texts: Divergent
Femininities*, edited by Emma Liggins and Daniel Duffy, Ashgate, 2001,
pp. 147–67.

Newman, Hilary. "'Eternally in Yr Debt': The Personal and Professional Relationship between Virginia Woolf and Elizabeth Robins." Cecil Woolf, n.d.

Niessen, Olwen Claire. *Aristocracy, Temperance and Social Reform: The Life of Lady
Henry Somerset*. Tauris Academic Studies, 2007.

Noble, Joan Russell, editor. *Recollections of Virginia Woolf by Her Contemporaries*. Ohio
UP, 1972.

Nord, Deborah Epstein. *The Apprenticeship of Beatrice Webb*. U of Massachusetts P, 1985.

——. *Walking the Victorian Streets: Women, Representation, and the City*. Cornell UP,
1995.

O'Day, Rosemary, and David Englander. *Mr Charles Booth's Inquiry: Life and Labour of
the People in London Reconsidered*. Hambledon Press, 1993.

Ormond, Leonee. "Vernon Lee as a Critic of Aestheticism in *Miss Brown*." *Colby
Library Quarterly*, vol. 9, no. 3, September 1970, pp. 131–54.

Outka, Elizabeth. *Consuming Traditions: Modernity, Modernism, and the Commodified
Authentic*. Oxford UP, 2009.

Parejo Vadillo, Ana. "Generational Difference in *To the Lighthouse*." *The Cambridge
Companion to* To the Lighthouse, edited by Allison Pease, Cambridge UP, 2015,
pp. 122–35.

——. *Women Poets and Urban Aestheticism: Passengers of Modernity*. Palgrave Macmillan, 2005.

Park, Sowon S. "Suffrage Fiction: A Political Discourse in the Marketplace." *English
Literature in Transition, 1880–1920*, vol. 39, no. 4, 1996, pp. 450–61.

——. "Suffrage and Virginia Woolf: 'The Mass behind the Single Voice.'" *Review of
English Studies*, N.S., vol. 56, no. 223, 2005, pp. 119–34.

Paul, Janis M. *The Victorian Heritage of Virginia Woolf: The External World in Her Novels*.
Pilgrim Books, 1987.

"Pauper's Beer." *Pall Mall Gazette*, 15 Oct. 1879, p. 5. *British Newspaper Archive*,
britishnewspaperarchive.co.uk/viewer/bl/0000098/18791015/007/0005.
Accessed 1 Jan. 2018.

Pawlowski, Merry M. "Exposing Masculine Spectacle: Virginia Woolf's Newspaper
Clippings for *Three Guineas* as Contemporary Cultural History." *Woolf Studies
Annual*, vol. 9, 2003, pp. 117–42.

Pennell, Elizabeth Robins. *Nights: Rome, Venice, in the Aesthetic Eighties; London, Paris,
in the Fighting Nineties*. J. B. Lippincott, 1916.

Peters, Catherine. *Thackeray: A Writer's Life*. Sutton Publishing, 1999.

Peterson, Linda H. *Becoming a Woman of Letters: Myths of Authorship and Facts of the
Victorian Market*. Princeton UP, 2009.

Phillips, Kathy J. *Virginia Woolf against Empire*. U of Tennessee P, 1994.

Pollock, Sir John. *Time's Chariot.* John Murray, 1950.

Poovey, Mary. *Uneven Developments: The Ideological Work of Gender in Mid-Victorian England.* U of Chicago P, 1988.

Pound, Ezra. "I Vecchii." *New Selected Poems and Translations,* edited by Richard Sieburth, New Directions, 2010, pp. 87–88.

Powell, Anthony. *Messengers of Day. To Keep the Ball Rolling: The Memoirs of Anthony Powell,* vol. 2. Heinemann, 1978.

Priestley McCracken, L. A. M. "Madame Sarah Grand and Women's Emancipation." *The Vote,* vol. 34, 25 Aug. 1933, pp. 265–66. Grand, *Sex, Social Purity and Sarah Grand,* vol. 1, pp. 323–26.

Prins, Yopie. *Ladies' Greek: Victorian Translations of Tragedy.* Princeton UP, 2018. *University Press Scholarship Online,* www.universitypressscholarship.com/view /10.23943/princeton/9780691141893.001.0001/upso-9780691141893. Accessed 8 Sept. 2019.

Pugh, Martin. *The March of the Women: A Revisionist Analysis of the Campaign for Women's Suffrage, 1866–1914.* Oxford UP, 2000.

Pykett, Lyn. *Engendering Fictions: The English Novel in the Early Twentieth Century.* Edward Arnold, 1995.

———. *The "Improper" Feminine: The Women's Sensation Novel and the New Woman Writing.* Routledge, 1992.

Ramusack, Barbara N. "Cultural Missionaries, Maternal Imperialists, Feminist Allies: British Women Activists in India, 1865–1945." *Western Women and Imperialism: Complicity and Resistance,* edited by Nupur Chaudhuri and Margaret Strobel, Indiana UP, 1992, pp. 119–36.

Randall, Bryony, and Jane Goldman, editors. *Virginia Woolf in Context.* Cambridge UP, 2012.

Raverat, Gwen. *Period Piece.* Norton, 1952.

Reid, Panthea. "Virginia Woolf, Leslie Stephen, Julia Margaret Cameron, and the Prince of Abyssinia: An Inquiry into Certain Colonialist Representations." *Biography,* vol. 22, no. 3, 1999, pp. 323–55.

Richardson, Angelique. *Love and Eugenics in the Late Nineteenth Century: Rational Reproduction and the New Woman.* Cambridge UP, 2003.

Ritchie, Anne. *Records of Tennyson, Ruskin, Browning.* New York, 1899.

Ritchie, Anne Thackeray. *Anne Thackeray Ritchie: Journals and Letters,* edited by Abigail Burnham Bloom and John Maynard, Ohio State UP, 1994.

Robinson, W. Sydney. *Muckraker: The Scandalous Life and Times of W. T. Stead.* Robson, 2012.

Rosenbaum, S. P. "Leonard and Virginia Woolf at the Hogarth Press." *Aspects of Bloomsbury: Studies in Modern English Literary and Intellectual History.* Macmillan, 1998, pp. 142–60.

Rosenberg, Beth Carole, and Jeanne Dubino, editors. *Virginia Woolf and the Essay.* St. Martin's, 1997.

Ross, Ellen. Introduction. *Slum Travelers: Ladies and London Poverty, 1860–1920,* edited by Ross, U of California P, 2007, pp. 1–39.

Rothenstein, William. *Men and Memories: A History of the Arts, 1872–1922.* Tudor, n.d. *Internet Archive,* www.archive.org/details/menandmemoriesah017669mbp. Accessed 14 July 2013. 2 vols.

Rubenstein, Roberta. *Virginia Woolf and the Russian Point of View*. Palgrave Macmillan, 2009.

Rubinstein, David. *A Different World for Women: The Life of Millicent Garrett Fawcett*. Ohio State UP, 1991.

Rudikoff, Sonya. *Ancestral Houses: Virginia Woolf and the Aristocracy*. The Society for the Promotion of Science and Scholarship, 1999.

Russell, Alys [Pearsall Smith]. "The Ghent School for Mothers." *The Nineteenth Century and After*, vol. 60, 1906, pp. 970–75. *HathiTrust Digital Library*, hdl.handle.net /2027/uiug.30112118706107?urlappend=%3Bseq=978. Accessed 7 Sept. 2018.

——. "The St. Pancras School for Mothers." *The Nineteenth Century and After*, vol. 63, 1908, pp. 763–70. *HathiTrust Digital Library*, hdl.handle.net/2027/uiug.301121 18706123?urlappend=%3Bseq=777. Accessed 8 Sept. 2019.

Schaffer, Talia. *The Forgotten Female Aesthetes: Literary Culture in Late-Victorian England*. U of Virginia P, 2000.

Schaffer, Talia, and Kathy Alexis Psomiades. Introduction. *Women and British Aestheticism*, edited by Schaffer and Psomiades, U of Virginia P, 1999, pp. 1–22.

Schlack, Beverly Ann. *Continuing Presences: Virginia Woolf's Use of Literary Allusion*. Pennsylvania State UP, 1979.

Scott, Bonnie Kime. *The Women of 1928. Refiguring Modernism*, vol. 1. Indiana UP, 1995.

Scott, David. "The Temporality of Generations: Dialogue, Tradition, Criticism." *New Literary History*, vol. 45, no. 2, 2014, pp. 157–81.

Sedgwick, Eve Kosofsky. *Epistemology of the Closet*. U of California P, 1990.

Seymour-Smith, Martin. *Rudyard Kipling*. St. Martin's, 1989.

Shaw, George Bernard. "Municipal Theatres." *The Drama Observed*, edited by Bernard F. Dukore, Pennsylvania State UP, 1993, vol. 2, pp. 545–50.

S[horter], C. K. "A Literary Letter." *The Sphere: An Illustrated Newspaper for the Home*, vol. 30, no. 398, 7 Sept. 1907, p. 228. *HathiTrust Digital Library*, hdl.handle.net /2027/nyp.33433096046655?urlappend=%3Bseq=242. Accessed 12 Feb. 2020.

Showalter, Elaine. *A Literature of Their Own: British Women Novelists from Brontë to Lessing*. Princeton UP, 1977.

——. *Sexual Anarchy: Gender and Culture at the Fin de Siècle*. Viking, 1990.

Siegel, Daniel. *Charity and Condescension: Victorian Literature and the Dilemmas of Philanthropy*. Ohio UP, 2012.

Silver, Brenda R. *Virginia Woolf Icon*. U of Chicago P, 1993.

——. *Virginia Woolf's Reading Notebooks*. Princeton UP, 1983.

Simpson, Kathryn. "Woolf's Bloomsbury." Randall and Goldman, pp. 170–82.

Smith, Alys W. Pearsall. "A Reply from the Daughters: II." *The Nineteenth Century*, vol. 35, 1894, pp. 443–50. *Google Books*, books.google.com/books?id =R90aAAAAYAAJ. Accessed 8 Oct. 2018.

Smith, Logan Pearsall. *Unforgotten Years*. Little, Brown, 1939.

Smyth, Ethel. *Female Pipings in Eden*. Peter Davies, 1934.

——. *Impressions That Remained*. 3rd ed., Longmans, Green, 1920. 2 vols.

——. *What Happened Next*. Longmans, Green, 1940.

Snaith, Anna. "Race, Empire, and Ireland." Randall and Goldman, pp. 206–18.

——. Letter to Florence Nightingale. 3 Feb. 1893. British Library. Manuscript.

——. Letter to Frances Willard. 29 Mar. 1897. Frances Willard House Library and Archives. Manuscript.

——. Letter to Frances Willard. 2 Apr. 1897. Frances Willard House Library and Archives. Manuscript.

——. Letter to Frances Willard. 18 June 1897. Frances Willard House Library and Archives. Manuscript.

——. "The Living Pictures: To the Women of England." *The Woman's Signal*, 2 Aug. 1894, p. 65. Microfilm.

——. "Pure Women." *The Watchman*, vol. 77, no. 24, 11 June 1896, pp. 9–10. *American Periodicals*, search-proquest-com.proxy.lib.miamioh.edu/docview /126949473? accountid=12434. Accessed 8 Oct. 2018.

——. "'Stray Guineas': Virginia Woolf and the Fawcett Library." *Literature and History*, vol. 12, no. 2, 2003, pp. 16–35.

——. *Under the Arch*. Doubleday Page, 1906. *Google Books*, books.google.com/books ?id=dIBBAAAAYAAJ. Accessed 8 Oct. 2018.

——. *Virginia Woolf: Public and Private Negotiations*. St. Martin's, 2000.

Somerset, Lady Henry. "Books of the Hour." Review of *The Armenian Crisis in Turkey*, by Frederick Davies Greene. *The Woman's Signal*, 9 May 1895, pp. 297–98. Microfilm.

——. "The Welcome Child." *The Arena*, vol. 12, no. 64, 1895, pp. 42–49. *Internet Archive*, archive.org/details/ArenaMagazine-Volume12. Accessed 8 Sept. 2019.

Southworth, Helen. Introduction. *Leonard and Virginia Woolf, the Hogarth Press and the Networks of Modernism*, edited by Southworth, Edinburgh UP, 2010, pp. 1–26.

Squier, Susan. *Virginia Woolf and London: The Sexual Politics of the City*. U of North Carolina P, 1985.

[Stead, W. T.]. "Against Compulsory Motherhood: Lady Henry Somerset Takes the Lead." *The Review of Reviews*, vol. 11, Apr. 1895, p. 328. *HathiTrust Digital Library*, hdl.handle.net/2027/uc1.b2900841?urlappend=%3Bseq=336. Accessed 7 Sept. 2019.

[——]. "Character Sketch: June. Lady Henry Somerset." *The Review of Reviews*, vol. 7, June 1893, pp. 606–22. *HathiTrust Digital Library*, hdl.handle.net/2027/uc1 .31210015370636?urlappend=%3Bseq=618. Accessed 7 Sept. 2019.

——. "The Dispute among the Women." *The Woman's Herald*, 4 May 1893, pp. 163–64. *Attacking the Devil: W. T. Stead Resource Site*, attackingthedevil.co .uk/steadworks/dispute.php. Accessed 4 Jan. 2017.

Steedman, Carolyn. "Fictions of Engagement: Eleanor Marx, Biographical Space." *Eleanor Marx (1855–1898): Life, Work, Contacts*, edited by John Stokes, Ashgate, 2000, pp. 23–39.

Stephen, Caroline Emelia. *The Service of the Poor; Being an Inquiry into the Reasons for and against the Establishment of Religious Sisterhoods for Charitable Purposes*. London, 1871. *HathiTrust Digital Library*, hdl.handle.net/2027/hvd.hn1ebh. Accessed 7 Sept. 2019.

Stephen, Julia Duckworth. ["Agnostic Women"]. Gillespie and Steele, pp. 241–47.

——. ["The Servant Question"]. Gillespie and Steele, pp. 248–52.

Stephen, Julia Prinsep. "Beer in Workhouses." *Pall Mall Gazette*, 4 Oct. 1879, p. 5. *British Newspaper Archive*, www.britishnewspaperarchive.co.uk/viewer /BL/0000098/18791004/005/0005. Accessed 1 Jan. 2018.

——. "Paupers' Beer." *Pall Mall Gazette*, 17 Oct. 1879, p. 3. *British Newspaper Archive*, www.britishnewspaperarchive.co.uk/viewer /bl/0000098/18791017/007/0003. Accessed 1 Jan. 2018.

Stephen, Leslie. "Art and Morality." *The Cornhill Magazine*, vol. 32, 1875, pp. 91–101.

——. "Balzac's Novels." *Hours in a Library (First Series)*, 2nd ed., London, 1877, pp. 299–348.

——. "Charlotte Brontë." *Hours in a Library (Third Series)*, pp. 325–64.

——. "The Decay of Literature." *The Cornhill Magazine*, vol. 46, 1882, pp. 602–12. *Internet Archive*, www.archive.org/details/cornhillmagazine46londuoft. Accessed 5 Mar. 2017.

——. "Fielding's Novels." *Hours in a Library (Third Series)*, pp. 50–92.

——. "Forgotten Benefactors." *Social Rights and Duties: Addresses to Ethical Societies*. 1896. Thoemmes Press, 2002, vol. 2, pp. 225–67. *HathiTrust Digital Library*, hdl .handle.net/2027/uc1.31970022730516?urlappend=%3Bseq=237. Accessed 8 Sept. 2019.

——. *Hours in a Library (Third Series)*. London, 1879.

——. Letter to Julia Duckworth. 23 July 1877. Berg Collection, New York Public Library. Manuscript.

——. Letter to Julia Stephen. 27 July 1893. Berg Collection, New York Public Library. Manuscript.

——. Letter to Julia Stephen. 3 Aug. 1893. Berg Collection, New York Public Library. Manuscript.

——. Letter to Thoby Stephen. 15 May 1897. Stephen Family Papers, 1888–1903. British Library. Manuscript.

——. Letter to Thoby Stephen. 17 Jan. 1903. Stephen Family Papers, 1888–1903. British Library. Manuscript.

——. *Life of Henry Fawcett*. London, 1885. *Internet Archive*, archive.org/details /cu31924028315426. Accessed 9 Sept. 2019.

——. "Richardson's Novels." *Hours in a Library (First Series)*, London, 1874, pp. 59–112.

——. *Selected Letters of Leslie Stephen*, edited by John W. Bicknell, Ohio State UP, 1996. 2 vols.

——. *Sir Leslie Stephen's Mausoleum Book*, edited by Alan Bell, Clarendon Press, 1977.

——. "Walter Bagehot." *Studies of a Biographer*, vol. 3. G. P. Putnam's Sons, 1907, pp. 144–74.

"Stephen-Duckworth Group, 1892." *Leslie Stephen's Photograph Album*, plate 38e. Mortimer Rare Book Room, www.smith.edu/libraries/libs/rarebook /exhibitions/images/stephen/large38e.jpg. Accessed 31 Aug. 2019.

Stetz, Margaret D. "Publishing Industries and Practices." Marshall, *Cambridge Companion*, pp. 113–30.

Stoddart, Jane T. "Lady Henry Somerset as an Englishwoman Knows Her." *Congregationalist and Christian World*, vol. 87, no. 36, 6 Sept. 1902, pp. 336–37. *ProQuest*, search.proquest.com.proxy.lib.miamioh.edu/docview/124180142 ?accountid=12434. Accessed 8 Oct. 2018.

Stokes, John. *In the Nineties*. U of Chicago P, 1989.

Strachey, Barbara. *Remarkable Relations: The Story of the Pearsall Smith Family*. Gollancz, 1980.

Strachey, Lytton. *The Letters of Lytton Strachey*, edited by Paul Levy and Penelope Marcus, Farrar, Straus and Giroux, 2005.

Strachey, Ray. *"The Cause": A Short History of the Women's Movement in Great Britain.* 1928. Kennikat Press, 1969.

———. *Frances Willard: Her Life and Work.* Fleming H. Revell, 1913.

———. *Millicent Garrett Fawcett.* John Murray, 1931.

Stutfield, Hugh. "Tommyrotics." *Blackwood's Magazine*, vol. 157, no. 956, 1895, pp. 833–45. *ProQuest*, search-proquest-com.proxy.lib.miamioh.edu/docview/6577358?accountid=12434. Accessed 9 Sept. 2019.

Sutherland, Gillian. "Clough, Blanche Athena." *Oxford Dictionary of National Biography.* Oxford UP, 23 Sept. 2004, doi.org/10.1093/ref:odnb/48434. Accessed 26 Feb. 2020.

Sutherland, John. "A Girl in the Bodleian: Mary Ward's Room of Her Own." *Browning Institute Studies*, vol.16, 1988, pp. 169–79. *JSTOR*, www.jstor.org/stable/25057834. Accessed 27 Feb. 2020.

———. *Mrs. Humphry Ward: Eminent Victorian, Pre-eminent Edwardian.* Clarendon Press, 1990.

Swanson, Diana. "With Clear-Eyed Scrutiny: Gender, Authority, and the Narrator as Sister in *Jacob's Room*." *Virginia Woolf Out of Bounds*, edited by Jessica Berman and Jane Goldman, Pace UP, 2001, pp. 46–51.

Swanwick, H. M. *I Have Been Young.* Victor Gollancz Ltd., 1935.

Symonds, John Addington. *The Letters of John Addington Symonds*, edited by Herbert M. Schueller and Robert L. Peters, Wayne State UP, 1969. 3 vols.

Tate, Trudi. *Modernism, History and the First World War.* Manchester UP, 1998.

Taylor, Clare L. *Women, Writing, and Fetishism 1890–1950.* Clarendon Press, 2003.

Taylor, D. J. *Thackeray: The Life of a Literary Man.* Carroll and Graf, 1999.

Tennyson, Alfred, Lord. "Merlin and Vivien." *The Poems of Tennyson*, vol. 3, edited by Christopher Ricks, U of California P, 1987, pp. 395–422.

Thackeray, William Makepeace. *The History of Pendennis.* 1848–50. Penguin, 1986.

———. *The Letters and Private Papers of William Makepeace Thackeray*, edited by Gordon N. Ray, vol. 4, Harvard UP, 1946.

Thomas, Gillian. "Hogarth [*married name* Courtney], Janet Elizabeth." *Oxford Dictionary of National Biography.* Oxford UP, 28 May 2015, doi.org/10.1093/ref:odnb/38617. Accessed 26 Feb. 2020.

Thomas, Katie-Louise. *Postal Pleasures: Sex, Scandal, and Victorian Letters.* Oxford UP, 2012.

Tickner, Lisa. *The Spectacle of Women: Imagery of the Suffrage Campaign, 1907–14.* U of Chicago P, 1988.

Tolley, Christopher. *Domestic Biography: The Legacy of Evangelicalism in Four Nineteenth-Century Families.* Clarendon Press, 1997.

"Trades Unions for East End Women." *Pall Mall Gazette*, 9 Oct. 1889, p. 6. *British Newspaper Archive*, www.britishnewspaperarchive.co.uk/viewer/bl/0000098/18891009/015/0006. Accessed 29 Sept. 2018.

Trevelyan, Janet Penrose. *The Life of Mrs. Humphry Ward.* Dodd, Mead, 1923.

Trodd, Anthea. *Women's Writing in English: Britain 1900–1945.* Longman, 1998.

Trollope, Anthony. *The Small House at Allington.* 1864. Penguin, 2005.

Troubridge, Laura. *Memories and Reflections.* Heinemann, 1925.

Turcon, Sheila. "A Quaker Wedding: The Marriage of Bertrand Russell and Alys Pearsall Smith." *Russell: The Journal of Bertrand Russell Studies*, vol. 3, no. 2, 1983, pp. 103–28.

Tusan, Michelle Elizabeth. *Smyrna's Ashes: Humanitarianism, Genocide, and the Birth of the Middle East*. U of California P, 2012.

——. *Women Making News: Gender and Journalism in Modern Britain*. U of Illinois P, 2005.

Tyrrell, Ian. "Somerset [*née* Somers-Cocks], Lady Isabella Caroline [Lady Henry Somerset]." *Oxford Dictionary of National Biography*. Oxford UP, 24 May 2012, doi.org/10.1093/ref:odnb/36188. Accessed 26 Feb. 2020.

——. *Woman's World/Woman's Empire: The Woman's Christian Temperance Union in International Perspective, 1880–1930*. U of North Carolina P, 1991.

VanArsdel, Rosemary T. *Florence Fenwick Miller: Victorian Feminist, Journalist, and Educator*. Ashgate, 2001.

Vanita, Ruth. *Sappho and the Virgin Mary: Same-Sex Love and the English Literary Imagination*. Columbia UP, 1996.

Walker, Dave. "The Hospital in Little Chelsea." *The Library Time Machine*, 23 Jan. 2014, rbkclocalstudies.wordpress.com/2014/01/23/the-hospital-in-little-chelsea/. Accessed 12 Sept. 2019.

Walker, Linda. "McLaren [*née* Müller], Eva Maria." *Oxford Dictionary of National Biography*, 8 Oct. 2009, doi.org/10.1093/ref:odnb/56261. Accessed 26 Feb. 2020.

Walkowitz, Judith R. *City of Dreadful Delight: Narratives of Sexual Danger in Late-Victorian London*. U of Chicago P, 1992.

——. "Going Public: Shopping, Street Harassment, and Streetwalking in Late Victorian London." *Representations*, vol. 62, 1998, pp. 1–30.

——. *Nights Out: Life in Cosmopolitan London*. Yale UP, 2012.

Waller, Philip. *Writers, Readers, and Reputations: Literary Life in Britain 1870–1918*. Oxford UP, 2006.

Walpole, Hugh. *The Apple Trees: Four Reminiscences*. Golden Cockerel Press, 1932.

Ward, Mrs. Humphry [Mary Augusta]. *Marcella*. 1894, edited by Beth Sutton-Ramspeck and Nicole B. Meller, Broadview Press, 2002.

——. *A Writer's Recollections*. Harper, 1918. 2 vols.

[Ward, Mrs. Humphry, and T. Humphry Ward]. "A Morning in the Bodleian Library." *Every Saturday*, vol. 1, no. 8, 24 Feb. 1872, pp. 204–6. *EBSCOhost*, search.ebscohost.com/login.aspx?direct=true&db=h9m&AN=59569501&site =ehost-live&scope=site. Accessed 12 Sept. 2019.

——. "A Morning in the Bodleian. By Two Fellows." *The Dark Blue*, vol. 2, Feb. 1872, pp. 683–91. *HathiTrust Digital Library*, hdl.handle.net/2027/ucl. b2983766?urlappend=%3Bseq=745. Accessed 7 Sept. 2019.

Ware, Vron. *Beyond the Pale: White Women, Racism and History*. Verso, 1992.

Waters, Chris. "New Women and Socialist-Feminist Fiction: The Novels of Isabella Ford and Katharine Bruce Glasier." *Rediscovering Forgotten Radicals: British Women Writers, 1889–1939*, edited by Angela Ingram and Daphne Patai, U of North Carolina P, 1993, pp. 25–42.

Waugh, Arthur. "Reticence in Literature." *The Yellow Book*, vol. 1, 1894, pp. 201–19. *The Yellow Nineties Online*, edited by Dennis Denisoff and Lorraine Janzen

Kooistra, Ryerson University, 2010, www.1890s.ca/HTML.aspx?s=YBV1 _waugh_reticence.html. Accessed 15 Sept. 2019.

Webb, Beatrice. *My Apprenticeship.* 1926. Cambridge UP, 1979.

Weihman, Lisa. "Virginia Woolf's 'Harum-Scarum' Irish Wife: Gender and National Identity in *The Years.*" *Comparative Critical Studies*, vol. 4, no. 1, 2007, pp. 31–50. *OhioLINK Electronic Journal Center*, rave.ohiolink.edu/ejournals/article /321060416. Accessed 15 Sept. 2019.

Wells-Barnett, Ida. *A Red Record: Tabulated Statistics and Alleged Causes of Lynchings in the United States.* Chicago, 1895. *Internet Archive*, archive.org/stream /theredrecord14977gut/14977.txt. Accessed 25 Jan. 2018.

West, Rebecca. "The Gospel According to Mrs Humphry Ward." *The Young Rebecca: Writings of Rebecca West, 1911–17*, edited by Jane Marcus, Viking, 1982, pp. 14–17.

———. "Mrs. Pankhurst." *The Post Victorians*, edited by W. R. Inge, Ivor Nicholson, and Watson, 1933, pp. 479–500.

White, Terence de Vere, editor. *A Leaf from the Yellow Book: The Correspondence of George Egerton.* Richards Press, 1958.

Whitworth, Michael H. *Virginia Woolf.* Oxford UP, 2005.

Whyte, William. "The Intellectual Aristocracy Revisited." *Journal of Victorian Culture*, vol. 10, no. 1, 2005, pp. 15–45.

Wilcox, Timothy. "Smith [née Dalrymple], Martha Mary [Eustacia]." *Oxford Dictionary of National Biography*, 23 Sept. 2004, doi.org/10.1093/ref:odnb /62864. Accessed 26 Feb. 2020.

Wilde, Oscar. *The Artist as Critic: Critical Writings of Oscar Wilde*, edited by Richard Ellmann, U of Chicago P, 1982.

———. Preface. *The Picture of Dorian Gray.* 1891. *Artist as Critic*, pp. 235–36.

———. "The Soul of Man under Socialism." 1891. *Artist as Critic*, pp. 255–89.

Williams, Harold. *Modern English Writers: Being a Study of Imaginative Writing 1890–1914.* Sidgwick and Jackson, 1918. *HathiTrust Digital Library*, hdl.handle .net/2027/uc2.ark:/13960/t1pg1mj60. Accessed 10 Sept. 2017.

Willis, J. H., Jr. *Leonard and Virginia Woolf as Publishers: The Hogarth Press, 1917–41.* U of Virginia P, 1992.

Wilson, Nicola. "Circulating Morals (1900–1915)." Bradshaw and Potter, pp. 52–70.

Wilt, Judith. *Behind Her Times: Transition England in the Novels of Mary Arnold Ward.* U of Virginia P, 2005.

Wollaeger, Mark. "The Woolfs in the Jungle: Intertextuality, Sexuality, and the Emergence of Female Modernism in *The Voyage Out, The Village in the Jungle*, and *Heart of Darkness.*" *Modern Language Quarterly*, vol. 64, no. 1, 2003, pp. 33–69.

"The Women's Protest against Sir Charles Dilke." *Women's Penny Paper*, vol. 1, no. 15, 2 Feb. 1889, p. 3. Microfilm.

Wood, Alice. "Made to Measure: Virginia Woolf in *Good Housekeeping* Magazine." *Prose Studies: History, Theory, Criticism*, vol. 32, no. 1, 2010, pp. 12–24. *Taylor and Francis Online*, doi:10.1080/01440351003747634. Accessed 15 Sept. 2019.

———. *Virginia Woolf's Late Cultural Criticism: The Genesis of* The Years, Three Guineas, *and* Between the Acts. Bloomsbury Academic, 2013.

Woolf, Leonard. *Beginning Again: An Autobiography of the Years 1911 to 1918.* Harcourt Brace Jovanovich, 1963.

——. *Letters of Leonard Woolf*, edited by Frederic Spotts, Harcourt Brace Jovanovich, 1989.

——. *Sowing: An Autobiography of the Years 1880–1904*. Harcourt, Brace, 1960.

Woolf, Virginia. *Between the Acts*. 1941, edited with explanatory notes by Mark Hussey, Cambridge UP, 2011.

——. *The Complete Shorter Fiction of Virginia Woolf*. 2nd ed., edited by Susan Dick, Harcourt, 1989.

——. *The Diary of Virginia Woolf*, edited by Anne Olivier Bell, with Andrew McNeillie, Harvest/HBJ, 1977–84. 5 vols.

——. *The Essays of Virginia Woolf*, edited by Andrew McNeillie (vols. 1–4) and Stuart N. Clarke (vols. 5–6), Harcourt Brace Jovanovich, 1987–2011.

——. *Freshwater: A Comedy*, edited by Lucio P. Ruotolo, Harvest/HBJ, 1985.

——. "Hampstead." *Carlyle's House and Other Sketches*, edited by David Bradshaw, Hesperus Press, 2003, pp. 10–11.

——. *Jacob's Room*. 1922. Harvest/HBJ, 1978.

——. *The Letters of Virginia Woolf*, edited by Nigel Nicolson and Joanne Trautmann, Harcourt Brace Jovanovich, 1975–80. 6 vols.

——. "The Mark on the Wall." *Complete Shorter Fiction*, pp. 83–89.

——. "Memoirs of a Novelist." *Complete Shorter Fiction*, pp. 69–79.

——. *Moments of Being: A Collection of Autobiographical Writing*. 2nd ed., edited by Jeanne Schulkind, Harcourt, 1985.

——. *Mrs. Dalloway*. 1925, edited with explanatory notes by Anne E. Fernald, Cambridge UP, 2015.

——. *Night and Day*. 1919, edited with explanatory notes by Michael Whitworth, Cambridge UP, 2018.

——. "Old Bloomsbury." *Moments of Being*, pp. 181–201.

——. *Orlando: A Biography*. 1929, edited with explanatory notes by Suzanne Raitt and Ian Blyth, Cambridge UP, 2018.

——. *The Pargiters: The Novel-Essay Portion of* The Years, edited by Mitchell A. Leaska, Harvest/HBJ, 1977.

——. *A Passionate Apprentice: The Early Journals, 1897–1909*, edited by Mitchell A. Leaska, Harvest/HBJ, 1990.

——. ["Phyllis and Rosamond"]. *Complete Shorter Fiction*, pp. 17–29.

——. *Pointz Hall: The Earlier and Later Typescripts of* Between the Acts, edited by Mitchell A. Leaska, University Publications, 1983.

——. "Reminiscences." *Moments of Being*, pp. 28–59.

——. *A Room of One's Own*. 1929. Harvest, 2005.

——. "A Sketch of the Past." *Moments of Being*, pp. 64–159.

——. "The String Quartet." 1921. *Complete Shorter Fiction*, pp. 138–41.

——. *Three Guineas*. 1938. Harvest, 2006.

——. *To the Lighthouse*. 1927. Harcourt, 2005.

——. "22 Hyde Park Gate." *Moments of Being*, pp. 164–77.

——. *The Voyage Out*. 1915, edited by Lorna Sage, Oxford UP, 1992.

——. *The Voyage Out*. 1915. Random House, 2001.

——. *Women and Fiction: The Manuscript Versions of* A Room of One's Own, edited by S. P. Rosenbaum, Blackwell, 1992.

——. *The Years*. 1937, edited with explanatory notes by Anna Snaith, Cambridge UP, 2012.

Woolf, Virginia, Vanessa Bell, and Thoby Stephen. *Hyde Park Gate News: The Stephen Family Newspaper*, edited by Gill Lowe, Hesperus Press, 2005.

Wussow, Helen. "Conflict of Language in Virginia Woolf's *Night and Day*." *Journal of Modern Literature*, vol. 16, no. 1, 1989, pp. 61–73.

——. *The Nightmare of History: The Fictions of Virginia Woolf and D. H. Lawrence*. Associated University Presses, 1998.

Younger, John G. "Ten Unpublished Letters by John Addington Symonds at Duke University." *Victorian Newsletter*, no. 95, Spring 1999, pp. 1–10. *EBSCOhost*, search.ebscohost.com/login.aspx?direct=true&db=hlh&AN=47852644&site=ehost-live&scope=site. Accessed 11 Feb. 2018.

Youngkin, Molly. *Feminist Realism at the Fin de Siècle: The Influence of the Late-Victorian Women's Press on the Development of the Novel*. Ohio State UP, 2007.

Zemgulys, Andrea P. *Modernism and the Locations of Literary Heritage*. Cambridge UP, 2008.

Zorn, Christa. *Vernon Lee: Aesthetics, History, and the Victorian Female Intellectual*. Ohio UP, 2003.

Zuckerman, Joanne. "Anne Thackeray Ritchie as the Model for Mrs. Hilbery in *Night and Day*." *Virginia Woolf Quarterly*, vol. 1, no. 3, 1973, pp. 32–46.

Zwerdling, Alex. "Mastering the Memoir: Woolf and the Family Legacy." *Modernism/modernity*, vol. 10, no. 1, 2003, pp. 165–88. *Project Muse*, doi:10.1353/mod.2003.0029. Accessed 6 Jan. 2013.

——. *Virginia Woolf and the Real World*. U of California P, 1986.

INDEX